A Developer's Guide to .NET in Azure

Build quick, scalable cloud-native applications and microservices with .NET 6.0 and Azure

Anuraj Parameswaran

Tamir Al Balkhi

BIRMINGHAM—MUMBAI

A Developer's Guide to .NET in Azure

Group Product Manager: Preet Ahuja

Senior Content Development Editor: Adrija Mitra

Technical Editor: Arjun Varma

Copy Editor: Safis Editing

Project Coordinator: Ashwin Dinesh Kharwa

Proofreader: Safis Editing

Indexer: Pratik Shirodkar

Production Designer: Jyoti Chauhan

Marketing Coordinator: Rohan Dobhal

First published: October 2023

Production reference: 1220923

Published by Packt Publishing Ltd.

Grosvenor House

11 St Paul's Square

Birmingham

B3 1RB, UK.

ISBN 978-1-83763-301-2

www.packtpub.com

To my beloved family, consisting of Sreeja, Sidhardh, and Sivaardra, and to my parents, Parameswaran Namboothiri and Saraswathi, I dedicate this book with heartfelt gratitude. Your unwavering support, guidance, and boundless love have been the driving force behind my journey. Thank you for being a constant source of inspiration in my life.

– Anuraj Parameswaran

To my amazing mother and sister, thank you for your unwavering support and resilience. You have inspired me to overcome challenges and reach for greatness. Your love and strength are my endless source of inspiration. I am forever grateful.

– Tamir AlBalkhi

Contributors

About the authors

Anuraj Parameswaran is a seasoned IT expert with over 19 years of experience, starting in 2004, with a strong focus on Azure and .NET technologies. Currently serving as the **Chief Technology Officer (CTO)** of Socxo Solutions Pvt. Ltd., he has received seven prestigious Microsoft MVP awards. Anuraj actively participates in mentoring programs, delivers speeches at various events, and contributes extensively to both Microsoft and Azure communities. His commitment to sharing knowledge and embracing lifelong learning is exemplified by his involvement as a technical reviewer for Packt books.

I am deeply grateful to my colleagues at Socxo Solutions Pvt. Ltd. for their invaluable support and unwavering encouragement during the creation of this book. Their expertise and collaborative spirit enriched my work, and I extend my heartfelt appreciation to each member of the team. Thank you for inspiring me to strive for excellence.

Tamir Al Balkhi is a technology problem solver with 15 years of experience developing innovative and effective solutions for clients across various industries, including healthcare, finance, and retail. From steering small to medium-sized business projects to overseeing large enterprise implementations, Tamir has consistently demonstrated exceptional leadership and technical prowess. As a cloud architect and **Chief Technology Officer** (**CTO**), Tamir specializes in designing and delivering best-in-class cloud solutions within the Microsoft Azure ecosystem. His agile-first mindset and commitment to a test-driven delivery approach have been instrumental in his ability to deliver projects on time, within budget, and beyond client expectations.

About the reviewers

Stéphane Eyskens started his career in 1999. Since a bit more than a decade ago, he has been at the forefront of cloud technologies, starting his Azure journey and embracing the emerging K8s platform. As a Microsoft Most Valuable Professional, Stephane contributes a lot by writing blog posts on Microsoft communities, as well as speaking at tech conferences. He has also authored multiple books on Azure and software architecture.

Matt R. Cole has functioned in many different roles over a career of more than 35 years. He was an early pioneer of VoIP. He architected and developed the VoIP system NASA used for all Space Shuttle launches and transmission out to the International Space Station. He worked with Microsoft on Azure Bonsai DRL. Matt led a digital transformation effort for MGM in Las Vegas. He has experience in C, C++, C#, .Net, Python, AI/ML, Swarm Technology, and computational neuroscience.

Matt has authored several books and contributed to several more. His current role is as a senior solutions architect for Dexian, where he works with one of the largest gas and oil companies in the world.

Table of Contents

3

Building Resilient Applications with Dapr   63

4

Designing Microservices with AKS and Containers in Azure   83

5

Building Serverless Apps with Azure Functions and Container Apps 105

Part 3: Data and Storage

6

Exploring Azure Blob Storage   163

7

Creating an Azure SQL Database   209

8

Creating Documents via .NET for Azure Cosmos DB   243

Part 4: Messaging Mechanisms and Security

9

Utilizing Azure App Configuration   297

10

Processing Data with Azure Event Hubs   315

11

Designing Ready-Made Solutions with Azure Service Bus   357

12

Enhancing Data Protection with Azure Key Vault   403

13

Managing Access with Azure Active Directory B2C   433

Index   461

Other Books You May Enjoy   480

Preface

Unlock the power of the cloud and propel your .NET development skills to new heights with this must-have guide to building cloud-native applications and services on Azure. In a world where over 95% of advanced digital workloads are shifting to cloud-native platforms by 2025, now is the time to equip yourself with the knowledge and expertise to stay ahead of the curve. Immerse yourself in a captivating journey as this comprehensive book takes you step-by-step through the exhilarating process of creating and deploying your cloud-native applications on Azure.

With a laser focus on .NET, you'll dive into the captivating world of containerization with Docker, harness the full potential of Azure Kubernetes Service, and master the art of building serverless apps with Azure Functions. But that's just the beginning. Prepare to be amazed as this guide unlocks the secrets of Azure's remarkable container technologies, paving the way for running microservices and containerized apps effortlessly.

Discover the sheer power and flexibility of Dapr, empowering you with APIs for building portable and rock-solid microservices. Resilience becomes your middle name as you explore a plethora of patterns and best practices, leveraging messaging services such as Azure Service Bus and Azure Event Hubs to construct robust applications that never falter. Delve into the world of SQL and NoSQL databases, mastering the art of storing and retrieving data with finesse.

Security takes center stage as you navigate the intricate realm of service implementation, APIs, and authentication with Azure AD B2C. With meticulous attention to detail, this book guides you through proper implementations, ensuring your applications are fortified against potential threats.

But it doesn't stop there. Unlock the secrets of the 12-factor app methodology as you delve into the realms of configuration and secrets management. Unearth the hidden gems of Azure Key Vault and configuration services, and witness their transformative power in creating harmonious and cohesive applications.

By reaching the final page, you will have conquered a myriad of Azure services, empowering you to construct awe-inspiring, scalable, manageable, and resilient applications and microservices with .NET and Azure. Take advantage of this extraordinary opportunity to embark on a journey that will elevate your skills and propel your career to new heights. Get your copy of *A Developer's Guide to .NET in Azure* today and unlock the limitless potential of the cloud-native world!

Who this book is for

Calling all .NET developers and architects ready to embark on an extraordinary journey into the realm of scalable and resilient applications. This book is tailor-made for you, equipping you with the skills and knowledge to develop and deploy awe-inspiring applications using .NET and Azure. With a basic understanding of .NET, you'll be guided through the enchanting world of Azure, unlocking the full potential of these cutting-edge technologies. Whether you're a seasoned developer or an aspiring enthusiast, this book is your gateway to mastering the art of building remarkable applications with .NET and Azure.

What this book covers

Chapter 1, *Setting Up Your Development Environment*, shows you how to set up your development environment for .NET and Azure, ensuring a smooth and efficient workflow.

Chapter 2, *Creating Docker Containers on Azure*, covers the power of containerization as you dive into creating and deploying Docker containers on the Azure platform.

Chapter 3, *Building Resilient Applications with Dapr*, explores the world of Dapr and harnesses its APIs to build highly resilient and portable microservices in your applications.

Chapter 4, *Designing Microservices with AKS and Containers in Azure*, teaches you how to master the art of designing and deploying microservices using **Azure Kubernetes Service** (**AKS**) for scalability and efficiency.

Chapter 5, *Building Serverless Apps with Azure Functions and Azure Container Apps*, shows you how to unleash the potential of serverless computing as you learn to build and deploy serverless applications on Azure.

Chapter 6, *Exploring Azure Blob Storage*, shows you how to efficiently store and retrieve data using Azure Blob storage for your application's data storage needs.

Chapter 7, *Creating an Azure SQL Database*, dives into the world of Azure SQL Database and discovers how to create and manage robust relational databases in the cloud.

Chapter 8, *Creating Documents via .NET for Azure Cosmos DB*, shows you how to unlock the power of Azure Cosmos DB and its document database capabilities as you build and manage documents using .NET.

Chapter 9, *Utilizing Azure App Configuration*, explores Azure App Configuration and shows you how to manage and control your application's configuration with ease.

Chapter 10, *Processing Data with Azure Event Hubs*, delves into the world of event-driven architectures and shows you how to process and manage data using Azure Event Hubs.

Chapter 11, *Designing Ready-Made Solutions with Azure Service Bus*, explores the capabilities of Azure Service Bus and shows you how to design robust and scalable enterprise solutions with ease.

Chapter 12, Enhancing Data Protection with Azure Key Vault, shows you how to master the art of securing sensitive data by leveraging Azure Key Vault and implementing robust data protection measures.

Chapter 13, Managing Access with Azure Active Directory B2C, explores the world of identity management and teaches you how to utilize Azure Active Directory B2C for secure access control.

To get the most out of this book

Software/hardware covered in the book	Operating system requirements
.NET 6.0, Microsoft Azure, Visual Studio Code, Visual Studio 2022, Docker, Dapr.	Windows, macOS, or Linux

If you are using the digital version of this book, we advise you to type the code yourself or access the code from the book's GitHub repository (a link is available in the next section). Doing so will help you avoid any potential errors related to the copying and pasting of code.

Download the example code files

You can download the example code files for this book from GitHub at `https://github.com/PacktPublishing/A-Developer-s-Guide-to-.NET-in-Azure`. If there's an update to the code, it will be updated in the GitHub repository.

We also have other code bundles from our rich catalog of books and videos available at `https://github.com/PacktPublishing/`. Check them out!

Conventions used

There are a number of text conventions used throughout this book.

Code in text: Indicates code words in text, database table names, folder names, filenames, file extensions, pathnames, dummy URLs, user input, and Twitter handles. Here is an example: "We will be using the `dotnet new mvc` command with some extra parameters for supporting authentication using Azure AD B2C."

A block of code is set as follows:

```
var builder = WebApplication.CreateBuilder(args);
var app = builder.Build();
app.UseStaticFiles();
app.MapFallbackToFile("index.html");
app.Run();
```

Any command-line input or output is written as follows:

```
> dotnet new mvc -o Chapter13.MVC --framework net6.0 --auth
IndividualB2C --aad-b2c-instance https://pakctchapter13.b2clogin.
com  --susi-policy-id B2C_1_SignupSignIn --domain pakctchapter13.
onmicrosoft.com --SignedOutCallbackPath /signout/B2C_1_
SignupSignIn  --client-id 43ce7f01-c5f0-4198-b3bc-fed398f319f9
--tenant-id f5aa067e-157b-4b56-b18b-8197479efea7 --callback-path /
signin-oidc
```

Bold: Indicates a new term, an important word, or words that you see onscreen. For instance, words in menus or dialog boxes appear in bold. Here is an example: "Once the Azure AD B2C resource is created, we can click on **View resource** and view the overview of Azure AD B2C."

> Tips or important notes
> Appear like this.

Get in touch

Feedback from our readers is always welcome.

General feedback: If you have questions about any aspect of this book, email us at customercare@packtpub.com and mention the book title in the subject of your message.

Errata: Although we have taken every care to ensure the accuracy of our content, mistakes do happen. If you have found a mistake in this book, we would be grateful if you would report this to us. Please visit www.packtpub.com/support/errata and fill in the form.

Piracy: If you come across any illegal copies of our works in any form on the internet, we would be grateful if you would provide us with the location address or website name. Please contact us at copyright@packt.com with a link to the material.

If you are interested in becoming an author: If there is a topic that you have expertise in and you are interested in either writing or contributing to a book, please visit authors.packtpub.com.

Share Your Thoughts

Once you've read *A Developer's Guide to .NET in Azure*, we'd love to hear your thoughts! Scan the QR code below to go straight to the Amazon review page for this book and share your feedback.

https://packt.link/r/1837633010

Your review is important to us and the tech community and will help us make sure we're delivering excellent quality content.

Download a free PDF copy of this book

Thanks for purchasing this book!

Do you like to read on the go but are unable to carry your print books everywhere?

Is your eBook purchase not compatible with the device of your choice?

Don't worry, now with every Packt book you get a DRM-free PDF version of that book at no cost.

Read anywhere, any place, on any device. Search, copy, and paste code from your favorite technical books directly into your application.

The perks don't stop there, you can get exclusive access to discounts, newsletters, and great free content in your inbox daily

Follow these simple steps to get the benefits:

1. Scan the QR code or visit the link below

https://packt.link/free-ebook/9781837633012

2. Submit your proof of purchase

3. That's it! We'll send your free PDF and other benefits to your email directly

Part 1:
An Introduction to
Your Environment

Kicking off our exploration of Microsoft Azure, this initial chapter aims to help you understand the Azure landscape. We introduce you to the Azure portal, where you can set up every resource that will be discussed in the upcoming chapters. We'll also help you set up your Azure development environment, including selecting and configuring your **integrated development environment (IDE)** for seamless Azure integration.

This part has the following chapter:

- *Chapter 1, Setting Up Your Development Environment*

1

Setting Up Your Development Environment

Welcome to the first chapter! This chapter will guide you through the steps to set up your development environment and create your first Azure project.

We will start by discussing how to create your Azure subscription, which is the first step in getting started with Azure development. We will provide you with a step-by-step guide on setting up your subscription, including selecting the right subscription type and configuring your account settings.

Next, we will dive into configuring your development environment. This includes setting up your machine with the software, tools, and dependencies required for Azure development. We will guide you through this process, ensuring you have a well-configured environment.

After that, we will set up your Visual Studio for success. Visual Studio is a robust **integrated development environment** (**IDE**) that provides the tools to build, test, and deploy your Azure projects. We will show you how to configure Visual Studio for Azure development, including how to set up your project templates and debugging tools.

Finally, we will walk you through creating your first project in Azure. We will provide a hands-on approach, guiding you through creating a new Azure project, setting up your project structure, and deploying your project to the cloud.

In this chapter, we will cover the following main topics:

- Creating your Azure subscription
- Configuring your development environment
- Setting up your Visual Studio for success
- Creating your first project

By the end of this chapter, you will have a solid understanding of how to create your Azure subscription, configure your development environment, set up Visual Studio for success, and create your first Azure project. So, let's get started!

Creating your Azure subscription

You need an Azure subscription to work with examples in this book. In this section, you will learn about how to create an Azure subscription. Let's get started with the steps:

1. Open the browser, and navigate to `https://azure.microsoft.com/en-in/free/`.

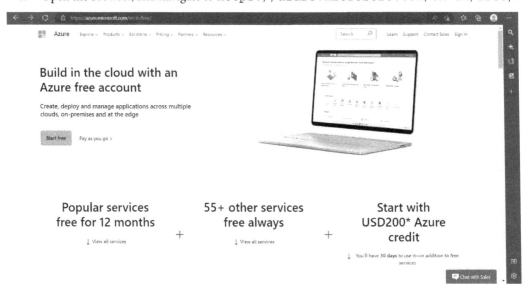

Figure 1.1 – Create your free Azure account screen

2. Click on the **Start free** button. On the second screen, you need to create an account. Click on the **Create one!** link.

Figure 1.2 – Azure account setup – signing in with a live account/signing up for a live account

3. You can use either your existing email address or you can create a new email address. We are using the existing email option.

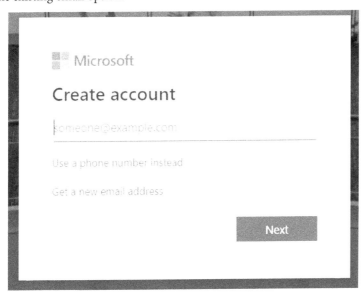

Figure 1.3 – Creating a live account – email address

4.   You need to create a password for your account and complete some CAPTCHA verification to create the account. Once it is completed, you will be redirected to an Azure account creation screen.

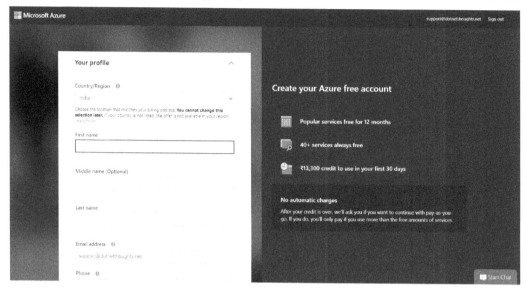

Figure 1.4 – Azure account profile creation

5.   On the screen, you need to provide your personal details, contact information, and your credit card information – for verification purposes. For verification purposes, $2 from your card will be charged and it will be credited to your card within one to two days.

Once the signup is successfully completed, you will be able to see the success page as follows. From this screen, you will be able to access the Azure portal.

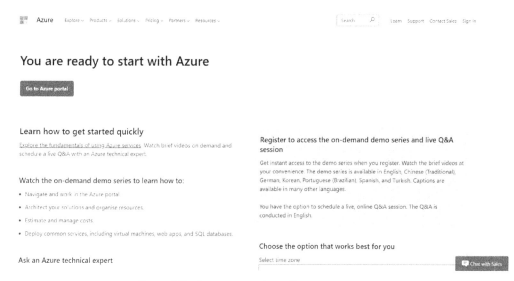

Figure 1.5 – Azure account creation – success page

6. Click on the **Go to Azure portal** button to access the Azure portal and you will be able to see a screen like this.

Figure 1.6 – Azure portal

The preceding screenshot shows the Azure portal where you can create and manage resources.

7. In the portal, you can search for resources in the middle search bar, which will help you to search for resources have you created; the available Azure services that you can create; the Marketplace, which you can use to access resources from third-party providers; and documentation on the Azure service you are looking for.

8.   In this example, I am searching for Storage since there is no storage account created. It does not show any existing resources, but the portal shows me services such as **Azure Storage Account** and **Storage browser**, and then it shows some Marketplace suggestions and finally, the documentation related to the Storage keyword.

Figure 1.7 – Searching for resources – the Azure portal

9.   In the portal, after the search bar, you can see a Cloud Shell icon, which helps you execute commands in either PowerShell or Bash shell – you can use this feature to create resources using the command line.

Figure 1.8 – Cloud Shell icon – Azure portal

10. The **Directories + Subscriptions** icon will help you switch between different active directories and subscriptions.

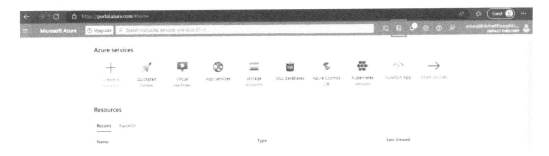

Figure 1.9 – Directories + Subscriptions – Azure portal

Once you click on the button, you will be able to see all directories.

Figure 1.10 – Directories + Subscriptions page – Azure portal

11. In the portal, the notifications icon will show different notifications, such as remaining credit, resource provisioning status, and so on.

Figure 1.11 – Notifications – Azure portal

12. Next is the settings icon, which helps you to customize the look and feel of the portal.

Figure 1.12 – Settings – Azure portal

Clicking on the settings icon will take you portal settings page where we have the following options:

- By default, it will open the **Directories + Subscriptions** page.

- You can click on the **Appearance + startup views** menu to configure the look and feel of the portal. In this section, you can also configure the first screen in terms of what you see on it when you log in.

Figure 1.13 – Configure appearance and startup view – Azure portal

- The **Language + region** option helps you to configure the currency format and date/time value.

Figure 1.14 - Setting up language, date, and currency format – Azure portal

- The **My information** section displays your email address and helps you to subscribe to different emails from Microsoft. You will be able to **Export** settings, which helps to export your current Azure portal configuration as a JSON file. The **Delete all settings and private dashboards** option helps you to remove all the settings and dashboards created.

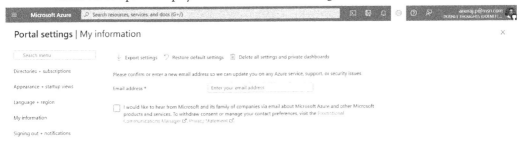

Figure 1.15 – My information – Azure portal

- Finally, the **Signing out + notifications** page helps you to configure notifications and sign-out options.

Figure 1.16 – Signing out and notifications configuration – Azure portal

13. Click on the **Support + troubleshooting** icon to learn about the health status of different Azure services. Also, you will be able to see different links to access billing FAQs, documentation, and the technical community.

Figure 1.17 – The Support and troubleshooting option – Azure portal

14. Click on the **Feedback** icon to share your experience with the Azure portal.

Figure 1.18 – Send feedback – Azure portal

15. Click on the **Show Portal Menu** option to see the Azure portal menu.

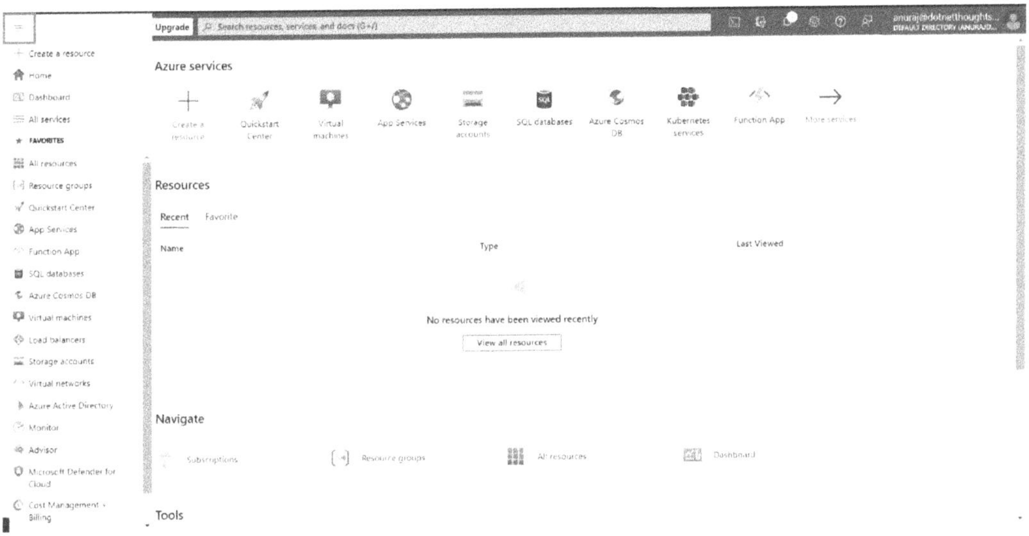

Figure 1.19 – Azure portal

You can customize this menu, which will help you to access different services quickly. The Azure portal comes with a Dashboard view as well. You will be able to create different dashboards and share them with your other team members.

Figure 1.20 – Azure portal

16. Click on the **Dashboard** button to see your private dashboard – by default, it will show as **My Dashboard**.

Figure 1.21 – Dashboard view – Azure portal

17. You can customize the dashboard. You can click on the **Edit** button, and on the screen, you can remove existing widgets and add different widgets.

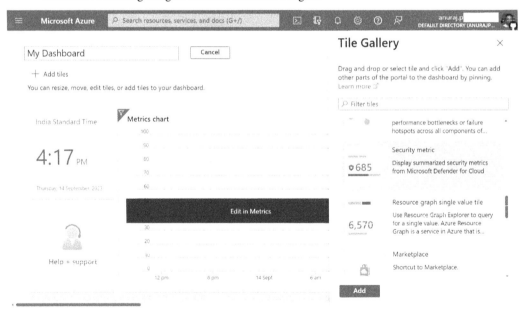

Figure 1.22 – Customizing the dashboard – Azure portal

18. Upon completing the customization, you can preview the changes, and then you will be able to save the changes by clicking on the **Save** button. You can share the dashboard with other users in the subscription using the **Share** button.

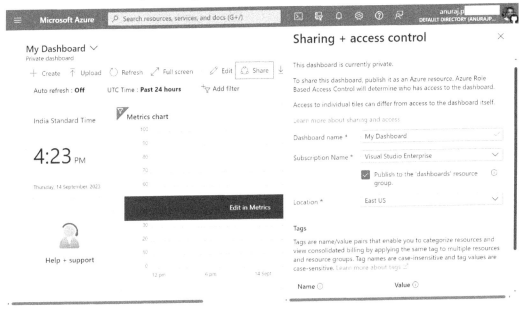

Figure 1.23 – Share dashboard – Azure portal

In this section, we learned about creating an Azure account and how to customize and configure the Azure portal. You will be able to create and manage different Azure resources from the Azure portal.

Creating resources in the Azure portal

Next, you will learn how to create a resource in the Azure portal:

1. You need to click on the + **Create a resource** button.

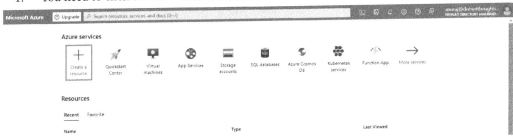

Figure 1.24 – Azure portal – + Create a resource

2.   On the next screen, you need to choose the resource you want to create.

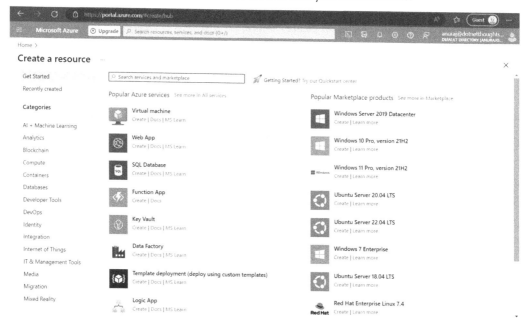

Figure 1.25 – Azure portal – Create a resource

For demo purposes, I will create a **resource group**. It's a container that contains related resources in an Azure solution. It is a best practice to create resources related to a project or product in the same resource group. You can search for `resource group` and click on the first result. Then, you will be able to see the details of the service/resource you're about to create.

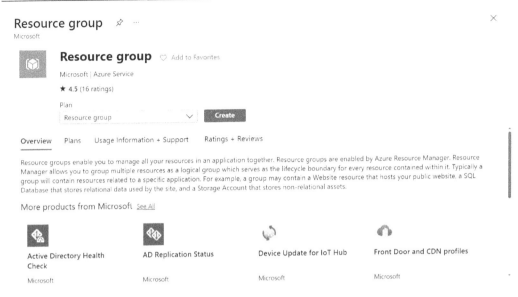

Figure 1.26 – Azure portal – new resource group

3.   Click on the **Create** button.

4.   On the **Create a resource group** screen, provide the name of the resource group – HelloWorld – set **Subscription** to **Free Trial**, and set **Region** to a region near your location.

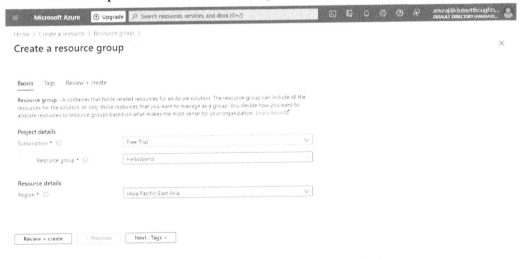

Figure 1.27 – Azure portal – Create a resource group – Basics screen

5.   Click on the **Review** + **create** button to view the details of the resource you're going to create, and then create the resource upon confirmation by clicking the button again. In the case of a resource group, you will only see the configuration values you created, but in the case of certain resources such as virtual machines or app services, you need to configure mandatory fields – then, you can click on **Review + create** – in such a scenario, you will be able to see the default values on this screen.

Or you can assign tags to the resource on the **Tags** tab. Tags are key-value pairs that act as metadata for Azure resources, which helps you to identify resources. Tags are helpful for tracking, organizing, grouping, and analyzing costs for resources. It is a best practice to add tags to your Azure resources.

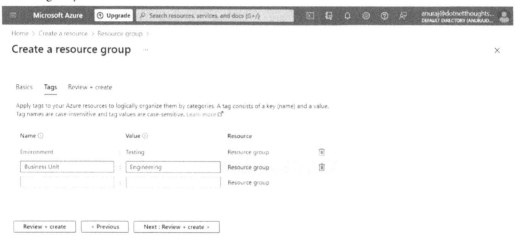

Figure 1.28 – Azure portal – associating tags

6.   Upon clicking the **Review + create** button again, you will be able to see the details of the resources and the tags:

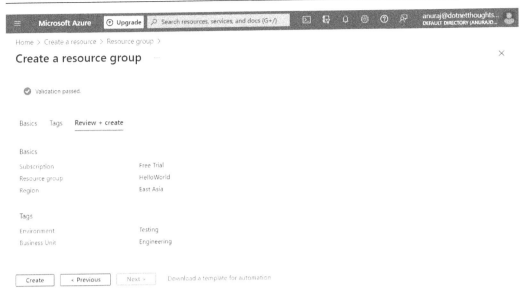

Figure 1.29 – Azure portal – Create a resource group confirmation screen

This screen will also help you to create an automation script. You can download the **Azure Resource Management (ARM)** script by clicking on the **Download a template for automation** link.

7. Once you click on the **Create** button, Azure will create the resource group and you will get a notification.

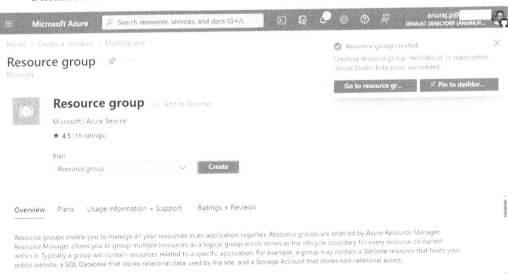

Figure 1.30 – Azure portal – Resource created notification

This way, you will be able to create resources in the Azure portal. Now you have learned how to create an account and create a free trial subscription in Azure portal. You also learned about how to create resources in Azure using the Azure portal. You will be able to create resources using the Azure CLI and Azure PowerShell as well. Next, you will learn about configuring your development environment.

Configuring your development environment

Setting up your development environment is essential for success because it provides you with the necessary tools and resources to efficiently and effectively develop, test, and deploy your software. A properly configured development environment allows you to streamline your workflow, automate tasks, and catch errors early on in the development process. If you're new to coding, I'm sure you're wondering how to set up the right environment for you so that you can get coding quickly and easily. You want to be able to focus on what matters most: creating great code!

There are many different ways to do this, but here is a simple guide that will show you how to set up an IDE for .NET programming on Azure. This guide will give you a solid foundation upon which you can build your knowledge of Python and other programming languages.

If you already have an environment setup, please note we will be working through examples utilizing .NET 6.0 in this book and that needs to be installed on your machine. If you are starting from scratch, follow the instructions below to get started.

Installing .NET 6.0

Follow these steps to install .NET 6.0:

1. Open your browser and go to this web page: `https://dotnet.microsoft.com/en-us/download/dotnet`. We will primarily be working in .NET 6.0 so make sure to choose the option related to the system you are using.

Figure 1.31 – .NET Download page

2. You need to download the .NET 6.0 SDK. Once the **Software Development Kit** (**SDK**) has been downloaded, execute the downloaded executable, which will bring up the following setup screen.

    In a Windows operating system, the executable will show a welcome screen as follows (see *Figure 1.32*) from where you can install the .NET SDK. In Windows, it will prompt for administrator access.

Figure 1.32 – .NET SDK – Windows installation

On Mac machines, it will show a welcome screen like this.

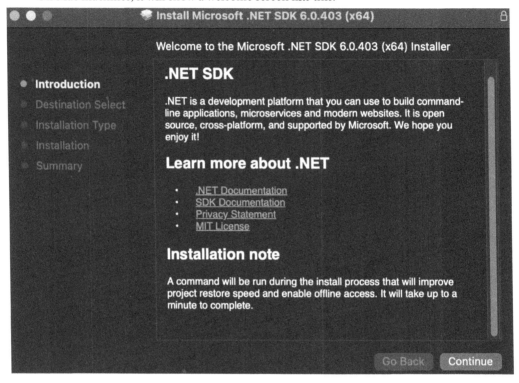

Figure 1.33 – .NET SDK – Mac installation

In Linux distributions, .NET SDK supports two types of installation – manual installation and script installation. With manual installation, we need to download the .NET SDK, execute the files, and configure paths. In script installation, we can download a .NET installation script from here: `https://dot.net/v1/dotnet-install.sh`. For developers or normal users, scripted installation is recommended. Once we have downloaded the script, we need to make it executable using the `chmod` command, and then execute the script.

Here are the bash commands to do this:

```
> wget https://dot.net/v1/dotnet-install.sh -O dotnet-install.sh
> chmod +x ./dotnet-install.sh
> ./dotnet-install.sh
```

This will install the .NET 6.0 SDK in most of the Linux distributions. You can find more details about the installation here: `https://learn.microsoft.com/dotnet/core/install/linux?WT.mc_id=DT-MVP-5002040`.

Now that we've successfully installed .NET 6.0, we can continue setting up our IDEs.

Setting up your local environment for Azure development

You need to set up and configure the development environment for building your applications in .NET and Azure. In this section, you will configure **Visual Studio Code (VS Code)** and Visual Studio. Visual Studio Code is an open source editor for building ASP.NET Core and C# applications.

Installing Visual Studio Code

Follow these steps to install Visual Studio Code:

1. Visit the Microsoft site to download Visual Studio Code: `https://visualstudio.microsoft.com/downloads/`

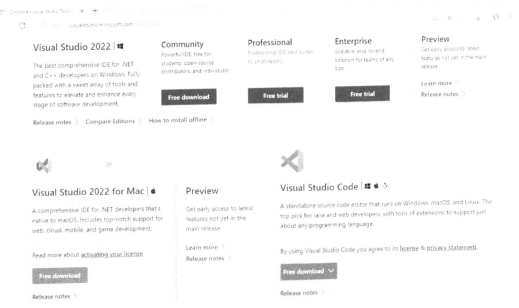

Figure 1.34 – Visual Studio/VS Code download page

2. Based on your development machine's operating system, download the applicable VS Code executable.

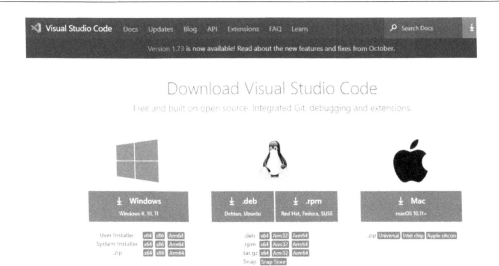

Figure 1.35 – VS Code – download page

3.   Accept the terms and conditions and continue with the installation:

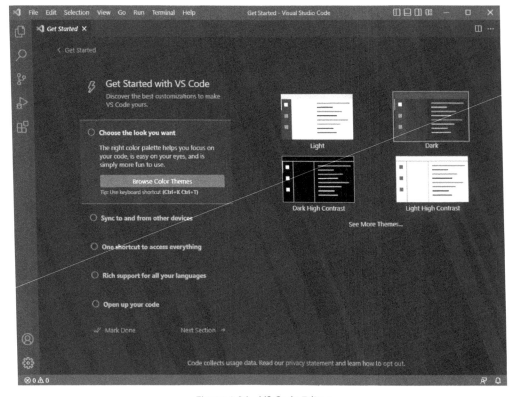

Figure 1.36 – VS Code Editor

4. Unlike on Windows and Mac, installing VS Code on Linux is easy – we just need to run the following command: `sudo snap install --classic code`. This will install VS Code on Linux. For more information on the VS Code installation, check out this page: `https://code.visualstudio.com/docs/setup/linux`.

5. Click on **Extensions** or press the *Ctrl + Shift + X* shortcut keys on Windows or *Cmd + Shift + X* on Mac and install the following extensions:

   - Azure Tools

   - Azure CLI Tools

   - Azure Pipelines

   - Azure Kubernetes Service

   - Azure Storage Explorer

   - C# Extension

Installing Visual Studio Community 2022

Follow these steps to install Visual Studio Community Edition 2022:

1. Visit the Microsoft site to download Visual Studio: `https://visualstudio.microsoft.com/downloads/`

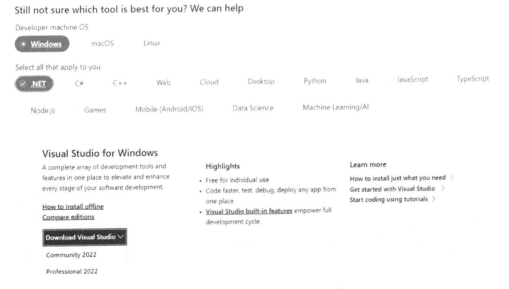

Figure 1.37 – Visual Studio download page

2. Install **Azure Development** and the accompanying packages for .NET development; the Visual Studio setup will prompt for different installation configurations or workloads.

Figure 1.38 – Visual Studio – installation configuration

3. Sign in to the cloud account you previously created to access the Azure resources within your IDE.

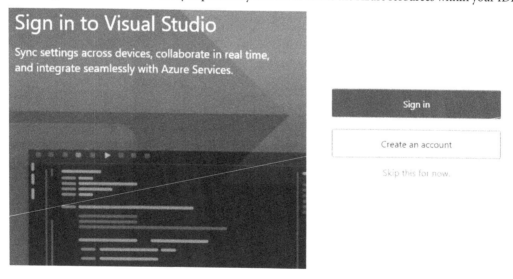

Figure 1.39 – Visual Studio – first screen

In this section, you learned about installing and configuring your development environment. VS Code is a cross-platform editor for debugging applications and Visual Studio is a fully featured IDE for building and debugging applications.

Now is the time to create our first project!

Creating your first project

After installing all of the prerequisite software listed in *step 2*, under the *Installing Visual Studio Community 2022* section, you should be able to begin building them without the need for any extra settings. To get things going, we'll write a straightforward function that we'll attempt to execute to make sure everything is set up and prepared. Start up Visual Studio 2022 Community Edition and select **Create a new project** to get started.

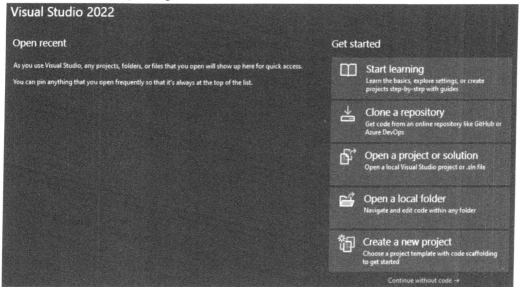

Figure 1.40 – Visual Studio – welcome screen

Now you can select an Azure Function from the list of choices and follow the steps to get started with the project. On the first screen, configure your new project screen. We need to set the project name, project location, and solution name. On the **Additional information** screen, we need to configure the framework, function trigger, and authorization level. Please see the following configuration values:

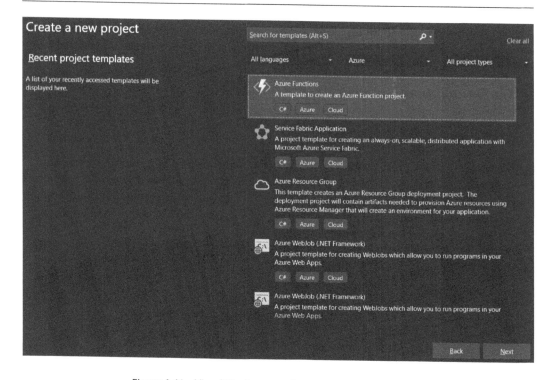

Figure 1.41 – Visual Studio – creating an Azure Functions app

Project Name: FunctionApp1

Project Location: C:\USER\PROJECTFOLDER

Solution Name: FunctionApp1

Functions Worker: .NET 6.0

Function: http trigger

Authorization Level: Function

After you click the **OK** button, you should see a screen similar to the following screenshot (see *Figure 1.42*). This indicates that a new function file has been created, and some standard code has already been added as a starting point. We will discuss how to create a function and its properties in the chapter of this book specifically related to Azure Functions (*Chapter 5*). For now, we won't go into too much detail.

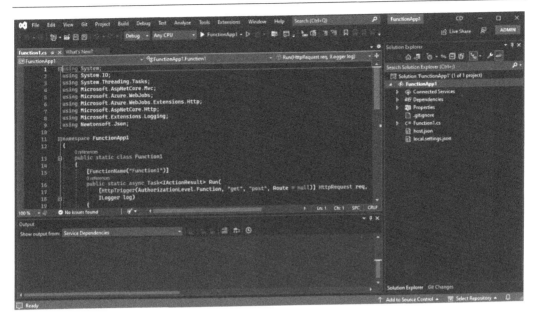

Figure 1.42 – Azure Functions project in Visual Studio

This is how, we can create an Azure Function using Visual Studio. We can other project types such as ASP.NET Core MVC, Blazor, and ASP.NET Core Web APIs. We will explore other project types in the upcoming chapters. Visual Studio will also help us to debug, deploy, and monitor the applications in Azure.

Summary

Congratulations on completing your first chapter on your Azure development journey! By now, you should have a solid understanding of how to set up your development environment, configure Visual Studio for Azure development, and create your first Azure project. These skills will serve as a foundation for your future Azure development work.

Remember, Azure is a powerful cloud platform with many services and solutions. By continuing to learn about and explore Azure, you can take advantage of its many benefits, including scalability, flexibility, and cost savings.

We hope this chapter has provided you with a valuable introduction to Azure development and inspired you to continue learning and exploring the world of cloud computing. The next chapter will dive deeper into Azure services and show you how to develop applications using some core services. In the next chapter, you will learn about containers, installing Docker, and building applications with container support. So, stay tuned and keep learning!

Part 2:
Serverless and Microservices

In this part, you will learn about the key aspects of Microsoft Azure. Initially, you'll dive into containerization and enrich your knowledge by understanding the **Distributed Application Runtime** (**Dapr**), enabling you to construct resilient, stateful microservices easily, and design microservices with **Azure Kubernetes Service (AKS)**. Finally, you'll be introduced to the power of serverless computing with Azure Functions and Azure Container Apps, and you will learn how to deploy practical, scalable applications that optimize cost. Each chapter promises a balance of theoretical understanding and practical application, paving the way for a holistic learning experience and equipping you with the necessary tools to develop scalable, resilient, and highly available applications.

This part has the following chapters:

- *Chapter 2, Creating Docker Containers on Azure*
- *Chapter 3, Building Resilient Applications with Dapr*
- *Chapter 4, Designing Microservices with AKS and Containers in Azure*
- *Chapter 5, Building Serverless Apps with Azure Functions and Container Apps*

2

Creating Docker Containers on Azure

Containers are a standard way of packaging application source code, dependencies, and configuration together so that it can be deployed anywhere without worrying about the dependencies and their versions. Docker is a company that offers a container platform. In this chapter, we will learn about Docker basics, how to create a Docker image, how to configure a private Docker registry, and finally, how to configure **continuous integration** (**CI**) and **continuous deployment** (**CD**) with a container registry. In later chapters, we will learn about Azure Container Apps and **Azure Kubernetes Service** (**AKS**) services that use Docker images and help us deploy Docker images at scale.

In this chapter, we're going to cover the following main topics:

- Installing Docker
- Exploring Docker and basic Docker commands
- Creating Docker images for your ASP.NET Core application
- Creating and configuring Azure Container Registry
- Deploying web apps to Azure App Service from Azure Container Registry
- Configuring CI/ CD with Azure Container Registry

Technical requirements

In this chapter, you'll see examples using ASP.NET Core, and you need the .NET SDK installed on your machine. If the .NET SDK is not installed, check out *Chapter 1* for instructions on how to do it. For building and debugging, you need either Visual Studio or VS Code.

Installing Docker

In this section, you will install Docker Desktop on your Windows machine. Docker is a software company that offers a containerization platform. There are other container software providers as well, but Docker is the most popular one.

In Windows, you can install Docker with the **WSL** (short for **Windows Subsystem for Linux**) backend or the **Hyper V** backend. The WSL backend is preferred, as WSL 2 provides better performance than the Hyper-V backend. You need a Windows 10 or Windows 11 computer with a 64-bit processor, 4 GB RAM, and hardware virtualization support must be enabled. You can find more details at `https://docs.docker.com/desktop/install/windows-install/`. You can also find the installation setup in this URL.

Once you download the Docker Desktop Installer (`Docker Desktop Installer.exe`) and execute it, the setup will check your system for the prerequisites and then show a prompt like this:

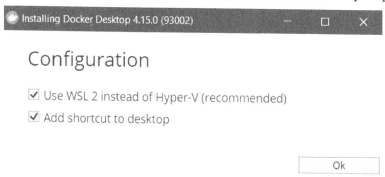

Figure 2.1: Docker Desktop installation screen

Since WSL is enabled in this machine, it is showing a prompt with WSL configuration. You can click **Ok** to continue. Next, the setup executable will download the required files. This may take some time based on your internet connection. Once the installation is complete, you will see a screen with a **Close** button. You can click on the **Close** button to finish the installation.

Next, from the desktop (if you selected the **Add shortcut to desktop** option in *Figure 2.1*), you're able to access the Docker Desktop icon. Double-click on the icon and it will start Docker Desktop. You need to accept the Docker subscription service agreement. Once you accept the agreement, Docker Desktop will start and will show the **Docker Desktop Tutorial** screen; you can skip this. You will then get the Docker Desktop dashboard screen.

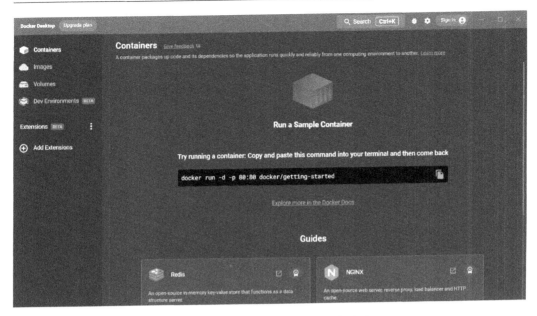

Figure 2.2: Docker Desktop dashboard window

You will be able to manage and configure Docker Desktop from this window. You can verify the installation by opening a Terminal or PowerShell or command window and executing the `docker version` command, which will display information like this:

```
> docker version
```

Once it is executed, you will be able to see the results in the console window, which will display the Docker client version and Docker server version.

To install Docker on other platforms, check out `https://docs.docker.com/get-docker/`.

In this section, we learned about what Docker is, how to install Docker Desktop on your machine, and how you can find out the Docker version by using the `docker version` command. In the next section, we will explore Docker in more depth and learn about basic Docker commands.

Exploring Docker and basic Docker commands

In this section, you will learn about Docker and a few Docker commands that are required to create and manage Docker images.

Containers provide a standard way to package your application source code, configurations, and dependencies into a single object. Containerization helps provide a separation of concerns – the development team can focus on implementing the business functionality and application logic, and the IT and operations teams can focus on deployment and management without bothering about the application dependencies, software versions, and configurations.

Docker architecture

Docker is written in the **Go** language and uses a client-server architecture. When you install Docker Desktop, you will be installing both the client and server, also known as **Docker daemon**, on your machine. The Docker client communicates to the Docker daemon through REST APIs. Here are some Docker architecture components:

- **Docker image** – This is a template that helps you to build a container. This contains the software dependencies and configuration of your application, which are used to create containers. The naming convention of Docker images is like this repository name: `tag` – if no version is specified, the latest tag is applied.

- **Docker container** – This is the instance of the Docker image. For example, if you consider a Docker image as a class in object-oriented programming, then the Docker container will be the instance of the class. It consists of your application code, dependencies, and configuration that helps to run your application.

- **Docker registry** – This is where you can store Docker images so that you can distribute them to Docker users. There are different registries available – Docker Hub is a Docker registry from Docker, **Azure Container Registry** (**ACR**) is from Azure, and **GitHub Container Registry** (**GHCR**) is from GitHub. You will be able to publish the images as public or private. Later in this chapter, you will learn more about ACR.

- **Docker daemon** – The Docker daemon runs as a service in your machine and listens for API requests from the Docker client – the Docker CLI or Docker Compose. Docker daemon manages the containers, images, volumes, and networking.

- **Docker client** – This is a command-line tool that helps you to interact with the The Docker daemon. You can connect to external Docker daemons as well.

Here is the basic architecture of Docker:

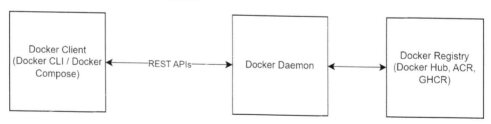

Figure 2.3: Docker Desktop architecture

When you execute the `docker version` command, in the result, you will be able to see the versions of both the Docker client and Docker server or Docker daemon.

Next, we will explore some Docker commands that you need to create, manage, and deploy a Docker image to ACR.

In the Terminal, if you execute the `docker help` command, you will be able to see all the Docker commands – certain commands are only available in certain versions . For example, Docker recently introduced a feature called **extensions**, so Docker commands to manage extensions are only available in the new versions.

Docker development life cycle

In this section, we will learn about the Docker development life cycle. It refers to the various stages and processes involved in developing and deploying applications using Docker. Docker allows you to package applications and their dependencies into containers, which can be easily moved between different environments, ensuring consistent behavior across development, testing, and production.

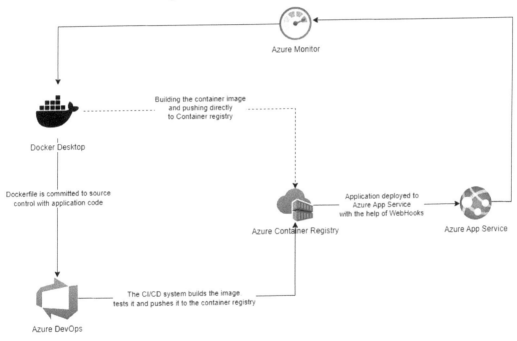

Figure 2.4: Docker development life cycle

Once we install and configure Docker Desktop in the development machine, we will create a Dockerfile along with the application code. We can either push the code to Azure DevOps or any other source control tools and the DevOps tool will build the Docker image and push it to the container registry, or we can build the Docker image from the development machine, test it, and push the image to the container registry. By using DevOps tools, we will be able to automate various tests, such as unit tests, integration tests, and security tests. From the container registry, by using Webhooks, we can automate the deployment to Azure App Service or any other hosting platform such as AKS or Azure Container Apps. We can use Azure Monitor or Azure Application Insights to monitor the performance and behavior of the containers. We can use Azure Monitor logs to troubleshoot any issues. Azure Monitor also helps to inspect the container state. We will be exploring the various components of the Docker life cycle in this chapter.

Docker commands

As mentioned earlier, there are a lot of Docker commands available. In this section, however, you will learn only a few of the ones that help to create and manage Docker images and containers:

- `docker run` – Runs a command in a new container
- `docker pull` – Pulls an image or a repository from a registry
- `docker images` – Lists all Docker images in the host machine
- `docker tag` – Creates a tag for the Docker image, which is required to deploy to the container registry
- `docker login` – Logs in to a container registry
- `docker build` – Builds a container from a Dockerfile

The docker run command

The `docker run` command helps you to run a Docker container. If you try to run a container that doesn't exist in your local host, Docker will download it from your configured container registry – by default, it will be Docker Hub. If the container image doesn't exist in the container registry, Docker will show an error message – either the image doesn't exist or it may require a login.

Here is an example. Run the `docker run` command with the `hello-world` image like this:

```
> docker run hello-world
```

When you execute this command, the Docker client will send the details to the Docker daemon. Since the container doesn't exist in your Docker host, it will download it from Docker Hub:

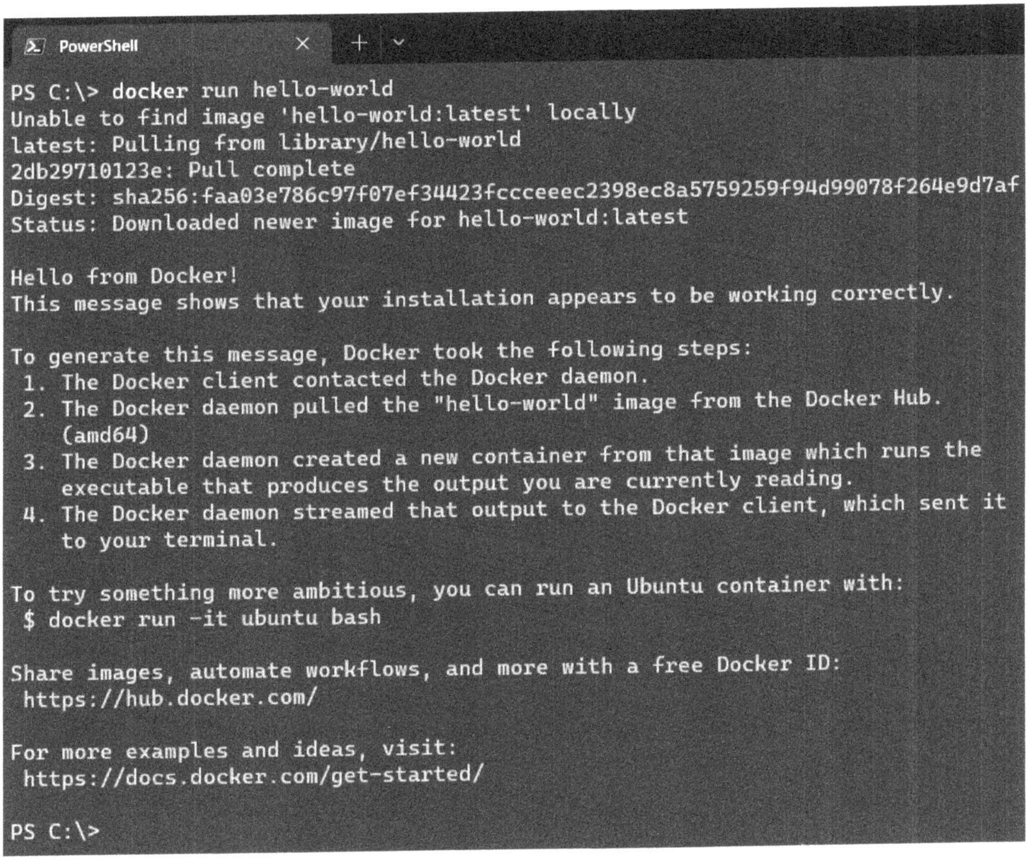

```
PowerShell                    ×    +   ∨

PS C:\> docker run hello-world
Unable to find image 'hello-world:latest' locally
latest: Pulling from library/hello-world
2db29710123e: Pull complete
Digest: sha256:faa03e786c97f07ef34423fccceeec2398ec8a5759259f94d99078f264e9d7af
Status: Downloaded newer image for hello-world:latest

Hello from Docker!
This message shows that your installation appears to be working correctly.

To generate this message, Docker took the following steps:
 1. The Docker client contacted the Docker daemon.
 2. The Docker daemon pulled the "hello-world" image from the Docker Hub.
    (amd64)
 3. The Docker daemon created a new container from that image which runs the
    executable that produces the output you are currently reading.
 4. The Docker daemon streamed that output to the Docker client, which sent it
    to your terminal.

To try something more ambitious, you can run an Ubuntu container with:
 $ docker run -it ubuntu bash

Share images, automate workflows, and more with a free Docker ID:
 https://hub.docker.com/

For more examples and ideas, visit:
 https://docs.docker.com/get-started/

PS C:\>
```

Figure 2.5: The docker run hello-world command result

Once it is downloaded, it will run the container, which basically prints out a **hello world** message on the screen. If you run the command again, you will see the container prints the message – it will not download the image again as it is already available.

When you're running web applications or databases, you may need to pass the port numbers as the parameter. To learn more about the docker run command, execute the command with the --help parameter – this parameter works with all Docker commands.

The docker pull command

This command helps you to pull the Docker images from the Docker registry. If the image exists in the local machine, it won't download the image again:

```
> docker pull hello-world
```

Here is an example; when you execute it for the first time, it can't find the image locally, so it is downloaded from Docker Hub:

```
PS C:\> docker pull hello-world
Using default tag: latest
latest: Pulling from library/hello-world
2db29710123e: Pull complete
Digest: sha256:faa03e786c97f07ef34423fccceeec2398ec8a5759259f94d99078f264e9d7af
Status: Downloaded newer image for hello-world:latest
docker.io/library/hello-world:latest
PS C:\> docker pull hello-world
Using default tag: latest
latest: Pulling from library/hello-world
Digest: sha256:faa03e786c97f07ef34423fccceeec2398ec8a5759259f94d99078f264e9d7af
Status: Image is up to date for hello-world:latest
docker.io/library/hello-world:latest
PS C:\>
```

Figure 2.6: The docker pull hello-world command result

But when you execute it for a second time, it is not downloaded from Docker Hub.

The docker images command

This `docker images` command or `docker image list` command will help you list all the images in your machine:

```
> docker images
```

It will display the repository (name), tag, image ID, when the image was created, and the size of the image:

```
PS C:\> docker image list
REPOSITORY      TAG       IMAGE ID        CREATED          SIZE
hello-world     latest    feb5d9fea6a5    14 months ago    13.3kB
PS C:\>
```

Figure 2.7: The docker image list command result

As you see, only one image exists – `hello-world` – and you can see the tag as `latest`. The image ID is a unique number, it was created 14 months ago, and the size is 13.3 KB. You can filter images with the name as the parameter, like this:

```
> docker images hello-world
```

This command will list all the `hello-world` images with different versions.

The docker tag command

This command helps you to tag a Docker container. This command is useful when you publish a Docker image to a container registry. To publish a Docker image, you need to follow a naming convention for the images, depending on the Docker registry. For Docker Hub, the naming convention is `dockerhub-username/repository:tag`. For ACR, it is `acrname.azurecr.io/repository:tag`. Unlike earlier commands, this command requires two parameters, *source name and tag*, and *target name and tag*. Here is an example:

```
> docker tag hello-world:latest packtpubebook.azurecr.io/hello-
world:1.0.0
```

When you execute this command, it doesn't display any message, but if you execute the `docker images` command, you will be able to see two container images:

Figure 2.8: The docker tag command result

If you notice, the details – the image ID, created time, and size – of both images are the same except for the repository name and tag.

The docker login command

The `docker login` command helps you to log in to a Docker container registry. You need to provide the registry as the parameter for this command.

You will log in to a container registry after you provision one in the *Creating and configuring Azure Container Registry* section of this chapter.

The docker build command

This is one of the most important commands, used to build an image from a Dockerfile.

Dockerfile

A Dockerfile is a regular text file that helps you to build container images. It contains different instructions or commands that you can execute in the Docker CLI. The format of a Dockerfile is like this:

```
INSTRUCTION arguments
```

A Dockerfile can have comments that start with a hash symbol (#). The instructions are not case-sensitive – it is the convention to use uppercase. The Dockerfile should start with a FROM instruction. The FROM instruction requires an image. Docker runs the instructions in the Dockerfile in the order of the commands written in the file. Here is an example of a Dockerfile:

```
FROM mcr.microsoft.com/dotnet/aspnet:6.0 AS runtime
WORKDIR /app
COPY published/ ./
ENTRYPOINT ["dotnet", "Chapter2.dll"]
```

This Dockerfile uses the ASP.NET Core 6.0 runtime as the base image – FROM mcr.microsoft.com/dotnet/aspnet:6.0. The WORKDIR instruction sets the working directory as /app. Then, the COPY instruction copies the contents of the published directory to the /app directory, and finally, the ENTRYPOINT instruction helps to execute the dotnet command with the Chapter2.dll file.

In this section, we explored Docker, looked at various Docker commands, and saw how to create a Dockerfile. In the next section, we will learn how to create a Dockerfile for your ASP.NET Core application and create a Docker image of the application.

Creating Docker images for your ASP.NET Core application

You can create, dockerize, or containerize your application using different tools. In this section, you will learn how to containerize your application with a Dockerfile, Docker CLI, VS Code, and Visual Studio.

Containerizing an ASP.NET Core application with the Docker CLI and Dockerfile

Follow these steps to get started:

1. First, you need to create an empty .NET Core 6.0 web app. Here is the command to create an empty web app; you can create any type of ASP.NET Core application – MVC, Web API, or Razor Pages:

   ```
   > dotnet new web -o Chapter02 --framework net6.0
   ```

   The -o parameter creates the project in the Chapter02 folder and the framework version is .NET 6.0 – this is required if you don't have multiple versions installed on your machine.

2. Next, in the project root folder, create a file with the name Dockerfile – no file extension. Then, paste the following code into the Dockerfile:

   ```
   FROM mcr.microsoft.com/dotnet/aspnet:6.0 AS runtime
   WORKDIR /app
   COPY published/ ./
   ENTRYPOINT ["dotnet", "Chapter02.dll"]
   ```

3. Next, you need to execute the command to publish the web app using the `dotnet publish` command. This is a very basic Dockerfile that is used to host the ASP.NET Core application. In the next section, you will learn about how to build the source code in a Docker container. Since the Dockerfile is using the `published` folder in the root folder, you need to execute the command with the `output` folder parameter, like this:

```
> dotnet publish --configuration Release --output published
```

4. Next, execute the `docker build` command like this:

```
> docker build -t packtbook.azurecr.io/chapter02:1.0.0 .
```

The `docker build` command's `-t` parameter builds and tags the Docker image. The dot (`.`) specifies the location of the Dockerfile – in our case, it is the `Chapter02` folder or the current directory. If the Dockerfile exists in a different directory, you need to mention it.

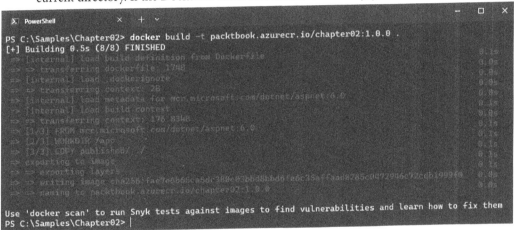

Figure 2.9: docker build command execution

5. Finally, you can run the container using the `docker run` command, like this:

```
> docker run --publish 5000:80 packtbook.azurecr.io/
Chapter02:1.0.0
```

This command runs the Docker container, which exposes port 5000. The application is running on port 80 inside the container, so the web app will be accessible via `localhost:5000`. This is a very basic Dockerfile. If you're using VS Code with a Docker extension or Visual Studio, you will be able to create a Dockerfile for your web application without writing any code.

> .NET 7.0 – bonus tip
>
> In .NET 7.0, Microsoft introduced a feature that helps publish Docker images without creating a Dockerfile. First, you need to add the reference of the `Microsoft.NET.Build.Containers` NuGet package to the project with the following command:
>
> ```
> > dotnet add package Microsoft.NET.Build.Containers
> ```
>
> Next, you can publish the Docker image using the following command:
>
> ```
> > dotnet publish --os linux --arch x64 -p:PublishProfile=DefaultContainer
> ```
>
> This will create a Docker image. You will be able to customize the name, tags, and so on with the project ile. Free to explore more at `https://learn.microsoft.com/dotnet/core/docker/publish-as-container?WT.mc_id=DT-MVP-5002040`

With VS Code and Visual Studio, you can add Docker support and the ability to debug your application running on Docker.

Containerizing your ASP.NET Core app with VS Code

Let's create a Docker image for your ASP.NET Core application using VS Code:

1. First, you need to create an ASP.NET Core project. You can create this project using the `dotnet` CLI command, like this:

    ```
    > dotnet new web -o Chapter02 --framework net6.0
    ```

2. Next, you need to open the project using VS Code. Either you can right-click on the **Project** button and click on **Open with Code** or you can execute the command, like this:

    ```
    > code Chapter02
    ```

3. If you're running VS Code for the first time, it will recommend some extensions such as C# since you're opening an ASP.NET Core project. If it is not prompting you, you may need to navigate to the **EXTENSIONS** tab on the VS Code main screen and install the following extensions:

    *   C# – `https://marketplace.visualstudio.com/items?itemName=ms-dotnettools.csharp`

    *   Docker – `https://marketplace.visualstudio.com/items?itemName=ms-azuretools.vscode-docker`

    The C# extension will help you to develop and debug ASP.NET Core apps. The Docker extension will help you to create and debug Docker images.

Figure 2.10: VS Code EXTENSIONS tab

Once it is installed, you may need to reload VS Code.

4. After you reload, VS Code will load the project again. Click on **View | Command Palette** or press the shortcut *F1* or *Ctrl + Shift + P*. Then, type `Docker:` and select the **Add Docker Files to Workspace…** option. You need to make sure that Docker Desktop is running on your machine; otherwise, it might not work properly.

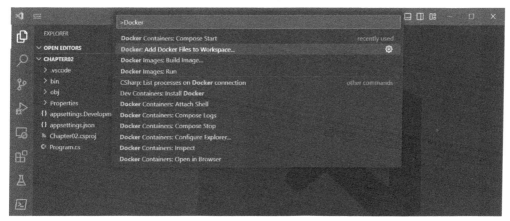

Figure 2.11: Add Docker Files to Workspace

5. Executing the previous step will prompt you to select the application platform – you need to choose **.NET: ASP.NET Core**.

6. Next, it will prompt you to select an operating system – you need to select **Linux** – by default, Docker Desktop will run Linux containers. There is an option to switch to Windows containers. Compared to Linux containers, Windows containers have a few limitations, such as you will get very few Docker images that support Windows containers, and the image size of Windows containers will be high compared to Linux containers.

7. Next, VS Code will show a port selection prompt; you can continue with the prepopulated one. Finally, VS Code will prompt you to include optional Docker Compose files; you can select the **No** option. Once it is completed, VS Code will generate a Dockerfile and show you; you can customize it if required.

8. You can again open the Command Palette and select Docker commands to build the image and run the Docker image. VS Code will also generate a `.dockerignore` file, which is similar to the `.gitignore` file, where you can specify the files or folders you don't need to copy to your containers – for example, the `Readme.md` file.

Containerizing your ASP.NET Core with Visual Studio

Similar to VS Code, Visual Studio offers containerization support for ASP.NET Core projects, and compared to VS Code, it is easy.

Create or open your ASP.NET Core application in Visual Studio. Once the project is loaded, right-click on the project node and select the **Docker Support...** menu. Visual Studio will prompt you to select the operating system of the container; similar to VS Code, select **Linux**. Visual Studio will create the Dockerfile in your project root.

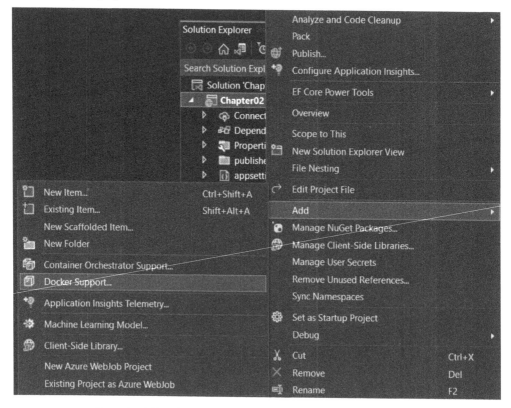

Figure 2.12: Visual Studio – adding Docker support for ASP.NET Core

Here is the Dockerfile generated by Visual Studio:

```
FROM mcr.microsoft.com/dotnet/aspnet:6.0 AS base
WORKDIR /app
EXPOSE 80
EXPOSE 443
FROM mcr.microsoft.com/dotnet/sdk:6.0 AS build
WORKDIR /src
COPY ["Chapter2.csproj", "."]
RUN dotnet restore "./Chapter2.csproj"
COPY . .
WORKDIR "/src/."
RUN dotnet build "Chapter2.csproj" -c Release -o /app/build
FROM build AS publish
RUN dotnet publish "Chapter2.csproj" -c Release -o /app/publish
/p:UseAppHost=false
FROM base AS final
WORKDIR /app
COPY --from=publish /app/publish .
ENTRYPOINT ["dotnet", "Chapter2.dll"]
```

VS Code will also generate a similar Dockerfile. This is a multi-stage build – unlike the earlier example, this Dockerfile contains multiple FROM statements. Multi-stage builds help you to reduce the build size.

In this section, you learned how to create Docker images for your application using the Docker CLI, VS Code, and Visual Studio. In the next section, you will learn how to create and configure ACR, and then how to deploy your Docker image to ACR and Azure App Service.

Creating and configuring Azure Container Registry

In this section, you will learn how to create an Azure container registry and different configuration options. You will also learn how to publish a Docker image to ACR and publish it to Azure App Service. So, let's get started:

1. Here, you will create all the resources using the Azure CLI. You need to install the Azure CLI if it is not already installed on your machine. You can download it from this URL: https://learn.microsoft.com/en-us/cli/azure/. The Azure CLI is cross-platform; you need to install it based on your operating system. Once installed, open your Terminal window and execute the following command:

    ```
    > az version
    ```

    This will display version information about the Azure CLI. If you're getting an error, you may need to restart the Terminal session or you may need to re-install the Azure CLI.

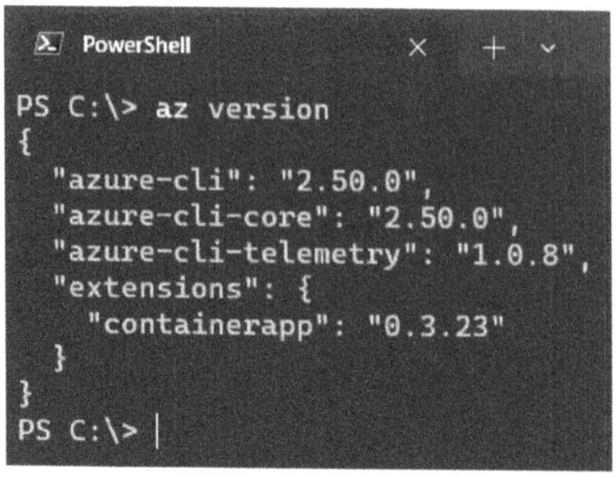

Figure 2.13: Azure CLI – az version command

2. Once the installation is complete, you need to associate the Azure CLI to your Azure account. To do this, execute the following command, which will open the Azure portal login window:

    > **az login**

    You can log in with your Azure portal credentials. If it succeeds, the Terminal will display information about your Azure subscription – name and subscription ID. The az login command can fail due to a number of reasons, such as invalid credentials, authorization issues, device login failure, expired or revoked tokens, or proxy or network issues. Based on the error message from the Azure CLI, try to troubleshoot or contact Azure support.

3. Now, you're ready to create the container registry. To create any resource in Azure, first, you need to create a resource group. We can execute the following command to create a resource group, which can be used to organize the various Azure resources we are creating in this chapter:

    > **az group create --name chapter2 --location centralindia**

    This command creates a resource group with the name chapter2 in the Central India region. Once it is executed, you will be able to see a JSON output and no errors.

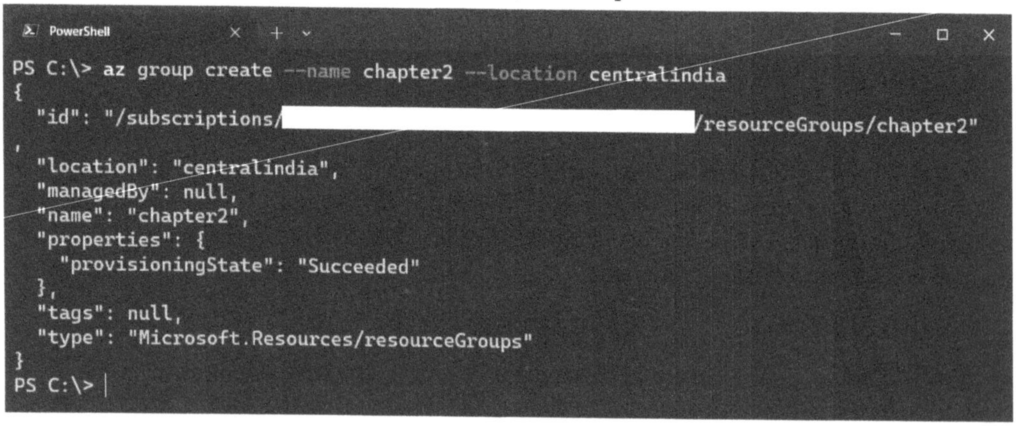

Figure 2.14: Azure resource group command output

4. Next, you can create the container registry using this command:

    ```
    > az acr create --resource-group chapter2 --name packtbook --sku
    Basic
    ```

    This command will create the container registry with the name `packtbook` with a `Basic` **Stock Keeping Unit (SKU)** or pricing tier, which is a cost-optimized solution for learning. The container registry name should be globally unique. So, you may need to add a unique number with the name. Once it is created, you will be able to see the details of the container registry in JSON format. You can log in to the container registry using the `docker login` command.

5. Since you're using the Azure CLI, it offers a command that helps to log in to ACR that is built on top of `docker login`. Here is the command to log in to ACR:

    ```
    > az acr login --name packtbook
    ```

    This command will log in to the `packtbook` container registry that we created in *Step 4*.

6. You need to execute it with your container registry name. And since you already logged into the account, the CLI will not prompt for any credentials and you will get a **Login Succeeded** message.

7. To publish the Docker image to the container registry, you need to tag the Docker image with the registry name if it is not already. You can use the Docker image that you created in the *Exploring Docker and basic Docker commands* section. Here is the command to build the Docker image with the registry name:

    ```
    > docker build -t packtbook.azurecr.io/chapter2:1.0.0 .
    ```

    This command will create the Docker image with the container registry name `packtbook.azurecr.io`.

8. And if you're using any other image, such as the `hello-world` image, you can tag it like this:

    ```
    > docker tag hello-world:latest packtbook.azurecr.io/ hello-
    world:latest
    ```

    Please note that you need to use your container registry name instead of `packtbook`. This command will help us to tag or configure the name of the container image with our container registry name.

9. Once you create the Docker image, you can execute the `docker push` command to publish the Docker image to your container registry:

    ```
    > docker push packtbook.azurecr.io/chapter2:1.0.0
    ```

    This command may take some time, depending on your internet connectivity.

10. Once it is executed, you can open the portal and search for container registries. Select the container registry you created, then select the **Repositories** menu, and you will be able to see the Docker image you published.

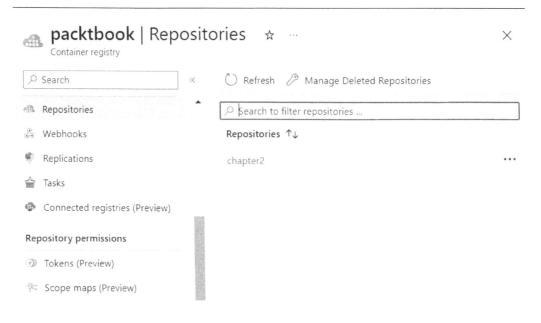

Figure 2.15: ACR – Repositories

11. You can also view the Docker images available in the container registry using the Azure CLI command, like this:

```
> az acr repository list --name packtbook --output table
```

This will display the Docker image name. In this command, you're listing the container images in the specified registry.

12. You can remove your existing Docker image using the following command:

```
> docker rmi packtbook.azurecr.io/chapter2:1.0.0
```

13. Next, you can consume the image from the registry using the docker pull or docker run command, like this.

```
> docker pull packtbook.azurecr.io/chapter2:1.0.0
> docker run --publish 5000:80 packtbook.azurecr.io/
chapter2:1.0.0
```

And you will be able to browse the app using the URL localhost:5000.

In this section, you learned how to create an Azure container registry using the Azure CLI and how to publish images to the container registry using Docker commands. In the next section, you will learn about deploying your ASP.NET Core application from the container registry to Azure App Service.

Deploying web apps to Azure App Service from Azure Container Registry

In this section, you will learn how to deploy an ASP.NET Core application to Azure App Service from ACR. There are two ways you can deploy images from ACR to other Azure services such as App Service, Container Apps, and Azure Functions. In this section, you will learn about enabling the **admin user** feature in ACR. This one is simple and easy to use. Another deployment option is using the **managed identity** feature in Azure. The managed identity feature is the recommended practice. You will learn about creating and configuring managed identity for ACR in the next section.

With the following steps, you will learn how to enable the admin user and work with username and password:

1. To enable the admin user of ACR, you can execute the following command:

    ```
    > az acr update -n packtbook --admin-enabled true
    ```

2. Once it is executed, Azure will enable the admin user for ACR with default passwords, which you can query and regenerate if required. To view the password, execute the following command:

    ```
    > az acr credential show --name packtbook --query
    [username,passwords[0].value]
    ```

    The preceding command will show the username and password for ACR. You can access the same from the portal as well.

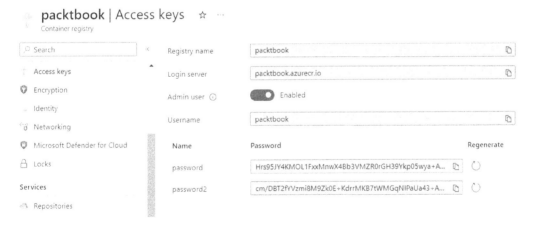

Figure 2.16: ACR – Access Keys

3. Next, you can create the Azure App Service. App Service resource provisioning can be done in three steps. First, you can create a resource group, then an App Service plan, and finally, the App Service. The resource group creation is optional, but it is recommended. Here are the Azure CLI commands to create a resource group and App Service plan:

    ```
    > az group create --name chapter2-example --location centralus
    > az appservice plan create --name chapter2-app-plan --resource-
    group chapter2-example --location centralus --is-linux --sku B1
    ```

    The first command will create a resource group with the name `chapter2-example` in the Central US region. The next command will create an App Service plan with the name `chapter2-app--plan` in the `chapter2-example` resource group. The App Service operating system is configured as Linux and the pricing tier is basic, `B1`, in the Central US region. Please note – the Linux-based app services are not available in all Azure regions and all SKUs. If you're getting any errors while provisioning, try changing the location or SKU. Currently, the `B1` SKU is free for one month.

4. Once the app service plan is created, you can execute the command to provision the app service. You can do this by executing the following command:

    ```
    > az webapp create --name packtbook-app-service --plan chapter2-
    app-plan --resource-group chapter2-example --deployment-
    container-image-name packtbook.azurecr.io/chapter2:1.0.0
    ```

    This will create a web app or Azure app service with the name `packtbook-app-service` (this name should be globally unique) in `chapter2-app--plan` inside the `chapter2-example` resource group. The deployment container image name configures the image to deploy. Once the deployment is completed, you will be able to access the app using the URL `https://packtbook-app-service.azurewebsites.net`. As mentioned earlier, you may need to use your own domain that you created. It will load the `hello world` page in a few seconds.

5. This command will show a warning such as no credentials given. Since you enabled the admin user, Azure automatically fetches the credentials and associates them to the Docker image. To fix this issue, you can provide ACR credentials as parameters in the command, like this:

    ```
    > az webapp create --name packtbook-app-service --plan
    chapter2-app-plan --resource-group chapter2-example
    --deployment-container-image-name packtbook.azurecr.
    io/chapter2:1.0.0 --docker-registry-server-password
    Hrs95JY4KMFxxMnwX4DD3VMZR0rGH39Ykp05wya+ACRBvnvxs  --docker-
    registry-server-user packtbook
    ```

    This way, you will be able to create an Azure App Service instance and deploy a Docker image from ACR using the Azure CLI.

In this section, you learned how to deploy your Docker image from ACR to your Azure App Service instance using the Azure CLI. In the next section, you will learn how to configure CI/CD with ACR.

Configuring CI/CD with ACR

In this section, you will learn about configuring CI/CD with ACR from Azure DevOps:

1. First, you need to create an organization in Azure DevOps – it is free and easy to create one. You can create an Azure DevOps organization from here: `https://dev.azure.com/`.

2. Once you have created an organization, you need to request free build agent resources, you can do this here: `https://aka.ms/azpipelines-parallelism-request`. This is a new change introduced by Microsoft. In this form, you need to fill in your Azure name, email, and DevOps organization, and select **Private** as the option for **Parallel increase** – since you're creating the projects as private.

3. Next, you need to create a project. Make sure you selected the visibility as **Private**. You will be using Azure DevOps as your source control. When you have created the project, navigate to the **Repos** menu. On the next screen, you will get instructions to clone your repository.

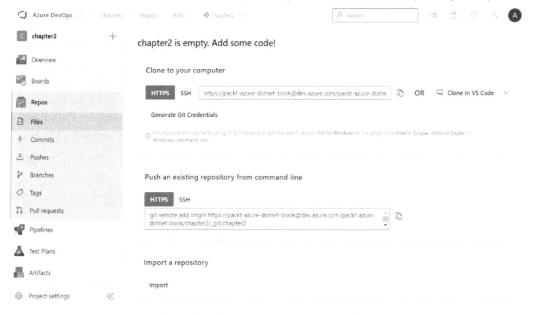

Figure 2.17: Azure DevOps – repository files

Before cloning the repository on your machine, you can initialize the repository with `.gitignore` and README files. You will be able to see the options to enable `.gitignore` and README files at the bottom of the screen. When you have initialized the repo, you will get two files inside the repository. There will be an option such as **Clone in VS Code** – click on the button to clone the repository using VS Code.

4. This will prompt a dialog to Open VS Code; click on **Open**. Once VS Code is open, it will show a **Select folder** dialog. Choose a folder in your machine so that the repo will be cloned in the local

machine. If VS Code is showing a window to enter credentials, you can click on the **Generate Git Credentials** button to get the username and password for the repository. Sometimes, VS Code will show another prompt to open the cloned folder in VS Code; you can open it.

5. Now you're ready with a cloned repository. There will not be any files in it. So, first, you need to create an ASP.NET Core app. You can do this by opening the Terminal window in VS Code. We can use the existing app we created earlier in this chapter if required. If the existing app code is used, then we can skip *Steps 6, 7*, and *8*, and go to *Step 9*, where we commit the code to source control.

6. In the window, run the command to create a new MVC application:

```
> dotnet new mvc --framework net6.0
```

7. To containerize the app, we need to add the Dockerfile using the VS Code Command Palette. Check the *Containerizing your ASP.NET Core app with VS Code* section if you need any clarifications on creating a Dockerfile using VS Code.

8. Next, to create a Docker image using the VS Code Command palette, type `Docker Images` and select the **Build Image...** option. This may take some time since it uses different base images for different steps and the code is compiled inside the container.

9. Once it is completed, you can commit the code to source control – since it is the first commit, you can directly push it to the main branch using VS Code. Click on the **Source Control** tab. You will be able to see the changes you made. You can commit the changes using the **Commit** button. Then, click on the three dots (Views and More Actions...) button, select the **Pull, Push** menu, and click on the **Sync** menu. This will commit and push the changes to Azure DevOps.

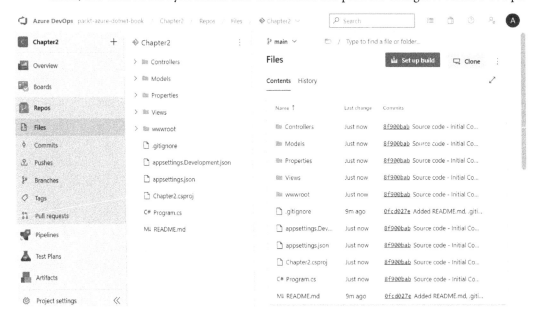

Figure 2.18: Azure DevOps – repository files – after committing the source

10. There are different practices related to source control workflows; the **feature branch workflow** is a common one, where for each feature, you will be creating a branch, and once the code implementation is complete, you will raise a `pull` request toward the `main` branch. In VS Code, on the **Source control** tab, provide a commit message – it can be anything but usually describes the change you did or about the feature you're implementing – and click on the **Commit** button, then click on the **Sync changes** button. Once the publishing is completed, you can open the DevOps portal and view your source code under the respective repositories.

11. Next, you can configure CI/CD by clicking on the **Set up build** button on the screen. This will redirect you to the **Configure your pipeline** screen.

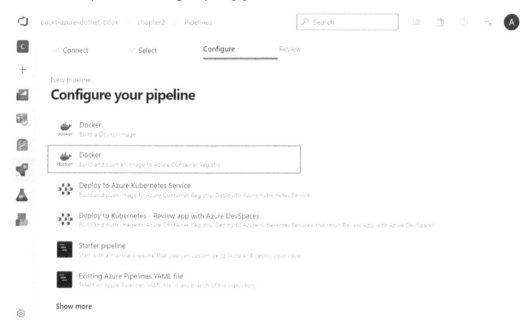

Figure 2.19: Azure DevOps – configuring the CI / CD pipeline

12. In the screen, you will notice that there is a template already available, which builds and pushes a Docker image to ACR. Clicking on the template will display a Docker sidebar, where you need to select your subscription and click on the **Continue** button.

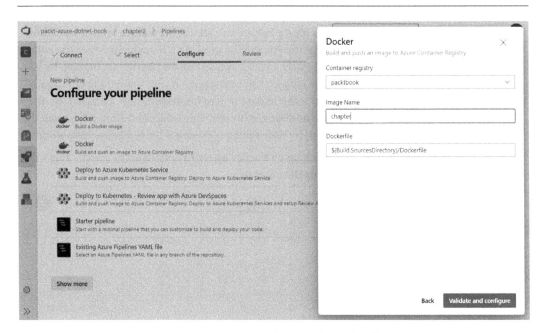

Figure 2.20: Azure DevOps – configuring the Docker deployment

13. You need to select the registry from the drop-down list, set a name, and specify the location of the Dockerfile. Once it is completed, click on the **Validate and configure** button, which will create the YAML build pipeline. You can view and modify it if required.

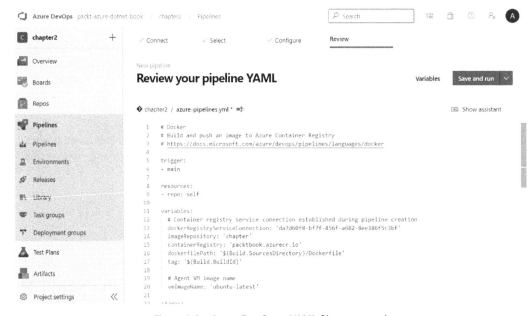

Figure 2.21: Azure DevOps – YAML file generated

14. Once you have made the changes, you can click on the **Save and run** button. The Azure DevOps portal will prompt for a commit message since you're adding the YAML file to the repository. You can keep the default message and click on the **Save and run** button. Once your build is executed and completed, you will be able to see the results, like this:

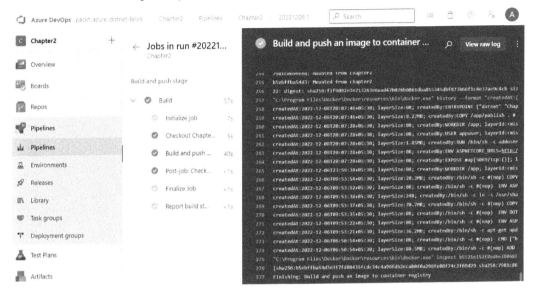

Figure 2.22: Azure DevOps – build running

15. If your build is failing with a message such as **No hosted parallelism has been purchased or granted. To request a free parallelism grant, please fill out the following form** https://aka.ms/azpipelines-parallelism-request, make sure you fill out the form by browsing the URL. Once the deployment is complete, you can view the new image on the ACR **Repositories** tab.

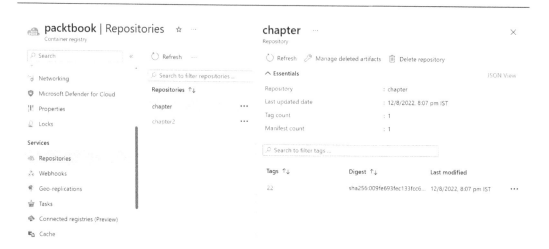

Figure 2.23: ACR – Docker image published from Azure DevOps

16. You can get the list of images using the command line as well:

```
> az acr repository list --name packtbook --output table
```

This way, you're able to configure CI/CD to ACR with Azure DevOps so, whenever you commit some code changes, Azure DevOps builds a container image and deploys it to AZR.

Deploying a Docker image to App service from ACR using managed identities

To enable deployment with identity, you need to create a managed identity in the Azure portal. The recommended method is using managed identities. The Azure App Service will use this managed identity to access ACR. So, let's get started:

1. You will be creating a user-assigned managed identity; to create it, execute the following command:

```
> az identity create --name chapter2-identity --resource-group
chapter2
```

Once it is created, please note down the `principalId` value from the JSON output, as you need this value to configure identity permission to the container registry.

2. To grant permission for the identity to access the container registry, you need to execute the `az role assignment` command. To execute this command, you need the identity's principal ID and the resource ID of the container registry. So, here is a set of commands that help you to get the principal ID of the identity and the resource ID of the container registry:

```
> $principalId=$(az identity show --resource-group chapter2
--name chapter2-identity --query principalId --output tsv)
```

This command will query Azure and store the value of the principal ID in a PowerShell variable, `principalId`.

3. Next, you can run the following command, which will query the resource ID of the container registry and store it in a variable:

```
> $registryId=$(az acr show --resource-group chapter2 --name
packtbook --query id --output tsv)
```

The registry ID is a long one with your subscription ID and resource group; because of that, it is recommended to use variables so that you can use the variable in the next command execution.

4. Finally, execute the `role assignment` command, like this:

```
> az role assignment create --assignee $principalId --scope
$registryId --role "AcrPull"
```

In this command, you're assigning an `AcrPull` role to the identity for ACR. Now, you're ready to create the app service and configure pulling the Docker image from ACR.

5. Next, you can create the app service plan and app service:

```
> az appservice plan create --name chapter2-app-plan --resource-
group chapter2-example --location centralus --is-linux --sku B1
> az webapp create --name packtbook-app-service --plan chapter2-
app-plan --resource-group chapter2-example --deployment-
container-image-name packtbook.azurecr.io/chapter2:latest
```

6. Next, you need to configure the `WEBSITES_PORT` environment variable. This is required because, by default, App Service expects the port to be `80` or `8080`. In the current Dockerfile, the port exposed is `5069`:

```
> az webapp config appsettings set --resource-group chapter2-
example --name packtbook-app-service --settings WEBSITES_
PORT=5069
```

7. Once the configuration is completed, you can enable the identity in the app service with this command:

```
> $id=(az identity show --resource-group chapter2 --name
chapter2-identity --query id --output tsv)
> az webapp identity assign --resource-group chapter2-example
--name packtbook-app-service --identities $id
```

8. After configuring the app service with the identity, you can configure the app service to pull the image from ACR:

```
> $appConfig=$(az webapp config show --resource-group chapter2-example --name packtbook-app-service --query id --output tsv)
> az resource update --ids $appConfig --set properties.acrUseManagedIdentityCreds=True
```

9. Next, you need to set the client ID of your web app:

```
> $clientId=$(az identity show --resource-group chapter2 --name chapter2-identity --query clientId --output tsv)
> az resource update --ids $appConfig --set properties.AcrUserManagedIdentityID=$clientId
```

This step is optional if you're using a system-managed identity in this section. If you're using the user identity, you have to execute the code.

10. Now it is configured to fetch the image from the ACR without enabling the ACR admin username and password. Currently, you're only deploying the Docker images to ACR from Azure DevOps – but the images are not getting deployed to the App Service.

To enable CI/CD to the App service, you need to enable CI/CD configuration – execute the following command:

```
> $cicdUrl=$(az webapp deployment container config --enable-cd true --name packtbook-app-service --resource-group chapter2-example --query CI_CD_URL --output tsv)
```

The CI_CD_URL variable is generated by the app service.

11. This URL will be configured in ACR as a Webhook URL – so ACR notifies this URL when an image is pushed. You can do this by executing the following command:

```
> az acr webhook create --name packtbookcd --registry packtbook --uri $cicdUrl --actions push --scope chapter2:latest
```

If you notice, in the commands, instead of using a fixed tag, the latest tag is used – this is required so that whenever a code is committed, Azure DevOps builds the Docker image and pushes it to ACR, which then invokes the Webhook configured from Azure App Service, and then App Service fetches the latest image from ACR. You might need to change the YAML file because, currently, the build number is used as the Docker image tag. You need to change it to latest instead of the build number.

In this section, we learned how to enable CI/CD from Azure DevOps to ACR by configuring Azure DevOps build pipelines. We also learned about configuring application deployment from ACR to Azure App Service.

Summary

In this chapter, you learned about containers, Docker, and the basics of Docker commands. Then, you learned how to create an Azure container registry, how to publish Docker images to ACR, and how to deploy a Docker image to Azure App Service. CI/CD is an essential skill when working with containers and microservices. So, you learned about creating and configuring version control and building CI/CD pipelines, which help you to build and deploy Docker images to ACR. In the last section, you learned about deploying the app service when a Docker image is pushed to ACR.

In the next chapter, you will learn about **Distributed Application Runtime** (**DAPR**), which is a framework that helps you to build scalable resilient microservices. When building microservices, developers often face challenges such as how to communicate between services, and where to store the state information. Through a pluggable architecture and components, DAPR helps developers to solve these challenges.

3

Building Resilient Applications with Dapr

Dapr, also known as Distributed Application Runtime, is a runtime environment that is event-driven and portable. It simplifies the process of building applications that are both stateful and stateless and can operate on the cloud or edge, enabling any developer to create resilient applications. Dapr was initiated and announced by *Microsoft* on October 16, 2019; however, Dapr is not owned by Microsoft and is being incubated at the **Cloud Native Computing Foundation** (**CNCF**). Dapr is an open source project and is hosted on GitHub. Dapr provides APIs or building blocks that help developers build microservices using industry best practices and patterns.

In this chapter, we will learn about the three main building blocks. In the context of Dapr, a building block refers to an HTTP or **Google Remote Procedure Call** (**gRPC**) API that can be accessed from code and utilizes one or more Dapr components. These building blocks are designed to tackle typical obstacles that are faced when building microservices applications that are resilient. They adhere to established best practices and patterns:

- **Service-to-service invocation**: This building block helps you communicate between two services
- **State management**: As its name implies, this building block helps developers manage state – applications can store state information as key-value pairs
- **Publish and subscribe** (**pub/sub**): This building block helps developers work with pub-sub messaging patterns

By the end of this chapter, you will have learned about Dapr and its building blocks, installed Dapr on your development machine, and be able to build resilient microservices with the help of Dapr.

In this chapter, we're going to cover the following main topics:

- Installing Dapr
- What is Dapr?

- Exploring Dapr's building blocks and how to use them in ASP.NET Core

- Enabling Dapr support in Azure Container Apps

Technical requirements

In this chapter, we will be installing Dapr and building applications in ASP.NET Core and Dapr. We need **Visual Studio Code** (**VS Code**) and the `dotnet` CLI to build ASP.NET Core apps. Dapr will be using Docker, so you need to install Docker Desktop if it's not installed already.

Installing Dapr

Dapr can be installed with and without administrative rights. In this section, we will learn how to install Dapr with administrative rights:

1. First, open the terminal as an administrator.

2. Next, execute the following command.

   ```
   powershell -Command "iwr -useb https://raw.githubusercontent.
   com/dapr/cli/master/install/install.ps1 | iex"
   ```

   Once you've executed this command, the script will create a directory called `Dapr` in your machine's system drive (usually, this is the C drive). Then, it will download and extract `dapr.exe` to the directory. Finally, add the directory to the `PATH` variable.

3. You can verify the installation using the following command:

   ```
   > dapr version
   ```

   This command will display the CLI version and runtime version.

   If you don't have administrator rights, you can execute the following command in the PowerShell terminal:

   ```
   > $script=iwr -useb https://raw.githubusercontent.
   com/dapr/cli/master/install/install.ps1;
   $block=[ScriptBlock]::Create($script); invoke-command
   -ScriptBlock $block -ArgumentList "", "$HOME/dapr"
   ```

   This command will install the Dapr CLI to your `$HOME` directory – usually, it will be `C:\Users\<YOUR_USERNAME>\dapr`. Next, you need to add this path to the user path environment variables manually. Once you've added the path to the environment variable, execute the `dapr version` command.

With that, we have installed Dapr on the Windows OS. You can find installation instructions for other OSs here: `https://docs.dapr.io/getting-started/install-dapr-cli/`.

Now, let's dig deeper into Dapr and try to understand what it is!

What is Dapr?

The opening sentence of the introduction pretty much defines Dapr for you. Dapr is currently available as an open source project on GitHub. Dapr works by using the **Sidecar** pattern. The Sidecar pattern is about separating cross-cutting operations (cross-cutting operations or cross-cutting concerns mean functionality that is important but should not be part of your application's business logic; for example, logging or authentication) from the microservice's implementation and reducing its complexity.

You can find more details about this pattern here: `https://learn.microsoft.com/azure/architecture/patterns/sidecar?WT.mc_id=DT-MVP-5002040`.

Dapr architecture

In this section, we will learn about the Dapr architecture. As mentioned earlier in this chapter, Dapr employs a Sidecar pattern, where a lightweight, separate process (the Dapr Sidecar) is attached to each microservice, enabling them to communicate, manage state, publish events, and handle service-to-service invocations seamlessly. This decoupled architecture abstracts away complexity, allowing developers to focus on application logic while Dapr handles cross-service concerns, making it easier to build resilient, portable, and interoperable applications:

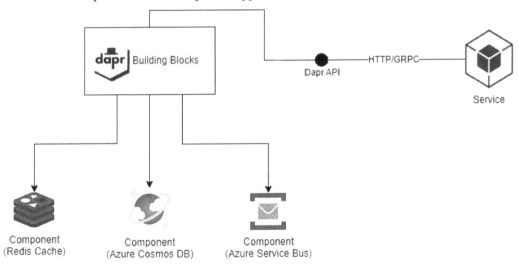

Figure 3.1 – Dapr architecture

Dapr can be hosted in two modes – **self-hosted** mode and **Kubernetes mode**. In this chapter, we are using **self-hosted** mode, which is easy to configure and can be used only for development purposes. In production, Dapr is always used with Kubernetes or Openshift. Using Bridge to Kubernetes, we can connect to Kubernetes clusters and debug Dapr applications from the development machine.

You can find more details about the Kubernetes hosting model here: `https://docs.dapr.io/operations/hosting/kubernetes/kubernetes-overview/`.

Once you've installed Dapr, you need to initialize it. You can do this by executing the following command:

```
> dapr init
```

You need to make sure Docker Desktop/Docker is running.

The `dapr init` command will download three Docker container images to your machine – these three Docker containers help us work with Dapr building blocks. The `Redis` container is used as a local state storage and message broker. The `Zipkin` container is for observability purposes. Finally, the `Dapr` container is used as a placement service container for local actor support. You can view the Docker containers with the `docker ps` command. Alternatively, you can use Dapr commands to view and understand the various Dapr components and services. First, you need to execute the following command:

```
> dapr run
```

Once it has been executed, this command will launch Dapr with default components. In a different terminal, execute the following command:

```
> dapr dashboard
```

This command will run the Dapr dashboard – this command will host the Dapr dashboard at `http://localhost:8080`. Open the URL and view the Dapr dashboard:

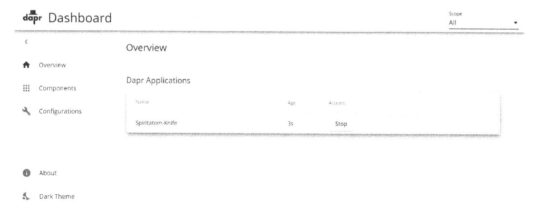

Figure 3.2 – Dapr dashboard

On this overview screen, you will be able to see the Dapr application – its name will be assigned randomly. Then, you can click on the **Components** menu and view the various Dapr components. You will see two components – `pubsub` and `statestore`. Finally, on the **Configurations** tab, you will be able to see the default Dapr configuration.

Running ASP.NET Core with a Dapr Sidecar

Before exploring Dapr's building blocks, we will explore how we can run ASP.NET Core applications with Dapr:

1. To run the application, first, you need to create an ASP.NET Core application. We can use any kind of application. In this section, we will be creating an ASP.NET Core Web API project with minimal API support:

    ```
    > dotnet new webapi --use-minimal-apis --output HelloWorldDapr
    --framework net6.0
    ```

2. Next, build the project and verify you can run it using the following command:

    ```
    > cd .\HelloWorldDapr\ ; dotnet run
    ```

3. Since we are running the default `dotnet` core web API project template, you can browse the `/swagger` endpoint and verify you're able to access the `/weatherforecast` method to confirm the `webapi` application is working. You need to note the port number. Stop the application using *Ctrl + C*.

4. We need to remove or comment on the `app.UseHttpsRedirection();` statement in `Program.cs`; otherwise, Dapr may not work as expected.

5. Next, run the following command to run the web app with Dapr support:

    ```
    >  dapr run --app-id helloworld --app-port 5262 --dapr-http-port
    35000 -- dotnet run
    ```

    In this command, we're running the ASP.NET Core application with the Dapr Sidecar, but we are not using any Dapr APIs or services. The `--app-id` parameter is required to uniquely identify the Dapr service. The `--app-port` parameter should be the port exposed by the application. By default, it will be `-1`, and the `--dapr-http-port` parameter will be the Dapr Sidecar port. Once you run the application with Dapr, you will be able to access the application through this port. The default for this port is also `-1`.

6. You can browse the API endpoint using the `curl` command, like so:

    ```
    > curl --request GET 'http://localhost:35000/weatherforecast'
    ```

7. If you execute the preceding command, you will get an error. This is because you need to access the URL with an HTTP header – `dapr-app-id` – with the value of the app ID when you run the `dapr run` command, like this:

    ```
    > curl --location --request GET 'http://localhost:35000/
    weatherforecast' --header 'dapr-app-id: helloworld'
    ```

    This will display the `weatherforecast` JSON response in the console. This way, you will be able to run the ASP.NET Core application with Dapr.

8. Alternatively, you can invoke the service like this:

```
> curl http://dapr-app-id:helloworld@localhost:35000/
weatherforecast
```

If you're using a different `dapr-app-id` parameter in the `dapr run` command, you need to replace `helloworld` with the `dapr-app-id` parameter.

Next, we will learn about various Dapr building blocks and how to use them with the ASP.NET Core Web API.

Exploring Dapr's building blocks

A building block refers to an HTTP or gRPC API that can be called from code and utilizes one or more Dapr components. These blocks are designed to tackle frequent hurdles encountered in constructing microservices applications that are robust and follow industry best practices and patterns. In this chapter, we will explore three building blocks.

Service-to-service invocation

The **service-to-service invocation** building block will help your application communicate with other applications and services reliably and securely. The service-to-service invocation building blocks help you address the following challenges:

*   Service discovery

*   Secure service communication

*   Handle retires and transient errors

*   Implement observability and tracing

*   Standardize API calls between services

As mentioned earlier, Dapr uses the Sidecar architecture. To communicate between services, your application needs to invoke an API in the Dapr instance. Each application or microservice communicates with its Dapr instance. These instances discover and communicate with the other Dapr instances:

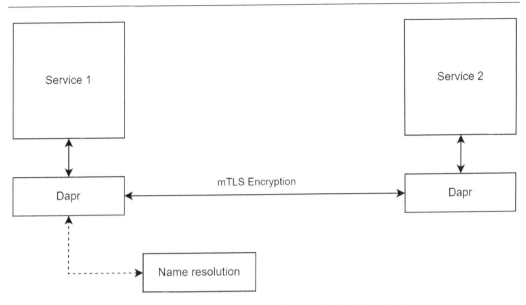

Figure 3.3 – The service-to-service invocation building block

Implementing the service-to-service building block in ASP.NET Core

Next, we will implement the service-to-service building block in the ASP.NET Core application:

1. To use the service-to-service building block, first, we need two Web API projects. The first Web API will interact with the second Web API using the service-to-service building block via Dapr.

    Here are the commands to build two services. In this example, the first service interacts with the second service through Dapr:

    ```
    > dotnet new webapi --use-minimal-apis --output Service1
    --framework net6.0
    > dotnet new webapi --use-minimal-apis --output Service2
    --framework net6.0
    ```

2. Next, you need to add the reference to the `Dapr.AspNetCore` NuGet package to the `Service1 web api` project. You can do this with the following command:

    ```
    > dotnet add package Dapr.AspNetCore --version 1.9.0
    ```

3. Open `Service1` in VS Code and remove the code inside the `/weatherforecast` endpoint. Then, update the code. This endpoint is getting the weatherforecast information from `Service2` via the `httpClient` object. Here is the implementation:

    ```
    app.MapGet("/weatherforecast", async (HttpClient httpClient) =>
    {
        var weatherForecasts = await httpClient
    .GetFromJsonAsync<WeatherForecast[]>("weatherforecast");
    ```

```
        return weatherForecasts;
    })
    .WithName("GetWeatherForecast");
```

An `httpclient` object is injected into this method. We are also calling the `weatherforecast` endpoint using the `GetFromJsonAsync` method. Finally, we are using the `Weatherforecast` record to receive the results and return them.

4. Next, we need to create and inject the `httpclient` object. Instead of using the `AddHttpClient()` method, we will be creating an `HttpClient` object with Dapr and then injecting it. Here is the implementation:

```
var httpClient = DaprClient.CreateInvokeHttpClient("backend");
builder.Services.AddSingleton(httpClient);
```

The `DaprClient` class is inside the `Dapr.AspNetCore` package. The `DaprClient.CreateInvokeHttpClient` method is used with `Service2`. We need to provide `dapr-app-id` as the backend while executing the `dapr run` command.

In both projects, remove the `HTTPS` redirection middleware – otherwise, you may receive some certificate error while accessing the services.

Now, we are ready to run both apps:

1. First, we need to run `Service2` and then `Service1`. Here are the commands – please note that the Web API port numbers may be different. You can execute the `dotnet run` command and use the HTTP port as the `app-port` parameter:

```
> dapr run --app-id backend --app-port 5140 --dapr-http-port
35001 -- dotnet run
> dapr run --app-id frontend --app-port 5053 --dapr-http-port
35000 -- dotnet run
```

2. Then, you can browse the frontend application using Postman or the `curl` command with the `dapr-app-id` header:

```
> curl --location --request GET 'http://localhost:35000/
weatherforecast' --header 'dapr-app-id: frontend'
```

Once you execute this command, you will be able to see the JSON response:

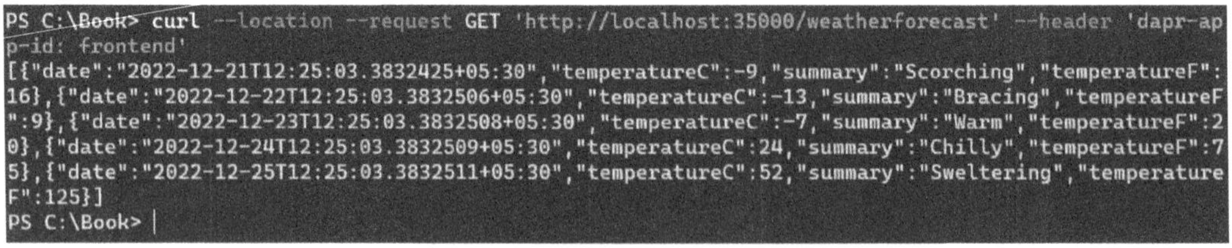

Figure 3.4 – JSON response from the API

This way, you can use the service-to-service invocation building block in ASP.NET Core, which helps you interact with other services without the need to worry about where the other service is running.

Observability in Dapr

As mentioned earlier, Dapr installs a Zipkin container for observability purposes. So, you can check the service invocation logs and traces from the Zipkin container. To access the Zipkin container, you can run the `docker ps` command:

```
> docker ps --format "table {{.Names}}\t{{.Ports}}"
```

This command will display the running containers in your machine:

```
PS C:\Book> docker ps --format "table {{.Names}}\t{{.Ports}}"
NAMES            PORTS
dapr_placement   0.0.0.0:6050->50005/tcp
dapr_redis       0.0.0.0:6379->6379/tcp
dapr_zipkin      9410/tcp, 0.0.0.0:9411->9411/tcp
PS C:\Book>
```

Figure 3.5 – Running Docker containers

Check the `PORTS` entry for the Zipkin container; you will be able to see two ports – usually, `9410` and `9411`. You will also see that the Zipkin console is running on port `9411`. Go to `http://127.0.0.1:9411/zipkin` in your browser to see the Zipkin console, where you can query the traces. By default, the screen will be empty; you can click the **Run Query** button to query all the traces.

Once it's loaded, you can look for the Dapr app ID and click on the **Show** button to see the execution details. At the time of writing, Dapr only produces telemetry data for the Dapr system services and Sidecars. Telemetry from your application code isn't automatically included. You can use a specific **software development kit (SDK)** such as the OpenTelemetry SDK for .NET to emit telemetry data from your application code.

On Zipkin's overview page, click the **Run Query** button to view all the traces:

Figure 3.6 – Zipkin overview page

This will display a screen like this:

Figure 3.7 – Zipkin traces display

As mentioned earlier, you can click the **Show** button to view details of the request, like this:

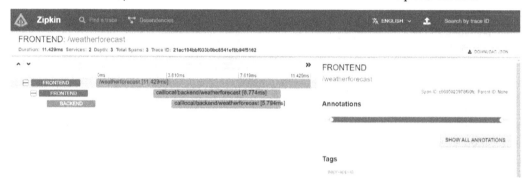

Figure 3.8 – Zipkin details of a request trace

In this section, you learned about the first Dapr building block – service-to-service invocation. Then, you learned how to use this building block in ASP.NET Core, as well as how to monitor and troubleshoot with a Zipkin container in Dapr. Next, we will explore the **state management** building block.

State management

This building block helps save, read, and query key/value pairs in the supported state stores. State management building block helps you create stateful and long-running services. Here is the architecture of the Dapr state management building block:

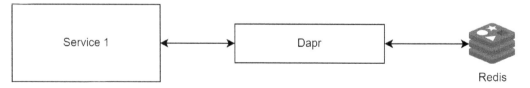

Figure 3.9 – State management architecture

Similar to the service-to-service invocation building block, state management building blocks also use the Sidecar pattern. To store and retrieve data, your application code needs to interact with its Sidecar. The Sidecar will create and retrieve data from the configured store. By default, Dapr uses **Redis** as the data store. You can configure other data stores such as **Azure Cosmos DB**, **Mongo DB**, **SQL Server**, and others.

Implementing state management in ASP.NET Core

Let's use the state management block in the current project. We will use the state management service to store the API response from the backend service:

1. To implement this, we need to use the `DaprClient` instance, which is used to save and read state information from the state store – in our installation, this is **Redis**. We need to inject `DaprClient` using the `AddDaprClient` method:

    ```
    builder.Services.AddDaprClient();
    ```

2. Next, we need to modify the `/weatherforecast` method, like this:

    ```
    app.MapGet("/weatherforecast", async (HttpClient httpClient,
    DaprClient daprClient) =>
    {
        var weatherForecasts = await daprClient.
    GetStateAsync<WeatherForecast[]>
            ("statestore", "weatherforecast");
        if (weatherForecasts == default)
        {
            weatherForecasts = await httpClient
    .GetFromJsonAsync<WeatherForecast[]>("weatherforecast");
            await daprClient.SaveStateAsync("statestore",
    "weatherforecast", weatherForecasts);
        }
        return weatherForecasts;
    })
    .WithName("GetWeatherForecast");
    ```

    In this method, the `daprClient` instance is used to get the state from the store with the store name and key name. If the state doesn't exist, it returns the null or default value of the `weatherforecast` array.

3. Now, we are ready to run the application with Dapr support. You can do this by executing the following commands:

    ```
    > dapr run --app-id backend --app-port 5140 --dapr-http-port
    35001 -- dotnet run
    > dapr run --app-id frontend --app-port 5053 --dapr-http-port
    35000 -- dotnet run
    ```

4. You can get the `weatherforecast` information with the `curl` command, like this:

    ```
    > curl --location --request GET 'http://localhost:35000/
    weatherforecast' --header 'dapr-app-id: frontend'
    ```

    Initially, the frontend service will check for the data in the state management component and if not, it will call the backend API and store the data in the state management store. If you execute it again, this data will be fetched from the store instead of the backend API. You can query the Redis data store with the Redis CLI. If you don't have the Redis CLI installed, you can query your Redis instance using Docker.

5. You need to execute the following command to start the Redis CLI with Docker:

    ```
    > docker exec -it dapr_redis redis-cli
    ```

    This will display a `redis-cli` prompt. This is where you can execute different Redis commands.

6. The first command you can execute is the `KEYS` command, which will display the stored keys:

    ```
    > KEYS *
    ```

7. Since the `weatherforecast` data is stored alongside the state management building block with the `weatherforecast` name, it will be displayed as `frontend||weatherforecast`. To view the contents inside the key, you can use the DUMP command alongside the key's name, which will display the serialized version of the value stored:

    ```
    > DUMP frontend||weatherforecast
    ```

8. To remove the data, you can use the DEL command, which can also be executed with the key name:

    ```
    > DEL frontend||weatherforecast
    ```

9. Now, if you invoke the frontend service again, it will fetch the data from the backend. You can execute the EXIT command to exit from the Redis CLI:

    ```
    > EXIT
    ```

This will bring you back to your terminal.

Changing the data store from Redis to SQL Server

So far, we have used the built-in Redis container as the state store. We can change this by using our own data storage components:

1. To do this, first, we need to create a folder named `components/local` in the `Service1` root folder. Next, we need to create a YAML file called `dapr-statestore-sqlserver.yaml` and paste the following code into it:

    ```
    apiVersion: dapr.io/v1alpha1
    kind: Component
    ```

```
metadata:
  name: statestore
spec:
  type: state.sqlserver
  version: v1
  metadata:
  - name: connectionString
    value: Server=YOUR-MACHINE;User Id=sa;Password=YOUR-
PASSWORD;
```

Make sure you're modifying your SQL Server connection string. You can specify the database name and table name, but those are optional. If you're not configured, the default values will be taken.

2. Next, when you execute the `dapr run` command, you need to provide your local component path, so instead of taking the Redis store, it can take the newly created SQL Server store, like this:

```
> dapr run --app-id frontend --app-port 5053 --dapr-http-port
35000 --components-path .\components\local -- dotnet run
```

Once you execute this command, you will be able to see a database called `dapr` on your machine. If you're getting any errors, make sure you're connecting to SQL Server with the proper credentials. This way, you can configure a different data store for the state management building block in Dapr.

In this section, you learned about the Dapr state management building block. You learned about verifying the data with the Redis CLI and learned about configuring a different data store for the state management building block.

In the next section, you will learn about the pub/sub building block.

Publish and subscribe

The pub/sub building block helps apps and services communicate with each other using messages for event-driven architectures. This pattern helps decouple services. The pub/sub building block provides APIs that allow applications to function both as publishers and subscribers. Similar to the pub/sub architecture, **publisher or producer** writes messages to a channel on a topic – this service doesn't have a clue about which services or applications are the recipient of this message. Finally, there's **subscriber or consumer**, which subscribes to a topic and receives messages from a channel – this service doesn't know which service created the message. There is a message broker component, which copies the messages from the publisher's channel to the subscriber's channels. Similar to the state management building block, Redis will be acting as the message broker. If required, we can change it to a different message broker such as Apache Kafka, RabbitMQ, Azure Event Hubs, or Azure Service Bus:

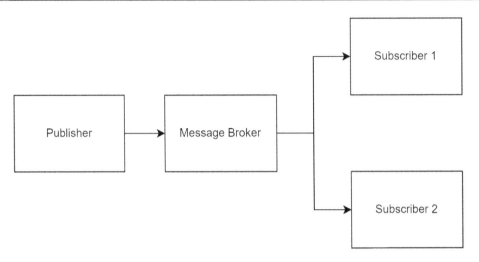

Figure 3.10 – The pub/sub architecture

Implementing pub/sub in ASP.NET Core

Let's implement pub/sub in the ASP.NET Core Web API project. The Service1 project will act as a publisher and the Service2 project will act as a subscriber:

1. In the Service1 project, let's add a method to create a weatherforecast event, like this:

    ```
    app.MapPost("/weatherforecast",
        async (WeatherForecast weatherForecast, DaprClient
    daprClient) =>
    {
        await daprClient.PublishEventAsync<WeatherForecast>
            ("pubsub", "weatherforecast", weatherForecast);
    });
    ```

    The first parameter in the PublishEventAsync method is the service name, and the second one is the topic name. Finally, the last one is the message object.

2. Similar to the earlier implementation, we need to configure DaprClient to perform dependency injection using the AddDaprClient() method, like this.

    ```
    builder.Services.AddDaprClient();
    ```

    With that, we've configured the Service1 project.

3. Next, we need to update the Service2 project. First, we need to add a reference to the Dapr.AspNetCore NuGet package. We can do this by running the following command in the Service2 project folder:

    ```
    dotnet add package Dapr.AspNetCore
    ```

4. Now, in the `Service2` project, we need to configure the subscription method, which can be implemented like this.

```
app.MapPost("/weatherforecast", async (WeatherForecast
weatherForecast) =>
{
    app.Logger.LogInformation("Create weatherforecast request
received");
    return weatherForecast;
}).WithTopic("pubsub", "weatherforecast");
```

This is a minimal API post method but the `WithTopic` method has been added – if you're using normal controllers, you can use the `WithTopic` attribute. In the `WithTopic` method, the first one is the pub/sub component's name, while the second one is the topic. So, when you post data to `Service1`, it will publish a message with a topic of `weatherforecast` using the `PubSub` component. `Service2` will subscribe to the topic and when a message is received, it will be processed.

5. We need to add one more middleware and map an endpoint to configure the subscription. We can do this by adding the following code:

```
var app = builder.Build();
if (app.Environment.IsDevelopment())
{
    app.UseSwagger();
    app.UseSwaggerUI();
}
app.UseCloudEvents();
app.MapSubscribeHandler();
```

The `UseCloudEvents()` method will add CloudEvents middleware to the pipeline, which helps us receive and process the requests in the **CloudEvents** format. You can find more details about the CloudEvents format here: `https://cloudevents.io/`. The `MapSubscribeHandler` method will expose the `/dapr/subscribe` endpoint, which helps find all the API endpoints with the topic configuration.

6. Next, run these two apps using the `dapr run` command:

```
> dapr run --app-id backend --app-port 5140 --dapr-http-port
35001 -- dotnet run
> dapr run --app-id frontend --app-port 5053 --dapr-http-port
35000 -- dotnet run
```

7. Now, you can execute the following command to post the data to the frontend service:

```
> curl --location --request POST 'http://localhost:35000/
weatherforecast' `
--header 'dapr-app-id: frontend' `
```

```
--header 'Content-Type: application/json' `
--data-raw '{
    "date": "2022-12-21T22:49:04.2508285+05:30",
    "temperatureC": 16,
    "summary": "Sweltering",
    "temperatureF": 60
}'
```

At this point, you will be able to see the log statements from `Service2` displayed on the console. You will be able to create multiple subscribers with the same topic and use it. This way, we can use the pub/sub building block.

So far, we've consumed the Dapr building blocks using the .NET SDK. However, we can directly interact with **REpresentational State Transfer** (**REST**) and **Google Remote Procedure Call** (**GRPC**) services as well. For example, you can store a key-value pair in the state management store by posting data to `http://localhost:3500/v1.0/state/statestore` and retrieve the data using the same endpoint by adding the key value as a parameter.

In this section, we learned about the pub/sub building block and how it can be implemented in ASP. NET Core. In the next section, we will learn how to deploy Dapr-enabled microservices to Azure Container Apps.

Enabling Dapr support in Azure Container Apps

Azure Container Apps is a service from Azure that is a fully managed serverless container service for building and deploying cloud-native apps and microservices. You will learn more details about Azure Container Apps in *Chapter 4*.

In this chapter, you will learn about creating an Azure container app, deploying container images, and enabling Dapr support. So, let's get started:

1. To create the container app, open the Azure portal and click on the **Create a resource** button. As we already know, it is a best practice to create a resource group before we create Azure resources, so first, we will be creating an Azure resource group. Then, click on the **Create** button inside the resource group and search for `Container App`.

2. Container apps require a Container Apps Environment, which acts as a boundary between different container apps. On the **Create Container App** screen, you need to provide the container app's name, resource group, and subscription. And we need to create a Container Apps Environment. (Figure 3.11)

3. Once you've configured these, click the **Next** button:

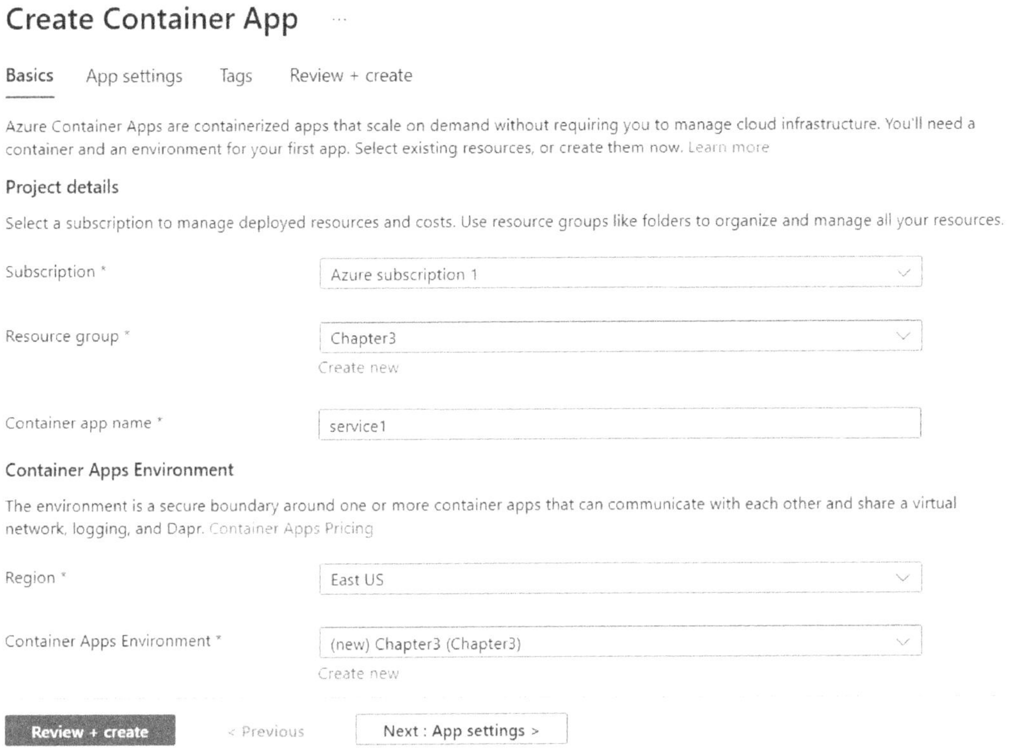

Create Container App ...

Basics   App settings   Tags   Review + create

Azure Container Apps are containerized apps that scale on demand without requiring you to manage cloud infrastructure. You'll need a container and an environment for your first app. Select existing resources, or create them now. Learn more

Project details

Select a subscription to manage deployed resources and costs. Use resource groups like folders to organize and manage all your resources.

Subscription *	Azure subscription 1 ⌄
Resource group *	Chapter3 ⌄
	Create new
Container app name *	service1

Container Apps Environment

The environment is a secure boundary around one or more container apps that can communicate with each other and share a virtual network, logging, and Dapr. Container Apps Pricing

Region *	East US ⌄
Container Apps Environment *	(new) Chapter3 (Chapter3) ⌄
	Create new

[**Review + create**]   < Previous   [Next : App settings >]

Figure 3.11 – Create Container App – Basics

4. On the **App Settings** screen, you need to choose the container image type and other networking configurations. As we are creating it for the first time, we can click the **Review + Create** button, which will create the container app and deploy the `helloworld` container. This might take some time because Azure has to provision a few resources, such as the **app environment**, **Log Analytics workspace**, and more.

5. Once the resource has been provisioned, you can click on the **Dapr** menu – by default, Dapr will not be enabled. Now, you can click on the **Enabled** option, which will display more configuration values, such as the App ID, App port, and more, all of which we used in the `dapr run` command.

Here, only **App Id** is mandatory; all the other fields are optional:

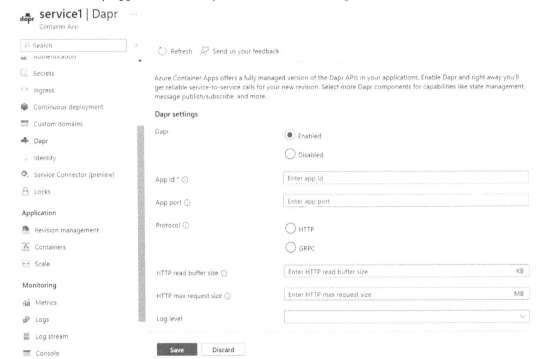

Figure 3.12 – Dapr configuration in Azure Container Apps

Unlike hosted mode, in Azure Container Apps, if you need to use a component such as state management, you need to add it to the Container Apps Environment. Once you've added a component, you will be able to access it via the Dapr configuration screen. Please note that the Dapr version in Azure Container Apps may not be the latest. Usually, the Dapr version in Azure Container Apps is updated 6 weeks after the Dapr release. For more details, check out the Dapr FAQ page: https://learn.microsoft.com/en-us/azure/container-apps/faq?WT.mc_id=DT-MVP-5002040.

6. To add a component, take the Container Apps Environment you created on the first screen and click on the **Dapr components** menu:

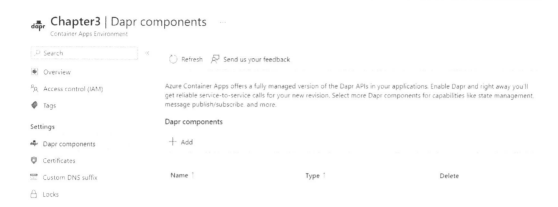

Figure 3.13 – Dapr components

7. Click the **Add** button to display the **Add Dapr Component** screen, where you can configure the component's type, name, and version. You can also configure the variable configuration values that are required for the component. For example, if we want to use state management in the ASP.NET Core application that is deployed in Azure Container Apps, we can add the state management component:

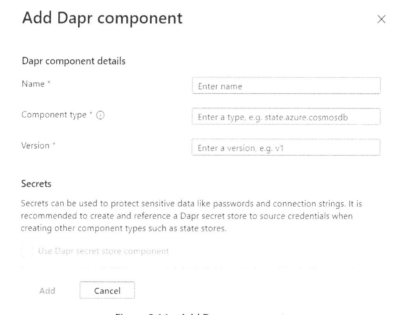

Figure 3.14 – Add Dapr component

This way, you can enable Dapr in Azure Container Apps. You will learn more about Azure Container Apps in *Chapter 4*.

Summary

In this chapter, you learned about Dapr, the different building blocks such as service-to-service invocation, state management, and pub/sub, and how you can use them in your ASP.NET Core apps and services. Then, you learned about customizing the state management building block data storage component. Finally, you created a container app on Azure Container Apps and enabled support for Dapr in Azure Container Apps.

Dapr is essential for modern application development as it abstracts the complexities of distributed systems, enabling us to focus on business logic. It offers a language-agnostic, event-driven architecture with built-in resilience, state management, and interoperability while fostering loose coupling and scalability. By incorporating Dapr, we can expedite development, ensure best practices, and navigate the challenges of distributed architectures with greater efficiency and simplicity.

In the next chapter, you will learn about **Azure Kubernetes Service** (**AKS**), a Kubernetes-as-a-service offering from Microsoft Azure, which helps you develop and deploy cloud-native applications to Azure. AKS also helps you get unified management and governance on Kubernetes clusters.

4

Designing Microservices with AKS and Containers in Azure

The objective of this chapter is to provide a thorough introduction to **Kubernetes**, an **open source framework** for managing **containerized applications**.

Kubernetes has fast become one of the world's most popular and widely used **container orchestration platforms**. It was created by Google and is now managed by the **Cloud Native Computing Foundation** (**CNCF**). It gives businesses of all sizes a robust set of tools for scaling and deploying containerized applications, which makes it a popular choice.

This chapter will cover the fundamentals of Kubernetes and how it is utilized to manage and coordinate containerized applications. We will start by going over the basic ideas and terms for Kubernetes. Then, we will move on to more complex topics, such as **scalability**, **self-healing**, and **rolling updates**. Familiar patterns and best practices for deploying and managing apps in a Kubernetes context will also be covered.

We will utilize hands-on examples and exercises throughout the book to explain how to use Kubernetes in a real-world situation. By the end of this chapter, you'll know how to use Kubernetes to deploy and manage containerized apps at a large scale.

The examples in this chapter cover the knowledge and skills required for a developer, systems administrator, or DevOps engineer to effectively utilize **Azure Kubernetes Service** (**AKS**) at scale. So, let's dive in and examine this robust platform.

In this chapter, we are going to cover the following main topics:

- What is Kubernetes?
- Self-hosted Kubernetes versus Azure Kubernetes Service
- Setting up an Azure Kubernetes Service cluster
- Troubleshooting Pods and Deployments
- Introducing containers

What is Kubernetes?

Kubernetes is a platform for managing applications that run in containers. It provides a comprehensive set of tools and features designed to simplify the process of scaling, deploying, and managing containerized apps in a production environment. With Kubernetes, you can harness the power of containerization while leveraging its advanced capabilities to enhance your application infrastructure. Here are some key advantages that Kubernetes brings:

- **Scalability**: Kubernetes makes it easy to add or remove copies of a container to make a containerized app bigger or smaller. This makes it easy for you to handle more traffic and demand.

- **High availability**: Kubernetes has features such as self-healing, **automatic failover**, and rolling updates that make it easy for you to ensure that your applications are always available.

- **Portability**: Kubernetes lets you deploy and manage your apps in different environments, such as **on-premises**, the **public cloud**, or a **hybrid environment**.

- **Automation**: Kubernetes automates many tasks in deploying and managing containerized applications, such as scaling, self-healing, and rolling updates.

- **Flexibility**: Kubernetes is a platform that can be extended and combined with other tools to make a complete solution for managing and deploying containerized apps.

How does Kubernetes achieve its goals?

Kubernetes achieves its goals in several ways. They are as follows:

- Kubernetes uses a set of abstractions to represent the desired state of a containerized application. It then repeatedly compares the actual state of the application to the desired state.

- Kubernetes is based on the following two main abstractions:

    - **Pods**: A Pod is a group of containers that should all run on the same host. Pods can also have storage and network resources that are shared.

    - **Services**: A Service is a logical grouping of Pods with a rule for how to get to them. Services give stable access points to the Pods for clients outside the Pods, and they can spread traffic across them.

- Kubernetes also has a set of controllers that keep an eye on the state of the Pods and make changes to bring containers closer to the desired state. For example, the **replication controller** ensures that the correct number of copies of a Pod is always running. In contrast, the **Deployment controller** lets you update the Pods in a replication controller in a declarative way. Kubernetes also uses **etcd**, a **distributed key-value store**, to store the cluster's configuration data. This lets all the parts of Kubernetes see the current state of the cluster in the same way.

- Kubernetes also lets you manage containerized applications with a wide range of features, such as automatic scaling, self-healing, rolling updates, service discovery, and load balancing.

- Kubernetes is a powerful and flexible platform for managing containerized applications in a production environment. It hides the infrastructure underneath and gives a consistent way to deploy, scale, and manage containerized apps in different environments.

Self-hosted Kubernetes versus Azure Kubernetes Service

Each approach offers distinct advantages and considerations for managing containerized applications. Self-hosted Kubernetes provides a hands-on, do-it-yourself experience where you have complete control over your Kubernetes environment. On the other hand, AKS delivers a managed Kubernetes solution that abstracts much of the infrastructure management, allowing developers to focus on their applications. In this comparison, we'll delve into the details of both approaches to help you understand which one aligns better with your needs and preferences.

Self-hosted Kubernetes

When it comes to managing your own Kubernetes infrastructure, there are important factors to consider that outline your responsibilities for overseeing different aspects of your cluster's performance and functionality. This section outlines what you need to take care of in a self-hosted Kubernetes environment:

- **Infrastructure management**: This involves setting up and maintaining the Kubernetes control plane and worker nodes. Users are responsible for manual updates, scaling, and maintenance of the Kubernetes cluster.

- **Networking and security**: Users configure networking components such as load balancers and network security policies. The user is responsible for implementing and managing security features such as **Role-Based Access Control (RBAC)**.

- **Deployment and scaling**: Users are responsible for deploying, managing, and scaling applications. Autoscaling needs to be set up by the user, which may require more configuration.

- **Monitoring and metrics**: Users must integrate monitoring tools and configure logging and metrics collection.

- **Backup and disaster recovery**: Users must create and manage backup and recovery strategies for the cluster and applications.

- **Initial setup and complexity**: Setting up a self-hosted Kubernetes cluster can be complex and time-consuming.

Azure Kubernetes Service

On the other hand, AKS transforms the landscape of Kubernetes management. It introduces a balanced ecosystem where Microsoft shoulders specific management tasks while you retain control over other facets. In the following list, we shed light on the scope of Azure's responsibilities and the areas where your input and guidance are essential within AKS:

- **Managed infrastructure**: Azure creates, scales, and manages the Kubernetes control plane and worker nodes. Azure handles automatic updates and maintenance.

- **Networking and security**: Azure manages network infrastructure and features such as load balancers and RBAC. Microsoft manages higher-level management tasks of the Kubernetes cluster, while users retain control over worker nodes and related infrastructure. Users configure internal security measures such as Pod-to-Pod communication and network security policies. Flexibility in network security configuration empowers users to tailor security settings to their application's needs.

- **Deployment and scaling**: Users deploy and manage applications, while Azure handles cluster scaling and autoscaling.

- **Monitoring and metrics**: AKS can be integrated with Azure Monitor for health checks, metrics, and insights into containers and applications.

- **Backup and disaster recovery**: Azure provides backup and recovery mechanisms for AKS clusters, streamlining disaster recovery.

- **Ease of use and adoption**: AKS abstracts much of Kubernetes' complexity, making it easier for developers to focus on applications. It is well suited for organizations that want to use Kubernetes without the full administrative burden.

Visualize managing a Kubernetes environment as tending to a garden. In the self-hosted approach, you're the sole gardener, responsible for every aspect—planting, watering, pruning, and protecting. You meticulously set up the garden, install irrigation systems, and monitor every plant's well-being. However, maintaining a thriving garden requires extensive gardening knowledge and constant attention.

Now contrast this with AKS. Here, you're still the gardener, but you have the assistance of a professional gardening team. Azure is responsible for preparing the soil, installing automated irrigation, and providing expert care for each plant. They also offer a weather monitoring system to ensure your garden thrives, intervening if a storm is detected. You can still select the plants, design the layout, and contribute your expertise, but the team handles the heavy lifting and routine maintenance.

Self-hosted Kubernetes is akin to cultivating your garden from scratch, managing every detail. In contrast, AKS empowers you to focus on designing your garden's beauty, while Azure's team ensures that the foundation and day-to-day care are expertly managed. This hybrid approach combines the advantages of Kubernetes orchestration with the convenience of managed services and user control.

Kubernetes Pods

The Pod is the smallest and most basic unit in the **Kubernetes object model**.

In Kubernetes, Deployments are done in tiny pieces called Pods. Each Pod has one or more containers, storage resources, and a unique network IP. In Kubernetes, Pods are the smallest units that can be deployed. They are created, deleted, and managed as a single unit. These containers share the same network namespace, so they can talk to each other using localhost. Also, they share the same storage, so another can read the data written by one container. To address concerns regarding data security, several key practices can be employed. Network policies enable controlled communication between Pods, mitigating risks. RBAC restricts resource access to authorized entities. Pod Security Policies enforce secure settings. Container sandboxing technologies such as gVisor enhance isolation. Sensitive data can be stored in Kubernetes Secrets, limiting access. Namespace isolation separates environments, and Services facilitate secure inter-Pod communication. Collectively, these measures ensure that Kubernetes Pods maintain a secure environment, addressing potential data access and security concerns.

The **Kubernetes control plane** can take care of Pods by using things such as **replication controllers**, **ReplicaSets**, and Deployments. These objects make sure that the number of Pods you want to run is running, and any Pods that fail are replaced automatically.

In short, Pods are the basic building blocks of Kubernetes. Each Pod represents a single process or container running in a cluster. Pods can contain one or more containers and are used to give containers shared resources and define the state they should be in. Pods are created, deleted, and managed as a single unit. They are used to make scaling easy and fix themselves when something goes wrong.

Kubernetes control plane

The control plane in AKS is a set of components that manage and coordinate the worker nodes in a cluster. In the context of Kubernetes, the control plane is not automatically managed. At its core, a control plane is a collection of processes that govern the state and behavior of a Kubernetes cluster. It makes sure that the user-specified desired state is in line with the system's actual state. This is achieved through a series of controllers, each tasked with overseeing specific components within the cluster. Imagine a symphony orchestra. The control plane is akin to the conductor, ensuring every instrument (or component) plays its part harmoniously to produce a cohesive performance (or desired state).

The term "desired state" often surfaces in Kubernetes discussions. Let's demystify it:

- **Pod-level desired state**: This pertains to individual application instances or Pods. Using constructs such as ReplicaSets or Deployments, Kubernetes ensures that a specified number of Pod replicas are always operational. If a Pod fails, Kubernetes springs into action to replace it, maintaining the desired state.

- **Cluster-level desired state via GitOps**: While Kubernetes itself doesn't define a holistic "cluster desired state," third-party tools such as Flux and Argo CD introduce this concept. They use GitOps, where a Git repository dictates the desired state of the cluster. These tools continuously monitor the cluster, ensuring its alignment with the state defined in the repository.

The control plane in AKS is made up of several components, which are as follows:

- **Kubernetes API server**: This component exposes the Kubernetes API, which allows users and other components to interact with the cluster. It handles **Create, Read, Update, Delete (CRUD)** operations on Kubernetes objects such as Pods, Services, and Deployments.

- **etcd**: This is a highly available key-value store that stores the configuration data of the cluster. It keeps track of the cluster's state and ensures it is the same on all nodes.

- **Kubernetes controller manager**: This component, which manages the control loop for built-in and custom controllers, watches for changes in etcd. Whether a state adjustment will be made for a given resource type will depend on the controller itself; some controllers might only observe resources for reporting purposes without amending their state. The objective is to ensure that the cluster's current state coincides with the desired state set forth by these controllers.

- **Kubernetes scheduler**: This component is responsible for scheduling Pods on the worker nodes. It considers the Pods' resource requirements and the available resources on the worker nodes to ensure that the Pods are placed on the appropriate nodes.

The control plane in AKS also handles the following tasks:

- **Configurable autoscaling**: In AKS, autoscaling is not enabled by default and must be explicitly configured. When enabled, AKS supports horizontal scaling, which involves adding or removing worker nodes (scale out/in) based on the resource requirements of the applications running on them. It is important to note that AKS does not automatically scale vertically (scale up), meaning it does not automatically adjust the CPU and memory allocations for individual nodes.

- **Importance of node selection**: Given that AKS does not automatically scale up, it is crucial to choose a suitable SKU for your worker nodes. If a single container requires more memory than any node in the cluster can allocate, the container will not start, and AKS will not automatically resolve this issue.

- **Versatile node pools**: To accommodate versatile and heterogeneous workloads, using different node pools with varying underlying SKUs is advisable. This allows for more granular control over the resources that different types of workloads can consume and ensures that the needs of diverse applications can be met effectively.

- **Monitoring**: The control plane integrates with Azure Monitor for container health monitoring and diagnostics, giving developers insight into the health and performance of their applications.

Kubernetes Service

How does Kubernetes know where to send network traffic to reach our application if the IP addresses of the Pods are constantly changing? The solution is a **Kubernetes Service**! A Service is a container that sits in front of a set of Pods and gives a static IP address. Traffic arriving at a Service is routed round-robin to a collection of backend Pods. The Service keeps track of how the IP addresses of the Pods change over time so that network traffic is still sent to the correct Pods.

Nodes

The backbone of a Kubernetes cluster, a node represents the foundation of your cluster. Imagine it as an individual computer within your system. These nodes can be physical machines in a data center or virtual machines hosted by cloud providers such as Microsoft Azure. Let's take an example. If you have a Kubernetes cluster with three nodes, each node contributes its CPU and RAM resources to the overall cluster capacity. This allows your applications to scale horizontally, effortlessly leveraging the combined resources of the nodes.

Persistent Volumes

Safeguarding data across nodes in Kubernetes can be challenging, especially when applications can run on any node within the cluster. To overcome this challenge, Kubernetes has introduced Persistent Volumes. Let's say you have a web application that requires a database. By utilizing Persistent Volumes, you can ensure that the data stored in the database remains intact even if the Pod running the database moves from one node to another. This ensures data durability and availability regardless of the Pod's location.

Deployments

While Pods serve as the fundamental computing units in Kubernetes, managing them individually can be cumbersome. That's where **Deployments** come in. Imagine you have a web application that needs to handle high traffic loads during peak hours. By creating a Deployment, you can define the state of your application, such as the number of replicas you want to run. Kubernetes will automatically manage the creation, scaling, and monitoring of these Pods to ensure your application runs smoothly.

Ingress

In a Kubernetes cluster, there is a need to enable external access to your application once you have deployed Pods and built a node cluster.

By default, Kubernetes provides separation between Pods and the outside world. To establish communication with a Service running inside a Pod, you must configure Ingress, which acts as the gateway for external traffic.

While it is possible to implement Ingress in your Kubernetes cluster through various methods, such as adding an Ingress Controller or a load balancer, these components are often used in conjunction. In practice, using an Ingress Controller without a load balancer is uncommon. Every Ingress Controller, whether it be NGINX, Traefik, or others, will deploy a Service of type **LoadBalancer**. This **LoadBalancer** Service is responsible for routing external traffic into your cluster and to the appropriate Services. It is worth noting that you can expose a Pod outside of the cluster using a **LoadBalancer** Service without deploying an Ingress Controller. However, this approach is rarely used for APIs and web applications in real-world scenarios. It might be a suitable solution for specific use cases, such as exposing an FTP endpoint or a database.

Therefore, while you are not forced to use an Ingress Controller, it is a standard and recommended practice for efficiently managing external access to Services in your Kubernetes cluster, especially for web applications and APIs.

Ingress serves as the entry point, allowing external traffic to reach the Services running within the cluster. For example, if you have a web application with multiple microservices, you can configure Ingress to route incoming traffic to the appropriate microservice based on the requested URL. In this way, Ingress enables efficient and secure communication between your application and external users.

In this section, we demystified the essential concepts of Kubernetes: nodes, Persistent Volumes, Deployments, and Ingress. By understanding these core components, you have gained the necessary foundation to build scalable and resilient microservice architectures. So far in this chapter, we've explored real-world examples, such as leveraging nodes for resource pooling, using Persistent Volumes for data durability, simplifying Pod management with Deployments, and enabling external access through Ingress.

As you continue your journey with Kubernetes, keep these concepts in mind, and explore how they can be applied to solve real-world challenges in your projects.

Setting up an Azure Kubernetes Service cluster

Now that we've learned a little about AKS, we will learn how to create a resource in the **Azure portal** as well as the **CLI** and **PowerShell**:

1. Start by logging in to your Azure portal and searching for Kubernetes:

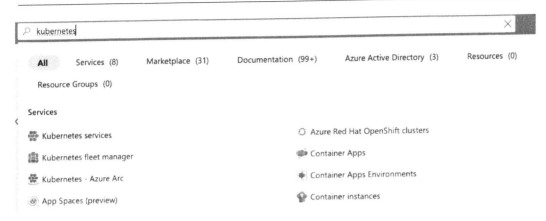

Figure 4.1 – Finding the Kubernetes service in Azure

2. Since this is your first time creating this specific resource, you will see an empty prompt with the **Create** button. Click the **Create** button to continue, and select **Create a Kubernetes cluster**.

No Kubernetes services to display

Use Azure Kubernetes Service to create and manage Kubernetes clusters. Azure will handle cluster operations, including creating, scaling, and upgrading, freeing up developers to focus on their application. To get started, create a cluster with Azure Kubernetes Service.

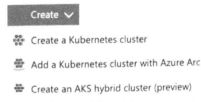

Figure 4.2 – Creating the Kubernetes cluster

3. Fill in the details for **Resource group**, **Kubernetes cluster name**, and **Region**.

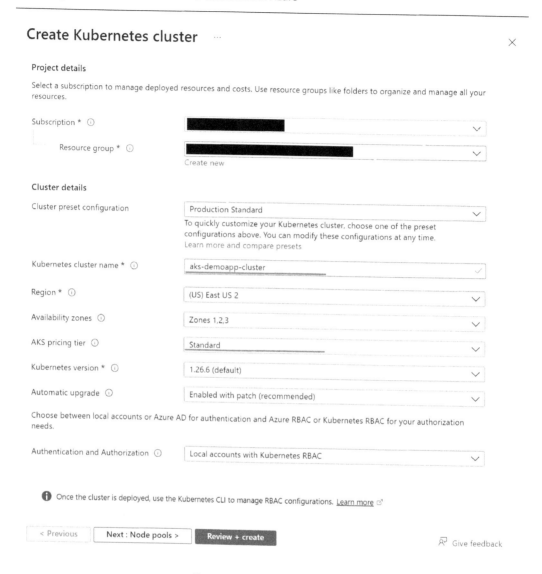

Figure 4.3 – Fill out cluster details

4.   Once the Kubernetes cluster is created, we can validate that the node pool was also initialized.

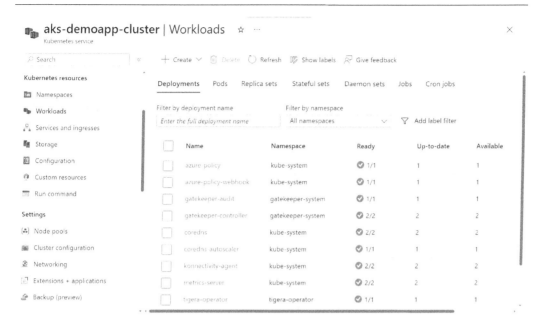

Figure 4.4 – Kubernetes cluster ready to use

Managing a Kubernetes cluster requires using the `kubectl` command-line client, an indispensable tool for interacting with Kubernetes environments. We need to configure it to communicate with our Kubernetes cluster. This can be achieved using the following `az aks get-credentials` command:

```
az aks get-credentials --resource-group aks-demoapp-rg
--name aks-demoapp-cluster
```

This command fetches the credentials required for authentication and configures kubectl to interact with your AKS cluster. It simplifies your ability to manage and monitor the cluster from your local development environment.

The preceding command serves multiple purposes:

- It retrieves the required credentials and configures kubectl to utilize them.
- By default, it uses `~/.kube/config` as the configuration file for Kubernetes. However, you can specify a different location for the configuration file using the `--file` argument.

Next, we need to validate that our connection to the cluster is successfully established and execute the `kubectl get` command, which retrieves a list of nodes in our cluster:

```
kubectl get nodes
```

When you run this command, you'll receive a list of nodes within your AKS cluster, along with their status. This verification step confirms that your AKS cluster has been successfully provisioned and is operational.

The output from this command should display the nodes you created earlier. Ensure that the status of each node is marked as `ready`, indicating that they are operational and ready to handle workloads.

Having the Azure CLI and kubectl in your toolkit equips you to tackle more advanced tasks within your Kubernetes environment. These tools provide efficiency and control, simplifying the management of your Kubernetes cluster and enabling you to optimize resources and applications hosted on AKS.

Now, moving on to the Deployment process, a critical component is required: the manifest file. This file outlines the intended state of your cluster, defining aspects such as the specific container images to be run. In the context of setting up a web application in AKS, we utilize a manifest file that specifies a Kubernetes Deployment. The manifest for the Deployment contains the following:

- **Deployment metadata**: This section provides a name for the Deployment, such as `aks-web-app-deployment`.

- **Deployment spec**: Details the number of replicas and the selector used to match labels for the `aks-web-app` app.

- **Template section**: Within the Deployment spec, the template metadata labels the app as `aks-web-app`. The template specification contains the container specifications to be executed. This includes the container's name (`aks-web-app-container`), the designated image (`nginx`), and port settings. Furthermore, the template specification defines the resource requests and limits for the container, determining CPU and memory allocations.

These manifests are used to define the desired state of your Kubernetes resources. Following this code block, I have provided an explanation of each manifest:

```
service.yaml

apiVersion: v1
kind: Service
metadata:
  name: aks-web-app-service
spec:
  type: LoadBalancer
  ports:
  - port: 80
  selector:
    app: aks-web-app
```

`service.yaml` defines a Kubernetes Service named `aks-web-app-service`:
- `apiVersion`: Specifies the version of the Kubernetes API to use.
- `kind`: Indicates the kind of Kubernetes resource, which in this case is a Service.
- `metadata`: Contains metadata about the Service, including its name.
- `spec`: Describes the desired state of the Service.

- `type`: Specifies the type of Service, which is `LoadBalancer`. This exposes the Service externally using a cloud provider's load balancer.

- `ports`: Specifies the ports to expose on the Service. In this case, port `80` is exposed.

- `selector`: Defines the labels that the Service selects Pods with. It matches the Pods with apps with the `aks-web-app label`.

Let's move on to the following `deployment.yaml` file:

```
apiVersion: apps/v1
kind: Deployment
metadata:
  name: aks-web-app-deployment
spec:
  replicas: 2
  selector:
    matchLabels:
      app: aks-web-app
  template:
    metadata:
      labels:
        app: aks-web-app
    spec:
      containers:
      - name: aks-web-app-container
        image: nginx
        ports:
        - containerPort: 80
          name: http
        resources:
          requests:
            cpu: 100m
            memory: 128Mi
          limits:
            cpu: 250m
            memory: 512Mi
```

`deployment.yaml` defines a Kubernetes Deployment named `aks-web-app-deployment`:

- `apiVersion`: Specifies the version of the Kubernetes API to use.

- `kind`: Indicates the kind of Kubernetes resource, which is a Deployment.

- `metadata`: Contains metadata about the Deployment, including its name.

- `spec`: Describes the desired state of the Deployment.

- `replicas`: Specifies the desired number of replicas (Pods) to maintain.
- `selector`: Defines the labels used to select the Pods managed by the Deployment. It matches the Pods with apps with the `aks-web-app` label.
- `template`: Describes the Pod template to create new Pods.
- `metadata`: Specifies labels for the Pods created from the template.
- `spec`: Describes the Pod's specification.
- `containers`: Specifies the containers to run in the Pod.
- `name`: Specifies the container name.
- `image`: Specifies the container image to use (in this case, `nginx`).
- `ports`: Specifies the ports to open in the container.
- `resources`: Specifies resource requests and limits for CPU and memory.

These YAML manifests define a Kubernetes Service and Deployment for an NGINX-based web application. The Service exposes the application to the external network, while the Deployment manages the desired number of replicas of the application.

Run the following command to create the Kubernetes Service:

```
kubectl apply -f service.yaml
```

After that completes, run the following command to create the Kubernetes Deployment:

```
kubectl apply -f Deployment.yaml
```

To ensure that the Service and Deployment have been created successfully, you can use the following commands:

- To view the Services, use the following:

  ```
  kubectl get services
  ```

- To view the Deployments, use the following:

  ```
  kubectl get deployments
  ```

  You should see the newly created Service and Deployment listed.

- To check the status of the Pods in the Deployment, use the following command:

  ```
  kubectl get pods
  ```

The Pods created by the Deployment should have a status of *Running* or *Completed*.

By following these steps, you successfully created a Kubernetes Service and a Deployment using the provided YAML manifests. These manifests define the desired state of your application's Deployment and Service in your Kubernetes cluster. This allows you to manage and scale your application effectively within your Kubernetes environment.

In conclusion, deploying your application using a Kubernetes manifest file is a powerful method for managing your application in Azure. Whether you're deploying a simple app or a complex microservices architecture, Kubernetes and Azure provide the tools you need to deploy, manage, and scale your application effectively.

Navigating the complexities of managing an AKS cluster can occasionally involve encountering hurdles that, in order to overcome, require effective troubleshooting techniques to maintain optimal performance and functionality. In this section, you'll find a set of essential Azure CLI commands for troubleshooting and managing your Azure resources effectively.

Troubleshooting Pods and Deployments

Managing a Kubernetes cluster involves overseeing the intricate interactions between various components, applications, and services. While Kubernetes simplifies container orchestration, occasional challenges may arise. This is where troubleshooting becomes a valuable skill. Whether it's diagnosing issues within Pods, ensuring Services are running optimally, or debugging networking problems, understanding how to troubleshoot effectively is crucial.

In this section, we'll delve into troubleshooting techniques to help you identify and address common issues that might occur within your AKS environment. From examining the status of your Deployments and Pods to investigating Service and networking concerns, we'll equip you with practical insights and commands to navigate and resolve challenges confidently. As you embark on your Kubernetes journey, having a strong troubleshooting foundation will empower you to maintain the health and performance of your applications and clusters. Below are essential commands that will enable you to meticulously evaluate and troubleshoot the status of your Deployments and Pods within your Kubernetes cluster:

- **Check the Deployment status**: After deploying your application, verifying the Deployment's status is crucial. Run the following command to assess the situation:

  ```
  kubectl get deployment aks-web-app-deployment
  ```

  This command will provide insight into the desired and current number of replicas. If these numbers are not equal, it could indicate a problem with the Deployment, such as scaling issues or resource constraints.

- **Check the Pod status**: To ensure that your Pods are running correctly within the Deployment, use the following command:

  ```
  kubectl get pods -l app=aks-web-app
  ```

  This command displays the status of all Pods labeled with `app=aks-web-app`. If a Pod is not in the *Running* state, it indicates there might be a problem with the container.

- **Inspect the Pod logs**: When troubleshooting, inspecting the logs of a specific Pod can provide valuable insights into any errors or issues within the container. Use the following command:

```
kubectl logs pod-name
```

Replace pod-name with the actual name of the Pod you want to investigate. This step can help you identify the root cause of any unexpected behavior.

- **Troubleshooting Services**: Services play a critical role in exposing your application. To check the status of your Service, execute the following:

```
kubectl get service aks-web-app-service
```

This command will reveal essential information about the Service type, external IP (if applicable), and port mapping.

- **Examine the load balancer**: For Services utilizing the LoadBalancer type, confirm the external IP or DNS name assigned to your Service:

```
kubectl get service aks-web-app-service
```

If the external IP is "Pending," give it time to allocate an IP address.

- **Node and network troubleshooting**: To delve into node issues and their conditions, run the following commands:

```
kubectl get nodes
kubectl describe node node-name
```

These commands offer valuable information about node health, conditions, and potential issues.

Network policies

If network communication isn't functioning as expected, ensure your network policies and firewall rules are correctly configured. Verify that Pods can communicate as intended based on your network setup.

- **Debugging with shell access**: When standard commands aren't sufficient, you can debug interactively by accessing a shell inside a container. First, access the container's shell:

```
kubectl exec -it pod-name -- /bin/sh
```

Once inside the shell, you can inspect environment variables, file paths, and log files and diagnose issues more effectively.

Remember to continuously monitor error messages, status conditions, and logs as you troubleshoot. Kubernetes offers robust tools for diagnosing issues, ultimately ensuring the reliable performance of your applications. As you gain experience, you'll become increasingly proficient at identifying and resolving various problems.

In conclusion, mastering the management of an AKS cluster empowers you to leverage the full capabilities of containerized applications, ensuring their uninterrupted operation. Through the step-by-step guide on creating, verifying, and troubleshooting your AKS cluster, you have acquired valuable insights into deploying applications, monitoring their status, and addressing potential issues.

Remember that AKS provides a powerful platform that abstracts away much of the underlying complexity of managing Kubernetes infrastructure. With the Azure CLI and `kubectl` commands, you've discovered efficient ways to interact with your cluster, streamline Deployments, and troubleshoot any unexpected behavior.

As you venture deeper into Kubernetes, you'll continue to uncover new features, configurations, and tools that can enhance your application's performance, resilience, and scalability. Whether you're scaling node pools, optimizing network policies, or diving into container logs, the knowledge you've gained will serve as a strong foundation for successful AKS management.

By understanding the nuances of AKS deployment and operation, you can confidently build, manage, and evolve your containerized applications. Embrace the learning journey, leverage the resources available, and unlock the full potential of AKS to create modern, dynamic, and resilient applications in the cloud.

Having delved deep into Kubernetes, we are ready to take our knowledge and dive into containers. In the upcoming section, we'll discuss the power of containers in Azure and arm you with the knowledge to identify what resource is the best one to use on your journey to developing enterprise-ready solutions in the cloud.

Introducing containers

Containers have become essential to modern software development as they provide a lightweight, portable, and consistent way to package and distribute applications. This section will explore what containers are, what a container image is, and how they differ from AKS.

Containers are lightweight, portable, and executable packages that include everything needed to run an application, including the code, runtime, system tools, libraries, and settings. They provide an isolated environment that separates the application from the underlying infrastructure, ensuring it runs consistently across different environments.

Containers are like the basic LEGO blocks for creating systems that can grow, work anywhere, and keep different parts separate from each other. They're super helpful for making and running software smoothly.

Containers are built on top of containerization technology such as **Docker**, which allows developers to create, manage, and run containers. Each container runs in its own isolated environment, separate from the host system and other containers. This isolation ensures that the application runs consistently, regardless of the underlying infrastructure.

Containers are different from virtual machines in that they share the host system's kernel and don't require an entire operating system to be installed. This makes them much more lightweight and efficient than virtual machines, as they don't require as much memory and storage.

They are charged on a per-second billing model that allows users to spin up a container quickly and use it for occasional workloads and testing but not continuously running workloads.

Consider a container as analogous to a briefcase you take on a business trip. It contains not only your laptop (the application) but also the charger, adaptor plugs, external drives (dependencies), and your itinerary (configuration files). All the essentials to ensure your laptop runs smoothly, regardless of the location, are included.

Just as it wouldn't matter whether your business meeting is in New York, London, or Singapore because your briefcase has everything you need, containers work similarly. The differences in infrastructure and operating systems are seamlessly handled.

A container is a comprehensive package with an application and everything required to function perfectly. This universality and portability mean your application can perform consistently, regardless of the environment in which it's deployed.

Difference between containers and AKS

In the evolving landscape of cloud computing and application deployment, two terms that frequently surface are containers and AKS. While they are both pivotal in modern software development, they serve distinct roles and functions in the life cycle of an application. Let's delve into the differences between these two concepts and understand how they complement each other in the broader context of application management and deployment.

Containers

Containers are lightweight, standalone, executable packages that contain everything needed to run a piece of software, including the code, runtime, system tools, libraries, and dependencies.

They are designed to provide a consistent and isolated environment for applications, ensuring that the software runs in the same way, regardless of where it is deployed.

In essence, containers are like lightweight virtual machines but without the overhead of running an entire operating system.

Azure Kubernetes Service

On the other hand, AKS is a managed service that simplifies using Kubernetes to deploy, manage, and scale containerized applications.

Think of AKS as a container orchestration platform. While individual containers are excellent for running a single application, real-world scenarios often involve multiple interconnected containers that need to work together, scale together, and recover from failures gracefully.

AKS organizes containers into logical units for easy management and discovery. It takes care of distributing containers across a cluster of machines, monitoring and maintaining the desired state of your applications, scaling up or down as necessary, and rolling out updates or rollbacks without downtime.

In simple terms, AKS is designed to help you run and manage containers at scale. It handles the complexity of coordinating and scheduling containers in your environment so you don't have to.

When to use Azure Container Instances

Azure Container Instances (**ACI**) can be used in several scenarios. In the following list, you will find some of the most common ones:

- Running short-lived, stateless workloads, such as batch jobs or **microservices**
- Scaling out containerized workloads, such as web apps, quickly and easily
- Running containers in situations where a full-fledged Kubernetes cluster is not necessary or desired
- For the testing and development of containerized applications as ACI allows for the easy and rapid deployment of containers
- Running a containerized application that does not require low-level control over the infrastructure
- Running specific workloads that require GPU resources
- Running event-driven workloads that require quick and efficient scaling
- Cost-effectively running containerized workloads as you only pay for the resources you consume

Remember that ACI is not a managed Kubernetes service and is unsuitable for long-term workloads, stateful workloads, or workloads requiring high availability.

Container groups

In ACI, a container group represents a set of one or more containers that are deployed together on the same host. Each container group has a single IP address and a single DNS name. Containers in the same group can talk to each other over `localhost`.

A container group can include multiple containers defined in the same configuration file, called a *Pod* in Kubernetes. This allows you to deploy and scale multiple containers together.

Each container in a container group can be set up with its CPU, memory, and other resource needs, as well as its own environment variables, ports, and volumes.

You can also set a restart policy for each container in a container group. This policy says if and how the container should be restarted if it quits or crashes.

By using container groups in ACI, you can deploy and manage multiple containers in a single deployment, making it easier to manage the containerized application and its dependencies.

ACI connector for Kubernetes

The integration of ACI with AKS through the Virtual Kubelet feature is a powerful combination that allows AKS clusters to burst into ACI when they need to scale quickly. This integration is designed to be seamless, providing a unified and consistent way to manage both virtual and physical nodes in a Kubernetes cluster.

Virtual nodes creation

When the Virtual Kubelet feature is enabled in an AKS cluster, it introduces a new type of node called a "virtual node." Unlike traditional nodes that represent physical or virtual machines, virtual nodes represent ACI instances in Azure.

This decoupling from underlying infrastructure enables rapid scaling and is especially useful for short-lived, CPU-intensive tasks.

Taints and tolerations

Virtual nodes are automatically tainted by Kubernetes, which prevents regular Pods from being scheduled onto them.

To deploy a Pod to a virtual node, the Pod specification must include a toleration for this taint. This ensures that only workloads that are suited for ACI execution are scheduled on virtual nodes.

The following is an example of part of a YAML file to explain toleration in a Pod security:

```
tolerations:
- key: "virtual-kubelet.io/provider"
  operator: "Exists"
```

ACI integration

When a Pod is scheduled onto a virtual node, the ACI connector, in conjunction with Virtual Kubelet, triggers the creation of an ACI container group.

This container group mirrors the Pod's specifications and runs in Azure as a first-class instance, making it, from a management perspective, indistinguishable from other Pods in the cluster.

Scaling and management

The ACI connector monitors the Kubernetes API for desired state configurations and ensures that the corresponding ACI resources are in sync.

For example, if a Kubernetes Deployment configured to run on virtual nodes is scaled up, the ACI Connector will automatically provision additional ACI instances to meet the desired state.

Exposing Services

ACI resources running as part of a virtual node can be exposed to external traffic using standard Kubernetes Services.

This is achieved in the same way as with traditional Pods, providing a consistent approach to network management, whether your workloads are running on physical nodes or ACI.

Networking considerations

To enable the integration of ACI with AKS through Virtual Kubelet, the AKS cluster must be configured to use Azure **Container Networking Interface** (**CNI**) as the network plugin.

Azure CNI provides **Virtual Network** (**VNet**) integration and high-performance networking with Azure VNets, a prerequisite for ACI connectivity.

It's important to configure this at the time of AKS cluster creation, as the network plugin cannot be changed after the cluster is deployed.

Practical use cases

This integration is particularly beneficial for scenarios requiring rapid scaling, such as unexpected traffic spikes for a web application.

It is also helpful for running batch jobs that require significant computing resources for a short period.

The integration of ACI with AKS through the Virtual Kubelet feature represents a significant advancement in the Kubernetes ecosystem. It combines Kubernetes' orchestration and management features with serverless containers' agility and efficiency. For developers and operators, this means a more flexible, responsive, and cost-effective environment for running containerized applications.

Summary

In this chapter, we undertook a comprehensive journey through the concepts of Kubernetes, AKS, and containers. These are critical building blocks that set the groundwork for our in-depth examination of serverless computing, a discussion that will continue in the forthcoming chapter with Azure Functions.

Kubernetes, fundamentally, is an open source orchestration platform conceived to streamline the deployment, scaling, and management of containerized applications. This potent platform organizes containers into logical clusters, thus ensuring the seamless management of containers across diverse cloud architectures – private, public, or hybrid. The true value proposition of Kubernetes resides in its proficiency to handle the complexities inherent to managing containers at scale, liberating developers to prioritize creating powerful and scalable applications.

While Kubernetes offers raw power and flexibility, AKS is the managed Kubernetes service provided by Microsoft Azure that simplifies leveraging this power. AKS alleviates many of the manual operations and complexities associated with managing a Kubernetes cluster. It deftly manages the Kubernetes infrastructure, empowering developers and system administrators to concentrate on the core activities of deploying and managing applications. This, in turn, results in operational cost reductions and boosts efficiency and productivity.

After that, we broached the topic of containers. In the software development universe, a container represents a standalone, lightweight, executable package encompassing everything necessary to run a piece of software – this includes the code, runtime, system tools, libraries, and settings. The power of containers emerges from their capacity to deliver a uniform and repeatable environment across varied stages of the development and deployment pipeline. This characteristic ensures that applications will operate seamlessly on any infrastructure in any environment, obviating the need for code modifications.

By comprehending these foundational elements, we are ready for the following chapter, where we will delve into Azure Functions. Azure Functions is Microsoft Azure's serverless computing service that enables the effortless execution of code fragments or "functions" in the cloud. This sets the stage for the evolving landscape of cloud services and underscores the importance of mastering core concepts such as Kubernetes and containers. Stay tuned for this exciting journey that promises to equip you with the tools and knowledge to harness the full potential of Azure.

Building Serverless Apps with Azure Functions and Container Apps

Welcome to an immersive journey into serverless application development, where the synergy of Azure Functions and Azure Container Apps brings unprecedented flexibility and efficiency to your projects. In this chapter, we will delve into the intricacies of serverless computing, explore the capabilities of Azure Functions, and immerse ourselves in the world of containerized applications using Azure Container Apps.

As we embark on this exploration, we will systematically navigate through the essential topics that serve as the foundation of this chapter, each contributing to your comprehensive understanding.

We'll start by gaining insight into the fundamental concepts of serverless computing and its significance in modern application development. Our next step will be to distinguish between monolithic and microservice architectures, understanding how the latter can enhance scalability, reliability, and maintainability.

Our journey will then shift to Azure Functions, where we'll delve into its runtime intricacies, explore its diverse use cases, and differentiate between process and in-process execution models. We'll also explore the world of Azure Functions triggers, enabling your applications to respond dynamically to various events and inputs.

Security is paramount, and we'll thoroughly examine the security aspects of Azure Functions, ensuring your applications are well-protected. We'll introduce you to Azure Durable Functions, offering insights into building stateful and orchestrating serverless workflows.

Practical guidance will be provided on setting up your first Azure function, giving you hands-on experience. You'll then transition into Azure Container Apps, understanding how they complement serverless applications. Finally, we'll guide you through seamlessly deploying Docker containers using Azure Container Apps, a key element in modern application development.

By the conclusion of this chapter, you will not only have a profound grasp of the intricate interplay between serverless computing, Azure Functions, and Azure Container Apps but also the practical knowledge and empowerment to architect and deploy sophisticated, responsive, and scalable applications. Welcome to the exciting world of serverless and containerization! Let us embark on this transformative journey together!

This chapter will cover the following main sections:

- Overview of serverless computing

- Monolithic architecture versus microservice architecture

- Introducing Azure Functions

- Azure Functions triggers

- Delving into Azure Functions security

- Azure Durable Functions

- Setting up an Azure function

- Getting started with Azure Container Apps

- Deploying Docker containers to Azure Container Apps

Overview of serverless computing

Referred to as a **Function as a Service** (**FaaS**) offering, serverless computing exemplifies a revolutionary, event-driven application design and deployment model. It facilitates developers in building and executing applications while the server management nuances are set aside.

In this scenario, it's not that servers are non-existent; it simply means the obligation of dealing with server operations, such as patching and upgrading, is shifted away from developers. Cloud service providers such as Amazon, Microsoft, or Google undertake these responsibilities, leaving developers to concentrate on their specific code or application.

A key characteristic of serverless computing is its pay-per-use billing model. You are charged strictly for the duration your code is in execution. One of the significant benefits of this architectural style is automatic scaling and load balancing. Managed by the cloud service provider, it ensures that your application adjusts to meet the demand and evenly distributes the incoming network traffic. This framework allows developers to focus on the most important task: developing their application. Meanwhile, the cloud service provider owns and maintains the server infrastructure, billing you for the resources utilized.

Serverless computing, embodying a paradigm shift in the technology sector, has replaced the traditional months-long application deployment on physical servers with a process that can be accomplished in just minutes. This change symbolizes a significant leap, boosting developer productivity and altering the standards of application development and deployment.

To summarize, serverless computing expedites the development process by eliminating server management, automatically adjusting resources to match demand, and enabling pay-per-use. This innovative approach offers an engaging entry point for those new to technology, striking an optimal balance between technical complexity and ease of comprehension. Next, we will dive into a quick introduction to the differences between monolithic and microservices architectures to get us in the right mindset for Azure Functions.

Monolithic architecture versus microservice architecture

Monolithic architecture and **microservice architecture** each present unique approaches to building applications. Traditionally, the monolithic approach held popularity, where the entire application – client-side, server-side, and database code – resided within one unified code base.

However, as time progressed, these monolithic applications grew in complexity and became increasingly challenging to maintain, especially when compared to the Agile development model. The monolithic design made applications more prone to bugs and deployment issues. Even in scenarios in which a bug arises in the client-side code, the design of monolithic architecture necessitates the redeployment of the entire server-side code post-bug-fix due to its single code base structure. This process leads to frequent application downtimes and mandates the need for expensive hardware infrastructure to ensure high availability.

Moreover, as the majority of applications transitioned to the cloud, the monolithic architecture posed difficulties in scaling, often resulting in higher expenses. DevOps processes became slow and complex, and the time required to deploy features, bugs, and hotfixes continually increased.

Here is where the concept of microservice architecture entered the scene as a potential solution. The microservice architecture decomposes a complex monolithic application into smaller, independent applications. This structure allows for easier and less expensive deployment and scaling of individual applications, streamlining DevOps processes.

In light of these observations, it becomes clear that a deeper understanding of alternative architectures is necessary. The next section will embark on a detailed exploration of serverless computing, an approach that eliminates many of the issues faced by traditional server-based architectures. The transition from monolithic to microservices represents a wider trend in the development world – a movement toward modular, scalable, and cost-effective solutions, exemplified by the rise of serverless computing. Let's delve into this transformative technology next.

Resource provisioning and management

In this section, we will delve into the transformation of architectural paradigms, moving from the conventional server-based architecture to a serverless model, as follows:

- **Traditional server-based architectures**: In a traditional architecture, managing resources involves manual provisioning, configuration, and maintenance of servers. This process can be time-consuming and error-prone, particularly in large-scale deployments. Developers are burdened with server monitoring, patching, and scaling tasks, diverting their focus from core application development.

- **Platform as a Service (PaaS)**: PaaS alleviates some of the management burdens by abstracting away much of the infrastructure complexity. Developers can concentrate on application logic and development while the cloud provider handles tasks such as server provisioning, load balancing, and database management. PaaS offerings require configuration and scaling decisions, often through autoscaling plans that need to be preconfigured based on anticipated demand.

- **Serverless technology (Azure Functions)**: Serverless technology takes resource abstraction to a higher level. With Azure Functions, for instance, you're relieved from server management and the intricacies of scaling configurations. The cloud provider dynamically allocates resources at runtime based on actual demand, ensuring optimal performance without manual intervention. Serverless technology is about allocating capacity on-demand, driven by the real-time workload. Unlike PaaS, you don't need to preconfigure scaling rules; the system automatically adapts to changes in load. This elasticity provides the utmost efficiency and cost-effectiveness, as you only pay for what you use. Moreover, you're completely isolated from server concerns, allowing you to focus solely on coding solutions that address business challenges.

Serverless technology goes beyond PaaS in terms of resource abstraction and dynamic scaling. While both PaaS and serverless relieve developers from traditional server management tasks, serverless allocates resources at runtime without requiring prior scaling configuration. The serverless approach offers efficiency, cost-effectiveness, and developer focus, as the cloud provider handles resource provisioning and scaling in response to the workload. Understanding these differences helps you choose the architecture that aligns with your application's scalability needs and development priorities.

Scaling

Scaling is another key difference between serverless technology and traditional server-based architectures. In a traditional architecture, scaling typically involves adding more servers or increasing the resources of existing servers. This can be an expensive and complex process, especially when dealing with unpredictable workloads.

In contrast, serverless technology and Azure Functions provide automatic scaling, enabling you to scale your applications seamlessly. Azure Functions automatically scales up or down based on the number of events that occur, ensuring that you only pay for the actual usage of resources.

Cost

Cost is another significant difference between serverless technology and traditional server-based architectures. In traditional architecture, you would need to pay for the resources you provision, regardless of whether you are using them or not. This can lead to high costs, especially when dealing with infrequent or unpredictable workloads.

In contrast, serverless technology and Azure Functions enable you to pay for the actual usage of resources, reducing costs and increasing flexibility. You only pay for the resources your functions consume while they are running, and you don't need to pay for idle resources.

Deployment and management

Deployment and management approaches vary significantly between serverless technology, traditional server-based architectures, and the evolving landscape of cloud services. Let's explore these differences to understand how each approach impacts application deployment and management:

- **Traditional server-based architectures**:

  - **Deployment complexity**: In a traditional architecture, deploying applications involves a complex and often manual process. This requires a deep understanding of server configurations, dependencies, and compatibility. Developers must consider various factors such as operating systems, runtime environments, and libraries. Deployment can become error-prone and time-consuming, especially for applications with intricate requirements.

  - **Management overhead**: Managing applications in a traditional environment requires ongoing efforts for monitoring, maintenance, and scalability. System administrators are responsible for hardware provisioning, patching, and scaling. As applications grow, so does the administrative burden, leading to potential downtime and operational challenges.

- **PaaS**:

  - **Abstracted deployment**: PaaS bridges the gap between traditional and serverless architectures. It abstracts the deployment complexity by providing predefined runtime environments, frameworks, and services. This simplifies deployment compared to traditional architectures but may not achieve the level of abstraction offered by serverless platforms.

  - **Managed services**: PaaS services manage underlying infrastructure to varying extents. While PaaS abstracts many operational tasks, it may still require manual scaling and configuration setup. Developers enjoy more focus on coding but may need to configure autoscaling rules and optimize resource allocation.

- **Serverless technology**:

  - **Streamlined deployment**: Serverless technology, exemplified by Azure Functions, offers streamlined deployment. Developers can focus solely on writing code without worrying about server configurations. With serverless, applications are packaged into functions, which are deployed individually. This modular approach simplifies deployment and enables incremental updates.

- **Managed infrastructure**: Serverless platforms abstract away infrastructure management. Azure Functions, for instance, automatically provision the necessary resources to execute functions. This managed infrastructure ensures optimal performance and scalability without manual intervention. Developers can rely on the cloud provider to handle server operations.

In summary, deployment and management approaches differ significantly across serverless technology, traditional server-based architectures, and PaaS. Serverless technology offers streamlined deployment, managed infrastructure, and an unparalleled focus on code development. Traditional architectures demand meticulous server configuration and manual management, while PaaS offers an intermediate level of abstraction and managed services. Understanding these distinctions is pivotal in selecting the right architecture for your application. Serverless technology and PaaS provide efficient deployment and management models, but the abstraction and control levels vary. The choice depends on your application's complexity, scalability needs, and the extent to which you want to offload infrastructure management.

Event-driven architecture

Finally, serverless technology and Azure Functions are based on an **event-driven architecture**, which is different from traditional server-based architectures. In a traditional architecture, applications typically run continuously, waiting for requests to arrive.

In contrast, serverless technology and Azure Functions are designed to execute code only when specific events occur. This event-driven architecture enables you to create highly scalable and efficient applications, reducing costs and increasing agility.

Introducing Azure Functions

Azure Functions is a versatile service that can help you build responsive, scalable, and cost-effective applications. One of the most common use cases for Azure Functions is event-driven processing. Azure Functions can be triggered by a wide range of events, including HTTP requests, messages from a queue, database changes, or timer schedules. This makes them ideal for building event-driven architectures that can respond to real-time events and process data streams as they arrive. By building applications this way, developers can make sure that their apps are always responsive and up to date, even if the amount of data and how it needs to be processed changes.

Another common way to use Azure Functions is to build small services that can run on their own and perform specific tasks. Microservices architecture is a modern approach to software development that divides large applications into smaller, more manageable components. This division allows developers to enhance scalability, reliability, and maintainability. Azure Functions is an excellent tool for building **microservices**, as it provides a serverless environment that can scale up or down based on demand. By using Azure Functions to build microservices, developers can make sure that each service is focused on a single task. This makes it easier to manage and deploy.

For example, an image processing microservice could be built using Azure Functions that takes an image as input, processes it, and then returns the processed image. This type of microservice is useful in a wide range of applications, from image recognition systems to e-commerce platforms. By building microservices using Azure Functions, developers can create scalable and responsive applications that can handle a wide range of workloads.

Azure Functions can be especially helpful for building APIs with low traffic, where the cost and complexity of managing a dedicated server infrastructure may be too much. It provides an excellent platform for building serverless APIs, as it provides a flexible and scalable environment that can handle a wide range of workloads. By using Azure Functions to build APIs, developers can make sure their APIs are responsive and scalable without having to worry about managing the infrastructure underneath. For example, Azure Functions could be used to build an API that gets weather information for a certain location. An HTTP request could start this API, and it would then use a third-party weather service to retrieve the weather data. By building this API using Azure Functions, developers can create a scalable and responsive API that can handle a wide range of workloads.

As we venture further into the intriguing landscape of serverless computing, the following sections will involve a deeper exploration of Azure Functions, a pivotal aspect of the Microsoft Azure platform. We'll delve into practical use cases where Azure Functions excel, showing you real-world applications of this powerful service.

Next, we will turn the spotlight on the Azure Functions runtime, which serves as the engine propelling these functions. Understanding its workings will provide invaluable insight into the heart of Azure serverless computing.

Finally, we'll compare the Azure Functions in-process and isolated process models, breaking down the benefits and potential considerations of each. This comparative analysis will provide a more rounded view of how Azure Functions can be utilized to their fullest potential. Get ready to dive into the nuances of Azure's serverless technology and unlock new horizons in your development journey.

Azure Functions use cases

Our next exploration will highlight the broad spectrum of Azure Functions usage. From enabling real-time responses to events, constructing efficient microservices, creating responsive APIs, and facilitating seamless integration across serverless environments to their instrumental role in automating DevOps tasks, Azure Functions exemplify an essential tool in modern development scenarios. The most common of these scenarios are as follows:

- **Event-driven processing**: Azure Functions can be triggered by a wide range of events, including HTTP requests, messages from a queue, database changes, or timer schedules. This makes them ideal for building event-driven architectures that can respond to real-time events and process data streams as they arrive. For example, an Azure Functions function could be triggered by a new message in a queue, and then process the message by running it through a machine learning model or updating a database. By building applications in this way, developers can ensure that their applications are always responsive and up to date, even as data volumes and processing requirements change.

- **Microservices**: Azure Functions can be used to build small, standalone microservices that perform specific tasks. By breaking down monolithic applications into smaller, more manageable pieces, developers can improve scalability, reliability, and maintainability. For example, an image processing microservice could be built using Azure Functions, which takes an image as input, processes it, and then returns the processed image.

- **Serverless APIs**: Azure Functions can be used to build lightweight APIs that respond to HTTP requests and provide data and services to other applications. This can be particularly useful for building APIs that have low traffic volume, where the cost and complexity of managing a dedicated server infrastructure may be prohibitive. For example, an API that retrieves weather data for a specific location.

- **Serverless integration**: Azure Functions can be used to integrate with other cloud services, such as **Azure Blob Storage**, **Azure Event Grid**, or **Azure Service Bus**. This makes it easy to build complex workflows that respond to events and triggers across multiple services without having to manage the underlying infrastructure. For example, an Azure Functions function could be triggered by a new file uploaded to Azure Blob Storage, and then process the file by sending an email notification or updating a database. By building these integrations using Azure Functions, developers can reduce the complexity and cost of managing a dedicated server infrastructure.

In some cases, there are better options than Azure Functions, such as Azure App Service, where the requirements are similar to a standalone service that is built for a specific task such as the following:

- **APIs and web applications**: If your primary focus is on building APIs or web applications, Azure App Service provides a more comprehensive environment. It offers better support for hosting full-fledged web applications with features such as continuous deployment, custom domains, and broader language and framework support.

- **Stateful applications**: If your microservice requires statefulness, such as maintaining a session state or utilizing WebSockets, Azure App Service might be a better fit. It provides the infrastructure and capabilities needed for managing stateful components.

- **Complex scenarios**: Azure App Service allows you to create more intricate applications for scenarios involving complex workflows or business logic that go beyond the scope of individual functions. Its support for full **Model-View-Controller** (**MVC**) frameworks and custom routing suits these scenarios.

- **Greater control over environment**: Azure App Service provides more control over the runtime environment, allowing you to install custom dependencies and configure various settings to suit your application's needs.

However, Azure Functions' capabilities extend beyond mere serverless execution. It shines in event-driven architectures, acts as the foundation for microservices, enables the creation of serverless APIs, and seamlessly integrates with other cloud services. Its adaptability as the glue in a process chain further highlights its versatility. With its event-driven focus and capability to serve as the connecting thread within modern architectures, Azure Functions represents a critical tool in the arsenal of modern developers seeking efficiency, responsiveness, and streamlined integration.

Azure Functions runtime

Different versions of the underlying software stack that Azure Functions uses to execute serverless functions are known as **Azure Functions runtime versions**. These versions include all the necessary components and libraries required to run and execute Azure Functions, such as the .NET Core runtime, Node.js, and Java.

Each version of the Azure Functions runtime is typically associated with a specific version of a programming language or framework. For example, Azure Functions runtime 1.x supports .NET Framework 4.7, while Azure Functions runtime 3.x supports .NET Core 3.1.

Developers can choose which version of the Azure Functions runtime to use based on their specific application needs and requirements. The latest version of the Azure Functions runtime, version 4.x, uses .NET Core 6.0 as its underlying technology. This version is the basis for the book's examples and provides a reliable and scalable environment for developers to build and deploy their applications.

Azure Functions – in-process versus isolated process

In Azure Functions, two hosting models are available: **in-process** and **isolated process**.

An in-process function runs within the same process as the Azure Functions host. This means the function shares the same resources as the host, such as memory and CPU. In-process functions can execute faster and are suitable for lightweight workloads that don't require a lot of resources. They can handle HTTP and other types of triggers and support a limited set of languages and frameworks, including **C#**, **JavaScript**, and **Python**.

Here are some of the key features of in-process functions:

- **Fast execution**: Because in-process functions are hosted within the same process as the Azure Functions host, they can execute faster and with lower latency than isolated process functions

- **Support for multiple languages**: In-process functions support a limited set of languages and frameworks, including C#, JavaScript, and Python

- **Simplified deployment**: In-process functions can be deployed as part of the Azure Functions app package, simplifying the deployment process

- **Seamless integration with other Azure services**: In-process functions can easily integrate with other Azure services, such as **Azure Storage** and **Azure Event Hubs**

However, in-process Azure functions have some limitations:

- **Limited resource allocation**: In-process functions share resources with the Azure Functions host, meaning they have limited access to CPU and memory resources. This can limit the amount of workload they can handle.

- **No support for long-running functions**: In-process functions are unsuitable for long-running functions requiring access to additional resources or external systems.

- **Limited language and framework support**: In-process functions support a limited set of languages and frameworks, which can limit the flexibility of the function.

The Azure Functions isolated process model, often referred to as the "out-of-process" model, is an execution model where the function execution happens in a separate worker process. This differs from the "in-process" model, where the function runs within the same process as the Azure Functions host. This isolation is achieved using two separate processes: one for the function host and another for the worker process where your functions actually run. This architecture also allows the host to maintain its life cycle separate from the functions, thereby providing robustness and reliability in the "isolated" model. The function execution is out-of-process and occurs in a separate worker process. This model enables you to target a different .NET version than the one on which the Azure Functions host is running.

Moreover, with the out-of-process model, exceptions in user code do not crash the host process but are instead contained within the separate worker process. The gRPC communication between the host and the worker also allows your app to be more resilient, as the host can restart the worker process if needed without impacting the overall app service.

As a .NET developer, these technical features empower you to build more resilient, flexible, and scalable Azure functions. You'll have more control over the execution environment and can ensure the stability of your overall application.

Here are some of the key differences between in-process and isolated process functions in Azure Functions in terms of the listed aspects:

- **Resource usage**: In-process functions share resources with the Azure Functions host, while isolated process functions have their own dedicated resources

- **Scaling**: In-process functions scale with the Azure Functions host, while isolated process functions can be scaled independently

- **Support for languages and frameworks**: In-process functions support a limited set of languages and frameworks, while isolated process functions support a wider range

- **Security**: Isolated process functions provide additional security controls, such as network and process isolation, which can be important in certain scenarios

- **Integration with other services**: Isolated process functions can more easily integrate with Azure services and systems due to their separate process environment

Now that we have a clearer understanding of the different processes in Azure Functions and their beneficial features, let's shift our focus to Azure plans, another significant aspect of Azure. These plans will give us insights into the different options available for resource usage and how we can optimize costs and scale effectively in Azure.

Azure Functions plans

In Azure Functions, we can choose from three plans: the Consumption plan, which scales automatically and charges only when functions run; the Premium plan, which auto-scales with pre-warmed workers for instant execution, operates on more powerful instances, and connects to virtual networks; and the Dedicated plan, which places functions in an App Service plan, suitable for extended operations where the Durable Functions extension isn't applicable. Beyond these, Azure Functions also supports three additional hosting plans for heightened control and isolation: the **App Service Environment** (**ASE**) for secure, dedicated environments at scale, Azure Container Apps leveraging **Azure Kubernetes Service** (**AKS**) for function execution, and Kubernetes for a fully isolated environment atop the Kubernetes platform.

The **Azure Functions Consumption plan** is a serverless hosting option designed to provide a cost-effective way to run small-scale or sporadically used applications in the cloud. It lets you deploy your functions without managing or setting up the servers or virtual machines that support them. With the Consumption plan, you only pay for your functions' computing time. This makes it an excellent choice for workloads that have traffic that comes and goes.

Here are some of the key features and benefits of the Azure Functions Consumption plan:

- **Cost-effective pricing**: The Consumption plan is based on a **pay-per-use pricing model**, meaning that you only pay for the actual compute time used by your functions. This makes it a cost-effective option for unpredictable or intermittent traffic applications, as you are not charged for idle resources.

- **Automatic scaling**: The Consumption plan automatically scales the number of instances of your function app based on incoming traffic. This means you don't have to worry about managing or provisioning additional resources during traffic spikes or high-demand periods.

- **High availability**: The Consumption plan provides high availability by automatically replicating your function app across multiple instances and data centers.

- **Scalable and flexible**: The Consumption plan allows you to scale your functions independently and provides flexibility to use any programming language or framework supported by Azure Functions.

While the Consumption plan provides several benefits, there are some limitations. For example, the Consumption plan has a **cold-start latency**, which means that the first request to a function may take longer to complete due to the need to initialize the underlying infrastructure. Additionally, the Consumption plan is not the best option for applications with long-running functions or requiring more granular control over the underlying infrastructure. Also, the Consumption plan does not allow for any virtual networking, and the function app is exposed to the internet.

However, the **Azure Functions Premium plan** is a serverless hosting option that gives you more features and resources than the Azure Functions Consumption plan. It is designed for larger-scale or mission-critical applications that require higher performance levels, scalability, and security. The Premium plan offers higher performance, greater scalability, and support for virtual network integration, dedicated instances, and hybrid connections.

Here are some of the key features and benefits of the Azure Functions Premium plan:

- **Higher performance**: The Premium plan offers higher performance than the Consumption plan. It uses faster CPUs and provides more memory and processing power, which enables it to handle larger workloads and more complex functions.

- **Greater scalability**: The Premium plan adapts to demand by dynamically adjusting its capacity, utilizing pre-warmed workers that launch applications without any delay when transitioning from idle status. It supports automatic scaling up to 100 instances per function app, which allows it to handle large traffic spikes and high demand periods.

- **Virtual network integration**: The Premium plan supports virtual network integration, which allows you to securely integrate your function app with other Azure resources, such as virtual machines, databases, and storage accounts.

- **Dedicated instances**: The Premium plan allows you to run your function app on dedicated instances, which provides more control over the underlying infrastructure and enables you to optimize performance for specific workloads.

- **Hybrid connections**: The Premium plan supports hybrid connections, which allows you to securely connect your function app to on-premises resources, such as databases or web services.

Even though the Azure Functions Premium plan has a lot of benefits, there are some things to keep in mind. For instance, it costs more than the Consumption plan and may not be needed for smaller or less important applications. Also, the Premium plan is not the best choice for applications with low traffic since you pay based on the number of running instances, not on how much you use.

The **Azure Functions Dedicated plan** is a hosting option that provides dedicated infrastructure for running Azure Functions. It is ideal for applications that require high levels of performance, scalability, and control. Compared to the Consumption plan, the Dedicated plan offers more flexibility and control over the underlying infrastructure, allowing you to optimize performance and security for specific workloads.

Some key features and benefits of the Azure Functions Dedicated plan include the following:

- **Dedicated infrastructure**: The Dedicated plan provides dedicated infrastructure for running Azure Functions. This gives you more control over the underlying resources, allowing you to optimize performance and security for specific workloads.

- **Customizable environment**: The Dedicated plan enables you to customize the runtime environment, including the operating system, middleware, and dependencies. This makes it easier to meet specific compliance requirements and integrate with other on-premises systems.

- **Scalability**: The Dedicated plan provides greater scalability compared to the Consumption plan. It supports automatic scaling of up to 30 instances per function app.

- **Virtual network integration**: The Dedicated plan supports virtual network integration, allowing you to securely integrate your function app with other Azure resources, such as virtual machines, databases, and storage accounts.

- **SLA-backed**: The Dedicated plan is **service-level agreement** (**SLA**)-backed, meaning that Microsoft guarantees a certain level of uptime and availability. This is crucial for mission-critical applications that require high levels of reliability and performance.

While the Azure Functions Dedicated plan provides several benefits, it also has some limitations to consider. For example, it is more expensive than the Consumption plan and may not be necessary for smaller or less critical applications. Additionally, the Dedicated plan may not be the best option for applications with unpredictable or intermittent traffic, as you are charged based on the number of instances running, regardless of actual usage.

Azure App Service has transformed web application hosting by offering a fully managed platform that simplifies deployment and scaling. For applications demanding enhanced isolation, scalability, and network control, the **Azure App Service Environment** (**ASE**) steps in as the ultimate solution. In this section, we'll delve into the key features and benefits of the Azure ASE.

Exploring the Azure ASE

The Azure ASE is a premium service offering a fully isolated and dedicated environment for hosting Azure App Service apps. It enables organizations to deploy and manage their applications within a controlled network environment, ensuring robust security, high availability, and optimal performance.

Some key features and benefits of the Azure ASE include the following:

- **Enhanced isolation and network control**: The ASE offers a dedicated environment isolated from the public internet. This isolation provides an added layer of security by minimizing exposure to potential threats. Furthermore, the ASE supports virtual network integration, allowing you to seamlessly integrate your app with other Azure resources while maintaining a private network environment.

- **Scalability and performance**: The ASE supports multiple VM sizes and easily scales your applications horizontally. The ASE can accommodate your needs, whether you're facing traffic spikes or gradual growth. This scalability ensures that your applications remain responsive and performant regardless of user load.

- **Secure deployment**: Security is a top priority for any application. The ASE enhances security by allowing you to deploy your applications directly into a **Virtual Network** (**VNet**). This isolation mitigates the risk of exposure to the public internet, making it an excellent choice for applications that handle sensitive data.

- **Hybrid connectivity**: The ASE seamlessly integrates with your on-premises network through an Azure VNet. This connectivity enables secure interaction between your cloud-based applications and on-premises systems, making the ASE a preferred option for hybrid scenarios.

- **High availability and reliability**: With multiple instances distributed across Availability Zones, the ASE ensures high availability and fault tolerance. This setup minimizes downtime and ensures continuous availability of your applications, even in the face of hardware failures.

- **Compliance and regulatory requirements**: Industries with stringent compliance and regulatory standards, such as finance and healthcare, benefit from the ASE's isolated environment. It allows you to meet compliance requirements by maintaining strict control over network traffic and data handling.

- **Custom domains and SSL certificates**: The ASE empowers you to use custom domains and SSL certificates, enhancing the user experience by establishing trust and improving SEO rankings. This feature is handy for applications that require branding and trustworthiness.

Considerations and limitations of the Azure ASE

Before choosing the Azure ASE, it's essential to carefully assess your application's requirements, budget, and the level of isolation and security needed. Here are some of the limitations of the Azure ASE:

- **Cost consideration**: While the ASE offers many benefits, evaluating the associated costs is crucial. The ASE is a premium service and may be more expensive than traditional Azure App Service plans. Assess your application's requirements and budget before making a decision.

- **Administrative overhead**: The ASE's advanced capabilities come with added administrative complexity. Setting up and managing the ASE requires networking, security, and Azure architecture expertise. Ensure you have the necessary skills or resources available.

The Azure ASE empowers organizations with advanced deployment and security capabilities. From enhanced isolation and network control to seamless hybrid connectivity and compliance adherence, the ASE provides a powerful platform for hosting business-critical applications. However, adopting the ASE should be based on a comprehensive analysis of your application's requirements, security considerations, and budget constraints.

> **Note**
>
> Azure ASE features and benefits may vary based on Azure updates and offerings. Always refer to the official Azure documentation for the most accurate and up-to-date information.

In this section, we learned about different Azure Functions hosting plans, and the pros and cons of different hosting plans. In the next section, we will learn about Azure Functions triggers, which will help us to invoke Azure Functions.

Azure Functions triggers

Azure Functions triggers are the mechanisms that invoke your .NET code. Triggers are a crucial aspect of Azure Functions, defining how and when your function runs. By setting up a trigger, you can configure your function to execute automatically in response to specific events or inputs, such as a message in a queue, a timer, or an HTTP request. The following list will provide a high-level overview of each currently available Azure Functions trigger:

- **HTTP trigger**: This trigger responds to HTTP requests and enables the function to be invoked via a URL endpoint

- **Blob trigger**: This trigger responds to new or updated blobs within Azure Blob Storage and starts the function execution

- **Queue trigger**: This trigger responds to new messages in Azure Storage queues and starts the function execution

- **Event Hubs trigger**: This trigger responds to messages sent to Azure Event Hubs and starts the function execution

- **Timer trigger**: This trigger enables the function to be executed on a timer or schedule

- **Cosmos DB trigger**: This trigger responds to changes in a Cosmos DB collection and starts the function execution

- **Service Bus trigger**: This trigger responds to new messages in an Azure Service Bus queue or subscription and starts the function execution

- **Event Grid trigger**: This trigger responds to custom or built-in events in Azure Event Grid and starts the function execution

With these trigger types, there are many ways to respond to events and run functions in Azure Functions. This allows developers to build and deploy serverless apps quickly and easily.

Triggers are defined in the function's code and configuration file, such as the `host.json` or `function.json` files. In the configuration file, you set the trigger type, its parameters, and the input and output bindings that your function will use. You can also set various options related to the trigger, such as the batch size or the polling interval.

The benefit of using triggers in Azure Functions is that they allow you to build highly scalable and responsive applications. Instead of running your code continuously, you can configure it to execute only when triggered by an event or input, reducing the overall resource usage and cost. Triggers also let you process data quickly, which is important in many production situations. By using triggers, you can make scalable, responsive, affordable applications that can process data in almost real time. As a .NET developer, understanding and using triggers in your Azure Functions code can help you build better and more efficient applications.

Let's take a closer look at one example of how Azure Functions triggers can be used.

HTTP trigger

An HTTP trigger is one of the most commonly used Azure Functions triggers. It is used to respond to HTTP requests, such as when a user interacts with a web page. Here's an example of how an HTTP trigger can be used to handle a user registration request:

```
using Microsoft.AspNetCore.Http;
using Microsoft.Azure.WebJobs;
using Microsoft.Azure.WebJobs.Extensions.Http;
using Microsoft.Extensions.Logging;
using System;
using System.Threading.Tasks;
namespace Mynamespace
{
public static class UserRegistrationFunction
[Function("UserRegistration")]
public static async Task<IActionResult> Run(
[HttpTrigger(AuthorizationLevel.Function, "post" Route = null)]
HttpRequestData req,
ILogger log)
{
log.LogInformation("UserRegistrationFunction triggered by HTTP POST
request.");
if (req.method != "POST")
{
log.LogWarning($"UserRegistrationFunction recieved an unsupported HTTP
method: {req.Method}");
return new StatusCodeResult(StatusCodes.Status405MethodNotAllowed);
}
```

We'll explore the purpose of each method, attribute, parameter, and property involved in the process – from defining the function name and triggering conditions to logging details and handling input request data. This dissection should shed light on how individual elements contribute to the overall functionality and set the stage for understanding error-handling scenarios:

- The code is a C# class named `UserRegistrationFunction`, which contains a single method named `Run`

- The `Run` method is decorated with the `[FunctionName("UserRegistration")]` attribute, which specifies the name of the Azure function

- The `Run` method takes two parameters: an `HttpRequest` object named `req` and an `ILogger` object named `log`

- The `[HttpTrigger(AuthorizationLevel.Function, "post", Route = null)]` attribute specifies that an HTTP POST request can trigger the function and that the authorization level is set to `Function`

- The `HttpRequest` object, `req`, represents the incoming HTTP request that triggers the function

- The `ILogger` object, `log`, is used for logging purposes

- The `log.LogInformation` method is called to log an informational message to the Azure Functions log:

```
try {
IFormCollection formData = await req.ReadFormAsync();
string username = formData["username"];
string email = formData["email"];
//TODO: Validate username and email
log.LogInformation($"UserRegistrationFunction processed new user
registration. Username: {username}, Email: {email}");
return new OKResult();
}
catch (Exception ex)
{
log.LogError(ex, "UserRegistrationFunction failed to process
user registration.");
return new StatusCodeResult(StatusCodes.
Status500InternalServerError);
}}}
```

- The `req.Form` property retrieves the form data submitted with the HTTP POST request

- The `username` and `email` variables are assigned the values of the `username` and `email` form fields, respectively

- A log message is added when the function is triggered by an HTTP POST request

- The code may return a *405 Method Not Allowed* error if the function is expecting a specific HTTP method (e.g., POST) but a different method is used to trigger the function (e.g., GET):

  - The [HttpTrigger] attribute on the Run method specifies that only HTTP POST requests can trigger the function, using the POST parameter in the constructor. If a different HTTP method is used, such as a GET request, the function will return a *405 Method Not Allowed* error.

  - To fix this error, make sure that the HTTP method used to trigger the function matches the method specified in the [HttpTrigger] attribute.

- Wrapped the function code in a try-catch block to catch and log any exceptions that might occur during processing.

- ILogger is used to log an informational message when a new user registration is processed and gives an error message if an exception is caught

- A TODO comment is added to validate the username and email input data

- The OkResult and StatusCodeResult classes are used to return the appropriate HTTP status codes for success and failure, respectively

Azure Functions bindings

Azure Functions bindings are a powerful feature of Azure Functions that allow developers to create serverless applications without the need for explicit integration code. Bindings provide a declarative way to connect input and output data sources to a function, allowing developers to focus on the business logic of their functions rather than the plumbing code to integrate with external services. In this subsection, I will explain what Azure Functions bindings are, how they work, and why they are beneficial for developers.

What are Azure Functions bindings?

Azure Functions bindings are a way to define how data is input to and output from a function. Bindings can connect to various data sources, including storage services, message queues, and other Azure services. Bindings are created by the Azure Functions runtime and can be used by the function without any additional code.

There are two types of bindings: **input bindings** and **output bindings**. Input bindings define how data is input into a function, and output bindings define how data is output from a function. Input bindings can be used to trigger a function, while output bindings can be used to store data, send messages, or update other services.

Azure Functions provides a variety of built-in bindings that can be used to connect to common data sources. These include **Azure Blob Storage**, **Azure Queue Storage**, **Azure Event Hubs**, **Azure Service Bus**, **Azure Cosmos DB**, and more. In addition, custom bindings can be created to connect to other services or data sources.

How do Azure Functions bindings work?

Azure Functions bindings are created and managed by the Azure Functions runtime. When a function is executed, the runtime reads the function configuration and creates the necessary bindings. The bindings are then used to connect to the specified data sources.

Input bindings can be used to trigger a function in response to an event, such as a message being added to a queue or a file being uploaded to a storage container. The input data is passed to the function as a parameter, which can be used in the function code. For example, an Azure Blob Storage input binding can be used to trigger a function when a new file is added to a storage container. The function can then read the contents of the file and process it as needed.

Output bindings can be used to store data, send messages, or update other services. The output data is passed to the binding as a parameter, and the binding handles the details of storing or sending the data. For example, an Azure Blob Storage output binding can be used to store the output of a function in a storage container. The function can pass the data to the binding as a parameter, and the binding will handle the details of storing the data in the specified container.

Why are Azure Functions bindings beneficial?

Now that we've learned about Azure Functions bindings, let's explore their benefits to you as a developer:

- **Simplified development**: Bindings provide a simplified way of interacting with external resources and services. You don't have to worry about writing code to handle low-level details of communication and connection management, which saves you time and effort.

- **Increased productivity**: By simplifying development, bindings allow developers to be more productive. They can focus on writing the core business logic for their functions instead of dealing with infrastructure-related tasks.

- **Improved maintainability**: Bindings make it easier to maintain your Azure functions over time. If you need to make changes to your code, you don't have to worry about breaking existing connections or modifying low-level communication protocols.

- **Enhanced flexibility**: Bindings allow you to connect your Azure functions to a wide range of external resources and services, including databases, message queues, event hubs, and more. This provides flexibility in designing and implementing your serverless applications.

- **Increased scalability**: Bindings provide a scalable way of interacting with external resources and services. Your functions can automatically scale up or down based on the incoming workload without you having to worry about the underlying infrastructure.

The host.json file

The `host.json` file is a configuration file used in Azure Functions that allows you to configure the host runtime behavior. It is located at the root of your Function app folder and is used to specify global settings that affect all functions within the app.

Here are some standard settings that can be configured in the `host.json` file:

- **extensions**: The `extensions` property allows you to configure extensions that are used in your Function app. An example of an extension is the `serviceBus` extension, which enables your functions to interact with Azure Service Bus. You can specify the version and configuration for each extension in this section.

- **version**: The `version` property specifies the version of the Azure Functions runtime that your app is using. You can use this to ensure that your app is running on the correct runtime version.

- **logging**: The `logging` property allows you to configure logging settings for your Function app. You can specify the logging level and where the logs should be written, such as a file or a remote logging service.

- **HTTP**: The `HTTP` property allows you to configure settings for the HTTP binding used by your functions. For example, you can specify the default route prefix or configure **Cross-Origin Resource Sharing (CORS)** settings.

- **functionTimeout**: The `functionTimeout` property specifies the maximum amount of time that a function can run before timing out. This is useful for preventing functions from running indefinitely and consuming too many resources.

It's important to note that not all of these settings are required in the `host.json` file, and some settings may not be applicable to your Function app. You can refer to the official Azure Functions documentation for more information on the available configuration options and their syntax located at `https://learn.microsoft.com/en-us/azure/azure-functions/`.

In summary, the `host.json` file is a powerful configuration file used in Azure Functions that allows you to configure global settings for your Function app, including extensions, logging, HTTP settings, and more. By properly configuring this file, you can optimize your function app ad its functionality. The `host.json` file is used to configure global settings for the Azure Functions host. It applies to all functions in the host and can be used to configure things such as logging, function timeouts, and CORS, HTTP-based mechanism settings. The `host.json` file is deployed along with the function code to Azure and is used to configure the runtime environment.

In addition, you will find a `local.settings.json` file, which is used to configure local development settings. It has the values for environment variables that the Function app needs to run locally, such as connection strings for external resources (e.g., databases or storage accounts). This file is not deployed to Azure along with the function code and is intended only for local development.

Note that there is also a `local.host.json` file, which is used to configure settings for local development that apply to the entire function host. This file has the same structure as the `host.json` file, but it only applies to the local development environment.

Wrapping up, the `host.json` file in Azure Functions acts as the core of configurations, streamlining how your functions interact with various services and systems. By simplifying your code, it enhances manageability and efficiency, which are key to creating successful serverless applications. As we pivot from understanding this configuration aspect, we'll journey into the pivotal area of Azure Functions security in our next topic. Secure implementation is indeed an indispensable facet in today's cloud-first development environment.

Delving into Azure Functions security

As .NET developers venture into Azure Functions, understanding the basics of the Azure Functions identity is crucial. It helps developers ensure their applications' security while providing seamless access to other Azure resources. This section will explore the fundamentals of Azure Functions **identity management features**, including **authentication**, **authorization**, and **managed identities**.

Authentication and authorization

Authentication and authorization are two critical aspects of application security. Although they are often used interchangeably, they serve different purposes, explained as follows:

- **Authentication**: Authentication is the process of verifying the identity of a user, system, or process. It establishes that the entity is who they claim to be. In Azure Functions, authentication can be implemented using various providers, such as Azure Active Directory, social media accounts, or custom identity providers.

- **Authorization**: Once the user or system is authenticated, authorization determines the level of access and permissions granted to the entity. Authorization controls what actions the authenticated entity can perform within the application or on specific resources. In Azure Functions, you can configure authorization at the function level using built-in roles or custom roles to grant or restrict access to specific functions.

Azure-supported authentication providers

Azure Functions supports various authentication providers to help developers build secure applications. These are some of the most popular providers:

- **Azure Active Directory** (**AAD**): AAD is a cloud-based identity and access management service that provides secure access to Azure Functions using organizational accounts. AAD supports **OAuth 2.0** and **OpenID Connect** protocols, enabling seamless integration with other services and applications.

- **Social media accounts**: Azure Functions can also authenticate users through their social media accounts, such as Facebook, Google, and Twitter. This option simplifies the authentication process for users and reduces the need for additional account management.

- **Custom identity providers**: In some cases, developers may need to use custom identity providers for authentication. Azure Functions allows you to integrate custom identity providers through OpenID Connect or OAuth 2.0 protocols, giving you the flexibility to meet unique authentication requirements.

Managed identities for Azure Functions

A managed identity is a feature of AAD that simplifies the authentication and authorization process for Azure resources. It eliminates the need for developers to manage credentials, such as client IDs and secrets, for accessing other Azure services by Azure. They come in the following two types:

- **System-assigned managed identity**: This type of identity needs to be explicitly created and tied to an Azure Functions app when you enable **Managed Identity**. When the app is deleted, the associated managed identity is also removed.

- **User-assigned managed identity**: This type of identity is created as a standalone Azure resource and can be assigned to multiple Azure Functions apps or resources that support it. The life cycle of a user-assigned managed identity is independent of any app it's associated with.

Benefits of using a managed identity

A managed identity offers several benefits for Azure Functions developers:

- **Simplified authentication**: It automates acquiring access tokens, eliminating the need to manually manage credentials. This simplifies the authentication process and reduces the likelihood of security vulnerabilities.

- **Secure access to Azure resources**: By using a managed identity, you can grant your Azure Functions app secure access to other Azure services, such as Azure Blob Storage, **SQL Database**, and **Key Vault**. This allows you to build more robust, integrated applications while ensuring security best practices are followed.

- **Reduced maintenance overhead**: A managed identity eliminates the need to store, rotate, and manage credentials for accessing Azure services. As a result, it significantly reduces the maintenance overhead and potential security risks associated with managing secrets manually.

- **Centralized identity management**: With a user-assigned managed identity, you can create a single identity that can be shared across multiple Azure Functions apps. This allows for centralized permissions and access control management, making managing and auditing your applications' access to Azure resources easier.

Understanding the basics of Azure Functions identity management is crucial for .NET developers working with Azure Functions. It enables them to build secure and scalable applications by leveraging Azure's authentication, authorization, and managed identity features. By using supported authentication providers, such as AAD, social media accounts, or custom identity providers, developers can ensure the identity of users and systems accessing their Azure Functions apps. Also, with a managed identity, developers can simplify authentication and authorization processes while securely accessing other Azure resources without manually managing credentials. These basics of Azure Functions identity management will help you make safe, reliable, and efficient applications in the Azure ecosystem. As you learn more about Azure Functions, you'll be able to handle identity management and access control scenarios that are more complicated. Next up, let's learn about Azure Functions access keys and authorization scopes to secure your environment.

Azure Functions access keys

Access keys are pivotal in fortifying your serverless applications in Azure Functions security. Function access keys act as the first line of defense, authenticating clients and regulating access to your functions. In this section, we'll delve into the intricacies of function access keys, their significance, and how to effectively manage them to ensure the integrity and privacy of your serverless applications.

Access keys are cryptographic strings that provide a secure method for clients to authenticate themselves when invoking Azure Functions. These keys are embedded in the HTTP request header, allowing the Azure Functions runtime to validate the authenticity of the requestor. Access keys act as a digital signature, ensuring only authorized clients can trigger your functions. Function access keys serve as a mechanism to control access to your functions. By requiring clients to present a valid access key with their requests, you can restrict usage to those with the proper credentials. This is particularly useful when enabling third-party applications or services to interact securely with your functions.

Generating access keys for Azure Functions is a straightforward process. Within the Azure portal, you can create and manage these keys from the Azure Function's **App Keys** settings. Each function within your app has its unique access key, allowing for granular control over access permissions. These keys can also be rotated periodically to enhance security.

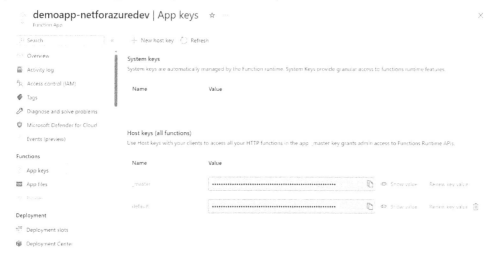

Figure 5.1: Access keys in Function app

Effectively managing access keys is essential for maintaining the security of your application. Following security best practices is recommended, such as keeping your code confidential and not hardcoding access keys. Azure can regenerate access keys if they are compromised, ensuring that your functions remain secure even in the face of potential threats.

Key authorization in requests

Clients requesting your Azure functions include the access key in the request header. The runtime validates this key against the access keys associated with the specific function. The function is invoked if the key is valid; if not, the request is denied. This process ensures that only authorized users with the correct key can interact with your functions.

Here are some best practices for managing function access keys:

- **Use the principle of least privilege**: Assign the minimum required permissions to each access key. This prevents unnecessary exposure of sensitive functions or data.

- **Rotate access keys**: Regularly rotate access keys to mitigate the risk of unauthorized access if a key is compromised.

- **Restrict key scope**: Assign access keys to specific functions rather than allowing blanket access. This provides a finer level of control over who can access each function.

- **Monitor and audit**: Keep track of access key usage and audit logs to identify any suspicious activities.

- **Secure storage**: Store access keys securely, avoiding hardcoded values in code repositories or public spaces.

In the dynamic landscape of serverless applications, securing your Azure Functions is non-negotiable. Function access keys are the initial gatekeepers, ensuring only authorized clients can interact with your functions. By understanding their role, generating and managing them prudently, and adhering to security best practices, you can bolster the security of your serverless applications and foster a trustworthy environment for your users. Next up, let's learn about authorization scopes and how they benefit the security of Azure Functions.

Authorization scopes in Azure Functions

In the realm of serverless computing, Azure Functions has gained widespread popularity for its agility and scalability. However, with the power of serverless comes the responsibility of ensuring robust security. One crucial aspect of securing Azure Functions is implementing authorization scopes at the function level. In this section we will delve deep into the world of authorization scopes, exploring their significance, mechanisms, and best practices for effectively utilizing them to fortify the security of Azure Functions.

Authorization scopes provide a granular level of control over who can access specific functions within your Azure Functions app. In essence, authorization scopes allow you to define different levels of access for different functions. This is particularly valuable when you have multiple functions within an application, each requiring varying degrees of access control.

While Azure Functions can be secured at the app level, applying authorization at the function level offers more flexibility and precision. Instead of granting blanket access to all functions within an application, you can assign specific permissions based on the principle of least privilege. This means that each function is only accessible by those roles or users requiring access, minimizing the attack surface and potential risks.

Configuring authorization scopes for Azure Functions involves a combination of defining roles and associating them with functions. Roles can be predefined (such as *Contributor* or *Reader*) or custom roles tailored to the requirements of your application. Azure Functions leverages AAD to manage roles and permissions.

Effectively managing access control within your application involves two fundamental steps:

1. **Defining roles**: Begin by defining the roles that align with your application's functional requirements. For instance, you might have functions that require administrative privileges and others that anonymous users can access.

2. **Assigning roles**: Once roles are defined, you associate them with specific functions. This process can be done programmatically using Azure **software development kits** (**SDKs**) or the Azure portal.

Imagine you have an e-commerce application with Azure Functions for order processing and customer management. In this scenario, you can define roles such as `OrderManager` and `CustomerServiceRep`. The `OrderManager` role might have access to functions related to order processing, while the `CustomerServiceRep` role can access functions dealing with customer inquiries.

For instance, a function responsible for processing refunds might require the `OrderManager` role. This ensures that only authorized personnel can initiate refund transactions, preventing unauthorized actions that could compromise financial integrity.

Best practices for implementing authorization scopes

Implementing authorization scopes effectively is crucial for ensuring the security and access control of your application. Here are some best practices for implementing authorization scopes:

- **Principle of least privilege**: Assign the least necessary privileges to perform each function's required actions. Avoid over-assigning permissions, which can lead to unintended vulnerabilities.

- **Regular auditing**: Review and audit roles and permissions to ensure they align with current business needs and security standards.

- **Immutable infrastructure**: Treat your Azure Functions app as immutable infrastructure. Any changes to roles and permissions should follow a well-defined process and undergo rigorous testing.

- **Role hierarchy**: Establish a clear hierarchy for roles, especially if your application has complex access requirements. This prevents role sprawl and simplifies management.

- **Logging and monitoring**: Implement robust logging and monitoring mechanisms to track role-based activities. Suspicious activities or unauthorized access attempts should trigger alerts.

In the era of cloud-native applications, securing serverless computing is paramount. Authorization scopes at the function level offer a potent tool for enhancing the security of Azure Functions. By tailoring access permissions to the specific needs of each function, you minimize risks and bolster the overall security posture of your serverless applications. Embracing authorization scopes isn't just a security measure – it's a strategic approach to safeguarding your serverless infrastructure and building a robust foundation for innovation. Next up, let's focus on creating an Azure function so that we can put our theory into practice.

Azure Durable Functions

Azure Durable Functions emerges as a transformative solution in the ever-changing serverless computing landscape, enabling developers to construct complex, reliable, and highly scalable workflows. This section explores the fundamentals of Azure Durable Functions, including its fundamental concepts, supported programming languages, development tools, and the distinction between stateful and stateless operations.

Fundamentally, Azure Durable Functions is a serverless orchestration platform. Durable functions are designed to seamlessly manage long-running and complex workflows, unlike traditional serverless functions, which execute brief duties. This suits them for scenarios requiring multistep coordination, asynchronous operations, and complex state management.

Elements of Azure Durable Functions

Azure durable functions embody three fundamental concepts that empower their orchestration capabilities:

- **Orchestrations**: Orchestrator functions serve as workflow command centers. They define the execution flow, coordinating and managing the numerous process steps and activities. Using a declarative approach, orchestrations allow developers to construct workflow logic that easily handles failures, retries, and parallelism.

- **Activities**: Activities are the discrete work elements within an orchestration. They carry out specified responsibilities such as data processing, API calls, and calculations. Activities are intended to be modular and reusable, enabling developers to partition functionality and improve maintainability.

- **Checkpoints**: Checkpoints play a crucial role in ensuring the durability of lengthy workflows. They facilitate the preservation of the execution state, allowing orchestrations to resume uninterruptedly after failures or scaling events. This factor is crucial for maintaining consistency and dependability in intricate workflows.

Stateful versus stateless workflows

Workflows in the domain of Azure Durable Functions can be classified as either stateful or stateless:

- **Stateful workflows** maintain and manage the process state across multiple phases and activities. This is accomplished using checkpoints, which store the workflow's intermediate state. Stateful workflows are optimal for situations where context and progress must be maintained, such as multistep approval processes and order processing systems.

- **Stateless workflows** do not necessitate the maintenance of intermediate states between steps. They respond to individual requests or occurrences without having to recall previous actions. Stateless workflows are appropriate for situations requiring high concurrency and low-latency processing, such as real-time data analysis or event-driven microservices.

The choice between these two workflow types depends on the specific requirements and objectives of the application. These workflows are particularly useful for scenarios demanding high concurrency and low-latency processing, such as real-time data analysis and event-driven microservices. As we delve deeper into application patterns, let's explore how these workflow types align with different use cases and development strategies.

Application patterns

Durable functions shine when simplifying intricate, stateful coordination requirements in serverless applications. Let's look at some typical application patterns that Durable Functions can enhance.

Function Chaining

In the ever-evolving landscape of cloud-based application development, orchestrating complex workflows has become integral to building scalable, reliable, and efficient systems. To address this need, Microsoft introduced Durable Functions – a serverless extension of Azure Functions that enables developers to design and manage workflows in a more streamlined and intuitive way. One of the fundamental patterns in Durable Functions is the **Function Chaining** pattern, which offers a powerful way to sequence and manage the execution of functions in a specific order.

Understanding function chaining

The Function Chaining pattern within Durable Functions involves utilizing an orchestrator function to call multiple activity functions in a predefined sequence. This sequence could represent a series of data transformations, processing steps, or any other logically related tasks. By chaining functions together, developers can create easier workflows to manage, maintain, and monitor.

Challenges addressed by Durable Functions

Before the advent of Durable Functions, developers had to resort to various methods to orchestrate function execution, often relying on techniques such as Service Bus queues. While these methods could achieve the desired outcome, they introduced several challenges:

- **Lack of visualization**: Orchestrating functions using Service Bus queues lacked clear visualization. It was difficult to comprehend the workflow at a glance, making monitoring and troubleshooting the sequence of functions cumbersome.

- **Conceptual overhead**: The introduction of middle queues to connect functions added conceptual overhead, making the overall architecture more complex and harder to maintain.

- **Complex error handling**: Error handling across multiple functions became intricate. Ensuring that errors in activity functions were accurately propagated back to the orchestrator function required additional effort.

Durable Functions tackles challenges of unclear visualization, conceptual overhead, and complex error handling in function orchestration, offering a comprehensive solution to streamline workflow management and improve efficiency.

Benefits of chaining functions with Durable Functions

The integration of the Function Chaining pattern within Durable Functions provides numerous advantages that significantly enhance workflow management:

- **Clear workflow visualization**: Durable functions offer a visual representation of the workflow, allowing developers to design and understand complex sequences of functions more efficiently. This visual depiction improves monitoring, debugging, and maintenance.

- **Streamlined orchestration**: The orchestrator function becomes the central hub for defining the order in which activity functions are executed. This eliminates the need to manage intermediate queues, reducing complexity and cognitive load.

- **Centralized error handling**: Durable functions centralize error handling. If an error occurs within an activity function, it is automatically communicated to the orchestrator, enabling informed decisions on whether to retry, continue, or terminate the workflow.

- **Simplified state management**: Durable functions manage the state of the workflow, ensuring that data and context are maintained throughout the execution of the chained functions. This simplifies data sharing between functions.

- **Scalability and parallelism**: Asynchronous execution and parallelism are inherent to Durable Functions. Chained functions can run concurrently when possible, optimizing performance and resource utilization.

The incorporation of the Function Chaining pattern in Durable Functions yields benefits, including clear workflow visualization, simplified orchestration, centralized error handling, streamlined state management, and enhanced scalability and parallelism, collectively elevating the capabilities of workflow execution and resource optimization.

Implementing chaining with Durable Functions

The following code exemplifies a powerful orchestration pattern using Azure Durable Functions, a framework designed to streamline the creation of robust and scalable workflows in serverless environments.

This code showcases the seamless coordination of multiple activity functions within an orchestrator to accomplish a complex task. Leveraging the orchestration capabilities, the code exhibits a holistic approach to managing and controlling the execution of a series of interrelated operations.

It showcases an orchestrator function implemented using Azure Durable Functions. This orchestrator efficiently coordinates the execution of three activity functions in parallel, passing an input value to each and collecting their results:

```
using Microsoft.Azure.WebJobs;
using Microsoft.Azure.WebJobs.Extensions.DurableTask;
using System;
using System.Threading.Tasks;
using Microsoft.Extensions.Logging;


public static class OrchestratorFunction
{
    [FunctionName("OrchestratorFunction")]
    public static async Task<string> RunOrchestrator(
        [OrchestrationTrigger] IDurableOrchestrationContext context,
ILogger log)
    {
        string name = "Alice";

        try
        {
            var parallelTasks = new[]
            {
            context.CallActivityAsync<string>("ActivityFunction1", name),
            context.CallActivityAsync<string>("ActivityFunction2", name),
            context.CallActivityAsync<string>("ActivityFunction3", name)
            };
```

By utilizing `Task.WhenAll` to synchronize parallel tasks, the orchestrator effectively orchestrates asynchronous operations. The code emphasizes structured error handling, logging, and exception propagation to ensure the integrity of the orchestration process. The orchestrator's capability to process activity functions concurrently highlights Durable Functions' ability to manage complex workflows. It is a powerful tool for orchestrating distributed and asynchronous tasks within a serverless environment:

```
        await Task.WhenAll(parallelTasks);
        string result1 = parallelTasks[0].Result;
        string result2 = parallelTasks[1].Result;
        string result3 = parallelTasks[2].Result;

        // You can perform more logic here with the results

        return $"Final Result: {result3}";
    }
    catch (Exception ex)
    {
        log.LogError($"Orchestration failed: {ex}");
        throw;          }}}
```

As we delve deeper into the capabilities of Azure Durable Functions, let's explore the dynamic orchestration prowess of the Fan-out/Fan-in pattern, where parallel execution and result aggregation synergize to enable intricate workflows in a highly scalable and efficient manner.

The Fan-out/Fan-in pattern with Durable Functions

In modern application development, orchestrating complex workflows efficiently is crucial for creating scalable and robust systems. Microsoft's Durable Functions, an extension of Azure Functions, provides an innovative approach to managing workflows with various patterns. One such pattern is the **Fan-out/Fan-in** pattern, which offers an elegant solution for executing multiple functions in parallel and aggregating their results. In this section, we will delve into the intricacies of this pattern, explore the challenges it addresses, and demonstrate its implementation using Durable Functions with .NET code examples.

Understanding the Fan-out/Fan-in pattern

The Fan-out/Fan-in pattern involves two distinct phases: the "Fan-out" phase and the "Fan-in" phase. During the Fan-out phase, a single function, often called the "orchestrator," spawns multiple parallel instances of activity functions. These activity functions run concurrently and independently, processing data or performing tasks. Once all activity functions are completed, the Fan-in phase comes into play. In this phase, the orchestrator gathers and aggregates the results from the various activity function instances, making it easier to perform subsequent tasks or produce a unified output.

Challenges addressed by Durable Functions

Implementing the Fan-out/Fan-in pattern without Durable Functions can be complex and error-prone. Challenges that developers might encounter include the following:

- **Concurrency management**: Ensuring smooth parallel execution of activity functions while managing synchronization and avoiding race conditions can be challenging

- **Result aggregation**: Collecting and aggregating the results from multiple activity function instances requires careful tracking and coordination

- **Error handling**: Handling errors across multiple parallel activity function instances, propagating the errors to the orchestrator, and deciding how to proceed can lead to intricate code

Benefits of Durable Functions

Durable Functions offers a comprehensive set of tools and abstractions that simplify the implementation of the Fan-out/Fan-in pattern:

- **Parallel execution**: Durable functions streamline the parallel execution of activity functions, allowing developers to focus on the logic of individual tasks rather than concurrency management

- **Result aggregation**: Durable functions automatically manage the aggregation of results from parallel instances, removing the burden of manual tracking

- **Error propagation**: Error handling becomes more straightforward as durable functions ensure that exceptions in activity functions are captured and reported to the orchestrator

- **Workflow visualization**: Durable functions provide visualization tools that make monitoring the progress of parallel instances and tracking their completion easier

- **Scalability**: The built-in scalability of durable functions ensures efficient execution of numerous parallel instances across distributed resources

Implementing Fan-out/Fan-in with Durable Functions

Let's consider a scenario where each task processed by `ActivityFunction` represents a sub-task that needs to be processed in parallel. The results of these sub-tasks are then aggregated and processed by another orchestrator. Here's how you can achieve this:

1. **SubOrchestrator**: Create a `SubOrchestrator` function that handles the fan-out and fan-in for a subset of tasks. This sub-orchestrator will call `ActivityFunction` for each task and aggregate their results:

   ```
   SubOrchestratorFunction.cs
   using Microsoft.Azure.WebJobs;
   using Microsoft.Azure.WebJobs.Extensions.DurableTask;
   using System.Collections.Generic;
   ```

```
using System.Threading.Tasks;


public static class SubOrchestratorFunction
{
    [FunctionName("SubOrchestratorFunction")]
    public static async Task<List<string>> RunSubOrchestrator(
        [OrchestrationTrigger] IDurableOrchestrationContext
context)
    {
        var tasks = new List<Task<string>>();


        for (int i = 0; i < 3; i++) // Process 3 tasks in
parallel
        {
            tasks.Add(context.
CallActivityAsync<string>("ActivityFunction", $"SubTask {i}"));
        }
        await Task.WhenAll(tasks);
        var results = new List<string>();
        foreach (var task in tasks)
        {
            results.Add(task.Result);
        }


        return results;
    }}
```

This sub-orchestrator efficiently manages the orchestration of three parallel tasks, invoking `ActivityFunction` for each `SubTask` in a dynamic manner. Subsequently, the results of these parallel operations are aggregated, aligning with the core principles of the Fan-In aspect of the pattern.

As we delve further into the orchestration landscape, let's transition to exploring how the main orchestrator leverages this sub-orchestrator to seamlessly orchestrate and aggregate diverse sets of tasks, embodying the complete Fan-In/Fan-Out pattern within the Azure Durable Functions framework.

2. **MainOrchestrator**: Modify the main orchestrator to call the SubOrchestrator function in parallel. This demonstrates the concept of fan-out at a higher level, where each SubOrchestrator instance processes multiple sub-tasks in parallel, and then MainOrchestrator aggregates their results:

```
MainOrchestratorFunction.cs
using Microsoft.Azure.WebJobs;
using Microsoft.Azure.WebJobs.Extensions.DurableTask;
using System.Collections.Generic;
using System.Threading.Tasks;


public static class MainOrchestratorFunction
{
    [FunctionName("MainOrchestratorFunction")]
    public static async Task<List<List<string>>>
RunMainOrchestrator(
        [OrchestrationTrigger] IDurableOrchestrationContext
context)
    {
        var subOrchestratorTasks = new
List<Task<List<string>>>();


        for (int i = 0; i < 2; i++) // Process 2 sets of
sub-tasks in parallel
        {
            subOrchestratorTasks.Add(context.
CallSubOrchestratorAsync<List<string>>(
                "SubOrchestratorFunction", null));
        }
        await Task.WhenAll(subOrchestratorTasks);
        var allResults = new List<List<string>>();
        foreach (var subOrchestratorResult in
subOrchestratorTasks)
        {
            allResults.Add(subOrchestratorResult.Result);
        }
        return allResults;
    }}
```

By introducing a sub-orchestrator and having the main orchestrator call it in parallel, you showcase a more intricate application of the Fan-out/Fan-in pattern. This example demonstrates the hierarchical nature of the pattern, where tasks are distributed and aggregated at different levels of the orchestration hierarchy. The Fan-out/Fan-in pattern, supported by Durable Functions, presents a powerful solution to the challenges of orchestrating parallel tasks and aggregating their results. By simplifying the parallel execution, result aggregation, error handling, and scalability aspects, Durable Functions enables developers to design and manage complex workflows more efficiently. The seamless integration of the Fan-out/Fan-in pattern within Durable Functions contributes to the overall agility and effectiveness of building modern cloud-based applications. Continuing our exploration of the capabilities offered by Azure Durable Functions, let's delve into the innovative realm of the HTTP Async Response pattern.

The HTTP Async Response pattern using Durable Functions

In the realm of modern web applications, interactions with external APIs play a crucial role in delivering dynamic and real-time experiences to users. However, when making API calls, uncertainties related to response time due to factors such as latency and varying request volumes can pose challenges, particularly in scenarios where functions are running in constrained environments or on consumption-based plans. To address this, the "HTTP Async Response" pattern comes into play, offering a solution that seamlessly integrates with the power of Durable Functions. In this section, we will delve into the intricacies of this pattern, explore its benefits, and provide insights into its implementation using Durable Functions.

Understanding the HTTP Async Response pattern

The HTTP Async Response pattern involves decoupling the synchronous request-response model of traditional API calls by introducing an asynchronous approach. Instead of waiting for an immediate response, the client receives an acknowledgment indicating that the request has been accepted and is being processed. The client can then monitor the status of the request and retrieve the actual response once it's ready. This pattern is particularly useful for long-running processes or when there's uncertainty about the response time due to various factors.

Benefits of Durable Functions

Durable Functions offers a well-suited framework for implementing the HTTP Async Response pattern due to several inherent benefits:

- **Built-in APIs for long-running operations**: Durable Functions provides built-in APIs that simplify the management of long-running function executions. This aligns perfectly with the asynchronous nature of the HTTP Async Response pattern.

- **State management**: Durable Functions manages the state of each execution, ensuring that functions remain stateless. This is crucial for maintaining the integrity of the asynchronous workflow.

- **Orchestrated execution**: Durable Functions allows developers to define and manage workflows that involve multiple steps and interactions. This orchestration capability is essential when implementing complex asynchronous operations.

Durable Functions presents an ideal foundation for implementing the HTTP Async Response pattern, driven by their inherent advantages that harmonize seamlessly with the requirements of asynchronous interactions. These benefits encompass streamlined APIs for managing long-running processes, sophisticated state management, and the robust capability to orchestrate intricate workflows. To bring these benefits to life, let's delve into a concrete .NET code example that illustrates the integration of the HTTP Async Response pattern using Azure Durable Functions.

Implementing HTTP Async Response with Durable Functions

The following examples will showcase how Durable Functions can transform the way we design and execute asynchronous operations in the context of API responses, enhancing user experiences and optimizing resource utilization:

- **HTTP trigger function**: In this example, we'll create an HTTP-triggered function that starts an orchestration, returns a task ID to the client, and then continues processing in the background:

```
using Microsoft.Azure.WebJobs;
using Microsoft.Azure.WebJobs.Extensions.Http;
using Microsoft.Extensions.Logging;
using Newtonsoft.Json;
using System.IO;
using System.Threading.Tasks;


public static class HttpAsyncFunction
{
    [FunctionName("HttpAsyncFunction")]
    public static async Task<IActionResult> RunAsync(
        [HttpTrigger(AuthorizationLevel.Function, "post")]
HttpRequest req,
        [DurableClient] IDurableClient client,
        ILogger log)
    {
        string requestBody = await new StreamReader(req.Body).
ReadToEndAsync();
        dynamic data = JsonConvert.
DeserializeObject(requestBody);
        string instanceId = await client.
StartNewAsync("OrchestrationFunction", data);


        return new OkObjectResult(new { InstanceId = instanceId
});
    }
}
```

The preceding code block represents an Azure Functions HTTP-triggered function called HttpAsyncFunction. When it receives an HTTP POST request, it initiates a new durable orchestration using IDurableOrchestrationClient, specifying the orchestration's name and optional input data. It then responds with an HTTP 200 OK status code and a message containing the ID of the newly started orchestration. This allows clients to trigger and monitor long-running workflows by making HTTP requests to this function, making it a crucial entry point for orchestrating asynchronous operations with Durable Functions.

- **Orchestration function**: Here's an example of the durable orchestration function, which will be invoked by HttpAsyncFunction:

```
using Microsoft.Azure.WebJobs;
using Microsoft.Azure.WebJobs.Extensions.DurableTask;
using System.Threading.Tasks;


public static class OrchestrationFunction
{
    [FunctionName("OrchestrationFunction")]
    public static async Task<string> RunOrchestrator(
        [OrchestrationTrigger] IDurableOrchestrationContext
context)
    {
        dynamic input = context.GetInput<dynamic>();
context.CallSubOrchestrator methods here
        return "Processing completed!";
    }
}
```

In this example, HttpAsyncFunction is triggered by an HTTP POST request. Instead of waiting for a response, it starts a new instance of OrchestrationFunction using Durable Functions. OrchestrationFunction represents a long-running process that might involve multiple steps, external events, or asynchronous operations. The client receives an acknowledgment containing the instance ID, and they can later use this instance ID to query the status or retrieve the final result of the orchestrated process.

The HTTP Async Response pattern, combined with the capabilities of Durable Functions, offers a robust solution for managing interactions with external APIs that involve uncertainty in response times. By embracing an asynchronous approach and leveraging the state management and orchestration capabilities of Durable Functions, developers can create responsive and resilient applications that handle long-running operations and varying workloads effectively. As the web application development landscape continues to evolve, Durable Functions is a testament to Microsoft's commitment to providing innovative tools that empower developers to address modern challenges.

In the following section, we explore the "Actors" pattern, a robust paradigm that navigates the complexities of orchestrating background tasks and managing recurring processes. This design pattern not only facilitates the efficient execution of parallel, independent tasks but also introduces a streamlined strategy for addressing state management and concurrency issues.

The Actors pattern with Durable Functions

In distributed systems and cloud-based applications, managing recurring processes and background tasks is critical to maintaining system reliability and efficiency. The "Actors" pattern, often referred to as "watchers" or "recurring processes," offers a solution for executing periodic tasks, such as cleanup processes or regular maintenance jobs. Durable Functions provides a powerful toolset for implementing this pattern seamlessly. In this section, we'll explore the nuances of the Actors pattern, address the challenges it overcomes, and illustrate its implementation using Durable Functions and pertinent .NET code examples.

Understanding the Actors pattern

The Actors pattern involves defining recurring processes, known as "actors" or "watchers," that periodically perform specific tasks. These tasks include data cleanup, cache expiration, and background data processing. Unlike traditional methods, the Actors pattern provides a more streamlined and organized approach to managing these tasks. Each actor operates independently, focusing on the task while following a predefined schedule.

Challenges addressed by Durable Functions

Implementing the Actors pattern without Durable Functions can present several challenges:

- **State management**: Traditional serverless functions need to be more stateless and short-lived, making it difficult to manage the state between invocations. This can be problematic for background tasks that require ongoing data.

- **Concurrency and synchronization**: Coordinating read and write access to shared external states, especially in recurring processes, can lead to synchronization and concurrency challenges.

- **Task scheduling**: Executing recurring tasks at specific intervals requires intricate scheduling mechanisms, often leading to complex code.

Implementing the Actors pattern without Durable Functions presents significant hurdles. Traditional serverless functions are often stateless and short-lived, making persistent state management challenging, especially for ongoing background tasks. Coordinating concurrent access to shared external states can result in synchronization issues. Additionally, crafting precise task scheduling mechanisms can lead to convoluted code.

The following section delves into Durable Functions' benefits. Addressing state management, concurrency, and task scheduling challenges, Durable Functions empowers efficient Actors pattern implementation. Enhanced state handling, synchronized access, and simplified task scheduling underscore Durable Functions' potency in orchestrating intricate workflows.

Benefits of Durable Functions

Durable Functions is well suited to implementing the Actors pattern due to their unique features and abstractions:

- **Flexible recurrence**: Durable Functions allows you to define recurrence intervals for actors with ease, ensuring that tasks are executed at the desired frequency

- **Task lifetime management**: Durable Functions manages the execution and lifetime of tasks, enabling them to run for the duration required by the recurring process

- **Multiple actors from one orchestration**: With Durable Functions, you can create multiple independent actors from a single orchestrator function, streamlining the management of recurring tasks

- **Simplified state management**: Durable Functions manages the state of each execution, removing the complexity of managing shared states and synchronization

Durable Functions proves to be exceptionally compatible with the Actors pattern due to its distinct advantages. These encompass the ability to define flexible recurrence intervals for actors, efficient task lifetime management, streamlined management of multiple actors from a single orchestrator function, and simplified state handling. These attributes amplify the efficiency and efficacy of implementing the Actors pattern.

Now that we've comprehensively understood how Durable Functions aligns with the Actors pattern and its benefits, let's put this knowledge into practice with a concrete example that showcases the seamless implementation of parallel, recurring processes using Durable Functions.

Implementing Actors with Durable Functions

With a solid grasp of the benefits that Durable Functions offers in implementing the Actors pattern, it's time to delve into a practical example that brings these concepts to life. In the following section, we'll walk through the step-by-step process of implementing the Actors pattern using Durable Functions, demonstrating how to efficiently orchestrate parallel and recurring tasks while leveraging the power of Durable Functions' unique capabilities.

Actor function

In the following code, we will be implementing an `Actor` function that executes the recurring task every 5 minutes using a `Timer` trigger:

```
using Microsoft.Azure.WebJobs;
using Microsoft.Extensions.Logging;
using System;
public static class ActorFunction
{
    [FunctionName("ActorFunction")]
```

```
public static void Run(
    [TimerTrigger("0 */5 * * * *")] TimerInfo myTimer,
    ILogger log)
{
    log.LogInformation($"C# Timer trigger function executed at:
{DateTime.Now}");
}}
```

In this example, `ActorFunction` uses `TimerTrigger` to execute the recurring task every 5 minutes. The recurring process is abstracted into this function, allowing it to perform tasks such as data cleanup.

The Actors pattern is a crucial aspect of maintaining the health and efficiency of modern applications. By leveraging the capabilities of Durable Functions, developers can simplify the implementation of this pattern, addressing challenges related to state management, synchronization, and task scheduling. The built-in support for recurrence intervals, task lifetime management, and simplified state handling makes Durable Functions a powerful tool for designing resilient and reliable background processes. As the landscape of distributed systems continues to evolve, Durable Functions stands as a testament to Microsoft's dedication to providing developers with innovative solutions to tackle complex challenges in cloud-based application development.

As we expand our exploration of Durable Functions' versatile capabilities, we now turn our attention to a crucial aspect of modern workflows: human interaction. In the upcoming section, we'll delve into how Durable Functions provides an elegant solution for orchestrating workflows that involve human decisions and interactions, offering a seamless approach to managing processes that require input and approvals from stakeholders.

Human interaction in workflows with Durable Functions

In the landscape of modern organizations, many processes involve a blend of automated actions and human decisions. Approvals, reviews, and other human interactions are integral to these processes. These processes must remain active for extended periods, awaiting input from various stakeholders. To manage these scenarios effectively, the **Human Interaction** pattern comes into play. This pattern requires a reliable mechanism for handling timeouts and escalations. Durable Functions provides a robust framework for implementing the Human Interaction pattern in a streamlined manner. In this section, we will delve into the nuances of this pattern, explore its benefits, and provide insights into its implementation using Durable Functions.

Understanding the Human Interaction pattern

The Human Interaction pattern involves scenarios where automated workflows or processes require human input or decisions. Examples include approval workflows, where a document needs approval from multiple stakeholders before progressing, or review processes that involve human validation. These processes might remain active for days or weeks, awaiting human intervention. A well-structured mechanism for timeouts and escalations is necessary to ensure efficiency and reliability.

Benefits of Durable Functions

Durable Functions offers several advantages that align well with the requirements of the Human Interaction pattern. From efficient management of extended processes to precise timeout handling and seamless escalation procedures, we'll explore these advantages step by step, showcasing how Durable Functions streamlines the orchestration of human-centric workflows:

- **Long-lived processes**: Durable Functions can manage long-lived processes efficiently. This is crucial when waiting for human input or decision-making that might take time.

- **Timeout handling**: Durable Functions provides mechanisms for setting timeouts on waiting for human interactions. If an expected input isn't received within a specified timeframe, predefined actions (such as escalations) can be initiated.

- **Escalation processes**: When the human interaction isn't completed within the expected time, Durable Functions can trigger escalation processes, ensuring that the workflow doesn't get stuck indefinitely.

- **State management**: Durable Functions manages the state of each workflow instance, allowing the process to remain active and resume where it left off after human input is received.

After gaining a thorough comprehension of the advantages that Durable Functions provides for efficiently managing human interactions within workflows, we will now transition to a practical perspective.

Implementing human interaction with Durable Functions

In this section, we will examine a real-world example that effectively illustrates the application of this pattern in the context of Durable Functions. Through this concrete example, we intend to illustrate how Durable Functions facilitates the orchestration of operations involving critical human input and decision-making processes.

Orchestrator function

With the following code example, we aim to demonstrate how Durable Functions streamlines the coordination of tasks that require significant human input and involve decision-making processes:

```
using Microsoft.Azure.WebJobs;
using Microsoft.Azure.WebJobs.Extensions.DurableTask;
using System;
using System.Threading.Tasks;


public static class HumanInteractionOrchestrator
```

```
{
    [FunctionName("HumanInteractionOrchestrator")]
    public static async Task<string> RunOrchestrator(
        [OrchestrationTrigger] IDurableOrchestrationContext context)
    {
        DateTime dueTime = context.CurrapprovalteTime.Add(TimeSpan.
FromDays(7));
        TimeSpan timeout = TimeSpan.FromDays(7);

        using (var cts = new CancellationTokenSource())
        {
            Task approvalTask = context.
WaitForExternalEvent<string>("ApprovalEvent", timeout, cts.Token);
            Task timeoutTask = context.CreateTimer(dueTime, cts.
Token);


            Task winner = await Task.WhenAny(approvalTask,
timeoutTask);
            if (winner == approvalTask)
            {
                return "Approved!";
            }
            else
            {
    approval // Timeout occurred, initiate escalation process
                return "Escalation Initiated!";
            }}}}
```

In this example, HumanInteractionOrchestrator waits for an external event (human approval) using the context.WaitForExternalEvent method. If the approval is received within the specified approval time (7 days), the process returns "Approved!". Otherwise, approval timeout occurs, and an escalation process is initiated, returning "Escalation Initiated!".

Triggering human interaction

Here's an example code snippet for triggering a human interaction Azure function that responds to an HTTP trigger:

```
using Microsoft.Azure.WebJobs;
using Microsoft.AspNetCore.Http;
using Microsoft.Extensions.Logging;
```

```
public static class TriggerHumanInteraction
{
    [FunctionName("TriggerHumanInteraction")]
    public static async Task<IActionResult> Run(
        [HttpTrigger(AuthorizationLevel.Function, "post")] HttpRequest
req,
        [DurableClient] IDurableOrchestrationClient starter,
        ILogger log)
    {
        string instanceId = await starter.
StartNewAsync("HumanInteractionOrchestrator");
        log.LogInformation($"Started orchestration with ID =
'{instanceId}'.");


        return new OkObjectResult($"Orchestration started with ID =
'{instanceId}'.");
    }
}
```

This example includes an HTTP-triggered function called `TriggerHumanInteraction` that initiates the orchestration of a human interaction. When this function is triggered, it starts a new instance of `HumanInteractionOrchestrator`.

The Human Interaction pattern, used where approvals or decisions are required from humans, is a critical aspect of many organizational workflows. With the capabilities offered by Durable Functions, developers can effectively manage and streamline these scenarios. By facilitating long-lived processes, providing timeout handling, and enabling escalation processes, Durable Functions is a robust tool for designing workflows involving human interaction. In the ever-evolving landscape of application development, Durable Functions is a testament to Microsoft's commitment to providing innovative solutions that empower developers to address complex challenges in a cloud-first world.

Azure Durable Functions is a potent set of tools for orchestrating complex operations in a serverless environment. By understanding the fundamental concepts of orchestrations, activities, and waypoints, developers can leverage Durable Functions to create scalable and resilient applications. The support for various programming languages and development tools increases their adaptability. At the same time, the distinction between stateful and stateless operations enables the optimal fit for a wide range of application scenarios. Azure Durable Functions paves the way for innovative solutions that depend on efficient orchestration and seamless coordination as technology evolves.

In the next section, we will see how to create an Azure function and set it up with authentication and authorization for it to be used in production settings.

Setting up an Azure function

This section will explore how to create an Azure function using the Azure portal. The Azure portal provides a user-friendly, visual interface that simplifies creating, configuring, and deploying Azure functions. Whether you're new to Azure or an experienced developer, the Azure portal offers an intuitive way to quickly set up and manage your serverless functions without the need for complex command-line operations or extensive coding. Let's dive into the step-by-step process of creating an Azure function using the Azure portal:

1. Log in to the Azure portal.

2. Click on the search bar and type in Function app. Select **Function app** from the drop-down list and then click the **Create** button.

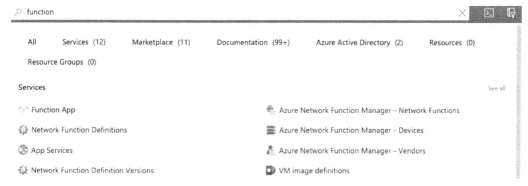

Figure 5.2: Searching for Function app in the Azure portal

3. On the **Create a resource** screen, search for Function app. In the first result, click on the **Create** button again, which will bring up a screen like this:

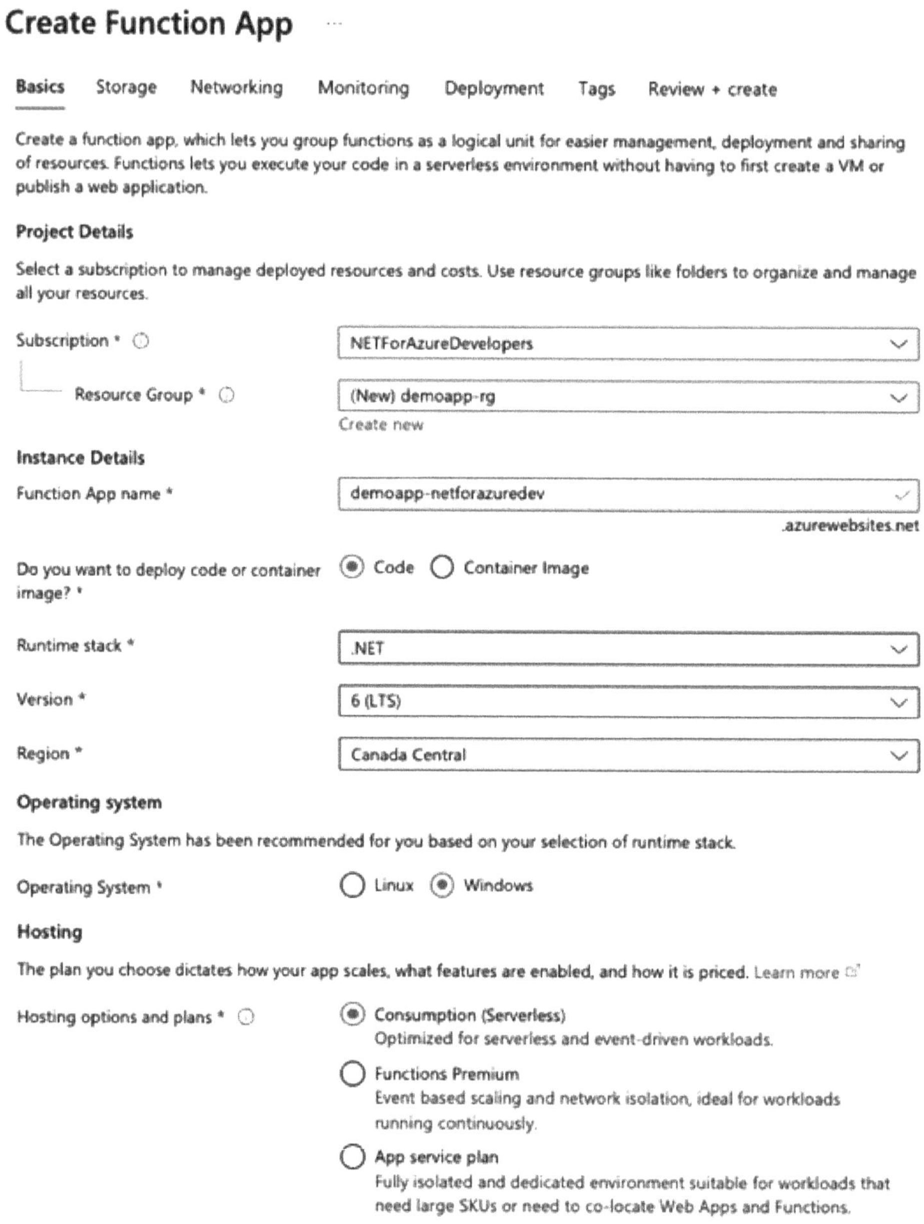

Create Function App ...

Basics   Storage   Networking   Monitoring   Deployment   Tags   Review + create

Create a function app, which lets you group functions as a logical unit for easier management, deployment and sharing of resources. Functions lets you execute your code in a serverless environment without having to first create a VM or publish a web application.

Project Details

Select a subscription to manage deployed resources and costs. Use resource groups like folders to organize and manage all your resources.

Subscription * ⓘ   [NETForAzureDevelopers   ∨]

└──── Resource Group * ⓘ   [(New) demoapp-rg   ∨]
                            Create new

Instance Details

Function App name *   [demoapp-netforazuredev   ✓]
                                                                              .azurewebsites.net

Do you want to deploy code or container   ⦿ Code   ◯ Container Image
image? *

Runtime stack *   [.NET   ∨]

Version *   [6 (LTS)   ∨]

Region *   [Canada Central   ∨]

Operating system

The Operating System has been recommended for you based on your selection of runtime stack.

Operating System *   ◯ Linux   ⦿ Windows

Hosting

The plan you choose dictates how your app scales, what features are enabled, and how it is priced. Learn more ☐

Hosting options and plans * ⓘ   ⦿ **Consumption (Serverless)**
                                   Optimized for serverless and event-driven workloads.

                                 ◯ **Functions Premium**
                                   Event based scaling and network isolation, ideal for workloads
                                   running continuously.

                                 ◯ **App service plan**
                                   Fully isolated and dedicated environment suitable for workloads that
                                   need large SKUs or need to co-locate Web Apps and Functions.

Figure 5.3: Create Function app – Basics

4. Fill in the details for the **Resource group**, **Function app name**, **Runtime stack**, **Version**, **Region**, **Operating System**, and **Hosting options and plans** fields as in the preceding screenshot with your specific details.

5. Click on **Review + create**, and the Function app will deploy in a few minutes. You can validate that it is completed by searching for the given function app.

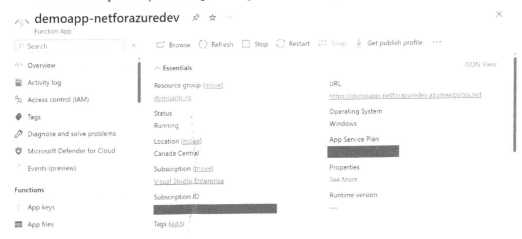

Figure 5.4: Deployed Function app

6. We can find the Azure function configuration by clicking on the **Configuration** menu. We will be able to configure different options such as the HTTP version, support for remote debugging, and the Visual Studio version.

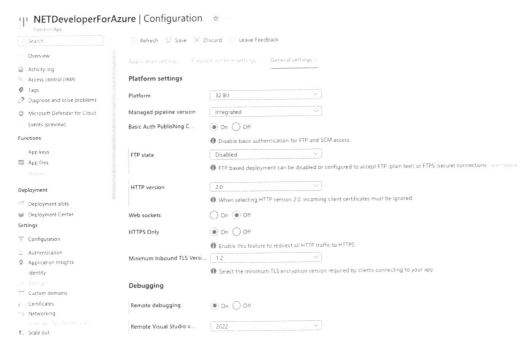

Figure 5.5: Azure function configuration

7. As mentioned earlier, we can create an identity using the Azure CLI with the following command:

    ```
    > az identity create -g demoapp-rg -n funcapp-mi
    ```

    In the command, we are creating the identity with the name `funcapp-mi` inside the `demoapp-rg` resource group.

    The output looks like this:

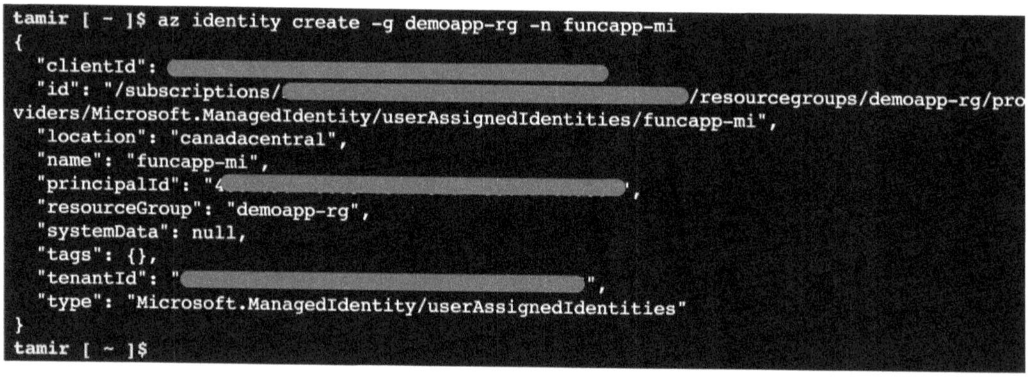

```
tamir [ ~ ]$ az identity create -g demoapp-rg -n funcapp-mi
{
  "clientId": "▮▮▮▮▮▮▮▮▮▮▮▮▮▮▮",
  "id": "/subscriptions/▮▮▮▮▮▮▮▮▮▮▮▮▮▮▮▮/resourcegroups/demoapp-rg/pro
viders/Microsoft.ManagedIdentity/userAssignedIdentities/funcapp-mi",
  "location": "canadacentral",
  "name": "funcapp-mi",
  "principalId": "4▮▮▮▮▮▮▮▮▮▮▮▮▮▮▮",
  "resourceGroup": "demoapp-rg",
  "systemData": null,
  "tags": {},
  "tenantId": "▮▮▮▮▮▮▮▮▮▮▮▮▮",
  "type": "Microsoft.ManagedIdentity/userAssignedIdentities"
}
tamir [ ~ ]$
```

Figure 5.6: Creating a user identity for the Azure function

8. To run and debug the Azure functions, we need to install Azure Functions Core Tools. We can install it using the following command:

    ```
    > npm i -g azure-functions-core-tools@4 –unsafe-prem true
    ```

    When we run this command, we are installing version 4 of Azure Functions Core Tools globally on our system while ensuring that `npm` has the necessary permissions to complete the installation by setting the `unsafe-perm` option to `true`. Here is the screenshot of the command execution:

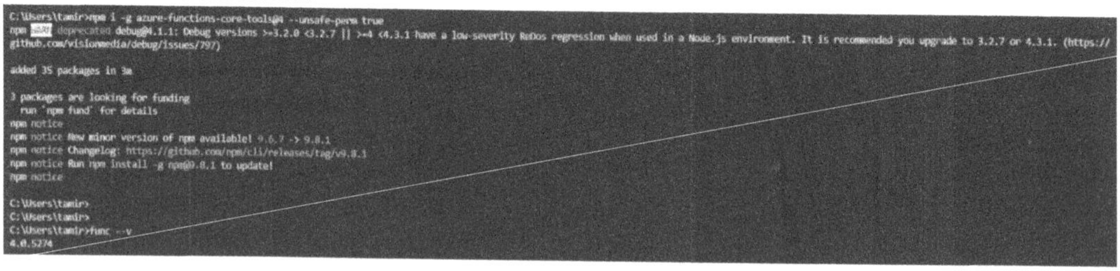

Figure 5.7: Installing Azure Functions Core Tools

9. Using Azure Functions Core Tools, we run the Azure function by running the `func start` command:

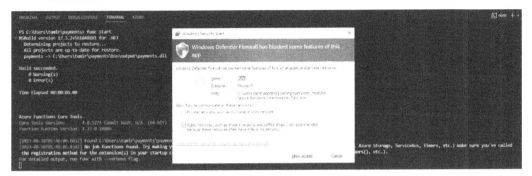

Figure 5.8: Running the Azure function using the Azure CLI

When we start the Azure function, if Windows Defender is enabled on the system, Windows Defender Firewall will prompt a security alert because Azure Functions Core Tools is trying to listen on port `7071`. Click on the **Allow access** option.

In conclusion, this section has illustrated creating an Azure function through the Azure portal, showcasing the platform's user-friendly and intuitive interface. By leveraging the Azure portal's streamlined approach, developers of all levels can effortlessly harness the power of serverless computing. As you move forward, remember that the Azure portal is a versatile tool that empowers you to build, manage, and deploy Azure functions efficiently, enabling you to focus more on your code and less on the infrastructure.

In the next section, we will look at Azure Container Apps – a serverless container service provided by Microsoft Azure that enables us to deploy and manage containerized applications without the need to manage the underlying infrastructure. We will learn about Azure Container Apps, and how we can create and deploy applications to Azure Container Apps using the Azure CLI.

Getting started with Azure Container Apps

Azure Container Apps is a container service offering from Azure that operates on a serverless model and is designed to support containerized applications and microservices. We already learned about how **Distributed Application Runtime** (**DAPR**) can be integrated with Azure Container Apps in *Chapter 3*. In this section, we will learn more about Azure Container Apps, how to deploy your Docker containers to Azure Container Apps, and how to configure **continuous integration and continuous delivery/continuous deployment** (**CI/CD**) to Azure Container Apps from Azure DevOps.

Azure Container Apps overview

As mentioned earlier, Azure Container Apps is a serverless offering from Microsoft Azure. With Azure Container Apps, applications packaged in any container can be executed without any restrictions on runtime or programming model. Azure Container Apps is built on top of the Kubernetes ecosystem, which is running on top of AKS, **Kubernetes Event Driven Autoscaling** (**KEDA**), DAPR, and Envoy. Unlike AKS, in Azure Container Apps, you don't need to manage the Kubernetes infrastructure.

Azure Container Apps offers the following features:

- Azure Container Apps can horizontally scale in or out using different scaling rules, such as the number of HTTP requests or based on CPU and memory utilization. Additionally, it can scale based on various event triggers, including Azure Service Bus, Azure Event Hubs, Redis, and Apache Kafka.

- You're able to run multiple revisions on the container and, based on requirements, you will be able to control traffic to the applications – this feature will help you to deploy your applications with zero downtime.

- Azure Container Apps helps you to expose your applications to the external internet or other container apps by enabling ingress. You don't need to manage any other Azure infrastructure, such as IP addresses or firewalls, to manage incoming HTTPS traffic.

- It provides out-of-the-box support for DAPR.

- It can deploy containers from any Docker registry (public or private), Docker Hub, or Azure Container Registry.

- Azure Container Apps can store application secrets and configuration values securely in the application.

- You can monitor your applications with the help of the Azure Log Analytics service.

In this section, we learned about various features of Azure Container Apps. In the next section, we will deploy a quick start container image using the Azure portal and an ASP.NET Core Web API application to Azure Container Apps using the Azure CLI.

Deploying Docker containers to Azure Container Apps

In this section, we will deploy container images to Azure Container Apps. First, we will deploy a quick start container from the Azure portal, which will help you to familiarize yourself with Azure Container Apps in the Azure portal. Then, we will deploy an ASP.NET Core Web API image to Azure Container Apps with the Azure CLI, which will help you to learn about the various Azure CLI commands to deploy your container image.

Deploying a container to Azure Container Apps via the Azure portal

In this section, we will be deploying a sample container to Azure Container Apps using the Azure portal:

1. Log in to the Azure portal.

2. Click on the **Create a resource** option – you can find it on your home page screen or the left sidebar or you can search for `all resources` in the search bar and click on the **Create** button.

3. On the **Create a resource** screen, search for `Container App`. In the first result, click on the **Create** button again, which will bring up a screen like this:

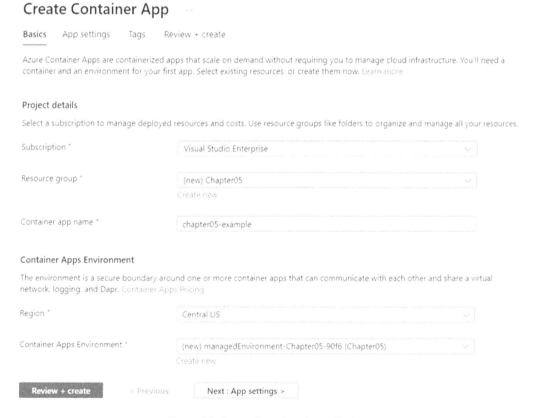

Figure 5.9: Create Container App – Basics

4. On the screen, like any other Azure resource, you need a resource group, a name for the resource, and a region. For container apps, we need to create a Container Apps environment, which will serve as a secure boundary for one or multiple container applications, enabling intercommunication and allowing for the sharing of virtual networks, logging, and DAPR. By default, the Azure portal populates a name, but we can customize it by clicking on the **Create**

new button, which will display a screen like the one shown in *Figure 5.10*. If we click on the **Monitoring** section, we will be able to customize where we can store the application logs – by default, it will log into Azure Log Analytics, which will create a Log Analytics workspace as well. For the demo, I am choosing the **Don't save logs** option and I am not modifying anything in the **Networking** tab.

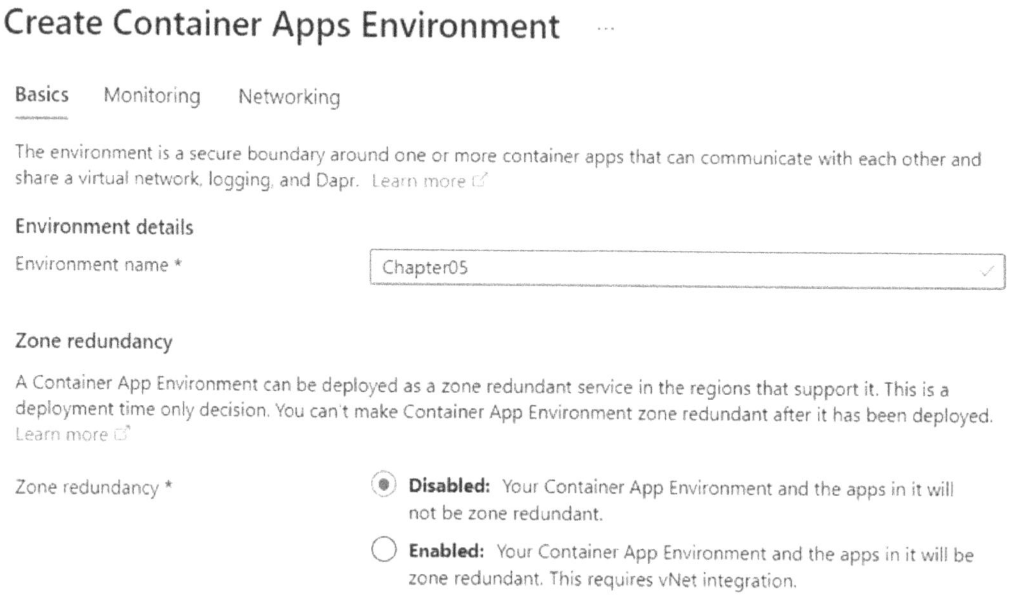

Create Container Apps Environment ...

Basics   Monitoring   Networking

The environment is a secure boundary around one or more container apps that can communicate with each other and share a virtual network, logging, and Dapr. Learn more ⌐'

Environment details

Environment name *

> Chapter05   ✓

Zone redundancy

A Container App Environment can be deployed as a zone redundant service in the regions that support it. This is a deployment time only decision. You can't make Container App Environment zone redundant after it has been deployed. Learn more ⌐'

Zone redundancy *   ⦿ **Disabled:** Your Container App Environment and the apps in it will
                                  not be zone redundant.

                              ◯ **Enabled:** Your Container App Environment and the apps in it will be
                                  zone redundant. This requires vNet integration.

Figure 5.10: Create Container Apps Environment

5.   Then, click on the **Create** button. This will redirect us back to the **Create Container App Basics** screen. Click on the **Next : App settings** button, which will display a screen like the one shown in *Figure 5.11*. In this screen, by default, the **Use quickstart image** option will be selected. We will be able to see the quickstart image – in this case, **Simple hello world container**. We will be able to configure the CPU cores, memory, and HTTP endpoints. For the quickstart image, we don't need to modify the default configuration. If you uncheck the **Use quickstart image** option, you need to configure the container registry details, Docker image name, tag, CPU, memory, any environment variables, and finally, ingress settings – from where all your applications can accept traffic. We will explore all these configuration options when we deploy the container image from the Azure CLI. Now, we will continue with the quickstart image option and accept the default configuration.

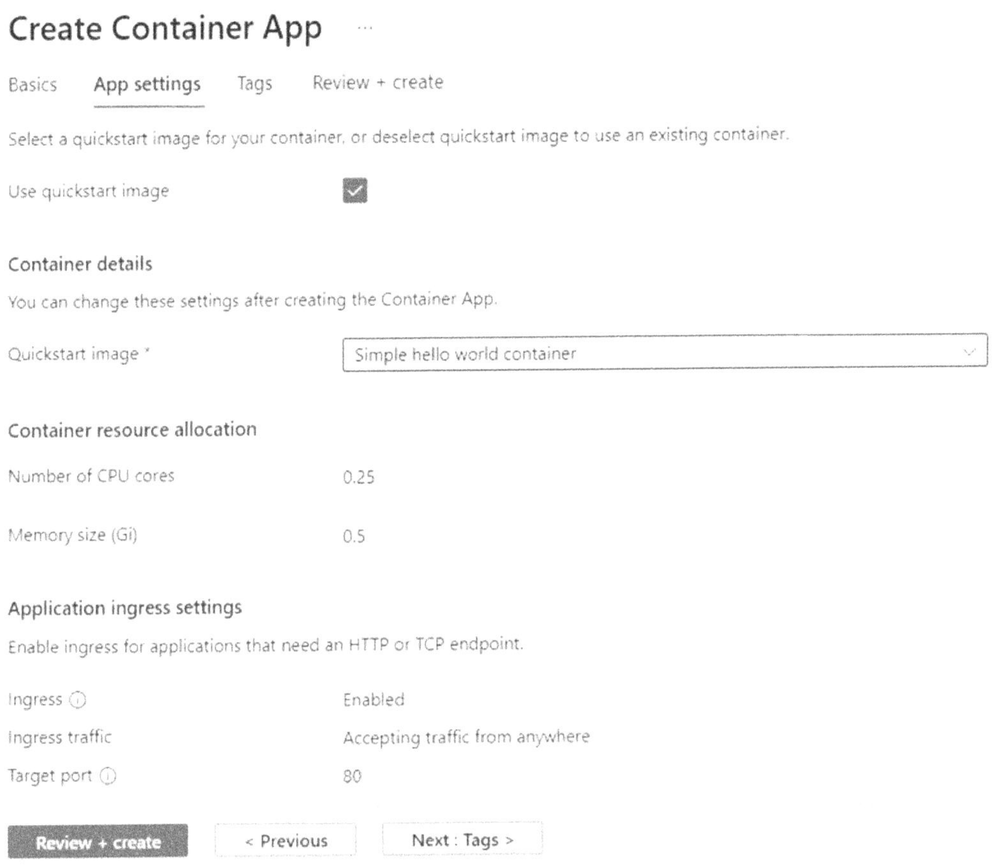

Create Container App ...

Basics   **App settings**   Tags   Review + create

Select a quickstart image for your container, or deselect quickstart image to use an existing container.

Use quickstart image   ☑

Container details

You can change these settings after creating the Container App.

Quickstart image * | Simple hello world container   ⌄ |

Container resource allocation

Number of CPU cores   0.25

Memory size (Gi)   0.5

Application ingress settings

Enable ingress for applications that need an HTTP or TCP endpoint.

Ingress ⓘ   Enabled

Ingress traffic   Accepting traffic from anywhere

Target port ⓘ   80

Review + create   < Previous   Next : Tags >

Figure 5.11: Create Container App – App settings

6. Now, click on the **Review + create** button, which will trigger the Azure portal to validate or verify all the configuration options and display a preview. Then, click on the **Create** button to create the Azure container app with the quickstart image. This will take one or two minutes. After that, we will be able to see the success message and we can click on the **Go to resource** button.

7. From the container app overview page, we will be able to see the application URL. We can click on the link to view the quickstart image running on the Azure container app, which will display an HTML page with a **Welcome** message and the Azure Container Apps logo.

In this way, we will be able to deploy a quickstart Docker image to Azure Container Apps using the Azure portal. We explored various configuration options for the quickstart image. To avoid Azure fees, once you complete your learning, you need to delete the resources. To do this, go to the resource group you created and select the **Delete resource group** option. In the next section, we will deploy an ASP.NET Core Web API image to Azure Container Apps.

Deploying a container to Azure Container Apps via the Azure CLI

In this section, we will deploy an ASP.NET Core Web API Docker image to Azure Container Apps using the Azure CLI. Make sure you have installed Docker, the Azure CLI, and .NET SDK 6.0 on your computer:

1. First, we need to create an ASP.NET Core Web API. We can do this by using the `dotnet new webapi -minimal -o Chapter05 --framework net6.0` command.

2. Next, we will add the Dockerfile to the application. This will help us to create the Docker image. Once the Dockerfile is added, we can enter the following code:

   ```
   FROM mcr.microsoft.com/dotnet/sdk:6.0 AS build
   COPY *.csproj ./source/
   WORKDIR /source
   RUN dotnet restore --no-cache
   COPY . .
   RUN dotnet publish -c release -o /app --no-restore
   FROM mcr.microsoft.com/dotnet/aspnet:6.0
   WORKDIR /app
   COPY --from=build /app ./
   ENTRYPOINT ["dotnet", "Chapter05.dll"]
   ```

3. Next, we need to build the Docker image. We can use this command to build the Docker image using the Dockerfile: `docker build -t chapter05:v1`.

4. We can verify whether the Docker image running or not using the following `docker run` command: `docker run -p 8080:80 chapter05:latest`. We can also browse the `http://localhost:8080/weatherforecast` endpoint and see the JSON results.

5. Once we have built the Docker image and verified it, we need to create an Azure Container Registry and publish the Docker image to the registry. We need to execute the following commands to create the resource group and Azure Container Registry:

   ```
   > az group create --name chapter05 --location centralus
   > az acr create --resource-group chapter05 --name
   packtbookchapter05  --sku Basic --admin-enabled true
   ```

6. Next, we need to tag the Docker image with the Azure Container Registry name so that we can push the Docker image to the Azure Container Registry:

   ```
   > docker tag chapter05:latest packtbookchapter05.azurecr.io/
   webapi:latest
   ```

7. After tagging the Docker image, we need to log in to the Azure Container Registry to publish the Docker image. We can execute the following command, which will authenticate the Azure CLI to publish the image to Azure Container Registry:

    ```
    > az acr login --name packtbookchapter05
    ```

8. When we have logged in, we can execute the following command to publish the Docker image to Azure Container Registry:

    ```
    > docker push packtbookchapter05.azurecr.io/webapi:latest
    ```

9. Now that we have published the Docker image to Azure Container Registry, next, we will create an Azure Container Apps environment and Azure container app to deploy the Docker image from Azure Container Registry:

    ```
    > az containerapp env create --name chapter05env --resource-
    group chapter05 --location centralus
    ```

    When we execute this command, it will prompt us to install the `containerapp` extension, and we do need to install it. This command will create the Azure Container Apps environment.

10. And finally, we need to execute the command to create the Azure container app. We can use the following command to create a container app and configure external ingress, which will help us to access the application from anywhere:

    ```
    > az containerapp create  --name webapi --resource-group
    chapter05 --environment chapter05env --image packtbookchapter05.
    azurecr.io/webapi:latest --target-port 80 --ingress
    'external'  --registry-server packtbookchapter05.azurecr.io
    --query properties.configuration.ingress.fqdn
    ```

    The `target port` option will configure the port that our application exposes. This command will configure the registry to pull the image from as well. Since no credentials are provided, the Azure CLI will get the registry password and create a secret in Azure Container Apps.

    When the preceding command is executed, it will display `ingress.fqdn` on the screen, which is the public endpoint for the application we deployed. You can also browse the `/ weatherforecast` endpoint, which will return the JSON response.

Now we've deployed the ASP.NET Core Web API application in Azure Container Apps, we can delete the resource using the following command: `az group delete --name chapter05`. This will delete the resource group and all the resources.

In this section, we learned how to deploy a Docker image to Azure Container Apps using Azure Container Registry and the Azure CLI. In the next section, we will learn how to configure CI/CD from source control to Azure Container Apps. You can find more details about configuring CI/CD to Azure Container Registry in *Chapter 2*, in the *Configuring CI/CD with Azure Container Registry* section.

Configuring CI/CD from source control to Azure Container Apps

In this section, we will create a build pipeline similar to the one in *Chapter 2*. In the build pipeline YAML file, search for `Azure Container Apps` in **Tasks**.

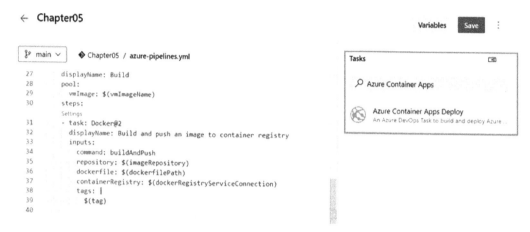

Figure 5.12: Searching for the Azure Container Apps Deploy task

Select the **Azure Container Apps Deploy** task; you will be able to see the configuration options for this task as shown here:

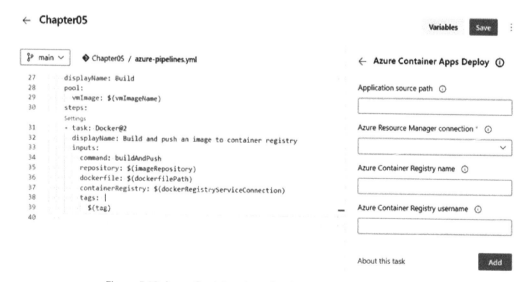

Figure 5.13: Azure Container Apps Deploy task configuration issue

We need to configure the values and then click on the **Add** button, which will push the configuration values to the build pipeline YAML file. Except for the **Azure Resource Manager connection** property, you can configure everything in the YAML file directly. For **Azure Resource Manager connection**, you can do it from its dropdown, or you can go to the project settings.

Here is the Azure Container Apps Deploy task:

```
AzureContainerApps@0
  displayName: Publish the Docker image to Azure Container Apps
  inputs:
    appSourcePath: '$(Build.SourcesDirectory)'
    azureSubscription: Pay As You Go Subscription'
    acrName: 'packtbookchapter05'
    imageToBuild: 'packtbookchapter05.azurecr.io/webapi:$(tag)'
    containerAppName: 'webapi'
    resourceGroup: 'chapter05'nt code for the YAML code.
```

Once the task is done, click on the **Save** button to save the build pipeline changes – this will trigger the build pipeline.

Once the build is completed, the source will be compiled, the Docker image built, the Docker image pushed to Azure Container Registry, and finally, the Docker image pushed to Azure Container Apps.

This way, we will be able to configure CI/CD from Azure DevOps to Azure Container Apps. To avoid Azure charges, once you complete your learning, you need to delete the resources. You can go to the resource group you created and select the **Delete resource group** option. Or you can execute the `az group delete --name chapter05` command to delete the resources.

In this section, we learned about Azure Container Apps – a container service offering from Azure that operates on a serverless model and is designed to support containerized applications and microservices. We learned how to deploy Docker images using the Azure portal and we also configured an Azure DevOps build pipeline to deploy the Docker image to Azure Container Registry, and from Azure Container Registry to Azure Container Apps.

Summary

In this chapter, we delved into the essentials of Azure Functions and Azure Container Apps for .NET developers. As we broadened our understanding of serverless computing, we also discovered the utility of Azure Functions triggers and bindings and addressed the important aspect of security within these functions. Our journey included the hands-on experience of deploying containerized applications using Azure Container Apps, providing practical knowledge to effectively utilize Azure's vast service landscape.

As we advance to the next chapter, we are poised to explore Azure Blob Storage. This new chapter will unravel the workings of Azure's robust, cost-effective cloud storage solution for handling vast amounts of unstructured data. Whether you're dealing with images, documents, or log files, mastering Blob Storage is an invaluable addition to your Azure toolkit. So, prepare yourself for a deep dive into Azure Blob Storage, as you continue to enhance your .NET developer skills in the Azure environment.

Part 3:
Data and Storage

In this part, you'll delve into Azure's data management services, starting with Azure Blob storage, a scalable solution for storing large amounts of unstructured data. You'll then explore Azure SQL Database, learning how to create, manage, and scale databases while utilizing its critical features for structured data storage. You'll also navigate Azure Cosmos DB, creating and managing document-oriented data using .NET while getting acquainted with advanced topics such as data partitioning and global distribution. Each stage will equip you with the tools to handle different data storage requirements effectively, promoting responsive and highly available applications on Azure.

This part has the following chapters:

Exploring Azure Blob Storage

This chapter will explore **Azure Blob Storage** and its significance for **.NET** developers. We will define Azure Blob Storage and discuss its key features and benefits. Next, we will delve into creating a storage account using the **Azure portal** along with best practices and tips for creating a storage account. We will then examine how to work with **blob containers**, including creating and organizing data effectively. Furthermore, we will discuss how to use the Azure Storage SDK for .NET to upload data to blob storage and highlight best practices for uploading data.

Security is essential, so we will explain the security model of Azure Blob Storage and discuss how to secure blob storage using **Shared Access Signatures (SAS)** and **Azure Active Directory (AAD)** authentication. We will also provide best practices for securing blob storage on Azure.

To help you avoid common pitfalls, we will identify common mistakes and challenges that .NET developers may encounter when working with Azure Blob Storage and provide tips for avoiding these issues. Finally, we will conclude by summarizing the key points covered in the chapter and emphasizing the importance of following best practices and tips for effectively writing, reading, and securing blob storage on Azure.

Throughout this comprehensive chapter, we will equip .NET developers with the knowledge and skills necessary to work with Azure Blob Storage effectively. By understanding the concepts of **storage accounts**, blob containers, **data uploading**, and **security**, developers can fully leverage the benefits of Azure Blob Storage for their applications. Additionally, by addressing common mistakes and pitfalls, developers can avoid potential issues and ensure a smooth experience when working with Azure Blob Storage.

As you progress through the chapter, remember to apply the best practices and tips discussed for each topic. These recommendations will help you achieve fluency in writing, reading, and securing blob storage on Azure, ultimately enhancing your applications' performance, scalability, and security. By the end of this chapter, you will have a strong foundation in Azure Blob Storage, empowering you to harness its full potential for your .NET projects.

In this chapter, we will cover the following topics:

- What is Azure Blob Storage?
- Types of blobs in Azure Blob Storage
- Pricing tiers
- Lifecycle management
- Blob Storage availability
- Avoiding common mistakes and pitfalls
- Understanding the .NET client library
- Azure Blob Storage security

What is Azure Blob Storage?

Microsoft Azure's cloud-based object storage service, Azure Blob Storage, makes storing and accessing unstructured data such as text, images, and videos easier. It presents a scalable and cost-effective cloud solution for businesses to store and manage data. As a .NET developer, you can utilize the Azure Storage SDK for .NET to programmatically interact with blob storage, seamlessly integrating it into your .NET applications.

The primary objective of Azure Blob Storage is to deliver a reliable and efficient method for storing and managing unstructured data in the cloud. It can accommodate varying storage requirements, scaling up or down as needed, and can store vast amounts of data. The service offers numerous advantages, including cost-effectiveness, scalability, durability, and security, making it an attractive option for businesses of all sizes.

One notable feature of Azure Blob Storage is its exceptional scalability, which enables effortless storage and retrieval of data ranging from a few bytes to several terabytes. Furthermore, it ensures high availability and data durability by distributing multiple copies of your data across different data centers.

Cost-effectiveness is another crucial aspect of Azure Blob Storage. With a **pay-as-you-use model**, you can select the storage tier that best aligns with your requirements. For example, the **hot storage tier** is designed for frequently accessed data, while the **cold storage tier** caters to infrequently accessed data.

Azure Blob Storage offers significant benefits to .NET developers. A primary advantage is its seamless integration with other Azure services, such as **Azure Functions** and **Azure Stream Analytics**, enabling the creation of highly scalable and reliable applications for processing vast amounts of data in real time.

Another advantage for .NET developers is the Azure Storage SDK for .NET, which supplies classes and methods for programmatic interaction with blob storage. This facilitates the development of highly customized and scalable applications that integrate with other Azure services.

Security features in Azure Blob Storage are essential for businesses handling sensitive data. Data access control can be achieved using **Shared Access Signatures** (**SAS**) or **Azure Active Directory** (**AAD**) authentication. SAS grants temporary access to specific users or applications, while AAD authentication manages storage account access through Azure Active Directory.

In addition to these benefits, Azure Blob Storage offers several other vital technical features, such as a **Representational State Transfer** (**REST**) **API** for data access from anywhere using **HTTP** or **HTTPS**. It also supports various data types, including **block**, **page**, and **append blobs**, further enhancing its utility and flexibility.

Types of blobs in Azure Blob Storage

Azure Blob Storage provides three specialized blob types – block blobs, page blobs, and append blobs – to cater to diverse data storage requirements. Each blob type has unique features and optimizations that suit specific use cases.

Understanding the different types of Azure Blob Storage is fundamental to achieving efficient data management and storage strategy in the cloud. These blob types (blob, page, and append) cater to diverse needs, accommodating varied data forms and access patterns, each having its own benefits and use cases. Let's delve into these types next.

Block blobs

Block blobs are the most commonly used blob type in Azure Blob Storage. They are designed for handling large files, such as images, videos, and text files, that can be broken into smaller chunks called blocks. This subsection will delve into the structure, features, and best practices of working with block blobs in Azure Blob Storage.

Block blobs are ideal for handling large files that can be divided into smaller blocks. This characteristic makes them an excellent choice for media storage, backup and restore operations, and big data processing. By leveraging block blobs, developers can optimize performance, minimize storage costs, and ensure data consistency.

Structure of block blobs

Block blobs consist of a series of blocks, each identified by a unique block ID. These blocks can be uploaded independently and in any order. Once all blocks have been uploaded, they can be committed in a specified order to form a complete blob.

Features of block blobs

Let's consider the following unique features that block blobs provide:

- **Scalability**: Block blobs support files up to 4.75 TB in size, making them suitable for storing large files, such as high-resolution images, videos, and large text files.

- **Efficient data transfer**: Block blobs enable the uploading and downloading of large files in parallel by breaking them into smaller blocks, thereby improving transfer efficiency and reducing the impact of network latency.

- **Resilient data transfer**: When uploading large files as blocks, if an individual block transfer fails, only that block needs to be retransmitted, not the entire file.

- **Data manipulation**: Block blobs allow the updating and modifying of specific blocks in the blob without needing to upload the entire file again. This is particularly useful when working with large files that undergo frequent changes.

Sample scenarios for block blobs

While there are a wide variety of scenarios in which you could utilize block blobs, the following are the most commonly encountered use cases:

- **Media storage**: Block blobs are ideal for storing images, videos, and audio files that require efficient data transfer and manipulation

- **Backup and restore**: Block blobs can be used to store large backup files and enable efficient restore operations by uploading and downloading only the necessary blocks

- **Big data processing**: Block blobs can store large datasets used in big data processing, machine learning, and analytics applications

Best practices for block blobs

When working with block blobs, consider the following best practices:

- **Optimize block size**: Choose an appropriate block size based on the given file size and network conditions. Larger block sizes can improve throughput, while smaller block sizes can provide better fault tolerance.

- **Parallel block transfers**: Leverage parallel block transfers by uploading or downloading multiple blocks simultaneously to improve upload and download performance.

- **Use access tiers**: Leverage access tiers (hot, cool, and archive) to optimize storage costs based on your data's access pattern and retention requirements.

- **Enable data redundancy**: Configure the appropriate level of data redundancy (locally-redundant storage, zone-redundant storage, or geo-redundant storage) based on your application's durability and availability requirements.

Page blobs

Page blobs are designed to store and manage **random access data**, making them ideal for scenarios that require frequent updates or modifications. They are optimized for scenarios where data is read or written in ranges, such as **virtual hard disk** (**VHD**) files for **virtual machines** (**VMs**) and large databases.

Structure and features of page blobs

A page blob is composed of pages, each with a size of 512 bytes. The maximum size for a page blob is 8 TB. Page blobs store data as a collection of individually addressable pages, allowing developers to perform read and write operations on specific pages, providing efficient access to data.

The following are key features of page blobs:

- **Random access**: Page blobs are designed to support random read and write operations. This means that you can directly read from or write to specific pages within the blob without needing to read or modify the entire blob. This capability is especially useful for scenarios where you need to make small, targeted changes to the data, such as updating specific sections of a VHD file.

- **Snapshot support**: Page blobs provide the ability to create snapshots. A snapshot is a point-in-time copy of the blob's data. Creating a snapshot captures the current state of the blob, allowing you to preserve data as it was at that specific moment. Snapshots are useful for creating backups and maintaining historical versions of data. They can also be used to recover from accidental data corruption or deletions, as you can revert to a previous snapshot.

- **Incremental copy**: Page blobs offer incremental copy operations, which enable efficient replication and data transfer between different page blobs. Incremental copy is particularly valuable when you want to replicate data from one blob to another without having to re-transfer the entire content. Instead, only the changes made since the last copy operation need to be transferred, reducing both time and network bandwidth usage.

Use cases for page blobs

Page blobs are well suited for the following scenarios:

- **Virtual hard disks**: Page blobs are the primary storage format for Azure VM disks, including both OS and data disks

- **Large databases**: Page blobs can be used for storing large databases that require frequent updates and modifications

- **Backup and restore**: The snapshot feature of page blobs can be used for creating backups and facilitating restore operations

Best practices for page blobs

When working with page blobs in Azure Blob Storage, incorporating best practices is essential to optimize storage efficiency and enhance performance. Two crucial practices that developers should bear in mind are **sparse allocation** and **aligning writes to page boundaries**. These practices address specific aspects of Page Blob management, offering strategies to effectively manage storage space utilization and data writing patterns. By implementing these best practices, you can not only minimize unnecessary storage consumption but also ensure optimal performance when interacting with page blobs, making them a fundamental component of efficient data storage strategies.

Use sparse allocation

Imagine you're setting up a page blob to serve as storage for log data produced by an application. Instead of upfront storage allocation based on the maximum possible log size, you can leverage **sparse allocation**. This approach allows you to assign storage only for specific pages as they become necessary. Consequently, if your log begins with just a handful of entries, you'll avoid occupying excessive storage space.

Here's an example using the Azure Storage SDK to establish a sparse page blob:

```
CloudPageBlob pageBlob = container.GetPageBlobReference("log-data.
blob");
pageBlob.Create(0); // Create an empty Page Blob without pre-allocated
storage
int pageIndex = 0;
byte[] logEntry = Encoding.UTF8.GetBytes("Log entry content...");
pageBlob.WritePages(new MemoryStream(logEntry), pageIndex * 512);
```

In this snippet, a page blob named `log-data.blob` is obtained using the Azure Storage SDK. By invoking `Create(0)`, an empty page blob is initialized without allocating storage beforehand. As log entries are generated by your application, storage space is assigned to accommodate the required pages, enhancing efficiency while economizing storage consumption.

Align writes to page boundaries

Imagine you're building a **virtual machine** (**VM**) image storage solution using page blobs. VM images are typically stored in fixed-size pages, so aligning writes to page boundaries is crucial for performance:

```
CloudPageBlob vmImageBlob = container.GetPageBlobReference("vm-image.
blob");
byte[] vmImageData = GetVmImageData();
int startingPageIndex = CalculateStartingPageIndex();
int alignedStartOffset = startingPageIndex * 512;
int alignedLength = (vmImageData.Length + 511) / 512 * 512;
vmImageBlob.WritePages(new MemoryStream(vmImageData,
alignedStartOffset, alignedLength), alignedStartOffset);
```

In the preceding example, `CalculateStartingPageIndex` determines the page index where the write operation should begin to align with page boundaries. `alignedStartOffset` is calculated to ensure the write operation aligns with a multiple of 512 bytes. This practice ensures that write operations don't span across page boundaries, optimizing performance.

By applying sparse allocation and aligning writes to page boundaries, you can efficiently manage page blobs in Azure Storage, reducing storage costs, improving performance, and maintaining data consistency.

Page blobs are designed for scenarios requiring random access data storage. Their structure and features make them well suited for storing virtual hard disks and managing large databases. By utilizing page blobs, developers can efficiently handle random access storage needs, optimize performance, and maintain data consistency.

Append blobs

Append blobs are optimized for append-only scenarios such as **log files** or **telemetry data**. They support efficient appending of data, making them suitable for use cases that require a growing data store.

Structure and features of append blobs

An append blob is composed of blocks, similarly to block blobs. However, unlike block blobs, the blocks in append blobs are always appended to the end of the blob. Append blobs have a maximum size of 195 GiB, with each block having a maximum size of 4 MiB.

The following are critical features of append blobs:

- **Efficient appends**: Append blobs support efficient data appending, making them ideal for growing data stores

- **Exclusive access**: Append operations on append blobs are atomic, ensuring that multiple clients can safely append data without the risk of data corruption

- **Snapshot support**: Much like page blobs, append blobs also supports snapshots, facilitating backups and versioning

Use cases for append blobs

Append blobs are well suited for the following scenarios:

- **Log files**: Append blobs are ideal for storing log files generated by applications, **web servers**, or any other system that produces incremental data. This allows for efficient storage and retrieval of logs while maintaining a growing data store.

- **Telemetry data**: Applications that generate telemetry data, such as **IoT devices** or **analytics systems**, can use append blobs to store time-series data. The efficient append operations make this type of blob suitable for capturing and storing large volumes of incoming data.

- **Event data**: Append blobs can store event data generated by event-driven systems, such as message queues, event hubs, and event-driven applications.

Best practices for append blobs

When working with append blobs, consider the following best practices:

- **Use a unique identifier for each append operation**: To ensure data consistency and prevent duplicate data, include a unique identifier, such as a **GUID** or **timestamp**, in each append operation

- **Monitor performance**: Regularly monitor append blob performance and adjust the configuration to optimize throughput and latency

- **Optimize data retrieval**: When retrieving data from append blobs, consider using range queries to retrieve specific data portions efficiently

- **Use snapshots for versioning and backup**: Leverage the snapshot feature of append blobs to create point-in-time copies of the data, which can be used for versioning and backup purposes

Understanding each blob type's unique features and best practices allows developers to choose the appropriate solution for their specific storage needs. By leveraging the respective strengths of block blobs, page blobs, and append blobs, developers can optimize their storage architecture, minimize costs, and maintain data consistency, ultimately contributing to a seamless and efficient application experience.

When navigating the vast landscape of Azure Blob Storage, one of the pivotal concepts that stands out is access tiers. Understanding these tiers is essential for optimizing both storage costs and data accessibility. Let's delve into the intricacies of these tiers and their significance.

Pricing tiers

Azure Blob Storage is a foundational element of Microsoft Azure's comprehensive cloud services, offering scalable and resilient object storage solutions. For .NET developers transitioning to the cloud, a deep understanding of Azure Blob Storage is indispensable. It is crucial to grasp the nuances of its access tiers and performance levels. Why? Because these tiers directly influence the cost and efficiency of your storage solutions. Before architecting any solution, being well versed in these tiers ensures that you're optimizing for performance and making cost-effective decisions. Missteps in tier selection can lead to unforeseen expenses, making it vital to choose wisely. Let's dive into the specifics of each access tier, providing you with the knowledge to build cost-efficient and high-performing .NET applications in the cloud.

Azure Blob Storage offers multiple access tiers and performance levels, each tailored for specific data access patterns and performance needs:

Access tiers

Azure Storage Account offers multiple access tiers, such as Hot, Cool, Cold and Archive:

- **Hot tier**:

  - **Usage scenario**: This tier is ideal for providing temporary storage for data that is in active use or frequently accessed, such as when being processed.

  - **Cost implications**: While the storage cost per GB in the hot tier is higher compared to other tiers, the transaction costs (i.e., read or write operations) are the lowest. This makes it cost-effective for data that's accessed or modified frequently.

  - **Performance**: Offers high throughput and low latency, ensuring rapid data access.

- **Cool tier**:

  - **Usage scenario**: The cool tier is designed for data that is not accessed as frequently as hot data but still needs to be readily available. Examples include monthly reports, data accessed seasonally, or short-term backups.

  - **Cost implications**: Storage costs in the cool tier are lower than in the hot tier, but access and transaction costs are slightly higher. It's also worth noting that there's a minimum storage duration of 30 days, meaning if you delete or move data out of this tier before the minimum of 30 days is up, you'll incur additional charges.

  - **Performance**: While still offering fast access, the cool tier is optimized for cost-effective storage of infrequently accessed data.

- **Cold tier**:

  - **Usage scenario**: Suitable for rarely accessed data where a wait of a few hours before being available is acceptable. An example might be yearly financial data or old logs retained for compliance but rarely accessed.

  - **Cost implications**: The cold tier offers even lower storage costs than the cool tier. However, data retrieval costs and transaction costs are higher. There's also a minimum storage duration of 180 days.

  - **Performance**: Data retrieval times can range from a few hours to a day, making it less suitable for time-sensitive applications.

- **Archive tier**:

  - **Usage scenario**: This tier is for data that is rarely accessed but needs to be retained for long periods, such as legal archives or old medical records.

- **Cost implications**: The archive tier offers the lowest storage costs of all tiers. However, the data retrieval costs are the highest, with a minimum storage duration of 180 days. Rehydrating (or accessing) data from the archive tier can also incur costs.

- **Performance**: Data in the archive tier is offline, meaning it needs to be rehydrated to an online tier (which can take several hours) before it can be accessed.

Performance Levels

For .NET developers, understanding the nuances of Azure Blob Storage's access tiers and performance levels is crucial:

- **Standard**: The Standard performance level is well-suited for a wide range of general-purpose storage needs. It is ideal for scenarios where a balance between performance and cost is required. Standard performance is cost-effective compared to Premium Storage options. It offers lower storage costs per gigabyte, making it a budget-friendly choice for businesses with moderate storage requirements:

  - **Performance**: Standard performance provides good overall performance for most common use cases. While it may not offer the ultra-low latency and high-throughput capabilities of Premium Storage, it still provides responsive and consistent access to data for typical applications.

  - **Supported Blob Types**: Standard performance is compatible with all types of blobs in Azure Blob Storage, including block blobs, append blobs, and page blobs.

  - **Provisioned Throughput**: Standard performance offers shared, multi-tenant throughput, which is generally sufficient for most workloads.

  - **Lifecycle Management**: Standard performance supports Azure Blob Storage's lifecycle management features. You can define policies to automatically transition or delete data based on criteria such as age or access patterns, helping you optimize storage costs and data retention.

  - **Regional Availability**: Standard performance is available in various Azure regions worldwide, making it accessible to users and businesses in different geographic locations.

- **Premium:**

  - **Usage scenario**: Premium level is designed for workloads that require high transaction rates or fast access times. It's ideal for high-speed data logging, real-time analytics, or bursty workloads in .NET applications.

  - **Cost implications**: While offering superior performance, it comes at a higher cost than standard tiers. It's billed based on provisioned GBs and transactions.

  - **Performance**: Backed by SSDs, Premium level offers significantly lower latency and higher transaction rates than standard performance tiers.

  - **Supported Blob types**: As of the last update, Premium performance level supports block blobs and append blobs.

- **Provisioned throughput**: You can provision a certain level of throughput, ensuring that your applications always have the necessary bandwidth.

- **Lifecycle management**: Transitioning data between Premium and standard tiers requires manual intervention. However, you can still apply lifecycle management policies within the Premium tier.

- **Regional availability**: It's essential to check its availability in your desired Azure region, as Premium Blob Storage might only be available in some places.

By choosing the right tier and performance level, developers can balance performance needs with cost considerations, ensuring optimal application efficiency. As data accumulates in Azure Blob Storage, effectively managing its lifecycle becomes paramount to ensuring both cost efficiency and data integrity. Let's dive into the concept of lifecycle management for blobs and explore how it can streamline storage strategies in the cloud.

Lifecycle management

.NET developers are no strangers to the challenges of managing data with varying lifecycles. With Azure Blob Storage's lifecycle management feature, these challenges can be addressed more efficiently.

Transitioning between tiers

Consider a scenario where you're building an application that allows users to upload, edit, and preview videos. During the initial phase post-upload, these videos are in high demand. They're accessed continuously for modifications, collaborative edits, or user previews. But as the novelty fades and weeks go by, the frequency with which these videos are accessed starts to decline.

To address this evolving data access pattern, one could adopt a tiered storage strategy in Azure Blob Storage:

- **Immediate storage in the hot tier**: Upon a user's video upload, it's optimal to store it in the hot tier. Designed for data that witnesses frequent access, this tier ensures high throughput and low latency. This means users can seamlessly edit and preview their videos without hiccups. While the storage cost in the hot tier might be on the higher side, the reduced access costs during this period of heightened activity make it a worthwhile investment.

- **Transition to the cool tier with time**: As the videos age and their access frequency drops, storing them in the hot tier might not remain cost-effective. This is where the magic of Azure Blob Storage's lifecycle management comes into play. By configuring a lifecycle policy, developers can automate the process, ensuring videos transition to the cool tier after a set period, such as 30 days. The cool tier, with its more economical storage costs, is the ideal choice for those older videos that are now accessed sporadically. This automated shift ensures all videos remain accessible without incurring excessive costs.

By harnessing the power of Azure Blob Storage's tiered approach combined with lifecycle management, .NET developers can craft applications that are not only responsive and efficient but also mindful of cost considerations. It's a strategic dance of placing data in the right storage tier at the right moment.

Let's build out a policy that we can set on our storage account:

```json
{
  "rules": [
    {
      "name": "moveToCoolAfter30Days",
      "enabled": true,
      "type": "Lifecycle",
      "definition": {
        "filters": {
          "blobTypes": ["blockBlob"],
          "prefixMatch": ["videos/"]
        },
        "actions": {
          "baseBlob": {
            "tierToCool": {"daysAfterModificationGreaterThan": 30}
}}}}]}
```

Let's break down the provided JSON, which represents a lifecycle management policy for Azure Blob Storage:

- `rules` – This is an array containing the rules that dictate how the lifecycle of blobs should be managed.

- `name: "moveToCoolAfter30Days"` – This is the identifier for the rule, providing a descriptive name that helps us understand its purpose.

- `enabled: true` – This indicates that the rule is currently active. If set to false, the rule would be ignored.

- `type: "Lifecycle"` – This specifies that the rule is of the `"Lifecycle"` type, meaning it's used to manage the lifecycle of blobs.

- `definition` – This section provides the specifics of the rule.

- `filters` – This section defines which blobs the rule will apply to.

- `blobTypes: ["blockBlob"]` – The rule is applicable to block blobs. Block blobs are optimized for streaming and storing cloud-native object data.

- `prefixMatch: ["videos/"]` – The rule will only be applied to blobs whose names start with `"videos/"`. This is useful for targeting specific directories or file types, in this case, likely video files.

- `actions` – This section specifies the actions to be taken on the blobs that match the filters.

- `baseBlob` – This section contains actions that apply to the base blob (the actual data object).

- `tierToCool: {"daysAfterModificationGreaterThan": 30}` – If a blob hasn't been modified for more than 30 days, it will be transitioned to the cool access tier. The cool tier is designed for storing data that's infrequently accessed but requires fast access when needed.

In essence, this policy states the following:

"For all block blobs under the videos/ directory, if they haven't been modified for 30 days, move them to the cool tier."

Transitioning through tiers in Azure Blob Storage is a powerful feature that allows developers to optimize storage costs based on data access patterns. By setting up lifecycle management policies such as the one just reviewed, developers can automate the process of moving data between tiers, ensuring that storage is both cost-effective and aligned with the data's relevance and access frequency. This dynamic management of data ensures that resources are utilized efficiently and costs are kept in check.

As we delve deeper into the intricacies of Azure Blob Storage management, another pivotal aspect emerges: automated data expiry. This feature ensures that data doesn't overstay its welcome, optimizing storage and costs. Let's explore this in more detail next.

Automated data expiry

Imagine building an application in .NET that handles transient user data, such as session logs or temporary files. This data, by its very nature, holds relevance only for a brief window of time.

To manage such ephemeral data efficiently in Azure Blob Storage, a two-pronged approach can be adopted:

- **Immediate storage in the hot tier**: When users generate temporary data, such as initiating session logs or creating temporary files, it's prudent to store this data in the hot tier. This tier is tailored for data that requires frequent and swift access, ensuring that any immediate operations on this data are seamless and efficient.

- **Scheduled data deletion**: Given the temporary relevance of this data, there's no need to store it indefinitely, leading to unnecessary storage costs. Azure Blob Storage's lifecycle management offers a solution. Developers can configure a lifecycle policy to automatically purge this data after a specific duration – say, 7 days. This ensures that the storage remains decluttered, holding only data that's currently pertinent.

By smartly combining Azure Blob Storage's hot tier with its lifecycle management capabilities, .NET developers can ensure their applications remain agile, efficient, and free from redundant data, optimizing both performance and cost. Let's work through another JSON file that we can set up on our container:

```
"rules": [
  {
    "name": "deleteTempAfter7Days",
    "enabled": true,
    "type": "Lifecycle",
    "definition": {
      "filters": {
        "blobTypes": ["blockBlob"],
        "prefixMatch": ["temp/"]
      },
      "actions": {
        "baseBlob": {
          "delete": {"daysAfterModificationGreaterThan": 7}
        }}}}]}
```

Here's the breakdown of the preceding JSON, which represents another lifecycle management policy for Azure Blob Storage:

- `rules`: This is an array containing the rules that dictate how the lifecycle of blobs should be managed.

- `name`: `moveToCoolAfter30Days`: This is the identifier for the rule. It provides a human-readable name to help you understand the purpose of this specific rule.

- `enabled`: `true`: This indicates that the rule is currently active. If it were set to false, the rule would be ignored.

- `type`: `Lifecycle`: This specifies that the rule is of the type `Lifecycle`, meaning it's used to manage the lifecycle of blobs.

- `definition`: This section provides the details of the rule.

- `filters`: This section defines which blobs the rule will apply to.

- `blobTypes`: `["blockBlob"]`: The rule is applicable to block blobs. Block blobs are optimized for streaming and storing cloud-native object data.

- `prefixMatch`: `["temp/"]`: The rule will only be applied to blobs whose names start with `temp/`.

- `actions`: This section specifies the actions to be taken on the blobs that match the filters.

- `baseBlob`: This section contains actions that apply to the base blob (the actual data object).

- `tierToCool`: `{ "daysAfterModificationGreaterThan" : 7 }`: If a blob hasn't been modified for more than 7 days, it will be deleted.

In simpler terms, this policy states:

"For all block blobs under the 'videos/' directory, if they haven't been modified for 30 days, move them to the cool tier. This rule is currently active and is named 'moveToCoolAfter30Days'."

In the vast ecosystem of Azure Blob Storage, understanding the nuances of data management is crucial. Especially when dealing with dynamic data, such as user-generated content, having a strategy in place can make all the difference – in terms of efficiently handling dynamic data such as user-generated content, ensuring data accessibility, security, cost-effectiveness, and compliance with regulations. Let's now delve deeper into a practical scenario to illustrate this point.

Rule definitions

In the context of .NET development, consider an application that manages user profile images. As users frequently update their profile pictures, older versions become obsolete and no longer serve a purpose.

To effectively manage such evolving data in Azure Blob Storage, a strategic approach can be employed:

- **Immediate storage in the hot tier**: When users upload or update their profile images, it's optimal to store these fresh images in the hot tier. This ensures that the latest profile pictures, which are likely accessed more frequently, benefit from swift and efficient access.

- **Lifecycle management for older images**: As newer profile images come into play, the older versions naturally see a decline in access frequency. Instead of letting these outdated images consume valuable hot tier space, Azure Blob Storage's lifecycle management can be leveraged. Developers can configure a policy that automatically transitions these older images to the cool tier after a set period, such as 60 days. Given that these images will eventually lose all relevance, the policy can also be set to automatically delete them after a longer duration, such as 180 days.

By marrying Azure Blob Storage's tiered storage with its lifecycle management features, .NET developers can ensure their applications remain streamlined, holding only relevant data and optimizing storage costs. This approach not only enhances application performance but also ensures efficient resource utilization. Consider an example where, as the users of a website update their profile images, the older versions may no longer be relevant, and storing them indefinitely might not be cost-effective. The following JSON policy provides a structured approach to handle such scenarios in Azure Blob Storage:

```
{
  "rules": [
    {
      "name": "manageProfileImages",
      "enabled": true,
      "type": "Lifecycle",
      "definition": {
        "filters": {
          "blobTypes": ["blockBlob"],
```

```
      "prefixMatch": ["profile-images/"]
    },
    "actions": {
      "baseBlob": {
        "tierToCool": {"daysAfterModificationGreaterThan": 60},
        "delete": {"daysAfterModificationGreaterThan": 180}
      }}}}]}
```

The preceding JSON is a representation of a lifecycle management policy for Azure Blob Storage. Let's break down its components:

- rules – This is an array that contains one or more rules that dictate how the lifecycle of blobs should be managed.

- name: "manageProfileImages" – This is the identifier for the rule. It's a human-readable name to help you identify what this specific rule is intended for.

- enabled: true – This indicates that the rule is active. If set to false, the rule would be ignored.

- type: "Lifecycle" – This specifies the type of rule. In this case, it's a lifecycle rule, which means it's used to manage the lifecycle of blobs.

- definition – This section contains the details of the rule.

- filters – This section defines which blobs the rule applies to.

- blobTypes: ["blockBlob"] – This rule applies to block blobs. Block blobs are optimized for streaming and storing cloud-native object data.

- prefixMatch: ["profile-images/"] – This rule will only apply to blobs whose names start with profile-images/. This is useful for targeting specific directories or file types.

- actions – This section defines what actions to take on the blobs that match the filters.

- baseBlob – This section contains actions that apply to the base blob (the actual data object).

- tierToCool: {"daysAfterModificationGreaterThan": 60} – If a blob hasn't been modified for more than 60 days, it will be moved to the cool access tier. The cool tier is a cost-effective option for storing data that's infrequently accessed.

- delete: {"daysAfterModificationGreaterThan": 180} – If a blob hasn't been modified for more than 180 days, it will be deleted.

In simple terms, this policy says the following:

"For all block blobs under the profile-images/ directory, if they haven't been modified for 60 days, move them to the cool tier. If they haven't been modified for 180 days, delete them. This rule is currently active and is named manageProfileImages."

By leveraging Azure Blob Storage's lifecycle management features, .NET developers can automate data management tasks, ensuring optimal performance and cost-efficiency for their applications.

Now it's time to implement what we've learned so far using the Azure CLI. Earlier, we discussed two JSON policies:

- `moveToCoolAfter30Days.json`: This policy was designed to transition videos that haven't been accessed for 30 days to the cool tier
- `manageProfileImages.json`: This policy aimed to handle user profile images, transitioning them to the cool tier after 60 days of inactivity and then deleting them after 180 days

Both of these policies are structured, easy to understand, and tailored to specific use cases. They encapsulate the logic of data management in Azure Blob Storage, ensuring that data is stored optimally based on its access patterns and relevance.

Implementing lifecycle management policies using the Azure CLI is straightforward. Once you have your JSON policy files ready, you can easily set them using the `az storage account management-policy create` command.

For instance, to implement the `manageProfileImages.json` policy, you'd use the following:

```
az storage account management-policy create \
--account-name <storage-account> \
--resource-group <resource-group> \
--policy @[path/to/your/manageProfileImages.json]
```

Similarly, the following command is used for the `moveToCoolAfter30Days.json` policy:

```
az storage account management-policy create \
--account-name <storage-account> \
--resource-group <resource-group> \
--policy @[path/to/your/moveToCoolAfter30Days.json]
```

For .NET developers, Azure Blob Storage, combined with the Azure CLI, provides a cohesive solution for adept data lifecycle management. By leveraging structured JSON policies, such as `moveToCoolAfter30Days` and `manageProfileImages`, developers can seamlessly automate data transitions based on specific access patterns. The ease of implementing these policies via the Azure CLI, coupled with Azure Blob Storage's tiered storage and lifecycle management, ensures optimal storage costs, swift data access, and efficient resource utilization. In essence, this synergy offers a cost-effective and intuitive approach to data management in the .NET development realm.

As we continue our exploration of Azure Blob Storage, up next on our agenda is a deep dive into creating and configuring Azure Storage Account using the Azure CLI.

Creating a Blob Storage account in Azure

This section will walk you through the step-by-step process of creating a Blob Storage account using the Azure **Command-Line Interface** (**CLI**). Following these instructions, you can set up a Blob Storage account, create a container within it, and prepare the foundation for managing your unstructured data efficiently.

> **Important**
>
> Please note that we'll create resources in the region closest to you to ensure optimal performance and latency for your storage account.

Let's start creating your Azure Blob Storage account and container using the Azure CLI.

Before creating the Blob Storage account, it's essential to create a resource group to logically group your resources together. A resource group helps in better management and organization. Run the following command to create a new resource group named `storage-rg` in the East US region:

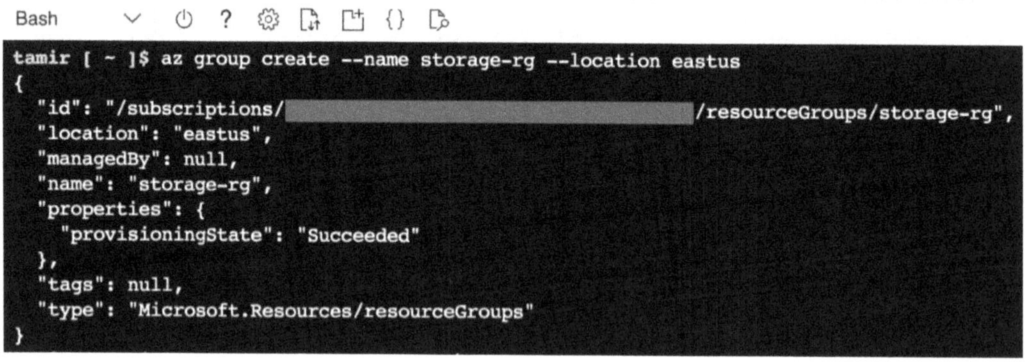

```
Bash        ∨   ⏻  ?  ⚙  ⌕  ⌸  {}  ⌙

tamir [ ~ ]$ az group create --name storage-rg --location eastus
{
  "id": "/subscriptions/                              /resourceGroups/storage-rg",
  "location": "eastus",
  "managedBy": null,
  "name": "storage-rg",
  "properties": {
    "provisioningState": "Succeeded"
  },
  "tags": null,
  "type": "Microsoft.Resources/resourceGroups"
}
```

Figure 6.1: Creating a resource group via the Azure CLI

The `storage-rg` resource group created by the preceding command will serve as a container for your Blob Storage account and associated resources, allowing you to manage them collectively.

Now that we have the resource group in placc, let's move on to creating the Blob Storage account. Use the following command to create an account named `netdeveloperforazuredemo` in the `storage-rg` resource group. This command includes specifying the account's location, SKU (`Standard_RAGRS`), kind (`StorageV2`), minimum TLS version (`TLS1_2`), and access tier (`Hot`):

```
tamir [ ~ ]$ az storage account create \
  --name netdeveloperforazuredemo \
  --resource-group storage-rg \
  --location eastus \
  --sku Standard_RAGRS \
  --kind StorageV2 \
  --min-tls-version TLS1_2 \
  --access-tier Hot
```

Figure 6.2: Creating the storage account

Let's break down the preceding command:

- `--name` specifies the name of the storage account you want to create

- `--resource-group` specifies the name of the resource group you created earlier

- The `--location` value should be replaced with the region that is closest to you

- `--sku` defines the desired SKU for the storage account, which affects replication and redundancy options

- `--kind` specifies the kind of storage account, with `StorageV2` being recommended for its latest capabilities

- `--min-tls-version` ensures a minimum TLS version is applied for secure communication

- `--access-tier` sets the access tier to `Hot`, which means the most frequently accessed data is stored in a performant storage tier

To organize and store your data within the Blob Storage account, you next need to create a container. Run the following command to create a container named `blob-content` within the `netdeveloperforazuredemo` storage account:

```
tamir [ ~ ]$ az storage container create \
    --account-name netdeveloperforazuredemo \
    --name blob-content \
    --auth-mode login
{
  "created": true
}
```

Figure 6.3: Creating a blob container

Let's examine the preceding command more closely:

- `--account-name` specifies the name of the storage account where the container will be created.

- `--name` specifies the name of the container you want to create.

- `--auth-mode` specifies the authentication mode. In this case, `login` is used to authenticate with the storage account.

With the above-mentioned command, you'll create a container named `blob-content` within the `netdeveloperforazuredemo` storage account using the specified authentication mode.

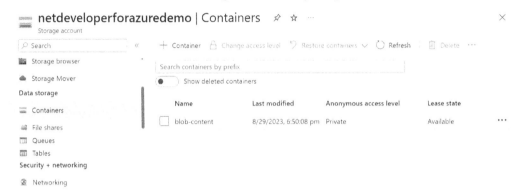

Figure 6.4: Showcasing the completed blob storage account and container

Following this step-by-step guide, you've successfully created a robust Blob Storage environment using the Azure CLI. You've established a resource group to group your resources logically, created a Blob Storage account with advanced capabilities, and organized your data with a dedicated Blob container. This storage account is now equipped to securely store and manage your blob data, catering to various application needs.

Now that you have a functional Blob Storage account, you can explore the many availability and accessibility options Azure offers. Blob Storage provides multiple tiers to meet specific performance and cost requirements, such as hot, cool, and archive tiers. Additionally, Azure offers redundancy options such as **locally-redundant storage (LRS)** and **geo-redundant storage (GRS)** to ensure data durability and availability across regions. With these features, you can optimize your Blob Storage setup to align with your application's needs, balance cost and performance, and enhance the resilience of your data. Let's now delve into the availability and durability options provided by Azure Blob Storage, ensuring your data remains secure, accessible, and highly available.

Blob Storage availability

An important consideration while using Blob Storage is the choice of replication strategy, which affects the durability of your data. There are four primary replication options: **locally-redundant storage (LRS)**, **zone-redundant storage (ZRS)**, **geo-redundant storage (GRS)**, and **read-access geo-redundant storage (RA-GRS)**, each one providing different levels of data resilience. In the sections ahead, we will delve deeper into these options, giving consideration to their nuances and discussing their appropriate use cases.

Figure 6.5: Setting up redundancy via the Azure portal

Locally-redundant storage

LRS is the most basic and cost-effective **replication method** available in Azure Blob Storage. Here's a closer look at what LRS brings to the table:

- **Data copies**: Three copies of your data are stored in a single data center.

- **Availability**: High availability within the same data center.

- **Durability**: Data copies stored within the same data center are designed to be extremely reliable and resistant to various forms of failure. Even if a hardware component fails or there's a temporary interruption, the system is designed to ensure that your data remains intact and available.

- **Data loss protection**: No protection against regional disaster.

- **Use cases**: Suitable when cost is a significant factor and high availability and durability within a single data center is sufficient.

- **Cost**: This is the most cost-effective replication method.

Zone-redundant storage

ZRS is a replication method that provides higher availability and durability than LRS. Considering more deeply the intricacies of ZRS, several key features and benefits come to the forefront:

- **Data copies**: Three copies of your data are stored across different data centers within a single region.

- **Availability**: High availability within the same region.

- **Durability**: The ability of your stored data to withstand failures and potential data loss, even in the face of unforeseen events or disruptions. In the ZRS configuration, your data is replicated and distributed across multiple data centers within the same Azure region.

- **Data loss protection**: Protection against single zone failures within the region.

- **Use cases**: Suitable when high availability and durability across different zones within a region are required, and the cost of replication is a significant factor.

- **Cost**: This method is more expensive than LRS but less expensive than GRS due to the increased availability.

Geo-redundant storage

GRS is a replication method that provides higher availability and durability than LRS and ZRS. Let's explore the distinct features of geo-redundant storage (GRS), setting it apart in Azure Blob Storage:

- **Data copies**: Six copies of your data are stored across two different regions

- **Availability**: High availability across two regions

- **Durability**: High durability across two regions

- **Data loss protection**: Protection against regional disasters

- **Use cases**: Suitable when high availability and durability across different regions are required, and the cost of replication is a significant factor

- **Cost**: This method is more expensive than both LRS and ZRS due to the increased data redundancy and protection

Read-access geo-redundant storage

RA-GRS is a replication method that provides the same level of availability and durability as GRS. However, it also provides read access to your data in the secondary region, enabling you to read it even during a regional disaster. Let us uncover the unique offerings it provides:

- **Data copies:** Six copies of your data are stored across two different regions

- **Availability**: High availability and read access across two regions

- **Durability**: High durability across two regions

- **Data loss protection**: Protection against regional disasters

- **Use cases**: Suitable when high availability, durability, and read access across different regions are required, and the cost of replication is a significant factor

- **Cost**: This is the most expensive method, as it provides the highest availability and redundancy, and read access in the secondary region

Choosing the right replication type for your application

It's also important to note that the replication method can be changed at any time, but it requires migrating your data to a new storage account, which can be time-consuming and expensive. Therefore, choosing the right replication method at the beginning is essential to avoid unnecessary downtime and costs. Another important consideration when selecting a replication method is the geographic location of your data and its intended audience. Suppose users primarily access your data in a specific region. In that case, choosing a replication method that stores copies of your data within that region may be more cost-effective. This can reduce latency and improve performance for your users.

On the other hand, if users across different regions access your data, choosing a replication method that provides high availability and durability across different regions may be necessary. It's also important to consider the performance implications of the replication method selected. **Replication** adds overhead and can affect the performance of your storage account. The more copies of your stored data, the more resources are required to maintain and synchronize those copies.

In addition to choosing the most appropriate replication method for your given context, it's also essential to regularly monitor your storage account to ensure it functions as expected. Azure provides several tools for monitoring your storage account, including **Azure Monitor** and **Azure Storage Analytics**. These tools provide metrics, logs, and alerts to help you detect issues and optimize performance.

When selecting a replication type for your Azure Blob Storage, it's essential to consider your application's specific requirements regarding performance, durability, and cost. The questions to consider when making this decision include the following:

- How critical is the data stored in Azure Blob Storage for your application?

- What level of data protection and durability does your application require?

- Are there any regulatory or compliance requirements that mandate data storage across multiple regions?

- What is your budget for storage costs?

You can choose the replication type that best aligns with your application's needs and requirements by evaluating the trade-offs between these factors.

In conclusion, choosing the proper replication method for your Azure Blob Storage account is an important decision affecting your data's availability, durability, and performance. It's essential to consider your business needs, budget, and the geographic location of your data and its intended audience when choosing a replication method. Regularly monitoring your storage account can help you detect issues early and optimize performance for your needs.

With your new understanding of what replication strategy will work best for different contexts under your belt, it's time to learn about the most common mistakes and pitfalls that new developers can run in to on Azure – and how to avoid them.

Avoiding common mistakes and pitfalls

Building a robust and secure cloud storage solution requires careful planning and adherence to best practices. It's essential not to rush the development process, instead focusing on understanding and circumventing common mistakes. Let's dive into some typical pitfalls in Azure Blob Storage and how to best avoid them for a smooth and efficient implementation:

- Storing secrets in plaintext:

  - **Mistake**: Storing your connection string in plaintext within your application's source code.

  - **Solution**: Leverage the power of **Azure Key Vault** or **Azure App Configuration** to store and efficiently manage your connection strings. Alternatively, adopt managed identities and **Azure Active Directory** (**AAD**) integration to eliminate the need for manual connection string management.

- Ignoring performance limitations:

  - **Mistake**: Using a general-purpose Azure Blob Storage account for large-scale data lake workloads. Such storage accounts aren't optimized for data analytics and the hierarchical data structures associated with a data lake. When used as a data lake, you may face challenges in data management, performance, and scalability, especially when dealing with many small files.

  - **Solution**: Use **Azure Data Lake Storage** (**ADLS**) Gen2, which offers capabilities optimized for analytics workloads. Enabling a hierarchical namespace in ADLS Gen2 allows for efficient data organization and management, and combining ADLS Gen2 and hierarchical namespace help to handle large-scale data workloads. This ensures you have a purpose-built solution for big data analytics scenarios.

- Not using the most appropriate access tier:

  - **Mistake**: Storing infrequently accessed data in the hot access tier, resulting in higher storage costs.

  - **Solution**: Move infrequently accessed data to the cool or archive tiers and use **lifecycle management policies** to automate these transitions.

- Using the wrong blob types:

  - **Mistake**: Storing log data as block blobs, causing slow append operations and inefficient storage consumption

  - **Solution**: Use append blobs for log data optimized for append-heavy workloads

- Poor error handling:

  - **Mistake**: Failing to handle errors when uploading a large file, causing the application to crash or hang

  - **Solution**: Implement proper error handling, including retries with exponential backoff, to ensure a more resilient application

- Poorly designed blob hierarchies:

  - **Mistake**: Storing all blobs in a single flat namespace makes navigating or querying the data challenging

  - **Solution**: Organize your blobs using virtual directories to create a hierarchical structure that is easy to navigate and query

- Insecure access control:

  - **Mistake**: Granting full read-write access to all users of your application, exposing your data to potential breaches

  - **Solution**: Use **Shared Access Signatures** with limited permissions and expiry times, and where possible, opt for **Azure AD-based authentication** to enforce **role-based access control**

- Not leveraging **Content Delivery Network (CDN)**:

  - **Mistake**: Serving frequently accessed images directly from Blob Storage increases latency and bandwidth costs

  - **Solution**: Enable Azure **Content delivery network (CDN)** to cache your blobs closer to your users, improving performance and reducing bandwidth costs

- Inefficient data transfer:

  - **Mistake**: Uploading a large blob sequentially in a single thread causes slow upload times and increased latency

  - **Solution**: Use parallel transfers and divide the blob into smaller chunks to optimize data transfer and improve upload performance

- Failing to monitor and optimize storage costs:

  - **Mistake**: Accumulating large amounts of unused data in your storage account increases costs.

  - **Solution**: Regularly review and delete unused blobs, optimize access tiers, and compress data to reduce storage costs.

By considering these examples and implementing the suggested solutions, you can avoid common mistakes and pitfalls when working with Azure Blob Storage and build efficient, secure, and cost-effective applications.

While avoiding common pitfalls helps create a solid foundation, truly mastering Azure Blob Storage involves leveraging the right tools. One such tool is the .NET client library, a crucial asset designed to streamline interactions between .NET applications and Blob Storage. The following section will allow us to take a closer look at this client library and its core concepts and classes.

Understanding the .NET client library

The .NET client library for Azure Blob Storage is a set of APIs designed to help developers interact with Blob Storage in their .NET applications. The client library simplifies connecting to and working with Azure Blob Storage by abstracting the underlying REST API calls and providing easy-to-use, **object-oriented APIs** for common operations including uploading, downloading, listing, and deleting blobs. Azure provides the .NET client library for **Azure Blob Storage.Storage.Blobs NuGet package**. This package is part of the **Azure SDK for .NET**, which includes libraries for various Azure services.

Here's an overview of some of the core classes and concepts in the .NET client library for Azure Blob Storage:

- **BlobServiceClient**: This class represents the Blob Storage service and acts as the entry point for interacting with it. With `BlobServiceClient`, you can do the following:

  - Create and delete blob containers using the `CreateBlobContainerAsync` and `DeleteBlobContainerAsync` methods

  - List blob containers using the `GetBlobContainersAsync` method

  - Retrieve and set service properties, such as logging, metrics, and CORS configurations, using the `GetPropertiesAsync` and `SetPropertiesAsync` methods

- **BlobContainerClient**: This class represents a blob container within the Blob Storage service. With `BlobContainerClient`, you can do the following:

  - Create, list, and delete blobs using the `UploadBlobAsync`, `GetBlobsAsync`, and `DeleteBlobAsync` methods

  - Retrieve and set container properties using the `GetPropertiesAsync` and `SetPropertiesAsync` methods

- Retrieve and set container metadata using the `GetMetadataAsync` and `SetMetadataAsync` methods

- Manage container access policies using the `GetAccessPolicyAsync` and `SetAccessPolicyAsync` methods

- **BlobClient**: This class represents a blob within a container and is a base class for other blob types. With `BlobClient`, you can do the following:

  - Upload a blob using the `UploadAsync` method

  - Download a blob using the `DownloadAsync` method

  - Delete a blob using the `DeleteAsync` method

  - Retrieve and set blob properties using the `GetPropertiesAsync` and `SetPropertiesAsync` methods

  - Retrieve and set blob metadata using the `GetMetadataAsync` and `SetMetadataAsync` methods

  - Create and manage snapshots of a blob using the `CreateSnapshotAsync` and `DeleteAsync` methods

- **BlockBlobClient**: This class represents a block blob and inherits from `BlobClient`. Block blobs are optimized for streaming and storing cloud objects such as documents, media files, and backups. With `BlockBlobClient`, you can do the following:

  - Upload a block blob using the `UploadAsync` method

  - Stage blocks for a block blob using the `StageBlockAsync` method

  - Commit staged blocks to create or update a block blob using the `CommitBlockListAsync` method

  - Retrieve the list of staged blocks for a block blob using the `GetBlockListAsync` method

- **AppendBlobClient**: This class represents an append blob and inherits from `BlobClient`. Append blobs are optimized for append operations, making them suitable for logging scenarios. With `AppendBlobClient`, you can do the following:

  - Create an append blob using the `CreateAsync` method

  - Append data to an append blob using the `AppendBlockAsync` method

  - Retrieve the list of append blocks for an append blob using the `GetAppendBlockPropertiesAsync` method

- **PageBlobClient**: This class represents a page blob and inherits from `BlobClient`. Page blobs are optimized for random read-write operations, making them suitable for storing **virtual hard disks (VHDs)** for **Azure VMs**. With `PageBlobClient`, you can do the following:

  - Create a page blob using the `CreateAsync` method
  - Upload pages to a page blob using the `UploadPagesAsync` method
  - Clear a range of pages in a page blob using the `ClearPagesAsync` method
  - Retrieve the list of page ranges for a page blob using the `GetPageRangesAsync` method

These core classes cover most of the operations you'll need to perform when working with Azure Blob Storage in your .NET applications. In addition to these core classes, there are also some helper classes and enumerations to make your work with the library more efficient and convenient:

- **BlobDownloadInfo**: This class represents the response returned when downloading a blob. It includes the blob's content, content type, content encoding, content length, and other properties. This class can access a downloaded blob's content stream and properties.

- **BlobUploadOptions, BlobDownloadOptions, and BlobDeleteOptions**: These classes configure optional parameters when uploading, downloading, or deleting a blob, respectively. For example, you can set the content type and content encoding or specify a range of bytes to download.

- **BlobRequestConditions**: This class represents the request conditions for a blob operation, such as specifying an access condition based on the blob's **ETag** or last-modified time. You can use this class to execute operations only when certain conditions are met conditionally.

- **BlobContainerEncryptionScopeOptions**: This class represents the encryption scope options for a blob container. You can use this class to specify an encryption scope when creating a new container or updating an existing one.

- **BlobSasBuilder**: This class helps you create a **Shared Access Signature** (**SAS**) for a blob, **container**, or **service**. With SAS, you can grant limited access to your storage resources without sharing your account keys.

To effectively use the .NET client library for Azure Blob Storage, it's crucial to understand the core classes and their responsibilities. By leveraging these classes and their methods, you can build robust .NET applications that easily interact with Azure Blob Storage to store, retrieve, and manage your unstructured data. Additionally, here are some other important classes and concepts in the .NET client library for Azure Blob Storage that you may find useful when working with blobs:

- **BlobLeaseClient**: This class represents a lease on a blob or container. Leases can be used to provide exclusive access to a blob or container for a specified period. With `BlobLeaseClient`, you can do the following:

- Acquire, renew, and release a lease on a blob or container using the `AcquireAsync`, `RenewAsync`, and `ReleaseAsync` methods

- Break a lease on a blob or container using the `BreakAsync` method

- Change the ID of an existing lease using the `ChangeAsync` method

- **BlobChangeFeedClient**: This class represents the Blob Storage change feed, a log of all changes made to blobs within a storage account. With `BlobChangeFeedClient`, you can do the following:

  - List change feed events using the `GetChangesAsync` method

  - Access change feed events for a specific time range using the `GetChangesForTimeRangeAsync` method

- **BlobQueryClient**: This class allows you to query the contents of your blobs using the **Azure Storage Data Lake Storage Query REST API**. With `BlobQueryClient`, you can do the following:

  - Run queries on the contents of your blobs using the `QueryAsync` method

These classes and concepts enhance the capabilities of the .NET client library for Azure Blob Storage, enabling you to perform more advanced operations and better manage your blobs and containers.

Here's a simple example of using the library to upload a file to Azure Blob Storage:

```
private static sync Task UploadFileToBlobStorage(string
coonectionString, string containerName, string blobName,string
localFilePath)
{
BlobServiceClient blobServiceClient = new
BlobServiceClient(coonectionString)
BlobContainerClient containerClient = blobServiceClient.
GetBlobContainerClient(containerName);
BlobClient blobClient = containerClient.GetalobClient(blobName);
using FileStream fileStream a File.OpenRead(localfilePath);
await blobClient.UploadAsync(fileStrean, true);
fileStream.Close();
}
```

In this example, we create a `BlobServiceClient` using a connection string, a `BlobContainerClient` for a specific container, and a `BlobClient` for a particular blob. We then upload a local file to the blob using the `UploadAsync` method.

By learning how to use the .NET client library for Azure Blob Storage effectively, you can build powerful applications that seamlessly integrate with Azure Blob Storage to store, manage, and access large amounts of unstructured data in the cloud.

As a .NET developer working with Azure Blob Storage, you can further optimize your applications by implementing best practices and taking advantage of advanced features. Here are some tips and techniques to consider:

- **Use the latest version of the SDK**: Always use the newest version of `Azure.Storage.Blobs` NuGet package to benefit from the latest features, improvements, and bug fixes.

- **Use asynchronous methods**: Whenever possible, use the asynchronous methods provided by the library (e.g., `UploadAsync`, `DownloadAsync`). Asynchronous operations can improve the performance and responsiveness of your applications, especially when dealing with large amounts of data or high-latency environments.

- **Handle errors and retries**: Implement proper error handling and retries when working with Azure Blob Storage. The library provides built-in support for retries through the `RetryPolicy` class, which you can customize to fit your application's needs.

- **Use parallelism for large uploads/downloads**: When uploading or downloading large blobs, you can improve performance by dividing the blob into smaller chunks and processing them in parallel. The `BlockBlobClient` class provides methods such as `StageBlockAsync` and `CommitBlockListAsync`, making it easy to implement parallel uploads for block blobs.

- **Use the appropriate blob type**: Choose the right blob type (block, append, or page) based on your application's specific requirements. Each blob type has unique characteristics and is optimized for different use cases.

- **Enable data encryption**: Protect your data at rest by enabling server-side encryption with Azure **Storage Service Encryption** (**SSE**) or client-side encryption with **Azure.Storage.Blobs.Cryptography NuGet package**. Please note that client-side encryption will add serious performance overhead to your solution.

- **Use Azure AD authentication**: For more robust and secure authentication, consider using **Azure Active Directory** (**AAD**) to authenticate your applications with Azure Blob Storage. The library supports Azure AD authentication through the `DefaultAzureCredential` class, which can be used to authenticate `BlobServiceClient` instances.

By following these best practices and taking advantage of the advanced features offered by the .NET client library for Azure Blob Storage, you can build efficient, secure, and scalable applications that fully leverage the power of Azure Blob Storage for storing and managing your unstructured data in the cloud.

Security in Azure Blob Storage

In today's digital landscape, securing data stored in the cloud is of paramount importance. Azure Blob Storage, a core offering of Microsoft Azure's storage solutions, provides a comprehensive suite of security features to ensure that data remains protected, yet accessible when needed. In this section, we will delve deep into the intricacies of Azure Blob Storage Security, exploring key topics such as **Public Access Levels**, which dictate how data can be accessed by the public, and the **Resource URI**, the foundational address pointing to specific Azure Storage resources. We'll also demystify the **Shared Access Signature (SAS)**, a powerful tool for granting temporary access, and discuss the role of **Azure Active Directory (Azure AD)** and **Role-Based Access Control (RBAC)** in managing access permissions. Furthermore, our exploration will encompass the various facets of **encryption**, including **Storage Service Encryption (SSE)** for data at rest, **client-side encryption** for data before it reaches Azure, and **encryption in transit** to safeguard data as it moves between the client and Azure Blob Storage. Join us as we navigate the robust security mechanisms Azure Blob Storage offers, ensuring data integrity and confidentiality in the cloud.

Public access levels

In the vast ecosystem of Azure Blob Storage, understanding and managing data accessibility is paramount. To cater to diverse needs, Azure Blob Storage delineates its data access through three distinct public access levels:

- **Private**:
  - **Description**: The most restrictive level. No public access is allowed, and all requests must be authorized.
  - **Use case**: This is ideal for sensitive data or any data that should not be publicly accessible. Examples include database backups, sensitive documents, or proprietary business data.

- **Blob**:
  - **Description**: Individual blobs can be accessed publicly, but container metadata and the list of blobs within the container remain private.
  - **Use case**: Let's say you're running a website or an application, and you need to serve or share individual files (such as images, stylesheets, or scripts) publicly, but you don't want users or services to list or find out what other blobs you have in that container. This can be useful for websites with static content where direct access to resources is given via a URL, often accelerated and distributed via a CDN for enhanced performance.

- **Container**:

  - **Description**: Both the container metadata and individual blobs can be accessed publicly.

  - **Use case**: This might be suitable for entirely public datasets or resources where you want users or services to view individual items and list all items in the container. An example could be a public dataset for research where researchers can view a specific dataset and see what other datasets are available.

For .NET developers, manipulating these access levels is straightforward using the Azure SDK. However, it's imperative to tread with caution. While flexibility is advantageous, it's crucial to ensure that only the necessary data is made public, particularly when it pertains to sensitive or confidential information. Azure Blob Storage offers versatile public access levels to cater to various scenarios; it's the responsibility of developers to judiciously set these levels, striking a balance between accessibility and security.

In the ever-evolving world of cloud storage, ensuring secure and controlled access to resources is paramount. Azure Blob Storage, a cornerstone of Microsoft Azure's vast storage solutions, offers a mechanism known as the **Shared Access Signature** (**SAS**) to achieve this. For developers and administrators, understanding the SAS URI structure is not just a technical requirement but a foundational aspect of ensuring data security in Azure Blob Storage.

Shared Access Signature

Azure Blob Storage's SAS stands out as a powerful tool in the arsenal of developers and administrators. It's designed to grant temporary, yet secure, access to storage resources without sharing the primary or secondary storage access keys. This access is encapsulated in a unique URI, commonly referred to as the SAS URI.

Anatomy of the SAS URI

The SAS URI is a harmonious blend of the resource's URI and the SAS token. Together, they define the scope and permissions of the access granted. Let's dissect the SAS URI to understand its components better.

Resource URI: This is the foundational address pointing to the specific Azure Storage resource you're aiming to grant access to. Whether it's a blob, a container, a file, a table, or a queue, the structure remains consistent. The following is an explanation of each part of the resource URI:

- `[account-name]` represents the name of your Azure storage account.

- `[service-name]` could be a blob, file, queue, or table, depending on the Azure Storage service in question.

- `[resource-path]` denotes the path to the specific resource. For blobs, this would typically be the container name followed by the blob name.

- Delimiter character (?): The delimiter character serves a simple yet crucial role. It acts as a boundary, separating the resource URI from the SAS token. This character, commonly used in URLs, signals the commencement of a query string. Within the SAS URI's context, this query string houses the SAS token.

Constructing a **Shared Access Signature** (**SAS**) URI involves combining the service endpoint, the shared resource path, and the SAS token. The process allows you to grant limited access to Azure Storage resources without needing to share the account key or other credentials.

Here's a step-by-step guide to constructing a SAS URI:

1. **Determine the resource type and endpoint**:

   - If you're creating a SAS for a blob, your endpoint would look like this: `https://myaccount.blob.core.windows.net/mycontainer/myblob`

   - For a container, it would use the following syntax: `https://myaccount.blob.core.windows.net/mycontainer`

   - Similarly, you'd use the appropriate given endpoint for tables, queues, or files

2. **Specify permissions**:

   Decide what type of permissions you want to grant:

   - **Blob**: Possible permissions include read (`r`), write (`w`), delete (`d`), and others

   - **Container**: Permissions could include list (`l`), read (`r`), write (`w`), and delete (`d`)

3. **Define the validity period**:

   - `st` is the start time

   - `se` is the expiration time

4. **Create the string-to-sign**:

   This string is constructed based on parameters including permissions, start and end times, and resource type. It is used to generate the signature.

5. **Generate the signature**:

   Sign the string-to-sign using the HMAC-SHA256 algorithm and your storage account access key. The result is the signature, which will be the sig parameter in the SAS token.

6. **Form the SAS token**:

   Combine all the parameters, including permissions (`sp`), start time (`st`), expiry time (`se`), and signature (`sig`), into a single string, which becomes your SAS token.

7. **Construct the SAS URI**:

   Append the SAS token to the resource URL.

Let's put this all together and try out an example:

```
https://myaccount.blob.core.windows.net/mycontainer/myblob?sv=2023-
08-24&st=2023-08-25T00:00:00Z&se=2023-08-25T00:00:00Z&sp=rw&sig=<
signature>
```

In the preceding example resource URL, we have the following elements:

- `sv` stands for the storage service version
- `st` and `se` define the valid time range for this SAS
- `sp` indicates the granted permissions (read and write in this case)
- `sig` is the generated signature

Azure provides SDKs in various programming languages (e.g., .NET, Python, Java, etc.) and tools (the Azure CLI or Azure portal) that help you generate SAS tokens and URIs programmatically or through a UI, which can greatly simplify this process.

Security note

Always ensure that you do not expose your account key or the generated SAS URI in an insecure manner. The SAS provides direct access to the resource for the specified duration and permissions, so handle it with the same care you'd give to your primary credentials.

The magic behind the SAS token

At first glance, a **Shared Access Signature** (**SAS**) token might appear as an intricate string of characters, but it's much more than that. A SAS token is a meticulously crafted string encapsulating the permissions granted, and its magic lies in the secure way it's generated and validated. Let's see how it works!

The SAS token is generated based on several **input parameters**:

- **Permissions granted**: This can include read, write, delete, and more.
- **Start and expiry time**: Specifies the duration for which the SAS is valid.
- **Targeted storage resource**: This can be a blob, file, queue, or table in the storage account.
- **IP Restrictions**: If defined, only specific IP addresses or IP ranges are allowed to use the SAS.
- **Other constraints**: Additional conditions or constraints defined during the SAS generation, such as the allowed HTTP methods or the protocols (HTTP/HTTPS).

- **Signature Creation**: Once these parameters are set, a string-to-sign is constructed. This string is then signed with the account's access key using the HMAC-SHA256 algorithm, producing a signature. This hashing mechanism uses the SHA-256 hash function, leveraging the account key as the secret. The resulting signature is appended to the SAS token as the sig parameter.

The SAS token is appended to the URL of the targeted storage resource, creating the SAS URI. When a request is made using this URI, Azure computes the signature on the server side using the same logic. If the computed signature matches the sig parameter in the SAS token, the request is legitimate, and the specified permissions are granted.

The security of the SAS token lies in the HMAC-SHA256 signature. As the signature is based on the shared key and the specified parameters, the SAS token can't be tampered with without invalidating the signature. Moreover, without the account's access key, no one can generate a new valid token. In essence, while complex in appearance, the SAS token is a beacon of meticulously crafted security, granting specified permissions to Azure Storage resources with precision and confidence.

Constructing the SAS URI – best practices

While tools such as the Azure portal, PowerShell, the Azure CLI, and the Azure Storage SDKs can generate the SAS URI, it's essential to understand the underlying structure. This knowledge ensures that even if you're crafting the SAS URI manually or just troubleshooting, you're well equipped.

When navigating the intricacies of Azure Blob Storage, it's crucial for security to adhere to best practices when constructing the SAS URI. The following pointers shed light on the essential guidelines to ensure optimal security and functionality:

- **Always use HTTPS**: When constructing or sharing the SAS URI, always use HTTPS to ensure the security of any data in transit

- **Limit the SAS lifespan**: The SAS should be time-bound, granting access only for the necessary duration

- **Review permissions**: Ensure that the SAS token grants only the required permissions, adhering to the principle of least privilege

Let us go through a quick visualization of what this looks like on the Azure portal.

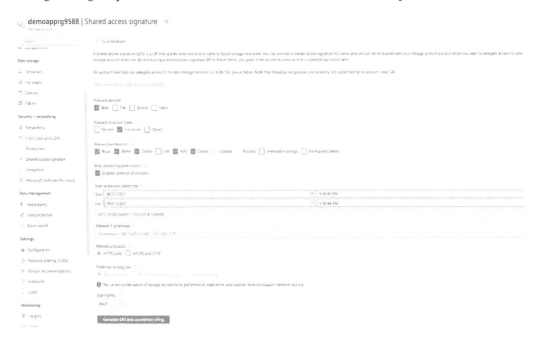

Figure 6.6: Creating a SAS token

The SAS URI structure in Azure Blob Storage is a testament to Azure's commitment to offering flexible yet secure data access mechanisms. By understanding its intricacies, developers and administrators can ensure that Azure Storage resources are accessed both securely and efficiently. As we venture deeper into the realm of cloud storage, tools such as SAS become invaluable. They not only offer granular access control but also empower developers to build robust and secure cloud-based solutions. Always remember, while the SAS URI offers flexibility, it's the responsibility of the developer to ensure its judicious use, striking the right balance between accessibility and security.

Crafting and using SAS in .NET – a practical approach

Azure's SDK for .NET has made generating SAS tokens a breeze. Let's now delve into a more detailed example to deepen our understanding.

Imagine you're developing a .NET application where users can upload photos. However, you want to grant temporary access to certain users to view a specific photo album without giving them blanket access:

```
var blobServiceClient = new BlobServiceClient(connectionString);
var blobClient = blobServiceClient.GetBlobContainerClient(albumName).
GetBlobClient(photoName);
```

```
BlobSasBuilder sasBuilder = new BlobSasBuilder
{
    BlobContainerName = albumName,
    BlobName = photoName,
    Resource = "b",
    StartsOn = DateTimeOffset.UtcNow,
    ExpiresOn = DateTimeOffset.UtcNow.AddHours(2),
    IPRange = new SasIPRange(IPAddress.Parse("192.168.1.1"),
IPAddress.Parse("192.168.1.255")), // Limiting access to a specific IP
range
    Protocol = SasProtocol.Https // Only HTTPS requests allowed
};
sasBuilder.SetPermissions(BlobSasPermissions.Read); // Only read
permission granted
string sasToken = sasBuilder.ToSasQueryParameters(new
StorageSharedKeyCredential(accountName, accountKey)).ToString();
string blobUrlWithSas = blobClient.Uri + "?" + sasToken;
```

This URL (`blobUrlWithSas`) can now be shared with the user, granting them temporary access to view the photo.

Advanced SAS considerations for .NET developers

For .NET developers diving deeper into Azure Blob Storage, mastering the nuances of SAS is paramount. The following are some advanced considerations to ensure a seamless and secure experience:

- **Stored access policies**: Instead of defining ad hoc permissions and durations for each SAS, .NET developers can define and manage stored access policies on a container. These policies can be reused, providing a consistent set of permissions and constraints.

- **User delegation SAS**: This is a special type of SAS that uses Azure AD credentials for authentication, allowing for more granular control and the ability to revoke tokens without affecting other services.

- **Revoking SAS tokens**: One inherent challenge with SAS is its revocation. Once issued, a SAS token is valid until its expiry. However, if there's a need to revoke it prematurely, you'd typically have to regenerate the storage account's access keys, which can be disruptive. Using a user delegation SAS or stored access policies can offer more flexibility in this regard.

Best practices and recommendations

When working with SAS in Azure Blob Storage, ensuring security and optimal configuration is critical. The following are some key best practices and recommendations to optimize your SAS implementations:

- **Minimal permissions**: Always grant the least amount of permissions necessary. If a user only needs to read a blob, don't provide them with write or delete permissions.

- **Short lifespans**: Keep the SAS token's lifespan as brief as feasible. If a user only needs access for 30 minutes, don't grant them access for 24 hours.

- **Logging and monitoring**: Use Azure Monitor and Azure Blob Storage's logging capabilities to track SAS token usage. This can help detect anomalies and potential security breaches.

Shared Access Signatures, while intricate, offer .NET developers a powerful mechanism to control access to Azure Blob Storage resources. Developers can craft secure, efficient, and scalable solutions by understanding their nuances and leveraging the Azure SDK for .NET. In cloud storage, where data access must be flexible and secure, SAS tokens stand as a testament to Azure's commitment to offering developers the tools they need to succeed. For instance, consider a scenario where an organization generates reports that external partners must access. The stipulation is that these reports can only be accessed for a maximum duration of one week after their production.

In this particular situation, SAS becomes an invaluable tool:

- **Time-bounded access**: With SAS, you can define a precise start and end time for access, making it straightforward to grant temporary access. Once the SAS expires, the data becomes inaccessible, adhering to the one-week stipulation.

- **No overhead of identity management**: When dealing with external partners or other situations that call for providing temporary access, managing identities via AAD might introduce unnecessary overhead. SAS provides a lean solution without registering or managing external identities in your directory.

- **Granular permissions**: SAS allows for specific permissions at the blob or container level. Whether it's read-only access to a report or the ability to upload new data, permissions can be finely tuned to the exact requirement.

- **Easy distribution**: SAS tokens can be easily shared with external partners as part of a URL, enabling them to access the data without additional authentication.

While AAD remains the gold standard for most Azure-related authentication scenarios due to its comprehensive security and management features, SAS shines in scenarios requiring short-term, granular access, particularly when engaging with external parties. Thus, while AAD is often cited as a best practice, it's essential to understand the unique strengths of each authentication method and apply them judiciously based on the specific requirements of the use case.

Azure Active Directory

In the modern cloud ecosystem, identity and access management constitutes a central pillar of security. Azure Blob Storage, with its vast capabilities for data storage, is no exception to this rule. For .NET developers, **Azure Active Directory (Azure AD)** integration with Blob Storage offers a robust framework for identity-based access control. This section delves deep into Azure AD's integration with Blob Storage, providing .NET developers with a comprehensive understanding and practical insights.

Azure AD is Microsoft's cloud-based identity and access management service. It allows organizations to manage users, groups, and applications in a centralized manner. When integrated with Azure Blob Storage, it provides a mechanism to authenticate and authorize users and services, ensuring that only valid entities can access the data.

Why Azure AD integration matters for .NET developers

For .NET developers, Azure AD integration with Blob Storage offers several advantages:

- **Centralized management**: Manage users, roles, and permissions from a single location, reducing administrative overhead.

- **Enhanced security**: Leverage Azure AD's features such as **multi-factor authentication** (**MFA**) and Conditional Access to bolster security.

- **Seamless integration**: The Azure SDK for .NET offers tools and libraries that make integrating Azure AD with Blob Storage straightforward.

Authentication mechanisms

Azure AD offers multiple authentication mechanisms, each catering to different scenarios:

- **Managed identities**: Azure services can use managed identities to request access tokens. These identities are automatically managed by Azure AD, eliminating the need for developers to manage credentials.

- **Service principals**: Service principals are identities created for applications, allowing them to access Azure resources. They act as the application's "user" in Azure AD.

- **User identities**: These are the regular user accounts in Azure AD. They can be members of an organization or external users.

Azure AD-based authentication in .NET

The Azure SDK for .NET simplifies Azure AD-based authentication. Here's a basic workflow for a .NET application accessing Blob Storage using Azure AD:

1. Register the application in Azure AD to obtain a client ID and client secret

2. Use the `Azure.Identity` library to authenticate against Azure AD

3. Access Blob Storage using the obtained token

To better illustrate the Azure AD-based authentication process in .NET, let's delve into a practical code example:

```
var clientId = "<Your Azure AD Application Client ID>";
var clientSecret = "<Your Azure AD Application Client Secret>";
var tenantId = "<Your Azure AD Tenant ID>";
```

```
var blobServiceEndpoint = new Uri("https://<YourAccountName>.blob.
core.windows.net/");
var tokenCredential = new ClientSecretCredential(tenantId, clientId,
clientSecret);
BlobServiceClient blobServiceClient = new
BlobServiceClient(blobServiceEndpoint, tokenCredential);
```

In this example, the .NET application uses the client ID and client secret to authenticate against Azure AD and access Blob Storage. Next up, we will be exploring role-based access control within Azure AD and how it can secure our data access.

Role-based access control with Azure AD

Azure's robust cloud infrastructure provides dynamic storage solutions and ensures that access to these storage resources is governed with precision and security. One of the critical aspects of Azure's security paradigm is its **Role-Based Access Control** (**RBAC**) system. Specifically, for Blob Storage, Azure offers several built-in RBAC roles. These roles enable granular permissions, ranging from reading blob data to more complex operations such as delegating access through Azure AD credentials. Such meticulous access management ensures that data is accessible to those who need it while being safeguarded from unauthorized access.

Assigning roles in .NET

The Azure SDK for .NET allows developers to programmatically assign roles. For instance, you can assign a user the Blob Data Reader role, enabling them to read blob data. Alternatively, a user delegation SAS is a type of SAS token that uses Azure AD credentials. It provides a way to delegate access to Blob Storage resources without sharing account keys. Using the Azure SDK for .NET, developers can generate a user delegation SAS, providing fine-grained, time-limited access to blob data.

Best practices for .NET developers

To maintain a secure and efficient environment, .NET developers should adhere to the following best practices:

- **Limit permissions**: Assign only the necessary permissions. If a user only needs to read data, don't grant them write or delete permissions.

- **Regularly review access**: Periodically review and audit access permissions, ensuring that only valid entities have access.

- **Use managed identities**: Wherever possible, use managed identities to eliminate the need to manage credentials.

- **Monitor and audit**: Utilize Azure Monitor and Azure Security Center to track access patterns and potential security threats.

Out-of-the-box RBAC accounts

Azure's built-in RBAC roles related to Blob Storage can be used to help streamline access management. To help you develop a more precise understanding, here's a brief explanation of each role:

- **Storage Blob Data Contributor**:

  - **Description**: Users assigned this role can read, write, and delete data in Azure Blob Storage.

  - **Use case**: This role is ideal for individuals or applications that need to modify data within Blob Storage, such as adding, updating, or removing blobs.

- **Storage Blob Data Reader**:

  - **Description**: Users with this role can only read data from Azure Blob Storage.

  - **Use case**: Best suited for applications, services, or users that only need to view or download blobs without the ability to modify or delete them.

- **Storage Blob Delegator**:

  - **Description**: Allows a user to obtain a user delegation key, which can be used to create a user delegation SAS. The SAS can then grant access to blob data based on Azure AD and OAuth.

  - **Use case**: Useful for scenarios where there's a need to delegate access to specific blobs or containers for a limited time without sharing the primary account key or using fixed SAS tokens. This can be especially useful when temporary access needs to be granted to third parties or other services.

Challenges and solutions

While Azure AD integration offers numerous benefits, it's not without challenges:

- **Challenge**: Managing a large number of users and roles:

  - **Solution**: Use Azure AD groups to group users and assign roles to groups instead of individual users

- **Challenge**: Ensuring timely revocation of access:

  - **Solution**: Implement policies for regular access reviews and leverage tools such as Azure AD Privileged Identity Management

In the world of cloud security, Azure AD stands as a beacon, guiding developers to ensure data remains in the right hands. Azure AD's integration with Blob Storage is a game-changer for .NET developers. It offers a robust framework for identity-based access control, ensuring data security in Azure Blob Storage. By understanding the nuances of Azure AD authentication, leveraging the power of the

Azure SDK for .NET, and adhering to best practices, .NET developers can craft secure, efficient, and scalable cloud storage solutions.

Encryption in Azure Blob Storage

In the digital realm, where data breaches and cyberattacks are becoming increasingly commonplace, encryption protects us as the stalwart guardian of our data. For .NET developers navigating the vast seas of Azure Blob Storage, understanding the intricacies of encryption is not just beneficial—it's a necessity. This section offers a comprehensive exploration of encryption within Azure Blob Storage, tailored specifically for the .NET developer.

Microsoft Azure's data storage solutions include Azure Blob Storage, which prioritizes security in its design. Encryption involves converting data into code to prevent unauthorized access, and Azure Blob Storage provides strong encryption mechanisms for both data at rest and data in transit.

Storage Service Encryption (SSE)

Storage Service Encryption, commonly known as SSE, is Azure's built-in mechanism to automatically encrypt data before it's stored and decrypt it upon retrieval. It acts silently in the background, ensuring that data at rest is always encrypted.

Azure uses the **Advanced Encryption Standard** (**AES**), a symmetric encryption algorithm, for SSE. AES is widely recognized for its security and has been adopted as a standard by the US Government. When data is written to Azure Blob Storage, it's encrypted using 256-bit AES encryption. Similarly, when data is read, it's decrypted automatically.

.NET developers and SSE

For .NET developers, the beauty of SSE lies in its transparency. Since SSE operates at the service level, there's no additional code or configuration required. When you use the Azure SDK for .NET to interact with Blob Storage, data is automatically encrypted and decrypted without any intervention. This is encryption made easy!

Client-side encryption

While SSE encrypts data at rest in Azure, what if you want to encrypt data before it even reaches Azure Blob Storage? Enter client-side encryption. As the name suggests, this method involves encrypting data on the client side before uploading it to Azure.

The Azure SDK for .NET provides tools to facilitate client-side encryption. Here's a basic workflow:

1. Use Azure Key Vault to manage encryption keys securely.

2. Before uploading data to Blob Storage, encrypt it using your chosen encryption method and the key from Azure Key Vault.

3.   Upload the encrypted data to Blob Storage.

4.   When retrieving the data, decrypt it on the client side using the same key.

When considering the security of data, especially sensitive information, many organizations opt to encrypt their data before uploading it to the cloud. Here's a simple demonstration of client-side encryption:

```
var key = GetEncryptionKeyFromKeyVault();
var encryptedData = EncryptData(originalData, key);
var blobClient = new BlobClient(connectionString, containerName,
blobName);
blobClient.Upload(new MemoryStream(encryptedData));
```

By encrypting the data on the client side before uploading, you ensure an added layer of security: the data remains encrypted throughout its transit and storage in Azure. However, while this method bolsters data security, it does come with performance implications:

- **Increased processing time**: Encrypting and decrypting data on the client side requires additional CPU time. This can result in slower application performance, especially when dealing with large amounts of data.

- **Increased complexity**: Developers need to manage the encryption process, handle key rotation, and ensure compatibility between encryption algorithms and libraries.

However, this method might be preferable in specific scenarios:

- **In the absence of BYOK**: **Bring Your Own Key** (**BYOK**) might not be an option if the organization lacks an internal **Public Key Infrastructure** (**PKI**), in which case client-side encryption would help to increase security

- **Trust concerns**: Organizations with reservations about trusting Microsoft completely, possibly fueled by concerns about governmental bodies such as the NSA, would be able to assuage their concerns by using client-side encryption

That said, developers should be aware that the preceding provided workflow used a simple key vault, which, while secure, doesn't guarantee absolute isolation from external access. Truly security-focused customers might shun this method in favor of even more secure options. A dedicated **Hardware Security Module** (**HSM**), whether on-premises or in Azure, offers heightened security. Using this solution guarantees that the encryption keys are never exposed, not even to Microsoft. This distinction is critical: while the simple key vault uses software-based keys that could technically be accessed by Microsoft under certain conditions, HSMs are designed to be impenetrable.

Encryption in transit

While data at rest is crucial, ensuring its security while it's being transferred between the client and Azure Blob Storage is equally vital. Azure achieves this using **Transport Layer Security** (**TLS**), a protocol that ensures data integrity and security during transmission. For .NET developers, the Azure

SDK for .NET automatically uses HTTPS (which is based on TLS) for all communications with Azure Blob Storage. This means that data is encrypted as it travels to and from Blob Storage. Developers should ensure that they always use HTTPS endpoints and avoid downgrading to HTTP, as this could expose data to potential eavesdropping.

Best practices for .NET developers

To fortify data against potential threats, .NET developers must adhere to these essential best practices:

- **Always use HTTPS**: Ensure all communications with Azure Blob Storage use HTTPS to leverage TLS encryption.

- **Use the latest TLS encryption**: It's crucial to stay up to date with the latest TLS encryption standards to ensure the security of your communications with Azure Blob Storage. **Transport Layer Security (TLS)** protocols provide encryption and authentication for data in transit.

- **Rotate keys**: Regularly rotate and refresh encryption keys in Azure Key Vault to enhance security.

- **Audit and monitor**: Use Azure Monitor and Azure Security Center to keep an eye on access patterns and potential security threats.

- **Stay updated**: Encryption standards and best practices evolve. Stay updated with the latest recommendations from Azure and the broader security community.

Encryption, in the context of Azure Blob Storage, is a multifaceted domain. From automatic encryption at rest with SSE to client-side encryption and ensuring data security during transit with TLS, Azure offers a comprehensive suite of tools for .NET developers. By understanding and effectively leveraging these tools, .NET developers can ensure that data in Azure Blob Storage remains secure, irrespective of where it resides or how it travels. In the ever-evolving landscape of cybersecurity, knowledge and vigilance are our best allies.

As we've journeyed through the multifaceted realm of Azure Blob Storage, it's become evident that Microsoft Azure has left no stone unturned in fortifying its storage solutions. From granular access controls such as public access levels and RBAC to the array of intricate encryption mechanisms encompassing SSE, client-side encryption, and encryption in transit, Azure Blob Storage stands as a beacon of security in the vast cloud storage landscape. For developers and administrators, understanding and leveraging these tools is not just a technical endeavor but a commitment to safeguarding data. As the digital world continues to evolve, with data becoming an increasingly valuable asset, the importance of robust security measures like those offered in Azure Blob Storage cannot be overstated. In essence, Azure Blob Storage offers a harmonious blend of flexibility and protection, ensuring that data remains both accessible and secure in an ever-changing digital environment.

Summary

In this chapter, we have explored Azure Blob Storage and its importance for .NET developers, providing a comprehensive understanding of its key features, benefits, and best practices. We have discussed how to create a storage account using the Azure portal and programmatically with the Azure Storage SDK for .NET, along with examining how to work with blob containers effectively. Additionally, we have addressed the process of uploading data to blob storage and highlighted best practices.

We have also emphasized the significance of security in Azure Blob Storage by explaining its security model and how to utilize SAS and Azure AD authentication to secure blob storage. Best practices for securing Azure Blob Storage were also discussed to help you ensure you keep your data safe and well protected.

To help you avoid commonly encountered challenges as you get in to Azure Blob Storage, we identified potential mistakes and pitfalls that can happen, offering tips and guidance to mitigate these issues. By following this chapter's best practices and tips, you can ensure a smooth, efficient, and secure experience when working with Azure Blob Storage in your .NET projects.

As a .NET developer, having a solid foundation in Azure Blob Storage enables you to fully harness its potential for your applications, optimizing performance, scalability, and security. Applying the knowledge and skills gained in this chapter will allow you to work with Azure Blob Storage effectively and confidently. Remember the best practices and tips provided throughout this chapter as you continue to develop and enhance your applications with Azure Blob Storage.

As we conclude our comprehensive exploration of Azure Blob Storage, our focus now shifts toward Azure SQL Database. This service is another key pillar of the Azure ecosystem and understanding it is crucial as you broaden your Azure expertise. While Blob Storage is ideal for handling unstructured data, Azure SQL Database offers a dynamic and scalable environment for storing, managing, and accessing structured data. In the next chapter, we'll guide you through creating your very first Azure SQL Database instance, thereby laying solid groundwork as we continue our exploration into the vast landscape of Azure.

7

Creating an Azure SQL Database

Azure offers SQL server databases in three different services. **Azure SQL Database** is a fully managed **Platform-as-a-Service** (**PaaS**) database engine. Since the database is a PaaS model, most of the database management tasks (such as backup, backup retention, monitoring, and so on) that are managed by Azure SQL Database consistently operate on the most recent stable release of the SQL Server database engine and are supported by a patched operating system. With an impressive availability rate of 99.99%, Azure SQL Database ensures a highly reliable and uninterrupted service. In the previous chapter, we learned about Azure Blob storage and how to store binary data such as images. We also learned how to access storage using a shared access signature. In this chapter, you will be creating an Azure SQL server and Azure SQL database, configuring security rules, connecting to Azure SQL Server using a .NET Core application, and finally, connecting to the SQL 2 server from Azure App Service and other Azure resources.

In this chapter, we're going to cover the following main topics:

- Introduction to Azure SQL Database
- Creating an Azure SQL database
- Writing and reading data from Azure SQL Database using .NET Core
- Configuring security in Azure SQL Database

Technical requirements

In this chapter, you'll see examples using **ASP.NET Core**, so you need to install the **.NET SDK**. For building and debugging, you need either **Visual Studio** or **VS Code**. To create an Azure SQL database, you need an **Azure subscription**. You can install **SQL Management Studio** or **Azure Data Studio** to explore the database. In this chapter, we will be using the Visual Studio **SQL** Object Explorer feature for viewing and managing data.

Introducing Azure SQL Database

Azure SQL is a family of fully managed, secure, and intelligent relational database services. Azure SQL supports different application patterns such as moving from existing on-premises SQL Server workloads to modern cloud-native application development.

The Azure SQL family consists of three main services:

- **SQL Server on Azure VMs**: This is an **Infrastructure-as-a-Service** (**IaaS**) offering from Microsoft Azure. As the name implies, this is an Azure **Virtual Machine** (**VM**) with **SQL Server** installed. This service is suitable in scenarios where you need 100% SQL Server compatibility and OS-level access. In the Azure portal, you can choose to set up SQL Server on Windows or Linux. Azure VMs are available with a free SQL Server license and you can use your own SQL Server license if you have one, also known as **Bring Your Own License** (**BYOL**). The advantage of this service offering is that you can move your existing on-premises database and application without having to make too many changes in the code. Since it is an IaaS offering, you're responsible for managing the server – backup management, availability, and so on.

- **Azure SQL Managed Instance**: This is another service offering for SQL Server from Azure. Unlike SQL Server on Azure VMs, this is a PaaS service. It supports almost all on-premises instance-level and database-level capabilities. Unlike SQL Server on Azure VMs, this service offers built-in backup, patching, and recovery options. This service also offers easy migration from SQL Server. So, this service is suitable for modernizing existing apps.

- **Azure SQL Database**: This is the service we will explore in this chapter. It is suitable for building modern cloud applications. This version of SQL Server doesn't support all the **Transact Structured Query Language** (**TSQL**) features. (TSQL is similar to SQL, but adds some extra functionalities that will only work in SQL Server.) The most commonly used SQL Server features are available, including T-SQL for querying and scripting, and tables and indexes for data storage and retrieval optimization, stored procedures, and views. This service offers 99.995% availability, whereas the other two services offer 99.99% availability only.

You can find more details about the Azure SQL family and a comparison here: `https://learn.microsoft.com/en-us/azure/azure-sql/azure-sql-iaas-vs-paas-what-is-overview`.

Azure SQL Database offers the following two deployment options:

- **As a single database**: In this deployment model, the database will run similarly to a contained or isolated database – with its own resources managed by a logical SQL server.

- **As an elastic pool**: This is a resource management feature in Azure that allows multiple databases to share and dynamically allocate resources based on usage needs. It provides cost-effective scalability and simplified administration for managing databases with varying workloads. It is a cost-effective solution for implementing multi-tenant **Software-as-a-Service** (**SaaS**) applications. Databases can be added and removed from the elastic pool.

The single database deployment option offers various service tiers and compute tier models, allowing you to select the most suitable option based on your workload requirements. There are two main service tier offerings available: **the vCore-based purchasing model** (newly introduced), and the **Database Transaction Unit (DTU)-based purchasing model**. In the vCore-based model, you will get a Serverless compute tier, in which compute resources are auto-scaled and billed per second based on the vCores used. The serverless tier dynamically adjusts its compute capacity based on workload demands. It offers cost savings through automatic pausing during inactivity, pay-per-use billing for actual compute resources used, and the ability to quickly scale up to handle spikes in activity. It's suitable for workloads with variable or unpredictable usage patterns, allowing efficient resource management across multiple databases while maintaining compatibility with other Azure SQL Database service tiers. Please note that when using the Serverless tier, Azure will pause the database if there is no activity. The application should implement retry logic while working with serverless databases.

Figure 7.1 – Azure SQL database pricing configuration

You can find a detailed comparison of vCore- and DTU-based purchase models here: `https://learn.microsoft.com/en-us/azure/azure-sql/database/purchasing-models?view=azuresql`.

In this section, you learned about the Azure SQL family and different SQL Server offerings from Azure. You also learned about different deployment options in Azure SQL Database and the different compute and service tiers. In the next section, you will learn about creating and managing an Azure SQL database.

Creating an Azure SQL database

As mentioned in earlier chapters (*Chapter 1* and *Chapter 2*), you can create Azure resources from the Azure portal using the **Azure CLI**, **Azure PowerShell**, or **ARM template**. First, we will create an Azure SQL database from the Azure portal and then we will look into creating it using the Azure CLI.

Creating an Azure SQL database using the Azure portal

As shown in the following figure, to create an Azure SQL database, click on the **Create Resource** button on the Azure portal home page. On the **Create a resource** page, **SQL Database** will usually be available under **Popular Azure Services**. Or you can type SQL Database in the search textbox, click on the **Create** button under the **SQL Database** card, and click on the **SQL Database** option under **Create**.

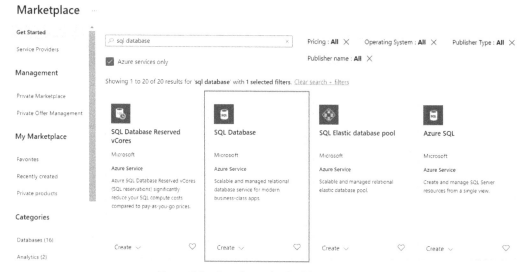

Figure 7.2 – Search results for SQL Database

You need to configure a few things in the Azure SQL database creation process. First, you need to select the subscription, then you need to either create a new resource group or select an existing resource group.

Figure 7.3 – Create database | Create SQL server

I am using my Visual Studio subscription and an existing resource group with the name `PacktBook`. For the database name, I kept the database name as `chapter7`. Since we don't have a SQL Server created in the subscription, we need to create one first. You can do this by clicking on the **Create new** link under the **Server** drop-down list.

When you click on the **Create new** button, you will see a screen like the following figure:

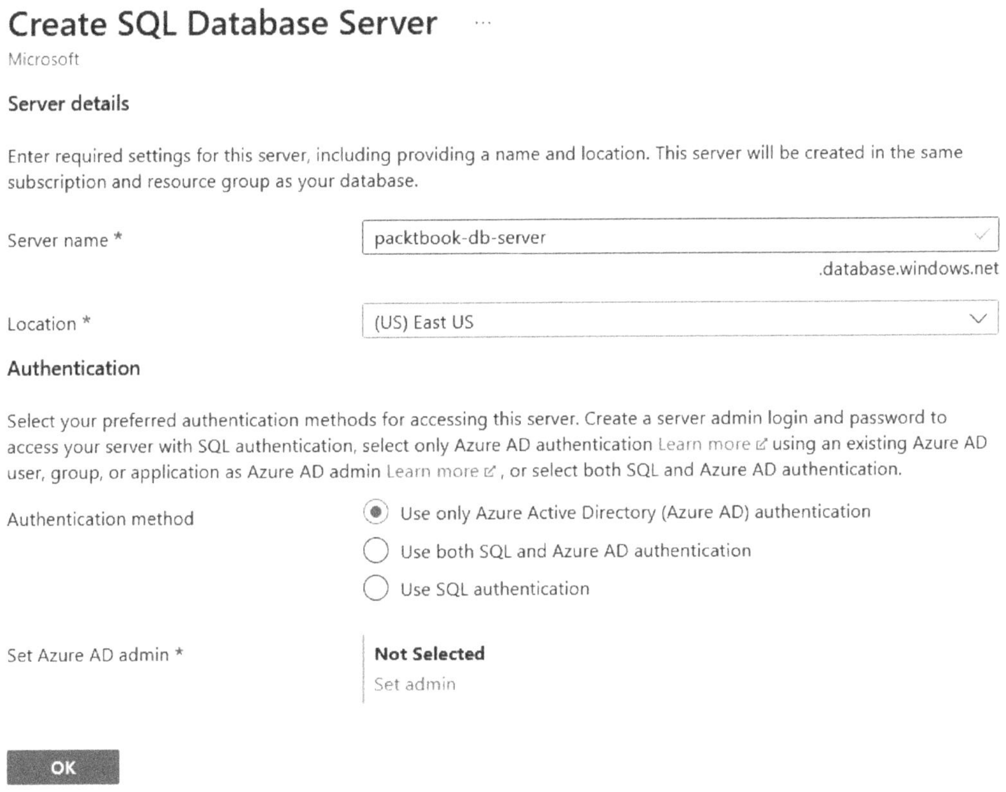

Create SQL Database Server   ···

Microsoft

Server details

Enter required settings for this server, including providing a name and location. This server will be created in the same subscription and resource group as your database.

Server name *	packtbook-db-server ✓
	.database.windows.net
Location *	(US) East US ⌄

Authentication

Select your preferred authentication methods for accessing this server. Create a server admin login and password to access your server with SQL authentication, select only Azure AD authentication Learn more ☑ using an existing Azure AD user, group, or application as Azure AD admin Learn more ☑ , or select both SQL and Azure AD authentication.

Authentication method	⦿ Use only Azure Active Directory (Azure AD) authentication
	◯ Use both SQL and Azure AD authentication
	◯ Use SQL authentication
Set Azure AD admin *	**Not Selected**
	Set admin

OK

Figure 7.4 – Create SQL Database Server

On this screen, you need to provide a globally unique name for your SQL server and a location – currently, I am using **East US** as the location and `packtbook-db-server` as the name for SQL Server.

The rest of the configuration is similar to the local SQL Server installation. You can choose **Use SQL authentication** or **Use only Azure Active Directory (Azure AD) authentication** or choose to use both. The best practice is to use Azure Active Directory authentication. Since SQL authentication is easy to configure, in this section, we are using SQL authentication. If we choose the **Use SQL authentication** option, we need to configure the username and password. I am creating a user with the name `packt-web-user`. We will be changing the authentication mode later in this chapter (in the *Configuring security in Azure SQL Database* section) to use Azure Active Directory instead of SQL authentication.

Click on the **OK** button to save the configuration, and you will see a screen like the following:

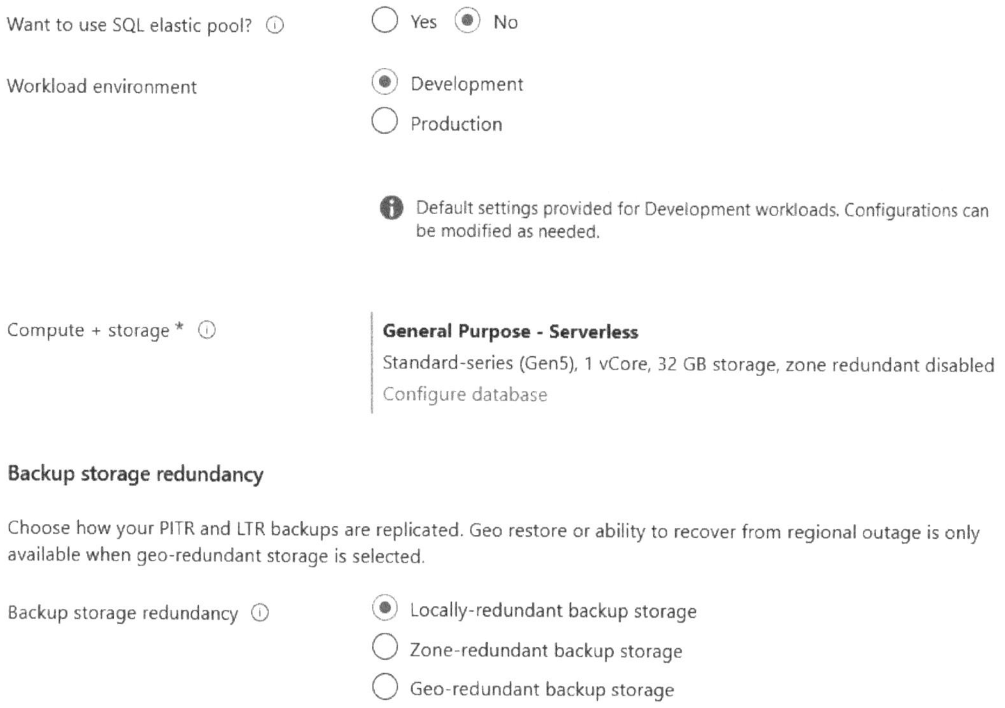

Want to use SQL elastic pool? ⓘ   ◯ Yes ◉ No

Workload environment   ◉ Development
                                            ◯ Production

                                            ❶ Default settings provided for Development workloads. Configurations can
                                               be modified as needed.

Compute + storage * ⓘ   **General Purpose - Serverless**
                                            Standard-series (Gen5), 1 vCore, 32 GB storage, zone redundant disabled
                                            Configure database

Backup storage redundancy

Choose how your PITR and LTR backups are replicated. Geo restore or ability to recover from regional outage is only
available when geo-redundant storage is selected.

Backup storage redundancy ⓘ   ◉ Locally-redundant backup storage
                                            ◯ Zone-redundant backup storage
                                            ◯ Geo-redundant backup storage

Figure 7.5 – Azure SQL configuration

Once SQL Server is configured, you need to change a few configuration settings. Select **No** for the **Want to use SQL elastic pool?** option. Set the workload environment to **Development**. It helps to reduce the cost of the resource. Set **Backup storage redundancy** to **Locally-redundant backup storage**.

Please note that the selected **Compute + storage** option is currently **General Purpose - Serverless**, but you can change this if required. Next, you can click on the **Review + create** button. This will display a **Review** screen where you will be able to find all the details of the resource getting provisioned with the default values. You can click on the **Create** button to create the SQL server and create an empty database. This process will take some time. If you're getting any errors such as **Not Found** after you click on **Create**, you might need to wait for some time and then try to create it again. Please note that you may not be able to create SQL Server or Azure SQL databases in all regions. If you're getting any errors related to the location, you may need to change the location and try again.

Currently, we have provisioned an empty SQL database; Azure offers an option to use a sample database as well. If we select this option, Azure will create an `AdventureWorksLT` database in the server, which will help us get started with an existing database. You can configure it from the **Additional Settings** tab. Once it is completed, you will see the SQL server and SQL database in your resource group.

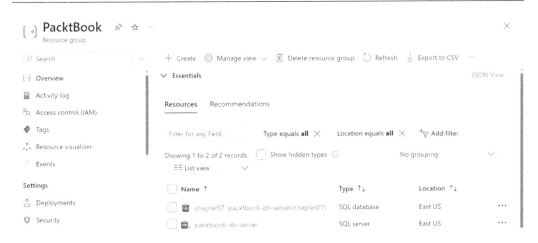

Figure 7.6 – SQL server and SQL database in the resource group

Next, we will look into provisioning a SQL database using the Azure CLI.

Creating an Azure SQL database using the Azure CLI

In this section, you will learn how to create an Azure SQL database using the Azure CLI. You already installed the Azure CLI in *Chapter 2*; if it is not available, you need to install it.

To use the Azure CLI, first, you need to log in to your subscription with the `az login` command:

```
> az login
```

This command will open the default browser with an Azure login screen; you need to log in to the portal. Once logged in, you can close the browser window. Your Terminal will display your subscription information.

Next, to view the already created SQL server, you can execute the following command:

```
> az sql server list -g packtbook -o table
```

This command will display output with SQL Server information in table format. The `-g` parameter is the resource group name (in our case, `packtbook`) and `-o table` will display the output in table format.

To create the database, you need to execute the `az sql db create` command. With the CLI, we will create the database with the `Basic` tier and sample database:

```
> az sql db create --resource-group PacktBook --server packtbook-db-
server --name Chapter7CliDemo --sample-name AdventureWorksLT --edition
Basic --compute-model Provisioned
```

Once you execute this command, this will provision a database in the `Basic` tier with sample data from the `AdventureWorksLT` database. The following figure displays the Azure SQL server and Azure SQL database created by the Azure CLI command.

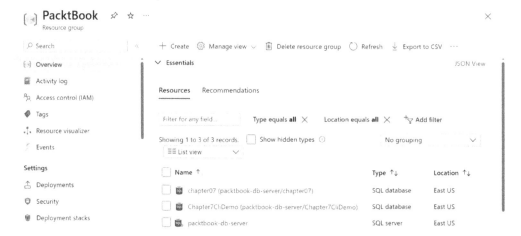

Figure 7.7 – Database created using the Azure CLI

Once created, make sure you delete the resources you created. There is an option to create a free SQL database as well: instead of using `Basic` as the edition, use `Free`.

Since we already created the database server, we use it in the command. If you need to create a SQL server, execute the following command:

```
> az sql server create --name packtbook-db-server --resource-group
packtbook --location eastus --admin-user packtuser --admin-password
YourSuperSecretPassword
```

This will create a server with the name `packtbook-db-server`, with SQL authentication in the `eastus` region and user credentials.

In this section, we created an Azure SQL database using the Azure CLI. In the next section, we will learn how to create an Azure SQL database using the Azure ARM template.

Creating an Azure SQL database using the Azure ARM template

Azure Resource Manager (**ARM**) templates are a form of **infrastructure-as-code** (**IaC**) offering from Azure. This is a concept in which you define the infrastructure you need to be deployed. The ARM template is a **JSON file** that defines the configuration and infrastructure for your solution. The template uses **declarative syntax**. In the template, you can define what you like to create and different associated configuration values. ARM templates are the recommended way to deploy resources because they provide repeatable results and are idempotent – you can write a template and deploy it in any environment and it will always give the same result. **Azure Bicep** is another IaC offering from Azure.

We can create the ARM template by exporting the ARM template file from the Azure portal's existing resource. The following screenshot shows what exporting an ARM template for SQL Database looks like. The code contains various JSON statements that describe which resources to provision with different configurations. For more details and to learn more about Azure ARM templates, visit `https://learn.microsoft.com/azure/azure-resource-manager/templates/?WT.mc_id=DT-MVP-5002040`.

Figure 7.8 – Exporting the template

We can also type `Custom Deployment` in the search bar, and select **Deploy** from a custom template option.

You can use the exported template from the last step or you can get Azure SQL database templates from **Quickstart template**.

The ARM template ZIP file you downloaded from the portal contains two files: `template.json` and `parameters.json`. The `template.json` file contains information about the resources getting provisioned – for example, SQL Server and SQL Database. The `parameters.json` file contains various parameters we can configure, such as the database/server name or location. You can modify the `parameters` file and add new parameters such as the `Compute` tier, so instead of deploying the `Basic` tier, Azure will prompt for a `Compute` tier when we import the file.

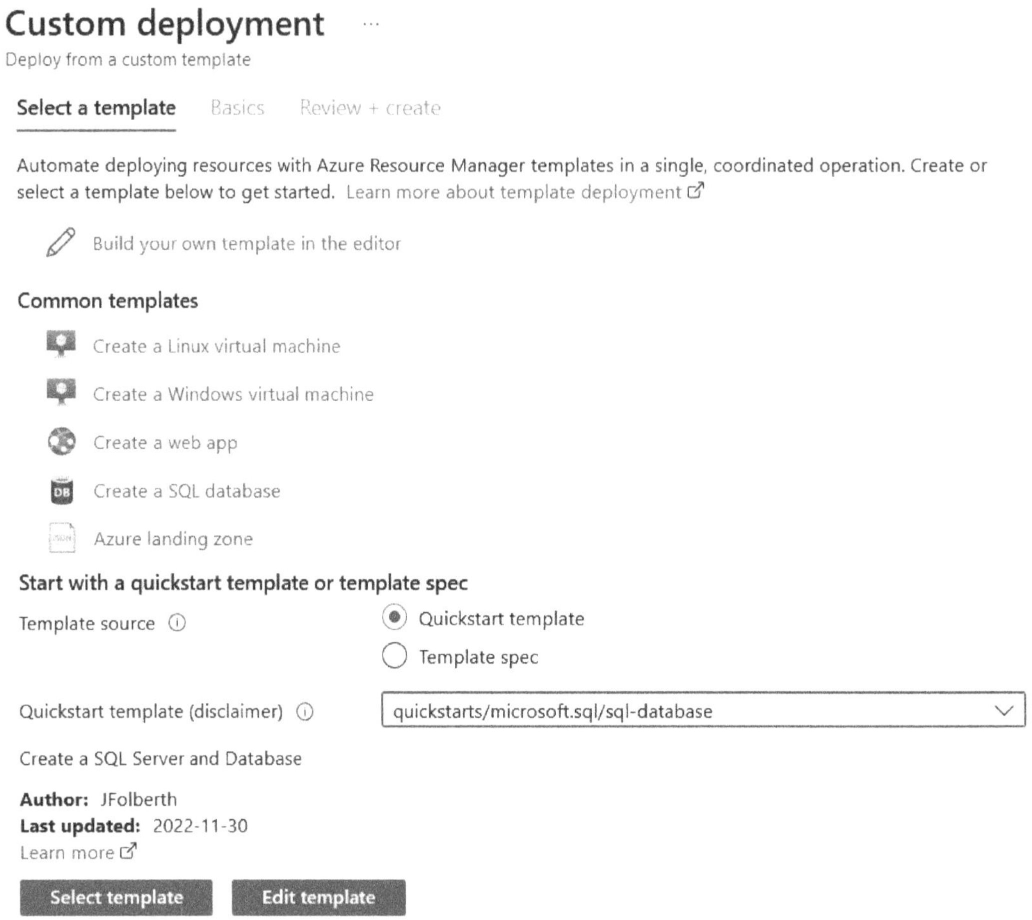

Custom deployment ···

Deploy from a custom template

Select a template   Basics   Review + create

Automate deploying resources with Azure Resource Manager templates in a single, coordinated operation. Create or select a template below to get started. Learn more about template deployment ☐

✎   Build your own template in the editor

Common templates

💻   Create a Linux virtual machine

💻   Create a Windows virtual machine

🌐   Create a web app

🗄   Create a SQL database

📄   Azure landing zone

Start with a quickstart template or template spec

Template source ⓘ   ⦿ Quickstart template

                             ◯ Template spec

Quickstart template (disclaimer) ⓘ | quickstarts/microsoft.sql/sql-database   ⌄ |

Create a SQL Server and Database

Author: JFolberth
Last updated: 2022-11-30
Learn more ☐

| **Select template** | | **Edit template** |

Figure 7.9 – Custom deployment

If you want to use your own, you need to click on the **Build your own template in the editor** option, and then you will be able to load the template file from the downloaded ZIP file. I am selecting the **Quickstart template** option. In the **Quickstart template** dropdown, search for sql-database, and you will get the template for creating the SQL server and database. Then, click on the **Select template** button.

Once you select the template, you will reach a screen similar to the following:

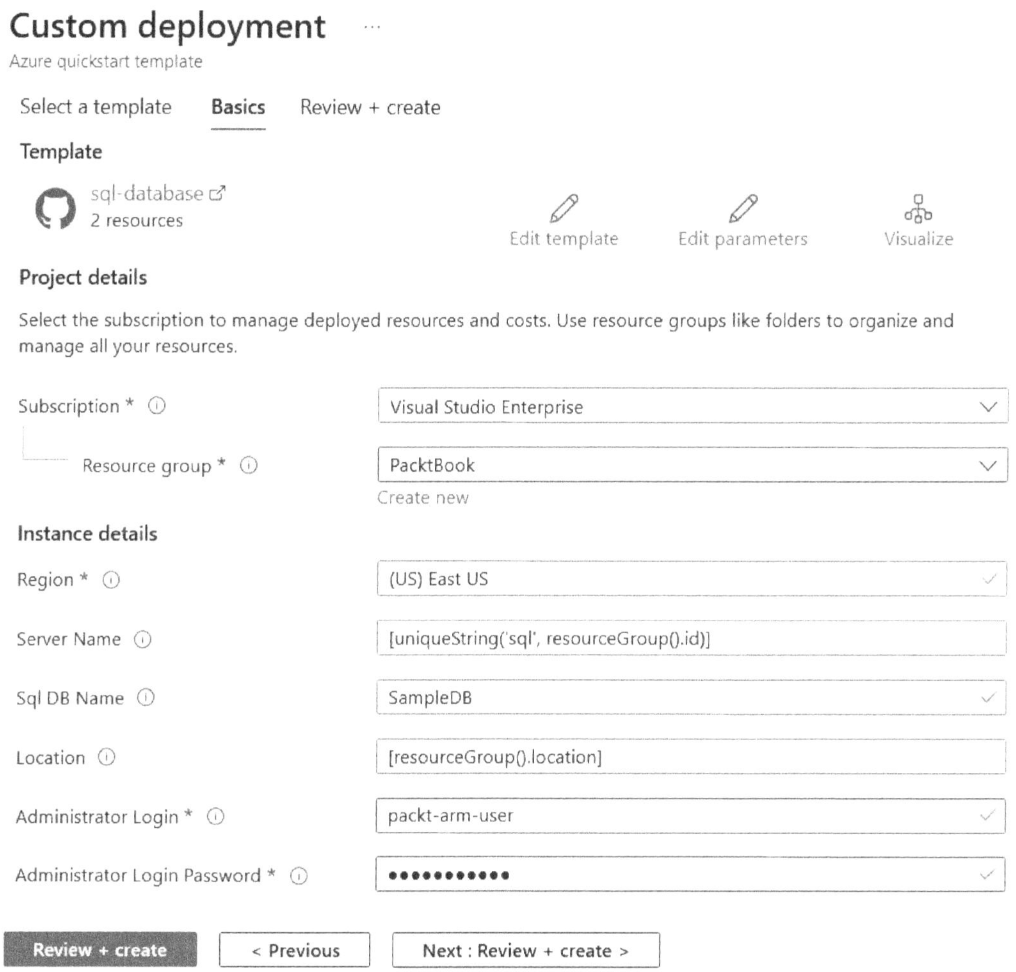

Custom deployment
Azure quickstart template

Select a template   **Basics**   Review + create

Template

sql-database ☐
2 resources

Edit template   Edit parameters   Visualize

Project details

Select the subscription to manage deployed resources and costs. Use resource groups like folders to organize and manage all your resources.

Subscription * ⓘ	Visual Studio Enterprise	∨

Resource group * ⓘ	PacktBook	∨

Create new

Instance details

Region * ⓘ	(US) East US	∨

Server Name ⓘ	[uniqueString('sql', resourceGroup().id)]	

Sql DB Name ⓘ	SampleDB	∨

Location ⓘ	[resourceGroup().location]	

Administrator Login * ⓘ	packt-arm-user	∨

Administrator Login Password * ⓘ	•••••••••••	∨

[Review + create]   [< Previous]   [Next : Review + create >]

Figure 7.10 – Custom deployment continued

You need to set some configuration values, such as **Resource group**, **Region**, **Server Name**, **Sql DB Name**, and SQL authentication credentials.

Once you filled in the details, you can click on the **Review + create** button. This will show a confirmation window with the license agreement and the provided details. Then, you can click on the **Create** button to provision the SQL server and database.

You can use the Azure CLI as well to import ARM templates. Here is the command to deploy with parameters:

```
> az deployment group create -g PacktBook --template-file .\template.
json --parameters serverName=packtbook-db-server --parameters
sqlDBName=Chapter7ArmDeployment --parameters location=eastus
--parameters administratorLogin=packt-web-user --parameters
administratorLoginPassword=SuperSecret@123456
```

The `template.json` file is the ARM template file I downloaded from the **Custom deployment** section of the Azure portal. In this way, you can deploy ARM templates using the Azure CLI.

So far, we have learned about the different ways to provision SQL Server and SQL Database in Azure. The Azure CLI and ARM templates are the recommended ways to deploy Azure resources. In the next section, we will learn how to connect to Azure SQL Database from .NET Core code.

Writing and reading data from Azure SQL Database using .NET Core and EF Core

In this section, we will learn how to interact with Azure SQL Database from the **.NET Core** application. We will learn about connecting to the SQL Server database using **Entity Framework Core (EF Core)** and implementing **Create**, **Read**, **Update**, **Delete** (**CRUD**) operations.

Connecting to Azure SQL Database from ASP.NET Core

In this section, we will learn about connecting to Azure SQL Database from an **ASP.NET Core Web API** application. We will be using the EF Core library to interact with Azure SQL Database.

Introducing EF Core

EF is an **object-relational mapping (ORM)** framework – a programming technique used to represent relational database entities to classes and objects, which helps developers work with databases without writing SQL code. Along with the .NET Core release, Microsoft introduced EF Core. Microsoft offers EF Core providers for databases such as **MS SQL Server**, **Cosmos DB**, and **SQLite**. Additionally, there are EF Core providers available for Oracle and MySQL databases from other vendors. We can use EF Core in two ways – **code first** and **database first**. In this section, we will be using the code-first approach.

In the code-first approach, you need to create a **database context** class, which should inherit from the `DbContext` class. The database context represents the database. For tables, we need to create simple **Plain Old Class Object** (**POCO**) classes, which we need to set as properties in the database context class with the `DbSet<T>` type. The database context class requires the database provider and connection string to interact with the database. To insert the data into the database, we need to set different properties of the `DbSet` property and need to invoke the `SaveChanges` or `SaveChangesAsync` method. We will explore these things in detail in this section.

First, we need to create an **ASP.NET Core Web API** project using either Visual Studio or the **dotnet CLI**. I am using the `dotnet` CLI here – except for the first step, everything else will be the same. We can use the following command to create the .NET Core Web API:

```
> dotnet new webapi --output AddressBook --framework net6.0
```

Next, you need to add a reference to the EF Core, EF Core SQL Server, and EF Core Design packages.

Here are the commands to do this:

```
> dotnet add .\AddressBook\AddressBook.csproj package Microsoft.
EntityFrameworkCore --version 6.0.13
> dotnet add .\AddressBook\AddressBook.csproj package Microsoft.
EntityFrameworkCore.SqlServer --version 6.0.13
> dotnet add .\AddressBook\AddressBook.csproj package Microsoft.
EntityFrameworkCore.Design --version 6.0.13
```

The `Microsoft.EntityFrameworkCore.Design` package is an optional one – we don't require this package to interact with the database. But since we are using the code-first approach, this package helps to create tables, called **Entity Framework migrations**.

Once the packages are added, we need to create POCO classes. In this example, we are creating a `Book` class, with the following properties. In the API project, first, we will create a `Models` folder and then an `Address.cs` file inside it. It is not mandatory – but this is the convention in Web APIs. Here is the code for the `Address.cs` class:

```
namespace AddressBook.Models;
public class Address
{
    public int Id { get; set; }
    public string? Name { get; set; }
    public string? Email { get; set; }
    public DateTime CreatedOn { get; set; } = DateTime.UtcNow;
}
```

Next, we need to create the database context class. I am using the name `AddressBookDbContext`, and I am creating a folder with the name `Data` and putting the database context file inside this folder. Here is the structure of the `AddressBookDbContext.cs` file:

```
using AddressBook.Models;
using Microsoft.EntityFrameworkCore;
namespace AddressBook.Data;
public class AddressBookDbContext: DbContext
{
    public AddressBookDbContext(DbContextOptions<AddressBookDbContext>
options) : base(options)
```

```
    {
    }
    public DbSet<Address> Addresses { get; set; } = null!;
}
```

In the code, the class is inheriting from the `DbContext` class. Next, we need to create a constructor that accepts a `DbContextOptions` object. The `Addresses` property is `DbSet<Address>` type. We have now completed the `DbContext` implementation.

Next, we will be creating a controller – `AddressBookController` – which implements CRUD operations. You can create a class inside the `Controllers` folder and add the following code:

```
using AddressBook.Models;
using Microsoft.AspNetCore.Mvc;
namespace AddressBook.Controllers;
[ApiController]
[Route("[controller]")]
public class AddressBookController : ControllerBase
{
    [HttpGet]
    public IActionResult Get()
    {
        throw new NotImplementedException();
    }
}
```

The preceding code is the `AddressBookController` controller. You can find the complete implementation in GitHub at `https://github.com/PacktPublishing/A-Developer-s-Guide-to-.NET-in-Azure/tree/main/Chapter07/AddressBook`.

You can delete `WeatherforecastController` and the associated model classes. If you're using Visual Studio, you can right-click on the `Controllers` folder and from the dialog, choose **API Controller – Empty template** or **API Controller with read/write actions** under **API**. In the next dialog, choose the same controller template and set the controller's name to `AddressBookController`.

Now, if we run the application using the dotnet `run` command and browse the URL displayed or debug through VS Code or Visual Studio, we will get a 404 page. This is expected as we are building a Web API and there is no **user interface (UI)** associated with the API. You can type `/swagger` in the browser address bar and it will display the Swagger/OpenAPI UI. **Swagger** is a documentation tool/framework that helps to document the APIs, and we can use it for testing the API endpoints as well. (Swagger has now changed its name to OpenAPI.) In earlier versions of ASP.NET Core, we had to enable Swagger explicitly by adding different **NuGet** packages. But from ASP.NET Core 3.1 onward, Swagger is enabled by default. The Swagger documentation helps to generate client libraries and helps to expose the API in various **API management solutions** such as **Azure API Management**, and exposes APIs to other Azure services and other applications. If you look into the code, you will see that Swagger is only enabled in a **development** environment.

Here is a screenshot of the Swagger UI:

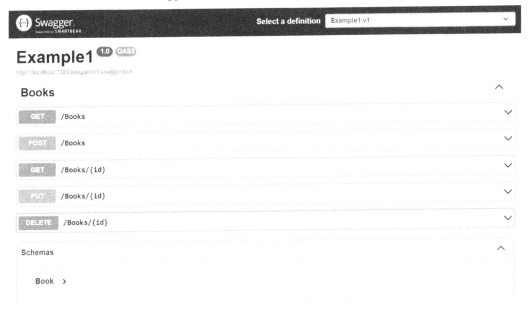

Figure 7.11 – Swagger/OpenAPI UI

Next, we will implement the first method – Get() - /AddressBook endpoint. In the Get action method, we can implement the following code:

```
[HttpGet]
public IActionResult Get()
{
    var addressBookDbContextOptions = new
DbContextOptionsBuilder<AddressBookDbContext>()
        .UseSqlServer("<your-azure-database-connection-string>").
Options;
    using var addressBookDbContext = new
AddressBookDbContext(addressBookDbContextOptions);
    var addresses = addressBookDbContext.Addresses.ToList();
    return Ok(addresses);
}
```

In the code, we are first building the `DbContextOptions` object, which is required as the constructor parameter for the `DbContext` class. While building the `DbContextOptions` class, we will be able to specify which database we are using and any other properties associated with that – the connection string in the current code. Once you implement the code, run the app again and browse for the `/AddressBook` endpoint or `/Swagger` endpoint, click on the **GET /AddressBook** endpoint downward arrow and click on the **Try it out** button:

Figure 7.12 – Swagger UI | AddressBook endpoint

Clicking on the **Try it out** button will display another button, **Execute**, and you can click on the **Execute** button to invoke the endpoint. If you invoke the endpoint, you will get a SQL exception. This exception appears because of a security feature in SQL Server.

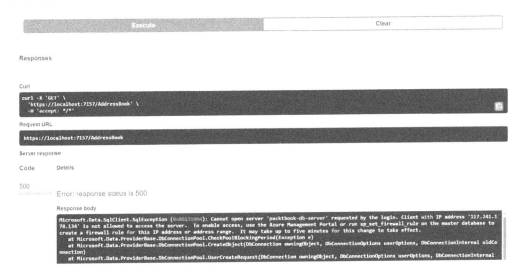

Figure 7.13 – SQL exception

> **Important note**
> You can get the connection string from your SQL Server Database **Overview** page in the portal. If you need to reset your password, go to the SQL Server **Overview** page.

You can fix this issue by adding your development machine IP address to the firewall configuration of Azure SQL Server. To do this, open the Azure portal, select the SQL server you would like to connect to, and select the **Networking** menu, as shown in *Figure 7.14*. Scroll to the **Firewall rules** section, and you will see there is an option called **Add your client IPv4 address** (your IP address). This will add a firewall rule – incoming traffic from the IP address will be allowed:

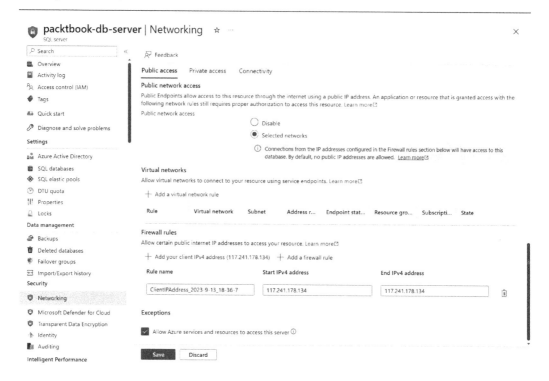

Figure 7.14 – Firewall rules configuration for Azure SQL Server

You can select the **Allow Azure services and resources to access this server** option as well. This will make sure that when you deploy your application in **Azure App Service** or **Azure Functions**, you don't need to configure firewall rules for the applications with the IP addresses associated with the Azure resources. Click on the checkbox and then click on **Save**. You can do the same with the Azure CLI as well. Here is the Azure CLI command to add any IP address to the SQL Server firewall rule:

```
> az sql server firewall-rule create --name mydevmachineip --resource-
group PacktBook --server packtbook-db-server  --end-ip-address
117.207.233.237 --start-ip-address 117.207.233.237
```

Once it is updated, run the app and invoke the /AddressBook endpoint again. This time, you will get a different exception – invalid object name Addresses – because we didn't create any Addresses table in the database. To do this, click on the **Query editor (preview)** menu item in the SQL Server Database; you will need to log in with your password. Once you have logged in, you will be able to execute any SQL queries in the editor.

Here is the SQL code to create the Addresses table in the SQL server:

```
CREATE TABLE Addresses
(
    Id INT PRIMARY KEY IDENTITY(1,1),
```

```
    [Name] NVARCHAR(MAX),
    [Email] NVARCHAR(MAX),
    [CreatedOn] DATETIME DEFAULT GETUTCDATE()
)
```

We will learn how to use EF Core migrations to create the **database schema** in the next section. When the table is created, invoke the endpoint again and we will see an empty result. So, we are able to successfully connect and query the Azure SQL database from an ASP.NET Core Web API project. We can add one or two addresses and execute the endpoint again and we will be able to see the results as JSON. We can create addresses with the following SQL query:

```
INSERT INTO [dbo].[Addresses]
(
[Name], [Email]
)
VALUES
(
'User 1', 'user1@example.com'
),
(
'User 2', 'user2@example.com'
)
GO
```

Execute the preceding code in the Query editor to insert two addresses into the database. Next, we can execute /Get endpoint to read all the addresses from the database using EF Core.

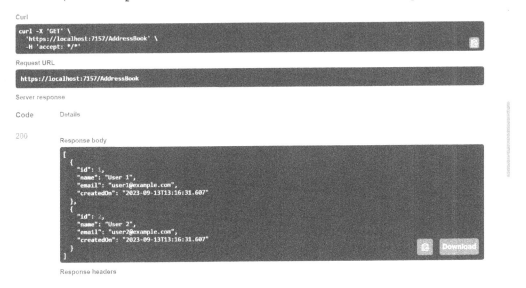

Figure 7.15 – Get endpoint results in the Swagger UI

Now we have implemented the Get endpoint and fetched records from the database. If we look into the implementation, we are creating an instance of the AddressBookDbContext class inside the Get method – which is not good because it creates a tight coupling between the controller and the AddressBookDbContext class. It also makes it harder to test the Controller class. To fix this issue, we are using a pattern called **dependency injection**. In this pattern, the dependency (in this scenario, the instance of the AddressBookDbContext class) will be provided to the method by the runtime or framework. So, the method can use the instance, and there is no need to take care of the instance creation logic. There are three types of dependency injection methods available – **constructor injection**, **property injection**, and **interface injection**. In ASP.NET Core, dependency injection is available out of the box – we don't need to install any other third-party libraries. ASP.NET Core uses the constructor injection type. So, in the Controller class, we can create a constructor with the AddressBookDbContext parameter and the framework will inject the AddressBookDbContext class.

So, let's create a constructor with the AddressBookDbContext parameter and modify the Get method as well. Here is the updated code:

```
public class AddressBookController: ControllerBase
{
    private readonly AddressBookDbContext _addressBookDbContext;
    public AddressBookController(AddressBookDbContext
addressBookDbContext)
    {
        _addressBookDbContext = addressBookDbContext;
    }
    [HttpGet]
    public IActionResult Get()
    {
        var addresses = _addressBookDbContext.Addresses.ToList();
        return Ok(addresses);
    }
}
```

In the HTTP GET – Get method, we can remove the AddressBookDbContext instance creation logic. Then, we can use the class-level AddressBookDbContext object in the Get method. Next, we need to configure the ASP.NET Core to inject AddressBookDbContext into the Controller constructor. We can do this by modifying the Program.cs class and adding the following code:

```
var builder = WebApplication.CreateBuilder(args);
builder.Services.AddDbContext<AddressBookDbContext>(options =>
    options.UseSqlServer("<your Azure Sql server connection
string>"));
builder.Services.AddControllers();
```

Currently, the connection string is hardcoded in the code; the best practice is to read it from the configuration. So, let's modify the appsettings.json file and add the following code:

```
"ConnectionStrings": {
  "AddressBookDb": "<Your Azure Sql Server connection string>"
}
```

Let's also modify the Program.cs file with the GetConnectionString method of the builder.Configuration object, which returns the connection string from the configuration file. The advantage of this method is that we can switch the configuration from appsettings.json to **Azure App Service** configuration or any other configuration provider:

```
var builder = WebApplication.CreateBuilder(args);
builder.Services.AddDbContext<AddressBookDbContext>(options
=>options.UseSqlServer(builder.Configuration.
GetConnectionString("AddressBookDb")));
builder.Services.AddControllers();
```

Now, let's run the application and verify the changes again – we should get the same results. Next, we will modify the other controller methods. First, we will implement the GetById method – this method returns an address from the database with the specified ID. If Address is not found, the controller returns a NotFound result. So far, we have implemented the Get method and looked at how to use dependency injection to access the database context. We will implement all the CRUD methods using the database context so that we can learn how to use C# to interact with the database.

Here is the implementation of the CRUD methods:

```
private readonly AddressBookDbContext _addressBookDbContext;
public AddressBookController(AddressBookDbContext
addressBookDbContext)
{
    _addressBookDbContext = addressBookDbContext;
}
[HttpGet]
public IActionResult Get()
{
    var addresses = _addressBookDbContext.Addresses.ToList();
    return Ok(addresses);
}
[HttpGet("{id}")]
public IActionResult GetById(int id)
{
    var address = _addressBookDbContext.Addresses.Find(id);
    if (address == null)
    {
```

```
        return NotFound();
    }
    return Ok(address);
}
```

In the preceding code, we are implementing the GET method – which is the READ operation in CRUD. The first GET method without any parameter returns all the addresses – it reads the Addresses table from the database using the EF Core database context, converts the data to a list, and returns Ok(). The Ok() method will return the Book list with an ok - HTTP 200 status response. The second GET method, with the id parameter, checks for the book with the ID and, if found, returns the book with an Ok – HTTP 200 status. If not found, it returns a Not Found – HTTP 404 status. The Address.Find method accepts the key of the table and returns the data if available. The following code implements the HTTP POST (create), HTTP PUT (update), and HTTP DELETE (delete) methods in the CRUD operations:

```
[HttpPost]
public IActionResult Post(Address address)
{
    _addressBookDbContext.Addresses.Add(address);
    _addressBookDbContext.SaveChanges();
    return CreatedAtAction(nameof(GetById), new { id = address.Id },
address);
}
```

The preceding method – Post – helps us to create an Address in the database. In the code, the Address object from the HTTP request body, ASP.NET Core run time, will process the input and invoke the method with the Address object as the parameter will be added to the DbContext class and DbSet property and to save the data, the SaveChanges method will be invoked – this method will commit the changes to the database. This is the create operation in the CRUD operations.

Next, we will learn about PUT – which is the update operation in the CRUD operations. This is a little complex compared to other methods. In the implementation, we will receive the book ID as the parameter we would like to update and the updated Book object. In the code, we will check that the ID of the book and the provided ID are the same – if not, we will return a Bad Request - HTTP 400 status response. Then, we will search for the book with the ID and if it is not found, it will return a Not Found – HTTP 404 status. If found, we will update the Book object and invoke the SaveChanges method to save the updated Book to the database:

```
[HttpPut("{id}")]
public IActionResult Put(int id, Address address)
{
    if (id != address.Id)
    {
        return BadRequest();
```

```
    }
    var existingAddress = _addressBookDbContext.Addresses.Find(id);
    if (existingAddress == null)
    {
        return NotFound();
    }
existingAddress.Name = address.Name;
existingAddress.Email = address.Email;
    _addressBookDbContext.Update(existingAddress);
    _addressBookDbContext.SaveChanges();
    return NoContent();
}
```

In the example, we used simple mapping; for a big object or complex object mapping, we can use a third-party mapping utility, such as the Automapper NuGet package. Based on REST API standards, after the Update method, we should not return a NoContent status. So, a No Content – HTTP 204 status response will be sent to the client. Next, we will learn about the Delete implementation, which helps to remove a book from the database. Similar to Update, the Delete operation also accepts the ID and checks for the book with the ID in the database. If not found, it returns a Not Found – HTTP 404 status response. If found, it removes the Book object and SaveChanges will commit the changes to the database:

```
[HttpDelete("{id}")]
public IActionResult Delete(int id)
{
    var book = _addressBookDbContext.Addresses.Find(id);
    if (book == null)
    {
        return NotFound();
    }
    _addressBookDbContext.Addresses.Remove(book);
    _addressBookDbContext.SaveChanges();
    return NoContent();
}
```

This operation also returns a No Content – HTTP 204 status response after success. After each of the operations, you need to call the SaveChanges() method to commit the change to the database.

> **Important note**
>
> If you're building a web application instead of writing the same CRUD operation code every time, Visual Studio and the dotnet CLI offers an option to generate code, controllers, Web API, **Model-View-Controller** (**MVC**), and Views. It is called **scaffolding**. You can find more information about this here: `https://learn.microsoft.com/en-us/aspnet/core/fundamentals/tools/dotnet-aspnet-codegenerator?view=aspnetcore-6.0`.

In the upcoming subsections, we will learn about EF Core migrations – this will help us to create and deploy database changes using C# code.

EF Core migrations

In the last section, we created a table by writing our own SQL statements. EF Core migrations will help you to generate C# and SQL scripts for the database changes and implementations so that you don't need to write any SQL statements – creating and maintaining the database schema will be managed by EF Core. To create migrations, first, we need to install the `dotnet` tool. If you're using Visual Studio, you can create migrations using PowerShell as well. I am using the `dotnet` tool in this chapter. To install the `dotnet` tool, we need to execute the following command:

```
> dotnet tool install --global dotnet-ef
```

If the tool is already installed, you can use the following command to update it:

```
> dotnet tool update --global dotnet-ef
```

Once it is installed or updated, you can execute the following command to learn about different options and commands:

```
> dotnet ef --help
```

Next, we need to make sure we're referencing the `Microsoft.EntityFrameworkCore.Design` NuGet package. Otherwise, we won't be able to create the migrations.

To create migrations, open the folder in your Terminal and execute the following command:

```
> dotnet ef migrations add Chapter7Migrations1
```

This command will build the project and create a folder called `Migrations`. Inside this folder, it will create three C# files. To apply migrations, execute the following command:

```
> dotnet ef database update
```

This command will create the database and tables based on the migration. Inside the `Migrations` folder, there will be a class with the migration name, which inherits from the `Migration` class.

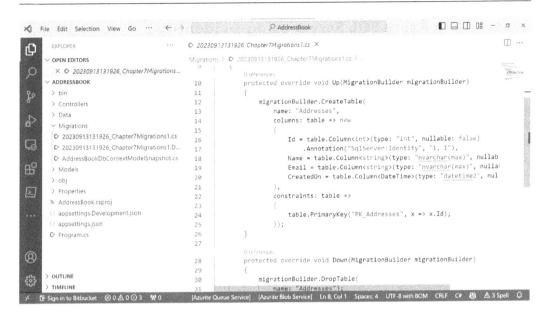

Figure 7.16: Migrations folder and files

Inside the class, there will be two methods – Up and Down. The Up method will be invoked when we apply a migration to the database. We can see the SQL script from the migrations using the following command:

```
> dotnet ef migrations script
```

The preceding command will print out the SQL script that will be generated and executed while we execute the dotnet ef database update command. Before executing the command, make sure you delete the existing Addresses table from the database.

In this section, we learned about working with Azure SQL Database from ASP.NET Core and C#. We learned about the database context class and how to use the dependency injection pattern to inject the database context object into the controller. We also implemented CRUD operations in the ASP.NET Core Web API. We also explored EF Core migrations, which help us to create database schema and tables in the database with the help of the database context class. In the next section, we will explore how to connect to SQL Server without a connection string – a more secure way – by using **identities**.

Configuring security in Azure SQL Database

In an earlier section, we learned about connecting to Azure SQL Database with ASP.NET Core code. In this section, we will learn about various ways to configure security in Azure SQL Database.

We will look at two main options. First, we will look into how to connect to Azure SQL using an identity and then we will look into firewall configuration.

Connecting to Azure SQL Server using an identity

In an earlier section, we connected to Azure SQL Server with a username and password, but Microsoft's recommended option to connect to Azure SQL is using identities – a feature that allows services to interact with each other without credentials. There are two types of identities available in Azure. The first one is system-assigned and the second one is user-assigned. System-assigned identities are removed when you remove the associated resource, which means that if we are creating a system-assigned identity for an Azure app service, the identity will be removed when you remove the app service. In the case of user-assigned managed identities, they can be used with multiple Azure resources – so we need to remove them explicitly.

Working with system-assigned managed identities

In this section, we will be creating system-assigned managed identities. To work with identities, first, we need to create an Azure app service. To create an app service, we need to create an **Azure App Service plan**:

```
> az appservice plan create --name PacktBookChapter7 --resource-group
PacktBook --sku FREE
```

By executing the preceding command, we are creating an Azure App Service plan with the Free SKU. Next, we create the Azure app service with the App Service plan using the following command:

```
> az webapp create --name PacktIdentityDemoWebApp --resource-group
PacktBook --plan PacktBookChapter7
```

This command will create an Azure app service with the Free App Service plan. Now we can deploy the Web API app – which will connect to SQL Server using a system-assigned managed identity. To deploy the Web API app, from Visual Studio, you can right-click and choose **Publish**, or from VS Code, with the Azure extension, log in to your Azure account and select **App Service** and **Publish**. Since I am using the command line, I am publishing the app using the dotnet CLI command and publishing to Azure using the Azure CLI. To publish the app, execute the following command:

```
> dotnet publish --configuration Release --output ./publish
```

In the preceding command, we are publishing the Web API project with release configuration and the output of the publish action will be copied to the publish folder.

To deploy to the Azure app service, we are using the **ZIP deployment** method. In this deployment method, we need to compress the publish folder to a ZIP archive and use that ZIP archive as a publishing artifact. Here is the command to compress a folder to a ZIP archive in PowerShell:

```
> Compress-Archive -Path .\publish\* -DestinationPath publish.zip
```

Once it is compressed, we can execute the following command to publish this ZIP file as the web app source:

```
> az webapp deployment source config-zip --src .\publish.zip --name
PacktIdentityDemoWebApp --resource-group PacktBook
```

Next, we need to configure the Web API to connect to Azure SQL Server. Here, I am using the Azure CLI to do the configuration change. Here is the command to configure the connection string to the app service:

```
> az webapp config connection-string set --connection-string-type
SQLAzure --resource-group PacktBook --name PacktIdentityDemoWebApp
--settings ConnectonStrings__Example1Db="YOUR_SQLAZURE_
CONNECTIONSTRING"
```

Now, if you browse the /AddressBook endpoint, it should return a 200 status code with information about two addresses in JSON format.

To use the identity, you need to configure the Azure App Service identity, modify the Azure SQL Database configuration to use the App Service identity, and finally, modify the connection string.

To enable the identity, navigate to Azure App Service and click on the **Identity** menu (*Figure 7.17*). Change the **Status** toggle from **Off** to **On** and save the change:

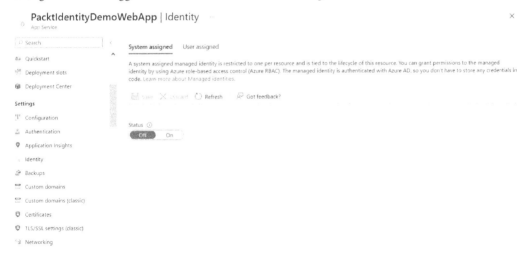

Figure 7.17 – Azure App Service | Enabling a system-assigned identity

Once you click on **Save**, the Azure portal will show a confirmation dialog; select **Yes** in the prompt. After the changes are saved, it will display an **Object (principal) ID** value, which we can use while assigning the identity to SQL Server.

Figure 7.18 – Azure App Service | Enabled system-assigned identity

Next, navigate to the SQL Server resource and select the **Azure Active Directory** option, as shown in the following figure:

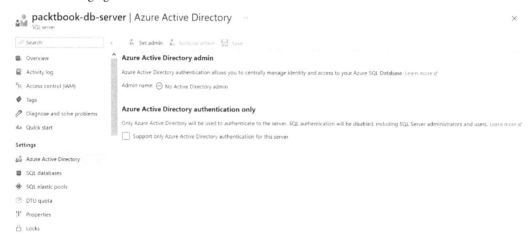

Figure 7.19 – Azure SQL Server | Enabling Active Directory admin

Then, click on the **Set admin** button, which will display an Azure Active Directory search option. We can use the object ID from the app service and paste it into the search textbox; this will display the Azure App Service name. Click on the name and then the **Select** button at the bottom.

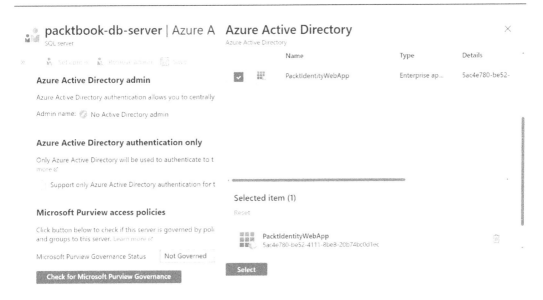

Figure 7.20 – Azure Active Directory – Search window

Then, click on the **Save** button. Once it is completed, we can modify the connection string like this:

```
Server=tcp:packtbook-db-server.database.windows.
net,1433;Authentication
=Active Directory Default; Database=chapter7;MultipleActiveResultSets
=False;Encrypt=True;TrustServerCertificate=False;Connection
Timeout=30;
```

Unlike the earlier connection string, we are not using any user credentials here. From the actual connection string, we removed the user ID and password values and replaced them with the `Authentication` option. Now, let us update the connection string like this in the app service and confirm whether it is working properly or not. Here is the command that will update the connection string for the Azure app service using the Azure CLI:

```
az webapp config connection-string set --connection-string-type
SQLAzure --resource-group PacktBook --name PacktIdentityDemoWebApp
--settings ConnectonStrings__Example1Db="Server=tcp:packtbook-db-
server.database.windows.net,1433;Authentication=Active Directory
Default; Database=chapter7;MultipleActiveResultSets=False;
Encrypt=True;TrustServerCertificate=False;Connection Timeout=30;"
```

Please note that we are using the updated connection string without the credentials hardcoded.

In the preceding section, we are configuring the identity as SQL Server admin. In production scenarios, the application doesn't require database management permissions or admin privileges. In this section, we will learn how to configure the identity to use only the permissions required to perform read and write operations on the database. To implement this, first, we need to create a user in Azure Active Directory. We can run the following command:

```
> az ad user create --display-name packtuser --password Password@123
--user-principal-name packtuser@yourazureaddomin.onmicrosoft.com
```

With the preceding command, we create a user in Azure AD with the display name packtuser, the password Password@123, and the user principal name packtuser@yourazureaddomin. onmicrosoft.com. This name uniquely identifies the user in our Azure Active Directory, so we should set it with the Azure Active Directory domain.

Next, we need to assign this user as SQL admin as we did earlier. Alternatively, we can execute the following commands, which will get the user ID and assign it as an admin user in SQL Server:

```
> $azureaduser=(az ad user list --filter "userPrincipalName eq
'packtuser@yourazureaddomin.onmicrosoft.com'" --query '[].id' --output
tsv)
> az sql server ad-admin create --resource-group PacktBook --server-
name packtbook-db-server --display-name ADMIN --object-id $azureaduser
```

The first command will get the user ID and the second command will assign the user as administrator in Azure SQL Server.

Next, we need to connect to Azure SQL Server with the credentials and execute a few SQL statements to grant permissions to Azure App Service. We can use any SQL Server management tool to connect with the server. For simplicity, I am using the SQLCMD utility. We can execute the following command in the Terminal, which will connect to SQL Server with Azure AD authentication:

```
> sqlcmd -S packtbook-db-server.database.windows.net -d
Chapter7CliDemo -U "packtuser@yourazureaddomin.onmicrosoft.com'" -P
"Password@123" -G -l 30
```

Once we have logged in successfully, we need to execute the following SQL commands. If there are any login failures, check that your machine IP has been added to the SQL Server as we did earlier in this chapter and that the credentials are correct:

```
CREATE USER [PacktIdentityDemoWebApp] FROM EXTERNAL PROVIDER;
ALTER ROLE db_datareader ADD MEMBER [PacktIdentityDemoWebApp];
ALTER ROLE db_datawriter ADD MEMBER [PacktIdentityDemoWebApp];
GO
```

The first SQL query creates a user in the SQL server. Since we enabled the system-managed identity, we need to use the application name as the username. Next, we assign different roles to the user. The db_datareader role helps to read data from tables and views. The db_datawriter role helps to perform write operations, such as `insert`, `update`, and `delete`. For our use case – CRUD operations – only these two roles are required. If the application requires more permissions, we need to add them.

Finally, we can update the connection string as we did earlier in this section and connect to SQL Server from our application.

You can find more details about managed identities and connecting to Azure SQL here: `https://learn.microsoft.com/en-us/azure/app-service/tutorial-connect-msi-sql-database?tabs=windowsclient%2Cefcore%2Cdotnet`.

In this section, we learned how to connect to Azure SQL Server from Azure App Service without SQL Server credentials. We also explored how to create an App Service plan and app service, how to deploy App Service from the local machine, and how to configure the connection string using the Azure CLI. We also learned how we can use the identity feature with more security.

Configuring an Azure SQL firewall

By default, when we create an Azure SQL server, public access will be disabled, which means other applications can't access it. To access the database from other applications, we need to enable the **Selected networks** option and configure the firewall rules.

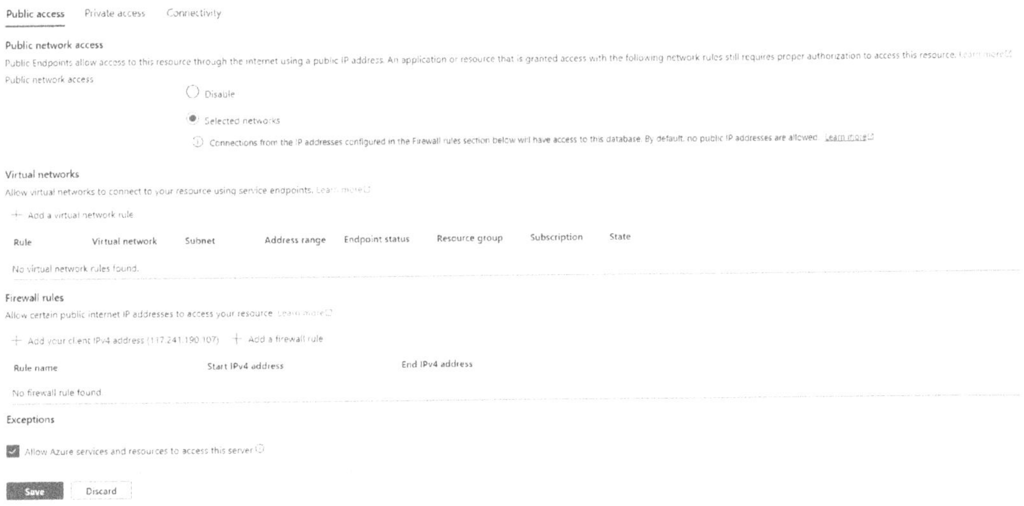

Figure 7.21 – Configuring Azure SQL Server networking

Once we enable the **Selected networks** option, we can select the **Allow Azure services and resources to access this server** checkbox, which will help other Azure resources to access the SQL server. If we want to configure specific resources, we need to add the IP addresses in **Firewall rules**. We can find the IP addresses of the Azure app service from the **Networking** tab, then select the outbound IP addresses and add them to the Azure SQL server.

Configuring the Azure SQL Server private endpoint

In the previous sections, we learned how to configure security for our Azure SQL database. But we are exposing the SQL server to the internet – by enabling the **Allow Azure services and resources to access this server** setting, any other app service in the same region can access the SQL server if they know the SQL server connection string. We can make the SQL server more secure by disabling public access and configuring private access. To achieve this, we will configure a **virtual network** (**VNet**) in Azure, configure a subnet inside the VNet for the SQL server, configure a private endpoint, and disable public access in the server. We need to configure VNet integration in Azure App Service to access the SQL server.

Here is the simplified architecture of the implementation:

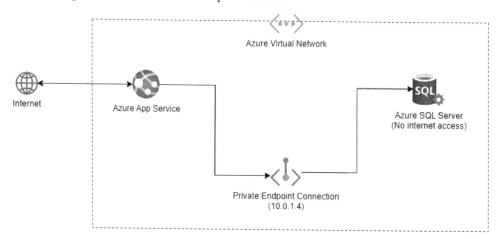

Figure 7.22 – SQL Server private endpoint architecture

To configure the private endpoint connection, we need an Azure VNet. This is an isolated cloud network that lets you securely run your Azure resources with controlled IP addressing and communication. We will be creating all the Azure resources in this section using the Azure CLI:

1. First, open your favorite Terminal window and log in to your Azure account using the `az login` command.

2. Once logged in, execute the following command to create an Azure resource group:

    ```
    > az group create --location "East US" --name "PacktBook"
    ```

    This command will create a resource group in the East US region with the name `PacktBook`.

3. Next, execute the following command to create an Azure VNet inside this resource group:

    ```
    > az network VNet create --resource-group PacktBook --name
    Chapter07
    ```

    This command will create an Azure VNet with the name `Chapter07`. We can specify the IP address range for the Azure VNet; if not specified, it will take the default one, which is `10.0.0.0/16`.

4. To configure the private endpoint, next, we need to configure a subnet. In a VNet, a subnet is a segmented IP address range that allows you to organize and control network traffic, helping to isolate and manage resources within the network. In this case, we are creating a subnet for the SQL server:

```
> az network VNet subnet create --name sql --resource-group
PacktBook --VNet-name Chapter07 --address-prefixes 10.0.1.0/24
```

We need to specify the address prefixes for this command, so I am using the IP 10.0.1.0/24 – this will create a subnet for the SQL server inside the Azure VNet.

5. We need to create an Azure private endpoint next. This is a network interface that establishes a private and secure connection to a service enabled by Azure Private Link. Utilizing a private IP address from your VNet essentially integrates the service within your VNet. This configuration ensures that data traffic between your VNet and the service is routed through Microsoft's internal network infrastructure, eliminating the need to expose your service to the public internet for added security. We can create an Azure private endpoint with the following Azure CLI command:

```
> az network private-endpoint create  --name
sqlprivatendpoint  --resource-group PacktBook --VNet-name
Chapter07 --subnet sql --private-connection-resource-id
$sqlserverId  --group-ids sqlServer  --connection-name
sqlconnection
```

6. In the preceding command, we are creating the Azure private endpoint with the resource group we created and the $sqlserverrId variable – which is the ID of the SQL server we created. We can get the value by executing the following command in PowerShell:

```
> $sqlserverId = (az sql server list --resource-group PacktBook
--query '[].[id]' --output tsv)
```

This command will query the IDs of SQL servers in the resource group and return the value as tab-separated. In this case, there is only one SQL server created in the resource group; if multiple servers are there, we need to execute the command and set the $sqlserverrId variable.

7. To complete the Azure private endpoint configuration for the SQL Server, we need to configure a private DNS zone. This allows for the resolution of custom domain names to private IP addresses within a VNet. This means that when you access Azure services through a private endpoint, such as Azure Storage or Azure SQL Database, the DNS resolution occurs privately within your VNet, enhancing security by avoiding public internet exposure and enabling you to use custom domain names for resource access, making it simpler for users and applications to interact with Azure resources. We need to execute the following commands to create a private DNS zone, associate it with an Azure private endpoint, and create a link between the private DNS zone and the VNet:

```
> az network private-dns zone create --resource-group
PacktBook  --name "privatelink.database.windows.net"
> az network private-dns link VNet create --resource-group
PacktBook --zone-name "privatelink.database.windows.net"  --name
appsqllink --virtual-network Chapter07 --registration-enabled
false
```

```
> az network private-endpoint dns-zone-group create  --resource-
group PacktBook --endpoint-name sqlprivatendpoint --name
appsqlzone --private-dns-zone "privatelink.database.windows.net"
--zone-name sqle
```

8. Finally, we need to disable public access to the SQL server. We can do this by executing the following command:

```
> az sql server update -n "packtbook-db-server" -g PacktBook
--set publicNetworkAccess="Disabled"
```

Now we have completely secured the SQL server.

9. Now, to configure Azure App Service to connect to the SQL server, we need to configure the VNet integration of Azure App Service. Without configuring the VNet integration, if we try to access the SQL server, we will get a **SQL server not available** error. To configure the VNet integration, we need to first create a subnet for the app service and then enable VNet integration in Azure App Service:

```
> az network VNet subnet create --name app --resource-group
PacktBook --VNet-name Chapter07 --address-prefixes 10.0.0.0/24
> az webapp VNet-integration add --resource-group PacktBook
--name chapter6-packt-web --VNet Chapter07 --subnet app
```

Now, both App Service and SQL Server are in the same Azure VNet, and Azure App Service will be able to access SQL Server without any configuration or code changes.

Summary

In this chapter, we learned about Azure SQL Server and Azure SQL Database, the two different relational database offerings from Azure. This will help you to choose which database type you need to select for a business problem. We learned how to provision Azure SQL databases using the Azure CLI, the Azure portal, and Azure ARM templates, giving you an understanding of a variety of different ways to create and configure Azure SQL Database. Next, we learned about Entity Framework – an ORM framework that helps to interact with SQL Server from ASP.NET Core. In that section, we implemented CRUD operations using the ASP.NET Web API and Entity Framework. We learned about the dependency injection pattern and how it can be used in ASP.NET Core. We also briefly explored EF Core migrations. Finally, we learned about Azure identities, how to create a system-assigned identity, and how identities can be used in Azure SQL Server.

In the next chapter, you will learn about **Azure Cosmos DB**, which is a **NoSQL database** offering from Microsoft Azure. We will learn about provisioning and configuring Azure Cosmos DB and how to connect to Cosmos DB from an ASP.NET Core web application.

8

Creating Documents via .NET for Azure Cosmos DB

Azure Cosmos DB is a powerful **NoSQL database service** that provides **.NET** developers with high flexibility, scalability, and performance for building modern, cloud-based applications. This chapter aims to provide .NET developers with a comprehensive understanding of Cosmos DB by introducing fundamental concepts, demonstrating data storage and retrieval, walking through the steps required to create a new Cosmos DB account, and highlighting essential configuration options.

Our guidance also includes how to query and manage data in Cosmos DB using the **.NET SDK**, along with tips and best practices for optimizing performance and developing with Cosmos DB. We emphasize the importance of adhering to guidelines and best practices when developing and managing Cosmos DB accounts. This includes tips for using Cosmos DB in production environments, such as the importance of monitoring and alerting and proper **disaster recovery planning**.

We also guide performance and scaling, covering the different performance characteristics of Cosmos DB, including **throughput**, **latency**, and **storage**. We explain how to configure and scale a Cosmos DB account to meet your application's needs, with examples of optimizing performance for various workloads.

Finally, we offer guidance on developing with Cosmos DB, including how to use the .NET SDK to create, read, update, and delete data in Cosmos DB and design and implement efficient data access patterns. We also cover **server-side programming** for stored **procedures**, **triggers**, **user-defined functions**, and how to implement logging for app insights in Cosmos DB.

In this chapter, we will cover the following topics:

- Introduction to Azure Cosmos DB
- Explaining containers in Azure Cosmos DB
- Understanding partition keys in Azure Cosmos DB

- Exploring indexes in Azure Cosmos DB

- Creating an Azure Cosmos DB database with the Azure CLI

- Querying and managing data in Azure Cosmos DB with the .NET SDK

- Performance and scaling in Azure Cosmos DB

- Developing with Azure Cosmos DB

Introduction to Azure Cosmos DB

In today's digital landscape, where data is generated at an unprecedented pace, the need for scalable and efficient database solutions has never been greater. **Azure Cosmos DB** is a groundbreaking NoSQL database service offered by Microsoft. Traditional relational databases have served us well, but a new approach was required with the surge in unstructured and semi-structured data. This is where NoSQL databases such as Azure Cosmos DB step in. These databases are designed to handle large volumes of diverse data types without sacrificing performance. They use flexible data models, making them ideal for applications that demand agility and scalability. At the heart of Azure Cosmos DB lies its unique distributed architecture. Unlike traditional databases that rely on a single server, Cosmos DB embraces a distributed model that spans multiple regions and offers global data distribution. This ensures high availability, low latency, and fault tolerance, making it a go-to choice for applications requiring constant uptime.

One of the most remarkable aspects of Azure Cosmos DB is its ability to provide various data consistency levels. From strong consistency, where data is guaranteed to be synchronized across all regions, to eventual consistency, which allows for the highest availability, Cosmos DB empowers developers to choose the level that aligns with their application's requirements. Gone are the days when developers had to choose between relational, document, key-value, or graph databases. Azure Cosmos DB supports multiple data models under a single service. This means you can work with your data in the way that makes the most sense for your application without the constraints of a one-size-fits-all approach. Imagine having your data accessible to users around the world with minimal effort. Azure Cosmos DB makes this a reality through its global distribution capabilities. By replicating data across regions of your choice, you can provide low-latency access to users regardless of their geographical location. Scalability is a cornerstone of modern applications, and Azure Cosmos DB takes this to heart. With tunable throughput, you can adjust resources based on workload demands. This dynamic scaling ensures optimal performance during peak and off-peak times, all while optimizing costs.

Azure Cosmos DB seamlessly integrates with various Azure services, enhancing its capabilities and making it an even more attractive choice for developers. Whether you are building web applications, IoT solutions, or AI-driven systems, combined with other Azure offerings, it can streamline your development process. Effective management of databases requires robust monitoring and insights. Azure Cosmos DB offers detailed telemetry and diagnostics, allowing you to gain deep insights into your database's performance and usage patterns. This proactive approach empowers you to optimize your application's performance.

In a world driven by data, the efficiency and scalability of your database solution can make or break your application's success. Azure Cosmos DB's revolutionary approach to database management, with its distributed architecture, multi-model support, and global distribution capabilities, empowers developers to create high-performing and responsive applications that cater to a global audience. By embracing the fundamental concepts discussed in this chapter, you will be well equipped to unlock the full potential of Azure Cosmos DB and stay ahead in the rapidly evolving digital landscape. In the upcoming section, we will explain containers in Azure Cosmos DB and work through examples utilizing the .NET SDK.

Azure Cosmos DB offers multiple API modalities to cater to various data storage and querying needs. Each modality provides unique features and benefits for different application scenarios. Let's have a comprehensive overview of the available modalities.

The Document API (SQL API)

The Document API, also known as the SQL API, is the most commonly used modality in Azure Cosmos DB. It is designed to work with JSON documents and provides a schema-less data model. Here is how it works:

- **Data model**: The Document API stores data as JSON documents. Each document can have different attributes, and there is no fixed schema that documents must adhere to.

- **Partitioning**: Documents are partitioned based on a specified partition key. This key determines how data is distributed across logical partitions within the Cosmos DB cluster.

- **SQL queries**: You can perform SQL-like queries using the Document (SQL API). This allows you to perform powerful queries on your data using familiar syntax.

- **Scaling**: Azure Cosmos DB offers automatic scaling of throughput and storage. You can scale up or down based on your application's demands.

- **Global distribution**: Cosmos DB allows you to replicate data across multiple regions to ensure low-latency access for users worldwide.

- **API compatibility**: The Document API provides SDKs for various programming languages, enabling developers to interact with Cosmos DB using their preferred language.

- **Use case**: The Document API is ideal for applications with evolving schemas and complex data structures, where flexibility is crucial. It is suitable for scenarios where data is semi-structured and different documents may have varying attributes.

- **Example**: E-commerce platforms that store product information, user profiles, reviews, and orders. Each of these documents might have different attributes, and the schema can evolve over time.

The Table API

The Table API is designed to provide a NoSQL key-value store similar to Azure Table storage. It is suitable for applications that require a simple schema with entities containing properties. Let's look at it in more detail:

- **Data model**: Data is organized into tables, where each table has rows with keys and associated properties. Each property is a key-value pair.

- **Scalability**: The Table API offers automatic partitioning and scaling of your data based on partition keys.

- **Query language**: While the primary access pattern is point lookups by keys, the Table API also provides a limited query language for range queries and filtering.

- **Global distribution**: Similar to other APIs, you can replicate your data globally to ensure low-latency access.

- **API compatibility**: It provides SDKs for multiple languages for easy integration with your application.

- **Use case**: The Table API is a great choice for applications that require high-speed, key-value access patterns, such as IoT telemetry data or sensor readings.

- **Example**: A sensor network generates a massive volume of timestamped data. Each sensor reading is a key-value pair, and you primarily need to perform quick lookups based on sensor IDs.

The MongoDB API

The **MongoDB API** allows you to use Cosmos DB as if it were a MongoDB database while leveraging Cosmos DB's global distribution and scalability features:

- **Compatibility**: You can run existing MongoDB workloads on Cosmos DB without code changes. Many MongoDB features are supported, but not all, due to differences in underlying architecture.

- **Data storage**: MongoDB documents are stored as JSON in Cosmos DB. The API supports BSON data types used in MongoDB.

- **Indexing**: The MongoDB API supports secondary indexes to optimize query performance.

- **Global distribution**: MongoDB API benefits from Cosmos DB's global distribution and multi-region replication capabilities.

- **Automatic scaling**: Cosmos DB's automatic scaling and provisioning features are available to MongoDB API users.

- **Use case**: The MongoDB API is well suited for applications that are migrating from a MongoDB environment or are designed to work with MongoDB's document model but require global distribution and scalability.

- **Example**: An application built on MongoDB that wants to take advantage of Cosmos DB's global distribution for worldwide availability while maintaining compatibility with their MongoDB query language and application code.

The Gremlin API (Graph API)

The Gremlin API allows you to build and execute graph queries on data stored in Cosmos DB, enabling graph database capabilities:

- **Graph Data Model**: Data is stored as vertices and edges, forming a graph structure. This is suitable for scenarios where relationships between entities are crucial.

- **Gremlin Query Language**: This API supports the Gremlin query language for traversing and querying graph data.

- **Property Graph Model**: It follows the property graph model, where vertices and edges can have properties associated with them.

- **Scalability**: Graph data is partitioned based on partition keys for efficient distribution.

- **Global distribution**: Like other APIs, you can replicate your graph data globally for low-latency access.

- **Use case**: The Gremlin API is perfect for applications that model complex relationships between data entities. It is suited for scenarios where analyzing connections and patterns in data is critical.

- **Example**: A social networking platform that needs to model friendships, followers, posts, and comments. Graph databases excel at representing and querying such intricate relationships.

In all cases, Azure Cosmos DB's global distribution, scalability, and low-latency access are powerful features that can benefit applications across various industries and use cases. It is important to choose the modality that aligns with your application's data model and access patterns to ensure optimal performance and flexibility.

Request units in Cosmos DB

Azure Cosmos DB, Microsoft's globally distributed, multi-model database service, has introduced an innovative way of measuring and billing performance: **Request Units** (**RUs**). As .NET developers dive into the world of Cosmos DB, understanding RUs becomes crucial for optimizing performance and costs. Let us delve into the intricacies of RUs, why they matter, and how they impact application development.

Demystifying RUs

At its core, an RU is a unit of measure representing the resource consumption of database operations. Think of RUs as the "calories" of a database request. Just as we measure food energy in terms of calories, Azure Cosmos DB measures CPU, **Input/Output Operations Per Second** (**IOPS**), and memory in terms of RUs. The beauty of RUs lies in their universality. Whether you are interfacing with Cosmos DB through SQL, MongoDB, Cassandra, Gremlin, or Table APIs, your costs and performance metrics remain consistent, always billed regarding RUs.

Understanding RU charges

There are three distinct modes to consider when attempting to comprehend the RU charges for Azure Cosmos DB. In **provisioned throughput mode**, developers can configure the number of RUs per second in advance. This method provides predictability to assignments with predictable or consistent traffic patterns. In increments of 100 RUs per second, scalability becomes flexible. On the other hand, the **serverless mode** is ideal for irregular or unpredictable workloads. This model has no predetermined RUs; instead, you are charged based exclusively on the number of RUs consumed by each database operation. The **autoscale mode** operates similarly to an "RU on-demand" system. Cosmos DB adjusts the assigned RUs based on actual usage, ensuring optimal performance without the danger of overprovisioning.

The science behind RU consumption

A multitude of factors play a role in determining the RUs consumed by an operation:

- **Item size**: As a rule of thumb, bigger items require more RUs. A 2 KB item consumes fewer RUs than a 5 KB item for similar operations.

- **Indexing**: Cosmos DB automatically indexes items for quicker query resolutions. However, this adds to the RU consumption. If you opt out of indexing, you save RUs at the cost of performance.

- **Item properties**: If you have items with numerous properties, they will naturally consume more RUs during **create, read, update, and delete** (**CRUD**) operations.

- **Query patterns**: Not all queries are born equal. A simple `SELECT` command may consume minimal RUs but introduce joins, multiple predicates, and user-defined functions, and your RU consumption can spike.

- **Consistency levels**: Cosmos DB offers five consistency levels. Opting for strong or bounded staleness levels means you are ensuring a higher degree of data accuracy, but this comes at a cost – twice the RUs for reads compared to more relaxed levels.

Navigating RUs in multi-region setups

When deploying Cosmos DB in multiple regions, understanding RU distribution becomes essential. Here is a simple formula: *Total RUs = RUs per container (R) x Number of regions (N)*. This ensures consistency in performance across regions. If you allocate 1,000 RUs for a container and deploy it across 3 regions, you ensure 1,000 RUs for each region.

Strategizing throughput settings

Let's look at two scenarios, which are setting RUs at the container level and the database level:

- **Container**: By provisioning RUs at the container level, you are ensuring a dedicated performance level for that container. It is ideal for scenarios requiring predictable performance.

- **Database**: When RUs are set at the database level, they are distributed amongst all containers in the database. This is advantageous for multi-tenant applications or when migrating NoSQL databases to Cosmos DB.

Throughput models

Azure Cosmos DB is versatile. You can combine throughput provisioning strategies. Imagine provisioning RUs for an entire database and allocating dedicated RUs for one specific, high-priority container. Other containers would share the database's RUs, but this one has its dedicated performance slice. For .NET developers, understanding Azure Cosmos DB's RUs is not only about cost management; it is also about ensuring optimal application performance. By strategically managing and allocating RUs based on workload, data size, query complexity, and deployment regions, developers can harness the full power of Cosmos DB, ensuring that applications are both performant and cost-effective.

Cosmos DB is the epitome of high-performance data storage and management, and in the next section, we will learn more about how to utilize it by understanding throughput, latency, and RUs.

Performance and scaling in Azure Cosmos DB

Performance and scaling are vital considerations when designing and deploying Cosmos DB applications. In this section, we'll explore the different performance characteristics of Cosmos DB, including **throughput**, **latency**, and **storage**, and discuss how to configure and scale a Cosmos DB account to meet your application's needs.

What are throughput, latency, and RUs in Cosmos DB?

Throughput, latency, and RUs are critical performance metrics in Cosmos DB that determine the speed and efficiency of data access and manipulation. Here's a brief overview of each concept:

- **Throughput:** This refers to the number of RUs that a Cosmos DB account can process per second. RUs measure the computational and storage resources required to perform a particular operation in Cosmos DB.

- **Latency:** This refers to the time a system takes to respond to a request. In the context of Cosmos DB, latency refers to the time it takes for the database to process a request and for the client to receive the response.

- **RUs:** These measure throughput and performance in Cosmos DB. They represent the resources consumed by each operation, such as queries or write operations, and are used to calculate the rate at which operations can be performed.

Having established the definitions of these critical metrics, we will explore strategies to optimize throughput, minimize latency, and efficiently utilize RUs for enhanced Cosmos DB performance in the subsequent section.

Optimizing for throughput in Cosmos DB

To achieve high throughput in Cosmos DB, .NET developers should optimize their data model for their application's specific queries and operations. This involves selecting appropriate **partition keys**, **consistency levels**, and **indexing strategies** to ensure that queries can be executed efficiently and that data can be distributed evenly across partitions. Let's dive in to learn a little more about each of these topics to ensure an optimized throughput in our Cosmos DB:

- **Partition keys**: A partition key divides a container's data into multiple partitions. Cosmos DB automatically partitions data based on the partition key selected by the developer. A good partition key should have high cardinality, be always used in queries, and evenly distribute data across partitions.

- **Consistency levels**: Consistency levels determine how quickly changes made to data in one region are propagated to other regions. By selecting the appropriate consistency level, .NET developers can balance the trade-off between consistency and availability and optimize their data model for the specific requirements of their application.

- **Indexing strategies**: Indexes can be created on specific properties of documents to speed up query execution. .NET developers should ensure that their queries are optimized to use the appropriate indexing strategies to minimize the number of RUs required to execute queries.

- **Scaling throughput**: Developers can scale up or down the throughput of a Cosmos DB account using the Azure portal, the Azure CLI, or the Cosmos DB .NET SDK. By increasing the throughput of an account, developers can ensure that their application can handle more requests per second, whereas decreasing the throughput can save costs.

For throughput in Cosmos DB, we will shift our focus to a key feature of Cosmos DB, which is its latency.

Optimizing for latency in Cosmos DB

To optimize for low latency in Cosmos DB, .NET developers should ensure that their queries are optimized using appropriate indexing strategies and consistency levels. This involves selecting appropriate partition keys, consistency levels, and indexing strategies to ensure that queries can be executed efficiently and that data can be distributed evenly across partitions. The following details are considerations when looking to optimize for latency:

- **Indexing strategies**: Indexes can be created on specific properties of documents to speed up query execution. .NET developers should ensure that their queries are optimized to use the appropriate indexing strategies to minimize the number of RUs required to execute queries.

- **Consistency levels**: Consistency levels determine how quickly changes made to data in one region are propagated to other regions. By selecting the appropriate consistency level, .NET developers can balance the trade-off between consistency and availability and optimize their data model for the specific requirements of their application.

- **Global distribution**: By replicating data across multiple regions, Cosmos DB ensures low-latency access to data from anywhere in the world. .NET developers can use Cosmos DB's global distribution to reduce latency by placing their data closer to users. Moreover, Cosmos DB's multi-master feature empowers developers to write data from any region, enhancing write availability and ensuring seamless data synchronization across all regional replicas. This capability is invaluable for applications requiring high availability and real-time data access from multiple geographies.

Now that we've covered latency and throughput, the last optimization we will worry about is cost. As cloud users and developers, we need to be conscious of how we interact with cloud services. Cosmos DB is efficient but without understanding the fundamentals, rampant usage of RUs will add significant cost fo your system. In the next section, we will discuss how to optimize cost by optimizing RUs.

Optimizing for RUs in Cosmos DB

To optimize for RUs in Cosmos DB, .NET developers should minimize the number of RUs required to execute queries. As discussed earlier, this can be achieved by selecting appropriate consistency levels, indexing strategies, and partition keys.

In addition, .NET developers can optimize for RUs by monitoring their application's RU consumption and scaling their Cosmos DB account appropriately. By increasing or decreasing the RUs of their account, developers can adjust the number of computational resources available and ensure that their application can handle the desired amount of throughput.

Cosmos DB also provides **auto-scaling**, which automatically adjusts the throughput of an account based on the workload. This feature can be helpful for applications with unpredictable traffic patterns or sudden spikes in traffic. While auto-scaling promises performance, it has potential pitfalls, particularly costs. Here's a common scenario: a development team eager to leverage the capabilities of a NoSQL database rushes to adopt Cosmos DB. Drawn by the convenience of auto-scaling, they set it up with a modest upper bound. As the application grows and faces performance hiccups, the upper bound increases, hoping to counteract these performance issues. But soon, the bill arrives, much higher than anticipated. The team is caught in a cycle of escalating costs and performance tuning.

This situation is all too familiar. In many cases, the root issue is more than just the scaling but also the initial design of the database. Sometimes, the application may not even be suitable for a NoSQL model. The rush to adopt newer technologies without a thorough analysis can lead to such mismatches.

Best practices for performance and scaling in Cosmos DB

Here are some best practices for achieving high performance and scaling in Cosmos DB:

- Before migrating to or starting with Cosmos DB, ensure your application is genuinely NoSQL-friendly. Understand the data model and query patterns. Poorly designed databases can lead to inefficient operations, consuming more RUs, and, by extension, incurring higher costs.

- Use the appropriate consistency level for your application's requirements. Strong consistency provides immediate and accurate results but can result in higher latency and lower throughput, while eventual consistency provides high throughput but may result in stale data.

- Optimize your partition keys to distribute data evenly across partitions. This can improve query performance and reduce latency.

- Use appropriate indexing strategies to speed up query execution and minimize the number of RUs required to execute queries.

- Ensure that everyone, from developers to decision-makers, understands the implications of auto-scaling, both in terms of performance and cost.

- Monitor your application's RU consumption and adjust the throughput of your Cosmos DB account as needed to ensure that your application can handle the desired amount of throughput.

- Leverage Cosmos DB's global distribution to reduce latency by placing your data closer to your users.

- Auto-scaling isn't a one-size-fits-all solution. It's essential to understand its nuances. Set realistic upper and lower bounds. Monitor them regularly and adjust them based on actual usage patterns, not just immediate performance issues.

Throughput, latency, and RUs are critical performance metrics in Cosmos DB that determine the speed and efficiency of data access and manipulation. By understanding these concepts and optimizing their data model, indexing strategies, partition keys, and consistency levels, .NET developers can achieve high application performance and scalability.

In addition, by monitoring their application's RU consumption and adjusting the throughput of their Cosmos DB account, developers can ensure that their application can handle the desired amount of throughput.

Continuing with our fundamentals, containers lie at the heart of the Azure Cosmos DB experience, serving as the fundamental units for data storage and management within this powerful globally distributed, multi-model database service. Let's now delve into the intricacies of containers to grasp their significance and optimize your data organization strategies.

Explaining containers in Azure Cosmos DB

Containers in Azure Cosmos DB serve as logical partitions for storing data, but they differ significantly from tables in a relational database. While a table in a **relational database** enforces a uniform structure for all records, a container in Azure Cosmos DB allows for more flexibility. The shared aspect across documents in a container is the partition key, which determines data distribution for scalability. Unlike relational databases, where strict schema adherence is essential, Azure Cosmos DB encourages a more adaptable approach. It's crucial to recognize that transitioning from relational concepts to NoSQL requires a fresh perspective to make informed choices and fully harness the benefits of this flexible data model.

Containers can store various data types, including **documents**, **key-value pairs**, **column-family data**, and **graphs**. Containers can also be partitioned across multiple physical nodes for improved scalability and performance. In Cosmos DB, a container is created within a database account, the top-level container for a Cosmos DB instance. Each container is associated with a specific partition key. This partition key determines how data is distributed and stored across the logical partitions within the Cosmos DB cluster. These logical partitions are managed by the system and influence how data is spread across the physical resources of the underlying infrastructure. While you can't directly control the data distribution on the physical level, the choice of partition key significantly affects how the logical partitions are created, sized, and distributed, thus influencing the overall performance and scalability of your Cosmos DB solution.

Developers can use containers to organize their data based on the application's requirements. For example, a container could be created for each data type the application needs to store, such as customer, product, and order information. The partition key is chosen based on the access pattern of the data, ensuring that data is distributed evenly across partitions and that queries are performed efficiently. One of the key benefits of using containers in Cosmos DB is the flexibility they provide for different types of applications. Containers can store various data types, allowing developers to choose the most appropriate container type for their applications. Additionally, containers can be scaled horizontally across multiple physical nodes, improving performance and scalability.

To create a container in .NET, developers can utilize the **Cosmos DB SDK for .NET**. The SDK provides several APIs for creating, updating, and deleting containers, including the Document API, the Table API, the Gremlin API, Cassandra API, and the MongoDB API.

To create a container, developers must create a Cosmos DB account and database. Then, they can create a new container using the `CreateContainerAsync` method of the `CosmosClient` class. The method takes several parameters, including the ID of the container, the partition key, and the throughput (measured in **RUs per second**, or **RU/s**) allocated to the container.

For example, here's how to create a container using the Document API in .NET:

```
using Microsoft.Azure.Cosmos;
using System.Threading.Tasks;
  string connectionString = "connection-string";
  CosmosClient cosmosClient = new
  CosmosClient(connectionString);
    DatabaseResponse database = await cosmosClient
CreateDatabaseAsync("myDatabase");

   ContainerResponse container = await database database.
CreateContainerAsync("myContainer", "/partitionKey");
```

In this example, the code creates a new `CosmosClient` object and connects to a Cosmos DB account using a connection string. Then, it creates a new database using the `CreateDatabaseAsync` method of the `CosmosClient` class. Finally, it creates a new container using the `CreateContainerAsync` method of the `Database` class, specifying the ID of the container, the partition key, and the throughput (which is optional and defaults to 400 RU/s).

In summary, containers are an essential concept in Azure Cosmos DB, providing a flexible and scalable way to store and manage data. Developers can create containers using the Cosmos DB SDK for .NET and choose the appropriate partition key and throughput to optimize performance and scalability. The next step in understanding Azure Cosmos DB is to learn about items. What they are, how they are stored in containers, why they are important, and much more will be covered in the following section.

Items in Azure Cosmos DB

In Azure Cosmos DB, an **item** is a single piece of data stored within a container. An item can represent a document, a row in a table, or any other type of data that can be stored in Cosmos DB. Items are essential for working with Cosmos DB, as they are the unit of storage and retrieval for the service. When working with items in Cosmos DB, developers can use the Cosmos DB SDK for .NET to create, read, update, and delete items. The SDK provides several APIs for working with items, including the Document API, the Table API, the MongoDB API, and the Gremlin API. Developers can choose the API that best suits their needs based on their programming skills and data model. One of the key benefits of using items in Cosmos DB is the flexibility they provide for different types of data.

In addition, items can be queried and retrieved efficiently using the Cosmos DB SDK for .NET. The SDK provides several APIs for querying data, including the **SQL API**, the MongoDB API, the Gremlin API, **SPARQL**, and the Table API. Developers can choose the API that best suits their needs based on their programming skills and data model. To create an item in .NET, developers need to use the Cosmos DB SDK for .NET. The SDK provides several APIs for creating, reading, updating, and deleting items, including the Document API, which is the most commonly used API for working with items. To create an item using the Document API in .NET, developers need to first create a new instance of the `CosmosClient` class and connect to a Cosmos DB account using a connection string. Then, they can use the `CreateItemAsync` method of the `Container` class to create a new item.

For example, here's how to create a new item using the Document API in .NET:

```
using Microsoft.Azure.Cosmos;
using System.Threading.Tasks;

string connectionString = "connection-string";
CosmosClient cosmosClient = new CosmosClient(connectionString);

string databaseId = "myDatabase";
string containerId = "myContainer";
Container container = cosmosClient.GetContainer(databaseId,
containerId);

dynamic newItem = new { id = "item1", name = "Tamir Al", age = 31 };
ItemResponse<dynamic> response = await container.
CreateItemAsync(newItem);
```

In this example, the code creates a new `CosmosClient` object and connects to a Cosmos DB account using a connection string. Then, it connects to a container using the `GetContainer` method of the `CosmosClient` class. Finally, it creates a new item using the `CreateItemAsync` method of the `Container` class, specifying the item data and receiving an `ItemResponse` object that provides information about the newly created item. If an item with the same ID value (`"item1"` in this case) already exists in the specified container, Cosmos DB will throw a `CosmosException` with a `StatusCode` property set to `409 Conflict`.

In summary, items are an essential concept in Azure Cosmos DB, providing a flexible and efficient way to store and manage data. Developers can use the Cosmos DB SDK for .NET to create, read, update, and delete items and choose the appropriate API based on their programming skills and data model.

Consistency in Azure Cosmos DB

Consistency refers to the level of agreement between replicas of data stored in Cosmos DB. Cosmos DB provides several levels of consistency, including **strong consistency**, **bounded staleness**, **session consistency**, **consistent prefix**, and **eventual consistency**. Consistency levels determine how data is replicated and how consistent the data is across replicas.

Strong consistency ensures that all data replicas are consistent at all times, meaning that all readers will see the latest write. Bounded staleness allows for a delay in consistency between replicas but guarantees that all replicas will eventually be consistent with each other. Session consistency ensures that reads and writes within a session are consistent but may allow for inconsistency between sessions. Consistency levels determine how data is replicated and how consistent the data is across replicas. Finally, eventual consistency allows for some delay in replicating data between replicas but guarantees eventual consistency.

Developers can choose a consistency level when configuring a Cosmos DB account or change the consistency level at any time. The consistency level chosen for an application depends on the application's requirements for consistency and **availability**. Here's how they can use each of the consistency models:

- **Strong consistency**: Developers can choose strong consistency for applications that cannot tolerate inconsistencies and need to reflect the latest data across all replicas. This model is suitable for applications where data integrity is of utmost importance, such as financial applications.

    It's tempting to view Cosmos DB's support for strong consistency as a way to treat it similarly to traditional SQL databases. However, this can be an anti-pattern. NoSQL's design philosophy is distinct from SQL, and Cosmos DB, despite its versatile features, is fundamentally a NoSQL database. Using strong consistency as a default, without assessing the specific requirements of the application, can result in inefficiencies and unexpected challenges.

    Cosmos DB's array of consistency options offers developers a broad toolset; it's imperative to approach it with a clear understanding of NoSQL philosophies. Embrace the characteristics of NoSQL where they fit best, and leverage Cosmos DB's advanced features in contexts where they add genuine value.

- **Bounded staleness**: For applications that require near-real-time data and can tolerate slight inconsistencies for a specified duration, developers can choose bounded staleness. This model is ideal for sensor data monitoring or live data feeds.

- **Session consistency**: When the application needs to maintain a consistent data view within a single session, developers can opt for session consistency. This model is ideal for applications such as e-commerce sites, where a user's data must stay consistent within a single session – for example, maintaining a shopping cart across multiple devices.

- **Consistent prefix**: Applications that need to read large volumes of data consistently can benefit from the consistent prefix model. This is particularly useful in applications such as log analysis, where the order of the data is essential.

- **Eventual consistency**: Developers can use eventual consistency for applications that can tolerate delays in reflecting the latest data but prioritize high availability. This model can be ideal for scenarios such as social media feeds or disaster recovery situations, where a delay in data propagation is acceptable.

In each case, the choice of consistency model can significantly impact the application's performance, latency, and user experience. Therefore, developers must understand the trade-offs and choose the most appropriate consistency model for their needs.

Choosing the right consistency level is important for achieving the desired balance between consistency and availability. Strong consistency provides the highest level of consistency but can also impact application performance. Eventual consistency allows for the highest level of availability but can also result in inconsistent data for a period of time.

To configure consistency in .NET, developers can use the Cosmos DB SDK for .NET. The SDK provides several APIs for configuring consistency, including the `CosmosClientOptions` class, which is used to configure the `CosmosClient` object.

For example, here's how to configure strong consistency using the `CosmosClientOptions` class in .NET:

```
using Microsoft.Azure.Cosmos;
using System.Threading.Tasks;

string connectionString = "connection-string"; CosmosClientOptions
options = new CosmosClientOptions { ConsistencyLevel =
ConsistencyLevel.Strong
};
CosmosClient cosmosClient = new CosmosClient(connectionString,
options);
```

In this example, the code creates a new `CosmosClientOptions` object and sets the `ConsistencyLevel` property to `Strong`. Then, it creates a new `CosmosClient` object using the connection string and the `options` object.

To summarize, consistency is a fundamental aspect of Azure Cosmos DB. It represents the degree of uniformity between the data replicas within the service. This concept plays a pivotal role in distributed systems, including databases, as it offers a mechanism to strike a balance between the consistency of data and its availability.

Developers can choose a consistency level when configuring a Cosmos DB account and can use the Cosmos DB SDK for .NET to configure consistency in their applications. Choosing the right consistency level depends on the application's requirements for consistency and availability.

To conclude, the various consistency models offered by Azure Cosmos DB cater to different application requirements and allow for a balance between consistency and availability. The most robust model, strong consistency, ensures that every replica of the data is always consistent. On the other hand, models such as bounded staleness, session consistency, and consistent prefix provide more flexibility with slight delays in consistency, allowing for more immediate data availability. At the furthest end of the spectrum, eventual consistency guarantees ultimate data consistency, albeit potentially after some delay. By understanding these models, developers can select the most suitable level of consistency for their specific use case, optimizing their applications for performance, availability, and user experience.

In the subsections ahead, we'll explore the different consistency levels offered by Cosmos DB and discuss the benefits and drawbacks of each level. We'll also provide examples of how each consistency level can be used in different types of applications.

Strong consistency

Strong consistency provides the highest level of consistency in Cosmos DB. With strong consistency, all replicas of the data are consistent with each other at all times, meaning that all readers will see the latest write. This consistency level provides a guarantee that a read operation is guaranteed to return the most recent write to the data, regardless of which replica it is read from.

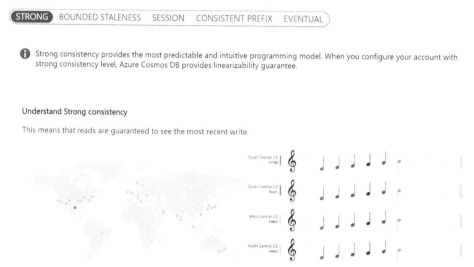

Figure 8.1 – Strong consistency in Azure Cosmos DB

While strong consistency provides the highest level of consistency, it can also impact application performance. Each write operation in a strong consistency model must be acknowledged by all replicas before the operation is considered complete. This can result in increased latency and reduced write throughput, particularly in scenarios with high write rates.

Let us take a real-world scenario such as a banking application; strong consistency ensures that all account transactions are instantly reflected across all replicas. When users withdraw funds from their account, the balance should immediately reflect the deduction across all regions. Strong consistency guarantees that any subsequent read operation will return the updated balance, providing users with real-time and accurate information, even in the case of concurrent transactions.

Bounded staleness

Bounded staleness allows for a delay in consistency between replicas but guarantees that all replicas will eventually be consistent with each other. With bounded staleness, developers can specify a maximum delay for data to be replicated between replicas, and read operations will return data that is no older than the specified delay.

This consistency level provides a balance between consistency and availability, allowing applications to provide **near-real-time data** while still ensuring that all replicas eventually become consistent. Bounded staleness can be useful in scenarios where near-real-time data is required, such as **sensor**

data monitoring, where data must be available for analysis as soon as possible. There's a limit or "bound" to the lag between the most recent write and subsequent reads. It offers a more predictable timeframe within which data replicas will synchronize, making it a middle ground between strong and eventual consistency.

If we take a social media platform as an example of **bounded staleness**, there may be a slight delay in replicating a user's post across all regions. However, the system guarantees that all followers' feeds will eventually be consistent. The trade-off here is that followers might see the post with a slight delay, but they will eventually receive the update, maintaining a smooth and engaging user experience.

Session consistency

Session consistency ensures that reads and writes within a session are consistent but may allow for inconsistency between sessions. With session consistency, all operations within a session will see the same data, regardless of which replica they are executed on. However, if a new session is started, the data may be inconsistent until all replicas are updated.

Session consistency is useful in scenarios where the application needs to maintain a consistent view of the data within a session. For example, in an e-commerce application, a user may add items to their shopping cart during a session. With session consistency, all operations within the session will see the same shopping cart data, regardless of which replica they are executed on. However, if the user logs out and logs back in, the data may be inconsistent until all replicas are updated.

Consistent prefix

Consistent prefix allows for reads to return a prefix of the data that is consistent across all replicas. With consistent prefixes, developers can specify a maximum prefix length, and read operations will return a prefix of the data that is consistent across all replicas.

A consistent prefix is useful in scenarios where the application needs to read a large amount of data in a consistent manner. For example, in a log analysis application, the application may need to read the latest log entries that are consistent across all replicas. With consistent prefixes, the application can specify a maximum prefix length, and read operations will return a consistent prefix of the log data.

Eventual consistency

Eventual consistency allows for some delay in replicating data between replicas but guarantees eventual consistency. With eventual consistency, read operations may return stale data, but all replicas will eventually become consistent.

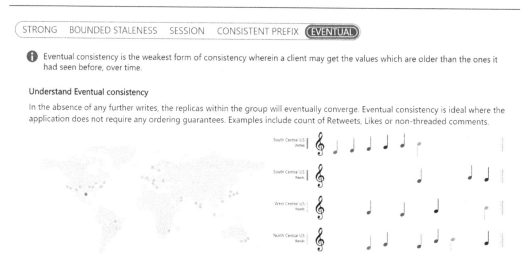

Figure 8.2 – Data replicating with a delay using eventual consistency

Eventual consistency is useful in scenarios where the application can tolerate some delay in reading the latest data. For example, in a social media application, when a user posts a new message, any subsequent read operation may not see the updated data immediately, but eventually, all replicas will become consistent with the latest write. Azure Cosmos DB's eventual consistency model doesn't directly notify readers when data is stale or updated. However, there are mechanisms to handle and be aware of data consistency:

- **Session tokens**: Ensure read-your-own-write consistency by using session tokens that are returned after write operations

- **E-tags**: Utilize e-tags for optimistic concurrency, which helps prevent overwriting of newer data with stale data

- **Change feed**: Track every change made to items in real time, allowing applications to respond to data modifications

- **Metrics and diagnostics**: Monitor the health and performance of Cosmos DB to understand data propagation delays

For critical applications, developers can employ additional Azure services or design patterns to actively notify clients of data changes or to detect stale data. Eventual consistency can also be useful in scenarios where availability is critical, such as in disaster recovery scenarios, where some data loss may be acceptable.

Understanding partition keys in Azure Cosmos DB

A **partition key** is a property of a document in Cosmos DB that is used to determine the physical partition in which the document is stored. When you create a container in Cosmos DB, you specify a partition key for that container. Cosmos DB then uses the partition key to distribute documents across multiple logical partitions based on the value of the partition key.

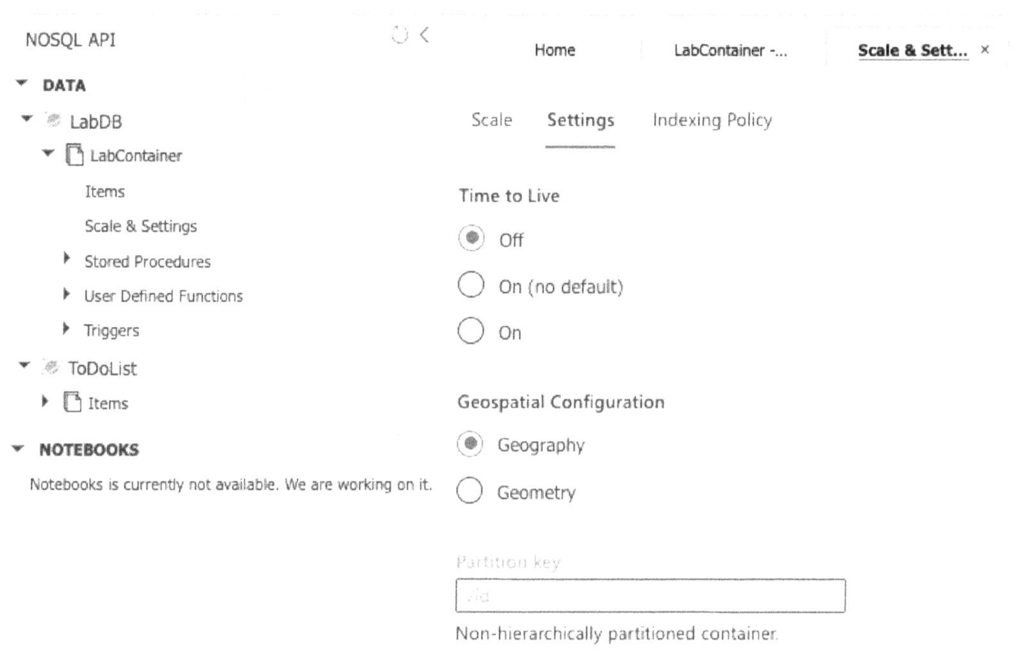

Figure 8.3 – Partition key in Cosmos DB

For example, let's say you have a container called `orders` in Cosmos DB, and you want to partition your data by customer ID. You can specify the customer ID as the partition key when you create the container. Cosmos DB will then use the customer ID to distribute orders across multiple physical partitions based on the value of the customer ID.

Currently, in Azure Cosmos DB, logical partitions have a maximum size limit of 20 GB. This limit is a "hard" limit, meaning that once reached, no more data can be added to that specific logical partition until some data is removed.

A logical partition consists of a set of items that have the same partition key value. For instance, if you've selected `userID` as the partition key for a container, all items with the same user ID will be stored in the same logical partition.

Here's why this is crucial:

- **Production halt**: If a specific logical partition reaches its size limit, any attempt to add more data will fail, which can halt operations in a production environment.

- **Hot partition**: Even before reaching the size limit, if one logical partition receives a disproportionately high volume of requests compared to others, it can become a "hot" partition. This can lead to rate-limiting, as each partition has a maximum request rate.

- **Redistribution is not automatic**: Cosmos DB won't automatically redistribute data once a logical partition fills up. Addressing an overfilled partition requires manual intervention, such as moving data or changing the partitioning strategy.

- **Repartitioning overhead**: If you ever need to change your partition key to address such issues, you'll face the overhead of creating a new container with the new partition key and migrating data, as discussed earlier.

Here's how to avoid these issues:

- **Anticipate Data Growth**: When choosing a partition key, consider the potential size each logical partition might grow to. Avoid partition keys that lead to a few very large partitions.

- **Monitor**: Regularly monitor the size and request rate of your logical partitions. Azure provides metrics to track these.

- **Balanced Partition Strategy**: Choose a partition key that distributes writes and reads evenly across all logical partitions. The key should also align with your most common access patterns to minimize more resource-intensive, cross-partition queries.

Understanding and respecting the hard limits of logical partitions is vital for maintaining smooth operations and performance in Cosmos DB.

Why are partition keys valuable?

Partition keys are valuable for building scalable, high-performance applications with Cosmos DB for several reasons:

- **Improved performance**: By distributing data across multiple physical partitions, Cosmos DB can improve **query performance** and reduce the impact of **hot partitions**. When a query is executed, Cosmos DB can parallelize the query across multiple physical partitions, improving query performance and reducing the amount of time it takes to return results.

- **Increased scalability**: By using partition keys, you can increase the scalability of your Cosmos DB solution. As your data grows, Cosmos DB can automatically distribute your data across additional physical partitions, allowing your application to scale horizontally to meet the needs of your workload.

- **Cost optimization**: Partition keys can also help to optimize the cost of your Cosmos DB solution. By choosing an appropriate partition key, you can minimize the amount of data that needs to be read or updated when executing queries, reducing the number of request units consumed and the overall cost of your solution.

Having understood the importance of partition keys in Cosmos DB, in the following section, we will delve into how to choose a practical partition key that can make the most of these benefits.

Creating partition keys in .NET

To create a partition key in .NET, you will need to use the Cosmos DB SDK for .NET. The SDK provides a set of classes and methods for interacting with Cosmos DB, including creating and managing partition keys.

Here's an example of how to create a partition key in .NET:

```
using Microsoft.Azure.Cosmos;
using System.Threading.Tasks;

string connectionString = "connection-string";
CosmosClient cosmosClient = new CosmosClient(connectionString);

Database database = await cosmosClient.CreateDatabaseAsync("my-db");
Container container = await database.CreateContainerAsync("my-container", "/partitionKey");
```

In this example, the code creates a new `CosmosClient` object using a connection string and then creates a new database and container using the `CreateDatabaseAsync` and `CreateContainerAsync` methods, respectively. The container is created with a partition key of `"/partitionKey"`, which means that the value of the `partitionKey` property will be used to determine the physical partition in which each document is stored. Once you've created a container with a partition key, you can start inserting and querying data using the Cosmos DB SDK.

Here's an example of how to insert data using the partition key:

```
using Microsoft.Azure.Cosmos;
using System.Threading.Tasks;
string partitionKey = "customer-123";
MyObject myObject = new MyObject
{
Id = "item-123",
PartitionKey = partitionKey,
Property1 = "value1",
Property2 = "value2"
};
Container container = cosmosClient.GetContainer("my-db", "my-container");
ItemResponse<MyObject> response = await container.
CreateItemAsync<MyObject>(myObject, new PartitionKey(partitionKey));
```

In this example, the code inserts a new object into Cosmos DB using the `CreateItemAsync` method. The object includes a partition key property (`PartitionKey`) with a value of `"customer-123"`, which is used to determine the physical partition in which the object is stored.

Once you have inserted data into Cosmos DB, you can start querying it using the Cosmos DB SDK. Here is an example of how to query data using a partition key:

```
using Microsoft.Azure.Cosmos;
using System.Collections.Generic;
using System.Threading.Tasks;

string partitionKey = "customer-123";
Container container = cosmosClient.GetContainer("my-db", "my-
container");
QueryDefinition query = new QueryDefinition("SELECT * FROM c WHERE
c.partitionKey = @partitionKey").WithParameter("@partitionKey",
partitionKey);


List<MyObject> results = new List<MyObject>();
using (FeedIterator<MyObject> iterator = container.
GetItemQueryIterator<MyObject>(query))
{
while (iterator.HasMoreResults)
{
FeedResponse<MyObject> response = await iterator.ReadNextAsync();
results.AddRange(response);
}
}
```

In this example, the code queries data from Cosmos DB using the `GetItemQueryIterator` method. The query includes a filter on the partition key property (`PartitionKey`) with a value of `"customer-123"`, which ensures that only data from the specified partition is returned.

Point-read operation

In Cosmos DB, a point-read operation refers to reading a single item (document) by its unique **identifier** (**ID**) and partition key value. Point-reads are the most efficient and lowest-cost read operations in Cosmos DB, targeting a specific item in a particular logical partition. Regarding performance and request charge (RU cost), point-reads are significantly more efficient than query operations that retrieve items based on other properties.

Let us assume you have a Cosmos DB container where each item represents a customer. The partition key for this container is `customerId`. To perform a point-read operation to retrieve a specific customer's data, you would provide both the unique `customerId` partition key value and the item's unique ID.

In C#, using the Cosmos DB SDK, it would look something like this:

```
string customerId = "12345"; string itemId = "A1B2C3";
Container container = cosmosClient.GetContainer("databaseName",
```

```
"containerName");
ItemResponse<Customer> response = await container.
ReadItemAsync<Customer>(itemId, new PartitionKey(customerId));
Customer customerData = response.Resource;
Console.WriteLine($"Customer Name: {customerData.Name}");
```

Let's look at this example in more detail:

- `customerId` is the partition key value that directs the SDK to the correct logical partition
- `itemId` is the unique identifier of the item within that partition
- The `ReadItemAsync` method performs the point-read operation
- The retrieved customer data is then available in the `response.Resource` object

Importance of point-reads

Understanding and leveraging point-reads is crucial for several reasons:

- **Efficiency**: Point-reads are the most efficient way to retrieve a single item based on RU utliziation
- **Performance**: Due to their specificity, point-reads are faster than general queries
- **Cost**: Since Cosmos DB billing is based on RUs, using point-reads when appropriate can lead to cost savings

When designing Cosmos DB-based applications, aligning your data access patterns to take advantage of point-reads whenever possible, especially for frequently accessed items or high-throughput scenarios, is essential.

Best practices for using partition keys

To get the best performance from Cosmos DB, it's important to choose the right partition key for your data. Here are some best practices for using partition keys in Cosmos DB:

- **Partition key selection**:

  - **Choose a high cardinality property**: Opt for a property with many distinct values to distribute data and avoid hot partitions. Understand your query needs up front, including read/write ratios.

  - **Cannot change the partition key**: Once chosen, you can't change the partition key without creating a new container. Plan for query types, data volume, and access patterns to save time and resources.

  - **Synthetic keys**: Composite keys formed by combining attributes can help distribute data across partitions when no single attribute is ideal.

- **Hierarchical keys**: Use hierarchical IDs for partition keys such as `/location/city` for organized data and efficient querying in hierarchical structures.

- **Redundancy with multiple containers**: Maintain multiple copies of data across containers with different partition keys for varied querying needs. This balances storage cost with query performance.

- **Monitoring and optimization**:

  - **Monitor partition size and performance**: Regularly check partition size and performance. Consider splitting a partition into multiple partitions if it is large or slow.

  - **Use hashing for uniform distribution**: When natural partition keys are lacking, use hashing to evenly distribute data across partitions, mitigating hot partitions.

  - **Plan for data growth**: Select a partition key that accommodates future data growth without causing hot partitions.

- **Performance and cost considerations**:

  - **RUs**: Optimal query performance depends on query alignment with partitioning. Single-partition queries usually outperform cross-partition queries.

  - **Query patterns**: Design queries to align with partition key strategy. Cross-partition queries may result in higher latencies.

  - **Provisioned throughput (RUs)**: Allocate RUs based on workload needs. Excessive provisioning leads to unnecessary costs, while low provisioning can result in poor performance.

  - **Storage costs**: Partition size impacts storage costs. Large partitions may require splitting, impacting both performance and RUs.

- **Tuning for performance and costs**:

  - **Monitor query performance**: Regularly track query performance and latencies. Adjust partitioning strategy based on higher RUs or slower performance.

  - **Indexing**: Proper indexing improves query performance. Create appropriate indexes aligned with query types.

  - **Avoid fan-out queries**: Minimize cross-partition queries (fan-out) as they tend to be less performant and consume more RUs.

  - **Query patterns**: Use the DocumentDB query analyzer to understand query patterns and ensure partitioning strategy alignment.

Balancing partition key selection, monitoring, and optimization is essential for achieving high performance, cost-effectiveness, and scalability in your Cosmos DB solution. Regularly tune and adjust based on evolving needs to maintain optimal operation.

Partition keys are critical to building scalable, high-performance applications with Cosmos DB. By using partition keys, you can distribute data across multiple physical partitions, improving query performance, increasing scalability, and optimizing costs. Choosing the right partition key for your data is essential and requires careful consideration of the cardinality and distribution of your data. For more details on how complex it can be to design Cosmos DB showcasing different iterations, visit `https://learn.microsoft.com/en-us/azure/cosmos-db/nosql/model-partition-example` for a more in-depth guide.

With the Cosmos DB SDK for .NET, creating and using partition keys is easy and intuitive. Whether you're building a high-traffic e-commerce site or a real-time gaming application, Cosmos DB provides the scalability, performance, and flexibility you need to build modern cloud-based applications with .NET.

In the dynamic landscape of application development, achieving peak performance and optimal cost-efficiency is a constant pursuit. Azure Cosmos DB's SQL API offers a powerful platform for building high-performance applications, but it's essential to navigate the intricate balance between performance optimization and cost-effective resource utilization. This next section delves into a comprehensive exploration of best practices that seamlessly blend performance enhancement and cost management, enabling you to create applications that are not only responsive but also fiscally prudent. Let's delve into the strategies that empower you to achieve both speed and economy in your Azure Cosmos DB deployments.

By following the best practices outlined in this chapter and carefully considering the partition key for your data, you can ensure that your Cosmos DB solution is optimized for performance, scalability, and cost. With Cosmos DB and .NET, you have the tools and technologies to build the next generation of cloud-based applications. To ensure an efficient system, we will dive into indexes in Azure Cosmos DB and explore what they are, why they are valuable, and how to implement them.

Exploring indexes in Azure Cosmos DB

Azure Cosmos DB is a **distributed database service** with high scalability, low latency, and global distribution. It is designed to be used with modern, cloud-based applications that require fast, responsive data access and the ability to scale to meet changing demands. One of Cosmos DB's key features is its indexing support, which allows data to be queried and retrieved more efficiently.

What are indexes?

An **index** is a data structure that is used to optimize the performance of queries by providing a faster way to retrieve data from the database. When you create an index on a container in Cosmos DB, it creates a separate data structure that contains a subset of the data in the container, organized to make it faster to search and retrieve data.

For example, let's say you have a container called `orders` in Cosmos DB, and you frequently query the container by customer ID. By creating an index on the customer ID property, Cosmos DB can create a separate data structure that contains only the customer ID property for each document in the container, organized to make it faster to search and retrieve data.

Why are indexes valuable?

Indexes are valuable for building scalable, high-performance applications with Cosmos DB for several reasons:

- **Improved query performance**: By using indexes, queries can be executed faster and with fewer resources. When a query is executed, Cosmos DB can use the index to quickly locate the data that matches the query, reducing the time it takes to return results.

- **Increased scalability**: By optimizing query performance, indexes can also increase the scalability of your Cosmos DB solution. As your data grows, Cosmos DB can continue to efficiently retrieve and query data from your container, allowing your application to scale horizontally to meet your workload's needs.

- **Cost optimization**: Indexes can also help optimize the cost of your Cosmos DB solution. By choosing appropriate indexes for your data, you can minimize the amount of data that needs to be read or updated when executing queries, reducing the number of RUs consumed and the overall cost of your solution.

However, there is also a downside that these indexes come with. It's a cost, both in terms of storage and performance. Maintaining an index for every column can have a particularly pronounced impact on databases with a high write ratio. Each write operation updates the document and potentially updates several indexes. This can lead to slower write operations and increased RU consumption, which, in turn, affects the cost.

For applications with a significant volume of write operations, disabling default indexing and adopting a more strategic approach is often recommended. By indexing only the frequently queried or critical columns for application performance, you can ensure faster write operations and reduced RU consumption.

The decision on which columns to index should be based on the application's read/write ratio and querying needs. More comprehensive indexing might be justified if a database has more reads. On the other hand, for databases dominated by write operations, minimizing indexes can lead to considerable performance and cost benefits.

Indexes are essential for enhancing query performance, but their maintenance comes with overheads. Developers should balance their application's querying needs and the associated costs and performance impacts of indexing. By carefully selecting which columns to index based on application usage patterns, you can optimize both performance and cost in Cosmos DB.

In the following section, we will learn how to create indexes in .NET and allow you to enhance your learning with a real-world example.

How to create indexes in .NET

To create an index in .NET, you'll need to use the Cosmos DB SDK for .NET. The SDK provides a set of classes and methods for interacting with Cosmos DB, including creating and managing indexes.

Here's an example of how to create an index in .NET:

```
static async Task Main(string[] args)
    {
        Container container = /* Get your container reference here */;
        string sqlQueryText = "SELECT * FROM c WHERE c.customerID =
'some_value'";
        QueryDefinition queryDefinition = new
QueryDefinition(sqlQueryText);
            try
        {
            FeedIterator<dynamic> queryResultSetIterator = container.
GetItemQueryIterator<dynamic>(queryDefinition);

            List<dynamic> results = new List<dynamic>();
            while (queryResultSetIterator.HasMoreResults)
            {
                FeedResponse<dynamic> currentResultSet = await
queryResultSetIterator.ReadNextAsync();
                foreach (var document in currentResultSet)
                {
                    results.Add(document);
                    Console.WriteLine($"Document ID: {document.id},
CustomerID: {document.customerID}, Details: {document}");
                }
            }
Console.WriteLine($"Total documents retrieved: {results.Count}");
        }
        catch(CosmosException cosmosEx)
        {
            Console.WriteLine($"An error occurred while querying:
{cosmosEx.Message}");
        }
        catch(Exception ex)
        {
            Console.WriteLine($"An unexpected error occurred: {ex.
Message}");
        }
    }
```

In this example, the code creates a new `CosmosClient` object using a connection string and then creates a new database and container using the `CreateDatabaseAsync` and `CreateContainerAsync` methods, respectively. The container is created with a partition key of `"/partition key"`. Then, we create an index on the `"customerID"` property using the `IndexAsync` method of the `container` object. The `RangeIndex` object represents a **range-based index** that can be used to index string, number, or date/time properties.

Once you've created an index on a container, you can start querying data using the Cosmos DB SDK.

Here's an example of how to query data using an index:

```
string sqlQueryText = "SELECT * FROM c WHERE c.customerID =
'customer-123'";
QueryDefinition queryDefinition = new QueryDefinition(sqlQueryText);
FeedIterator<dynamic> queryResultSetIterator = container.
GetItemQueryIterator<dynamic>(queryDefinition);
List<dynamic> results = new List<dynamic>();
while (queryResultSetIterator.HasMoreResults)
{
    FeedResponse<dynamic> currentResultSet = await
queryResultSetIterator.ReadNextAsync();
    foreach (var document in currentResultSet)
    {
        results.Add(document);
    }}
```

In this example, the code queries data from Cosmos DB using the `GetItemQueryIterator` method. The query includes a filter on the `customerID` property with a value of `"customer-123"`, which ensures that only data matching the filter is returned. Let's dive into best practices for using indexes up next.

Best practices for using indexes

To get the best performance from Cosmos DB, choosing the right indexes for your data is important. Here are some best practices for using indexes in Cosmos DB:

- **Choose the right indexing mode**: Cosmos DB supports two indexing modes: consistent and lazy. The **consistent indexing mode** ensures that all writes are indexed before they are acknowledged, while the **lazy indexing mode** allows for the eventual consistency of indexes. Choose the indexing mode that best suits your application's performance and consistency requirements.

- **Choose the right index types**: Cosmos DB supports several types of indexes, including **range**, **spatial**, and **composite indexes**. Choose the index type that best matches the data you're querying and executing.

- **Use composite indexes for complex queries**: If you're querying data using multiple filters or sorting criteria, consider using a composite index. A composite index combines multiple properties into a single index key, allowing for faster query performance when filtering or sorting by multiple criteria.

- **Monitor index usage and performance**: To ensure that your indexes provide optimal performance, monitor their usage and performance over time. If an index is not being used or is causing performance issues, consider modifying or removing the index to optimize performance.

- **Plan for data growth**: When choosing indexes for your data, plan for future data growth. Ensure that the chosen indexes can accommodate future data growth and won't result in slow query performance as data grows.

- **Understand the query patterns**: To choose the proper indexes for your data, you need to understand your application's query patterns. Analyze your queries to determine which properties are being filtered or sorted, and use that information to choose the proper indexes.

- **Test query performance**: Before deploying your application, test the performance of your queries using the **Cosmos DB Explorer**. This tool allows you to test different query configurations and see how they perform against your data, giving you valuable insights into the best index configuration for your application.

- **Use the query metrics feature**: Cosmos DB provides a query metrics feature that allows you to monitor the performance of your queries in real time. Use this feature to identify performance bottlenecks and optimize your query configuration for optimal performance.

By following these best practices, you can ensure that your Cosmos DB solution is scalable, performant, and cost-effective. With the right indexes and careful planning, you can build a Cosmos DB solution that can handle the needs of modern, cloud-based applications.

Indexes are critical to building scalable, high-performance applications with Cosmos DB. By using indexes, queries can be executed faster and with fewer resources, improving query performance, increasing scalability, and optimizing cost. Choosing the proper indexes for your data is essential and requires careful consideration of the types of indexes available and the queries you'll be executing.

Creating and using indexes with the Cosmos DB SDK for .NET is easy and intuitive. Whether you're building a high-traffic e-commerce site or a real-time gaming application, Cosmos DB provides the scalability, performance, and flexibility you need to build modern cloud-based applications with .NET.

In conclusion, indexes are critical to building scalable, high-performance applications with Cosmos DB. Using indexes can optimize query performance, increase scalability, and minimize costs. By following the best practices outlined in this chapter and carefully considering the indexes for your data, you can ensure that your Cosmos DB solution is optimized for performance, scalability, and cost. With Cosmos DB and .NET, you have the tools and technologies to build the next generation of cloud-based applications. With all the theory we've gained in the previous sections, we will now move on to creating an Azure Cosmos DB database using the Azure CLI.

Creating an Azure Cosmos DB database with the Azure CLI

Azure Cosmos DB is a powerful distributed database service that offers high scalability, low latency, and global distribution. In this section, we will walk through creating a new **Cosmos DB SQL API** account using the **Azure CLI**. We will discuss essential configuration options, such as choosing a location and configuring the consistency level.

Before we begin, make sure you have the following prerequisites in place:

- **Azure subscription**: You need to have an active Azure subscription to create and manage resources in Azure.

- **Azure CLI**: Install the Azure CLI on your machine. You can download it from the official Azure CLI website found here: `https://learn.microsoft.com/en-us/cli/azure/install-azure-cli`.

With these prerequisites in place, let's proceed with creating a Cosmos DB SQL API account in the following steps:

1. **Sign in to Azure**: Open your Command Prompt and sign in to your Azure account by running the following command:

   ```
   az login
   ```

   This will open a browser window where you can enter your Azure credentials and complete the sign-in process.

2. **Create a resource group**: A **resource group** is a logical container for **Azure resources**. It helps organize and manage related resources. To create a resource group, run the following command:

   ```
   az group create --name <resource-group-name> --location
   <location>
   ```

   Replace `<resource-group-name>` with a unique name for your resource group, and `<location>` with the desired Azure region for your Cosmos DB account.

3. **Create a Cosmos DB account**: To create a Cosmos DB SQL API account, run the following command:

   ```
   az cosmosdb create --name <account-name> --resource-group
   <resource-group-name> --locations regionName='Canada
   Central' failoverPriority=0 isZoneRedundant=false
   --locations regionName='Canada East' failoverPriority=1
   isZoneRedundant=false --default-consistency-level <consistency-
   level> --kind GlobalDocumentDB
   ```

   Replace `<account-name>` with a unique name for your Cosmos DB account, `<resource-group-name>` with the name of the resource group created in the previous step, and `<consistency-level>` with the desired default consistency level for your account (e.g., "Session", "BoundedStaleness", etc.).

4. **Retrieve connection information**: Once the Cosmos DB SQL API account has been successfully created, you can retrieve the connection information needed to connect to your account programmatically. Run the following command:

```
az cosmosdb show --name <account-name> --resource-group
<resource-group-name>
```

Replace <account-name> with your Cosmos DB account name and <resource-group-name> with your resource group name. This command will provide information such as the URI endpoint, primary and secondary keys, and other relevant details.

Congratulations! You have successfully created a Cosmos DB SQL API account using the Azure CLI. You can now start utilizing the power of Cosmos DB to build scalable and globally distributed applications.

Querying and managing data in Azure Cosmos DB with the .NET SDK

The .NET SDK for Azure Cosmos DB offers easy querying and data management for modern, cloud-based applications. In this section, we'll explore how to use the .NET SDK to query and manage data in Cosmos DB. We'll cover how to use Language Integrated Query (**LINQ**) and the SQL API for data filtering and querying, as well as how to use the **change feed** to receive real-time updates.

Querying data with the .NET SDK

The .NET SDK for Cosmos DB provides two main ways to query data: the SQL API and LINQ. Both methods are powerful and flexible and can be used to retrieve and manipulate data in Cosmos DB.

Using the SQL API

The SQL API provides a powerful query language for querying data in Cosmos DB. The SQL language is similar to SQL used in relational databases but has a few key differences. For example, instead of using joins to combine data from multiple containers, you can use the Cosmos DB JOIN operator to combine data from multiple collections or documents.

Here's an example of how to query data using the SQL API in .NET:

```
using Microsoft.Azure.Cosmos;
using System.Linq;
using System.Threading.Tasks;

string connectionString = "connection-string";
CosmosClient cosmosClient = new CosmosClient(connectionString);

Container container = cosmosClient.GetContainer("my-db", "orders");
```

```
string customerID = "customer-123";
QueryDefinition query = new QueryDefinition("SELECT * FROM c
WHERE c.customerID = @customerID") .WithParameter("@customerID",
customerID);

FeedIterator<MyObject> iterator = container.
GetItemQueryIterator<MyObject>(query);
while (iterator.HasMoreResults)
{
FeedResponse<MyObject> response = await iterator.ReadNextAsync();
foreach (MyObject item in response)
{
} }
```

In this example, the code queries data from the `"orders"` container using the SQL API. The query includes a filter on the `customerID` property with a value of `"customer-123"`, which ensures that only data matching the filter is returned.

Using LINQ

The .NET SDK for Cosmos DB also supports LINQ, a powerful query language that allows you to retrieve and manipulate data using a familiar syntax. LINQ can be used to query and filter data in Cosmos DB and supports a wide range of operations, including filtering, sorting, and grouping.

Here's an example of how to query data using LINQ in .NET:

```
using Microsoft.Azure.Cosmos.Linq;
using System.Linq;
using System.Threading.Tasks;
string connectionString = "connection-string";
CosmosClient cosmosClient = new CosmosClient(connectionString);
Container container = cosmosClient.GetContainer("my-db", "orders");
string customerID = "customer-123";
IQueryable<MyObject> query = container.
GetItemLinqQueryable<MyObject>()
.Where(x => x.customerID == customerID);

foreach (MyObject item in query)
{ // Do something with the item }
```

In this example, the code queries data from the `"orders"` container using LINQ. The query includes a filter on the `customerID` property with a value of `"customer-123"`, which ensures that only data matching the filter is returned.

Managing data with the .NET SDK

In addition to querying data, the .NET SDK for Cosmos DB also supports managing data in Cosmos DB. You can use the SDK to insert, update, and delete data and manage containers, databases, and other resources.

Inserting data

To insert data into Cosmos DB using the .NET SDK, you can use the `CreateItemAsync` method of the Container object. Here's an example:

```
using Microsoft.Azure.Cosmos;
using System.Threading.Tasks;
string connectionString = "connection-string";
CosmosClient cosmosClient = new CosmosClient(connectionString);
Container container = cosmosClient.GetContainer("my-db", "orders");
MyObject item = new MyObject
{
customerID = "customer-123",
orderID = "order-456",
orderTotal = 100.00
};
ItemResponse<MyObject> response = await container.
CreateItemAsync(item);
```

In this example, the code inserts a new item into the `"orders"` container using the `CreateItemAsync` method. The item is created using a custom object with properties for `customerID`, `orderID`, and `orderTotal`.

Updating data

To update data in Cosmos DB using the .NET SDK, you can use the `ReplaceItemAsync` or `UpsertItemAsync` methods of the container object. The `ReplaceItemAsync` method updates an existing item with a new version of the item. In contrast, the `UpsertItemAsync` method inserts a new item if it doesn't exist or updates an existing item if it does.

Here's an example of how to update an item in Cosmos DB using the `ReplaceItemAsync` method:

```
using Microsoft.Azure.Cosmos;
using System.Threading.Tasks;

string connectionString = "connection-string";
CosmosClient cosmosClient = new CosmosClient(connectionString);
```

```
Container container = cosmosClient.GetContainer("my-db", "orders");

string itemID = "item-123";
ItemResponse<MyObject> response = await container.
ReadItemAsync<MyObject>(itemID, new PartitionKey("partition-key"));

MyObject item = response.Resource;
item.orderTotal = 200.00;
response = await container.ReplaceItemAsync<MyObject>(item, itemID);
```

In this example, the code updates an existing item in the `"orders"` container using the `ReplaceItemAsync` method. The item is retrieved using the `ReadItemAsync` method and then updated with a new value for the `orderTotal` property. The updated item is then passed to the `ReplaceItemAsync` method to update the item in Cosmos DB.

Deleting data

To delete data from Cosmos DB using the .NET SDK, you can use the `DeleteItemAsync` method of the Container object. Here's an example:

```
using Microsoft.Azure.Cosmos;
using System.Threading.Tasks;

string connectionString = "connection-string";
CosmosClient cosmosClient = new CosmosClient(connectionString);


Container container = cosmosClient.GetContainer("my-db", "orders");

string itemID = "item-123";
ItemResponse<MyObject> response = await container.
DeleteItemAsync<MyObject>(itemID, new PartitionKey("partition-key"));
```

In this example, the code deletes an item from the `"orders"` container using the `DeleteItemAsync` method. The item is identified using its ID, and the partition key for the item is specified to ensure that the correct item is deleted.

Managing containers and databases

In addition to managing data, the .NET SDK for Cosmos DB also provides support for managing containers, databases, and other resources in Cosmos DB. You can use the SDK to create new containers, delete existing containers, and modify the properties of containers and databases.

Creating a new container

To create a new container in Cosmos DB using the .NET SDK, you can use the CreateContainerAsync method of the Database object. Here's an example:

```
using Microsoft.Azure.Cosmos;
using System.Threading.Tasks;

string connectionString = "connection-string";
CosmosClient cosmosClient = new CosmosClient(connectionString);

Database database = cosmosClient.GetDatabase("my-db");

string containerName = "new-container";
string partitionKeyPath = "/partitionKey";

ContainerProperties properties = new
ContainerProperties(containerName, partitionKeyPath);
ContainerResponse response = await database.
CreateContainerAsync(properties);
```

In this example, the code creates a new container in the "my-db" database using the CreateContainerAsync method. The container is created with the name "new-container" and a partition key path of "/partitionKey".

Deleting a container

To delete a container in Cosmos DB using the .NET SDK, you can use the DeleteContainerAsync method of the Database object. Here's an example:

```
using Microsoft.Azure.Cosmos;
using System.Threading.Tasks;

string connectionString = "connection-string";
CosmosClient cosmosClient = new CosmosClient(connectionString);

Database database = cosmosClient.GetDatabase("my-db");

string containerName = "old-container";
Container container = database.GetContainer(containerName); await
container.DeleteContainerAsync();
```

In this example, the code deletes an existing container from the "my-db" database using the DeleteContainerAsync method. The container is identified using its name, and the GetContainer method is used to retrieve a reference to the container object.

Modifying container properties

To modify the properties of a container in Cosmos DB using the .NET SDK, you can use the `ReplaceContainerAsync` method of the Database object. Here's an example:

```
using Microsoft.Azure.Cosmos;
using System.Threading.Tasks;

string connectionString = "connection-string";
CosmosClient cosmosClient = new CosmosClient(connectionString);

Database database = cosmosClient.GetDatabase("my-db");

string containerName = "existing-container";
Container container = database.GetContainer(containerName);
ContainerProperties properties = container.Properties;
properties.DefaultTimeToLive = 86400; // 1 day
await container.ReplaceContainerAsync(properties);
```

In this example, the code modifies the properties of an existing container in Cosmos DB using the `ReplaceContainerAsync` method. The container is identified using its name, and the `GetContainer` method is used to retrieve a reference to the Container object. The container properties are then modified, and the updated properties are passed to the `ReplaceContainerAsync` method to update the container in Cosmos DB.

Using the change feed

The **change feed** is a powerful feature of Cosmos DB that allows you to receive updates in real time as data changes in Cosmos DB. With the change feed, you can monitor changes to data, trigger events based on changes, and keep your applications up to date with the latest data.

To use the change feed in .NET, you can use the Cosmos DB **change feed processor library**, a high-level library providing a simple API for working with the change feed. The library takes care of many details of working with the change feed, such as checkpointing and resuming from failures, so you can focus on writing your business logic.

Here's an example of how to use the change feed in .NET:

```
using Microsoft.Azure.Cosmos;
using Microsoft.Azure.Cosmos.ChangeFeed;
using System;
using System.Threading.Tasks;

string connectionString = "connection-string";
CosmosClient cosmosClient = new CosmosClient(connectionString);
```

```
Container container = cosmosClient.GetContainer("my-db", "my-
container");

ChangeFeedProcessor changeFeedProcessor = container
.GetChangeFeedProcessorBuilder<MyObject>("processor-name",
HandleChangesAsync).WithInstanceName("instance-name") .Build();

await changeFeedProcessor.StartAsync();
async Task HandleChangesAsync(IReadOnlyCollection<MyObject> changes,
CancellationToken cancellationToken)
{
foreach (MyObject item in changes)
{
// Do something with the item
} }
```

In this example, the code uses the Cosmos DB change feed processor library to create a change feed processor for the `"my-container"` container in the `"my-db"` database. The processor is configured with a unique name (`"processor-name"`) and an instance name (`"instance-name"`) to identify the processor. The `HandleChangesAsync` method handles changes to the data and is called each time the change feed receives new data.

The Cosmos DB .NET SDK is a powerful tool for .NET developers to query and manage data in Cosmos DB. With support for SQL API, LINQ, and the change feed, you can easily interact with your data and take advantage of the database's high scalability, low latency, and global distribution. By optimizing your data model with partition keys, consistency levels, and indexing, you can ensure maximum performance and scalability. With complete control over containers, databases, and resources in Cosmos DB, you can make changes as your application evolves. Whether building a new cloud-based application or migrating an existing one, the Cosmos DB .NET SDK is an excellent choice for fast, responsive data access in the cloud.

Cosmos DB provides a powerful and flexible database platform for .NET developers, and understanding the concepts of throughput, latency, and RUs is critical to building high-performing and scalable applications.

Developing with Azure Cosmos DB

The .NET SDK for Cosmos DB is your gateway to seamless and intuitive interactions with this fully managed NoSQL database service. With the .NET SDK at your disposal, you'll find yourself effortlessly adding data to Cosmos DB and harnessing the full potential of the SQL API for powerful and precise data retrieval. With a quick introduction to CRUD via the .NET SDK and data patterns, you will be equipped to dive deeper into the SDK and create custom code to fit your every need.

Working with the .NET SDK

The .NET SDK for Cosmos DB provides a set of APIs and client libraries, making it easy for .NET developers to interact with Cosmos DB. The SDK supports **synchronous** and **asynchronous** programming models and provides a wide range of functionality for working with data in Cosmos DB. To optimize connectivity from an API to Cosmos DB, one of the most useful patterns you may find yourselves utilizing is the Singleton pattern. The Singleton design pattern ensures that a class has only one instance and provides a centralized access point to this instance. Essentially, it restricts a class from instantiating multiple objects and offers a global point of reference. This is achieved by making the default constructor private and introducing a static method that manages the instantiation. This method either creates a new instance or returns the existing one, thus guaranteeing a single object throughout a program's runtime. The Singleton pattern can be likened to a government structure in a country; no matter the individuals in power, there's only one recognized government at any time, serving as a unique point of authority. This pattern safeguards against inadvertent multiple instantiations and ensures that the instance can't be overwritten, maintaining data consistency.

Why is the Singleton pattern important?

The Singleton design pattern is especially beneficial for managing unique resources and maintaining consistency across various parts of an application. Specifically, it offers advantages in the following areas:

- **Resource management**: Some resources should have only a single point of control. For instance, a configuration manager, which reads a configuration file, should ideally be instantiated once to ensure that configurations stay consistent throughout the app's life cycle.

- **Shared state**: A Singleton can be crucial in scenarios where multiple objects need to share the same state. Every object accessing the Singleton will access the same shared state.

- **Reduce overhead**: Since the object is only instantiated once, you reduce the overhead of repeatedly creating and destroying the same object.

- **Database connections**: Often, applications use the Singleton pattern for database connections to ensure that the system uses a consistent and efficient connection mechanism without the overhead of establishing new connections frequently.

- **Logger**: An application logger is often implemented as a Singleton, ensuring that log entries from different parts of an application can be consolidated effectively.

- **Third-party integrations**: When integrating with third-party services or APIs that require a unique connection or access token, the Singleton pattern can be helpful to ensure there is a single point of access and control.

While the Singleton pattern offers many advantages, there are some concerns and caveats to be aware of:

- **Global state**: Since the Singleton pattern introduces a global state to the application, it can make the system harder to test because different parts of the program can change its state unpredictably.

- **Concurrency issues**: Ensuring that a Singleton remains single in multi-threaded environments can be challenging. You must handle concurrency to ensure that two threads do not create separate instances simultaneously.

- **Flexibility**: When using the Singleton pattern, there can be limitations in extending or modifying the behavior of the Singleton class because it ensures that only one instance of the class exists throughout the application's lifetime.

- **Misuse**: Due to its seeming simplicity, it can be overused. Not every shared resource needs to be a Singleton. Overuse can lead to issues related to global state and tight coupling.

In conclusion, the Singleton pattern is a powerful tool in the best-case scenario. As with any tool, it is essential to understand when and where to use it to get the most benefit without introducing unintended complexities.

Implementing Singleton for CosmosClient

`CosmosClient`, inherently thread-safe, is optimized for repeated usage. This reusability helps reduce latency and amplify efficiency by reusing connections and evading the overhead of ceaselessly initializing new clients. Integrating .NET Core 6's **Dependency Injection (DI)** into an API makes it easier to use the Singleton pattern for services.

The following are the steps to implement the Singleton pattern for our `CosmosClient` that we will be reusing in future examples:

1. **Service definition**: Start by encapsulating the Cosmos DB connection and its operations within a service:

```
public class CosmosDbService
{
    private readonly CosmosClient _cosmosClient;
    private readonly Database _database;
    private readonly Container _container;
    public CosmosDbService(string connectionString, string
databaseId, string containerId)
    {
        _cosmosClient = new CosmosClient(connectionString);
        _database = _cosmosClient.GetDatabase(databaseId);
        _container = _database.GetContainer(containerId);
    }
}
```

2. **Service registration**: In the `Program.cs` file of .NET Core 6, register this service as a Singleton:

```
var builder = WebApplication.CreateBuilder(args);
var services = builder.Services;
services.AddSingleton(x => new CosmosDbService(
```

```
        builder.Configuration["CosmosDb:ConnectionString"],
        builder.Configuration["CosmosDb:DatabaseId"],
        builder.Configuration["CosmosDb:ContainerId"]));
```

3. **Service consumption**: Inject this service into controllers or other required services:

```
public class SomeController : ControllerBase
{
    private readonly CosmosDbService _cosmosDbService;
    public SomeController(CosmosDbService cosmosDbService)
    {
        _cosmosDbService = cosmosDbService;
    }
}
```

There are a few key takeaways you must remember when working with the Singleton pattern:

*   Singleton ensures one-instance-only but is cautious about managing the global state within it in a thread-safe fashion

*   Prefer DI for easier testing and reduced coupling

*   For configurations, especially sensitive ones such as connection strings, employ .NET Core's configuration providers

*   While initializing CosmosClient, you can define connection policies for better control over performance and reliability

*   Equip your Cosmos DB service with logging mechanisms and use tools such as Azure Monitor for overseeing performance and issues

*   Although Singleton ensures one-time instantiation, always be mindful of resource cleanup

*   Leverage DI for easier mocking during unit testing, allowing simulation of Cosmos DB operations without actual calls

By adhering to the preceding guidelines, the integration of your API with Cosmos DB can be made robust, efficient, and maintainable in the context of .NET. Let us expand our knowledge by creating and querying data utilizing what we've set up previously.

Creating and querying data

To create data in Cosmos DB using the .NET SDK, developers can use the CreateItemAsync() method provided by the Container class. This method takes a document as input and adds it to the specified container. In the following code, we further demonstrate the Singleton pattern's application in interacting with Azure Cosmos DB, building upon the foundational CosmosDbService class introduced in the previous section.

To query data in Cosmos DB using the .NET SDK, developers can use the GetItemQueryIterator() method provided by the Container class. This method takes a query as input and returns an iterator that can be used to enumerate the query results. Let's extend with a code example to explain it further:

```
public sealed class CosmosDbService {
    private readonly CosmosContainer _container;
    public CosmosDbService(string authorizationKey, string
containerId) {         CosmosClient cosmosClient = new
CosmosClient("your_cosmos_db_endpoint", authorizationKey);
        Database database = cosmosClient.GetDatabase("your_database_
id");
        _container = database.GetContainer(containerId);
    }
    public async Task<ItemResponse<dynamic>> CreateItemAsync(dynamic
item) {
        return await _container.CreateItemAsync(item);
    }

    public async IAsyncEnumerable<dynamic> ExecuteQueryAsync(string
sqlQueryText)
    {
        QueryDefinition queryDefinition = new
QueryDefinition(sqlQueryText);
        await foreach (var document in _container.
GetItemQueryIterator<dynamic>(queryDefinition))
        {
            yield return document;
        }}}
```

Let us break down how the CosmosDbService class encapsulates an array of operations, laying a sturdy foundation for engaging with Azure Cosmos DB in a structured, modular, and efficient manner:

- **The CosmosDbService class**: This sealed class encapsulates the interaction with Azure Cosmos DB.

- **Constructor**: The constructor initializes the _container field, essential for working with the Cosmos DB container. It takes two parameters: authorizationKey for security and containerId to specify the container.

- **CosmosClient and database initialization**: Inside the constructor, CosmosClient is instantiated with the provided authorization key and a placeholder for the endpoint URL. The GetDatabase method fetches the database using the provided database ID.

- **Container initialization**: The _container is obtained using the GetContainer method from the database. This is the primary entity for performing operations on the data within Cosmos DB.

- **The CreateItemAsync method**: This asynchronous method adds a new item (provided as a dynamic item) to the container using `_container.CreateItemAsync(item)`.

- **The ExecuteQueryAsync method**: This asynchronous method yields the results of a query. It accepts a SQL query as `sqlQueryText` and processes results using the `_container.GetItemQueryIterator<dynamic>(queryDefinition)` method. The yield return statement returns each document one by one.

Now that we've explored the capabilities of the `CosmosDbService` class, let's transition our focus to the pivotal `Program` class. This class houses the program's entry point, orchestrating the execution and showcasing the practical utilization of the functionalities offered by the `CosmosDbService` class here:

```
public class Program {
    public static async Task Main(string[] args) {
        string authorizationKey = "your_authorization_key";
        string containerId = "your_container_id";
        dynamic newDocument = new
        {
            id = Guid.NewGuid().ToString(),
            name = "Tamir AlBalkhi",
            age = 99,
            occupation = "Architect"
        };
        using (CosmosDbService cosmosService = new
CosmosDbService(authorizationKey, containerId))
        {
            await cosmosService.CreateItemAsync(newDocument);
            string sqlQueryText = "SELECT * FROM c WHERE c.occupation
= 'Architect'";
            await foreach (var document in cosmosService.
ExecuteQueryAsync(sqlQueryText))
            {
                // Process each document here
            }}}}
```

Navigating through the mechanics of the program, let's delve into the intricacies of each stage:

- **Initialization**: Prior to engaging, essential parameters such as `authorizationKey` and `containerId` are meticulously provided, offering crucial access to the Cosmos DB container.

- **Creating a new document**: The spotlight shifts to the creation of a dynamic `newDocument`, introducing a blend of distinct properties, `CosmosDbService`.

- **Initialization**: The orchestration continues with the inception of a `CosmosDbService` instance within a well-structured `using` block. This encapsulation ensures impeccable resource management throughout.

- **CreateItemAsync**: As the narrative unfolds, the `CreateItemAsync` method comes to life, skillfully integrating `newDocument` into the Cosmos DB container.

- **Query execution**: A defining moment arrives with the formulation of a SQL query (`sqlQueryText`) for specific document retrieval. The `ExecuteQueryAsync` method emerges, poised to execute the query and embrace results within a gracefully executed `foreach` loop.

This explanation gives you a clearer understanding of the code! Next, we will explore how to update and delete data using the same pattern.

Updating and deleting data

To update data in Cosmos DB using the .NET SDK, developers can use the `ReplaceItemAsync()` method provided by the `Container` class. This method takes a document as input and updates the specified document in the container. To delete data in Cosmos DB using the .NET SDK, developers can use the `DeleteItemAsync()` method provided by the `Container` class. This method takes the ID and partition key of the document to be deleted and removes it from the container. Now, let's see how to do this in a sample code example:

```
public async Task<ItemResponse<dynamic>> UpdateItemAsync(string
documentId, string partitionKey, dynamic updatedDocument)
{
  return await _container.ReplaceItemAsync<dynamic>(updatedDocument,
documentId, new PartitionKey(partitionKey));
}
public async Task DeleteItemAsync(string documentId, string
partitionKey)
{
    await _container.DeleteItemAsync<dynamic>(documentId, new
PartitionKey(partitionKey));}
```

By adding these methods to our `CosmosDbService` Singleton class, we ensure that all Cosmos DB interactions are managed through a single instance of the service, maintaining consistency and efficiency.

Now that we have established the significance of maintaining a **Singleton instance** when interacting with Cosmos DB, let us shift our focus to another critical aspect of working with the service. As applications grow and evolve, a challenge known as the "Cosmos DB cold start problem" may emerge. This issue pertains to the initialization phase of the Cosmos DB SDK and its impact on application performance. In the next section, we will delve into what exactly happens during this slow initialization phase and explore strategies to mitigate it.

Cosmos DB cold start problem

Azure Cosmos DB, offers seamless horizontal scaling, global distribution capabilities, and multi-model support. However, like many services in the realm of cloud computing, it faces what is termed the "cold start problem." For developers, especially those working in serverless environments, this can pose significant challenges. Let us deeply understand this issue and how .NET developers can navigate it effectively.

Imagine you are trying to start an old car on a chilly morning. It hesitates, taking a moment before roaring to life. That hesitation? That is analogous to the "cold start" in the digital world of databases, especially in the serverless paradigm. The "cold start" delay in Cosmos DB arises when initializing an instance, especially with many containers, databases, and partitions. This initialization phase becomes conspicuously prolonged when Cosmos DB instances are frequently spun up and dismantled. Such a scenario is common in serverless computing, where functions are ephemeral, coming to life upon a trigger, doing their work, and disappearing.

Why does this delay happen? It's due to a series of essential steps that `CosmosClient` takes during initialization to ensure optimal and efficient interaction with the Cosmos DB service, such as the following:

- **Endpoint discovery**: Given that Cosmos DB is designed for global distribution, the first step upon initialization is for `CosmosClient` to fetch the list of regions your database resides in. This ensures future operations target the closest and most appropriate region.

- **Connection establishment**: As you would expect with any other database client, `CosmosClient` initiates connections with the Cosmos DB service. Depending on configurations, this can involve setting up TCP or HTTPS connections.

- **Metadata retrieval**: Metadata pertinent to your databases, containers, and other configurations is fetched to facilitate operations.

- **Caching**: To optimize and expedite future operations, specific metadata and configurations are cached within the client. This reduces the need for round trips to the database for frequently repeated operations.

Tackling the cold start issue in .NET

Understanding the challenges posed by cold starts, Azure has offered potential remedies. One notable approach is the use of `CosmosClient.CreateAndInitializeAsync`. This function instructs the client to perform the heavy lifting of initialization upfront rather than postponing it until the first database operation. By doing so, most of the background preparations will have been accomplished when your first operation is triggered.

Here is a glimpse of how you might integrate this in a .NET environment:

```
CosmosClientOptions options = new CosmosClientOptions
{
    // Insert desired configurations here
```

```
    };

    CosmosClient client = await CosmosClient.CreateAndInitializeAsync(
        "YOUR_ENDPOINT_URL",
        "YOUR_PRIMARY_KEY",
        options
    );
```

The actual advantages of this method shine in scenarios demanding immediate readiness of CosmosClient post-startup, a common expectation in serverless environments.

Cold starts, while a natural part of cloud computing, can sometimes be a thorn in the side for developers, especially when immediate responsiveness is a necessity. However, armed with knowledge and the right tools, .NET developers can ensure that their applications remain performant and efficient. As cloud computing continues to evolve, developers must stay informed, adapt, and make the best architectural decisions for their applications. Whether you are just starting or are a seasoned .NET developer, understanding the nuances of the Cosmos DB cold start and how to mitigate it can significantly elevate the efficiency of your applications.

Gateway versus direct mode connection

Azure Cosmos DB SDKs offer two distinct connection modes: gateway and direct. Selecting the appropriate mode for your application is paramount to achieving the desired balance between performance and compatibility with network environments:

- **Gateway mode**: Gateway mode is geared toward scenarios where connectivity might be restricted by firewalls or network policies. It operates solely over HTTPS (port 443), which is commonly allowed for outbound traffic in most enterprise networks. This mode is optimal for ensuring compatibility with stringent firewall configurations.

- **Direct mode**: Direct mode, on the other hand, is designed to maximize performance by using a combination of HTTP and TCP traffic. While this mode offers superior performance benefits, it utilizes a broader range of ports, which might be subject to network restrictions. Direct mode can lead to quicker data access and reduced latency, particularly for data-intensive workloads.

While recent versions of the Azure Cosmos DB SDKs default to direct mode, it is prudent to explicitly define the connection mode in your application code. This practice ensures that your application remains resilient even if defaults change in the future. By explicitly specifying the connection mode, you retain control over your application's performance characteristics.

The choice between gateway and direct mode necessitates a trade-off between performance and network compatibility. Developers must consider the nature of their application, the network environment it will operate in, and the potential impact of port restrictions. By making an informed decision, you can tailor the connection mode to align with both performance optimization and network configuration requirements. There are two important considerations when making a choice between each mode:

- **SDK version**: Recent versions of the Azure Cosmos DB SDK default to direct mode. However, it is always recommended to explicitly define the connection mode to avoid potential changes in default behavior in future versions.

- **Client initialization**: When you initialize the `CosmosClient` instance, the connection mode is set. To switch the connection mode, you need to create a new instance of `CosmosClient` with the desired connection mode and reinitialize any other relevant components.

The networking landscape can evolve over time, with firewall rules and network policies subject to change. What might be the optimal choice today could differ in the future. By explicitly defining the connection mode, you ensure your application retains its performance advantages even if defaults shift due to network updates.

Let us look at how to implement both using a code example. For the gateway mode, we can establish a connection as follows:

```
using Microsoft.Azure.Cosmos;
ConnectionPolicy connectionPolicy = new ConnectionPolicy
{
    ConnectionMode = ConnectionMode.Gateway
};
CosmosClient cosmosClient = new CosmosClient("connectionString",
connectionPolicy);
```

Moving on to the direct mode, we can set up a connection using the sample code as follows:

```
using Microsoft.Azure.Cosmos;
ConnectionPolicy connectionPolicy = new ConnectionPolicy
{
    ConnectionMode = ConnectionMode.Direct
};
CosmosClient cosmosClient = new CosmosClient("connectionString",
connectionPolicy);
```

These examples provide you with a straightforward way to explicitly define the connection mode when working with the Azure Cosmos DB SDK for .NET. In both examples, by explicitly setting the `ConnectionMode` property in the `ConnectionPolicy` object, you ensure that the specified mode, `Gateway` or `Direct`, is used when establishing connections to Azure Cosmos DB. This provides you with control over the connection behavior of your application, allowing you to optimize for either performance or compatibility with your network environment.

Awareness of these techniques provides a well-rounded perspective on the significance of choosing the right connection mode between `Gateway` and `Direct`, and how explicit definition can help strike the right balance between performance and network compatibility. Unlocking the full potential of Azure Cosmos DB hinges on crafting efficient data access patterns, which we will learn about next. By tailoring your approach to retrieving and manipulating data in this globally distributed, multi-model database service, you can achieve exceptional performance and responsiveness in your applications.

Designing efficient data access patterns

Designing efficient **data access patterns** is critical to achieving high performance and scalability in Cosmos DB. Here are some best practices for designing efficient data access patterns:

- Use partition keys effectively to distribute data evenly across partitions. This can improve query performance and reduce latency.

- Use appropriate indexing strategies to speed up query execution and minimize the number of RUs required to execute queries.

- Use appropriate consistency levels to balance the trade-off between consistency and availability.

- Avoid **cross-partition queries** whenever possible, as they can be more expensive in terms of RUs and result in higher latency.

- Use the change feed to receive real-time updates to data in Cosmos DB.

- Use stored procedures and triggers to encapsulate business logic and improve performance by reducing the number of round trips between the client and the database.

Examples of data access patterns

Here are some examples of common data access patterns in Cosmos DB:

- **CRUD operations**: These are the basic `Create, Read, Update,` and `Delete` operations that are performed on data in Cosmos DB. These operations can be performed using the .NET SDK and combined with other data access patterns to build more complex applications.

- **Point reads and writes**: These operations involve reading or writing a single document using its ID and partition key. Point reads and writes are efficient and can be performed using the `ReadItemAsync()` and `ReplaceItemAsync()` methods provided by the `Container` class.

- **Range queries**: These operations involve querying a range of documents based on a specific property. Range queries can be optimized using appropriate indexing strategies and consistency levels.

- **Aggregations**: These operations involve performing calculations on data in Cosmos DB, such as summing or averaging values across multiple documents. Aggregations can be performed using the SDK's `GroupBy()` and `Aggregate()` methods.

Developing with Cosmos DB using the .NET SDK is a powerful and flexible way to build high-performing and scalable applications. By understanding the basic CRUD operations, designing efficient data access patterns, and using appropriate indexing strategies and consistency levels, .NET developers can build fast, reliable, and efficient applications.

Examples of typical data access patterns, such as point reads and writes, range queries, and aggregations, can help developers understand how to use the .NET SDK to perform common operations on data in Cosmos DB. In addition, best practices for designing efficient data access patterns, such as using partition keys effectively, appropriate consistency levels, and avoiding cross-partition queries, can help developers optimize their applications for high performance and scalability. Finally, leveraging advanced features of Cosmos DB, such as the change feed, stored procedures, and triggers, can help developers encapsulate business logic and improve performance by reducing the number of round trips between the client and the database.

Considerations for performance and cost optimization

In an effort to optimize performance and manage costs within Azure Cosmos DB, striking a delicate equilibrium is paramount. Organizations leveraging this powerful database for large-scale applications must navigate the intricate interplay between resource efficiency and swift query response.

A series of considerations emerge to guide this endeavor, offering actionable insights for achieving performance and cost optimization. These insights empower users to navigate resource allocation intricacies, supercharge query responsiveness, and fully leverage Azure Cosmos DB's capabilities.

Central to this optimization journey is understanding RUs, a crucial metric that wields influence over both performance and expenditure. By using Azure Cosmos DB's query metrics and monitoring, users can pinpoint and optimize high-RU queries. Additionally, recognizing the impact of partitioning on RU distribution is vital, as cross-partition queries can be more resource-intensive.

As the focus shifts to performance enhancement, the connection between cost awareness and optimization remains foundational. The spotlight turns to harnessing RUs for dual performance and financial efficiency benefits. These considerations underline the importance of informed decision-making and strategic resource utilization in achieving the best possible balance between performance and cost within Azure Cosmos DB.

Cost optimization

As organizations increasingly rely on Azure Cosmos DB for their large-scale applications, it becomes crucial to strike the right balance between efficient resource usage and fast query response times. In the following sections, we will explore actionable insights and best practices that enable you to understand the intricacies of resource utilization, enhance query performance, and make the most of what Azure Cosmos DB has to offer.

Understanding RUs and costs

Effectively managing costs is a fundamental aspect of any database solution. We will kick off by examining how to understand and optimize RUs, which play a pivotal role in determining both performance and cost:

- **Query metrics and monitoring**: Leverage the query metrics and monitoring features of Azure Cosmos DB to understand the RUs consumed by your SQL queries. This helps you identify high-RU queries and optimize them.

- **Partitioning impact**: Remember that partitioning impacts the distribution of RUs. Some queries might be more resource-intensive due to cross-partition queries, which consume more RUs.

Performance optimization

Effectively managing costs is a fundamental aspect of any database solution. We will kick off by examining how to understand and optimize RUs, which play a pivotal role in determining both performance and cost. Let us look at some key considerations in the following subsections:

Query optimization

Let's now explore fundamental strategies that hold a crucial role in optimizing the efficiency of your queries within Azure Cosmos DB:

- **Indexing strategies**: In the SQL API, defining appropriate indexes is key to query performance. Use single-field indexes for simple queries and composite indexes for more complex ones that involve multiple fields in WHERE clauses.

- **Composite indexes**: Composite indexes allow efficient querying on multiple fields. When designing composite indexes, consider query patterns that involve filters on multiple properties.

- **Covered queries**: A covered query is one where all the fields needed are available in the index, eliminating the need to fetch data from the documents. This reduces both RUs and response times.

Data modeling

Let's dive into strategies that can shape your data model for enhanced performance:

- **Denormalization**: Just as with other APIs, denormalizing your data model in the SQL API minimizes the need for joins, improving query performance.

- **Hierarchical data**: Utilize nested documents to represent hierarchical data structures. This reduces the need for separate collections and simplifies queries.

Monitoring and performance tuning

To ensure your Azure Cosmos DB queries are running efficiently, proactive monitoring and performance tuning are crucial. Let's delve into methods to fine-tune your setup:

- **Query diagnostics**: Enable query diagnostics to capture query execution details. This helps you identify slow queries, inefficient index usage, and other bottlenecks.

- **Tuning slow queries**: Use diagnostic insights to identify queries with high RU consumption. Optimize these queries by adding appropriate indexes or modifying the query structure.

Testing and iteration

Achieving the best query performance involves a cycle of testing, refining, and iterating. Let's look at how testing with real data and query profiling can lead to performance enhancements:

- **Query profiling**: Profiling tools within Cosmos DB provide insights into query execution steps. This information aids in identifying areas for query optimization.

- **Real data testing**: As with any database system, it is important to test query performance using real data. Synthetic workloads might not accurately represent the complexities of actual queries and data distribution.

In summary, understanding the cost implications of your queries and optimizing for both performance and cost are essential aspects of effectively using the SQL API in Azure Cosmos DB. By addressing both cost and performance considerations, you can ensure efficient resource utilization while delivering optimal query response times.

Summary

This chapter delved into the key concepts and benefits of using Azure Cosmos DB, a distributed database service, for .NET developers. We began by introducing the fundamental aspects of Cosmos DB, including its flexibility, scalability, and performance, which make it an excellent choice for building modern, cloud-based applications.

We discussed the importance of selecting the appropriate API. We highlighted the support for the SQL API, which enables developers to leverage their existing SQL skills and easily query data using SQL-like syntax. We also touched upon other supported APIs, including the MongoDB, Cassandra, Gremlin, and Table APIs, that offer developers the flexibility to choose the best API for their application needs.

In addition, we explored the global distribution and low-latency capabilities of Cosmos DB, which ensure that data is accessible and available even during regional outages. We emphasized the significance of consistency levels, allowing developers to balance data consistency and availability based on their application requirements. To optimize performance, we explored partitioning strategies, such as range-based and hash-based partitioning, and emphasized the importance of evenly distributing data across partitions to avoid hot partitions. We covered essential aspects such as indexing, which enhances query performance, and the importance of selecting the appropriate consistency level for efficient data retrieval.

Furthermore, we touched upon performance optimization, scalability, and pricing aspects, guiding developers on configuring and scaling Cosmos DB accounts to meet application demands effectively.

To encourage further exploration and learning, we provided resources for developers to dive deeper into Cosmos DB.

In conclusion, Azure Cosmos DB is a robust and feature-rich database service that offers .NET developers unparalleled flexibility, scalability, and performance for building modern, cloud-based applications. By understanding the key concepts, benefits, and best practices highlighted in this chapter, developers can harness the power of Cosmos DB to create resilient, highly available, and globally distributed applications.

We urge you to continue your exploration of Cosmos DB, leveraging the resources and tools provided and staying up to date with the latest advancements in this ever-evolving technology. Embracing Azure Cosmos DB empowers .NET developers to unlock the full potential of their applications in the cloud.

Our next chapter will shift away from databases and focus on Azure App Configuration. As your applications evolve, managing configurations becomes critical to maintaining efficiency and adaptability. Azure App Configuration simplifies this process by centralizing all your configurations in one place, making it a breeze to update settings without needing application redeployment. Whether building a new cloud-native app or modernizing an existing one, Azure App Configuration provides the flexibility and reliability needed to streamline configuration management.

Join us as we delve into the core features of Azure App Configuration, exploring how it seamlessly integrates with your .NET applications and reveals the magic of dynamic configuration updates. Get ready to harness the power of feature flags to enable easy toggling of features, ensuring smooth deployments and A/B testing without breaking a sweat.

Part 4: Messaging Mechanisms and Security

Immerse yourself in the world of messaging mechanisms and security within Azure. Gain invaluable insights to enhance your .NET development journey. Begin with Azure App Configuration, a service that centralizes configuration management and supports application scalability and reliability. Dive into Azure Event Hubs, a powerful platform for data processing that refines analysis and decision-making. Explore Azure Service Bus, mastering advanced messaging patterns for robust and secure application development. Elevate data protection through Azure Key Vault, safeguarding secrets and controlling access. Finally, discover Azure Active Directory B2C, a stronghold for identity management in consumer-facing applications, ensuring privacy and compliance. Elevate your Azure expertise with messaging and security mastery tailored for .NET developers.

This part has the following chapters:

- *Chapter 9, Utilizing Azure App Configuration*
- *Chapter 10, Processing Data with Azure Event Hubs*
- *Chapter 11, Designing Ready-Made Solutions with Azure Service Bus*
- *Chapter 12, Enhancing Data Protection with Azure Key Vault*
- *Chapter 13, Managing Access with Azure Active Directory B2C*

Utilizing Azure App Configuration

In the **cloud-native architecture**, application settings and configurations play a key role. The **Azure App Configuration** service helps developers manage application settings and configuration in a central location. Azure App Configuration also helps us to implement **feature flags** or **feature toggles** – a software development technique that helps with turning on and off application features without redeploying code.

In this chapter, we will learn about Azure App Configuration, and then we will learn how to use Azure App Configuration from **Azure App Service**. Finally, we will learn about feature flags and how to implement and use them in **ASP.NET Core**.

In this chapter, we're going to cover the following main topics:

- Introducing Azure App Configuration
- Using Azure App Configuration in ASP.NET Core
- Exploring feature flags

Technical requirements

In this chapter, you'll see examples using ASP.NET Core, so you need to install the **.NET SDK**. For building and debugging, you need either **Visual Studio (VS)** or **VS Code**. And to create an Azure App Configuration instance, you need an active Azure subscription.

Introducing Azure App Configuration

One of the key recommendations in the *Twelve-Factor app guidance* (`https://12factor.net/`) is to keep the configuration separate from the application code. Azure App Configuration offers a solution for managing application settings or configuration and feature flags in a centralized manner out of the application code. The Azure App Configuration service helps us to manage application settings or configurations for distributed applications securely and easily. Azure App Configuration can be used by any application. There are SDKs available from Azure to connect to Azure App Configuration for **.NET**, **.NET Core**, **Python**, **Node.js**, and **Java Spring**. Other languages or platforms can make use of the **REST API** provided by Azure to access Azure App Configuration.

In the upcoming sections, we will be creating an Azure App Configuration instance, which will help us to set up our application configuration, and then we will explore how to consume the Azure App Configuration service from an ASP.NET Core application using the Azure App Configuration SDK.

Creating Azure App Configuration instance using the Azure portal

We will create an Azure App Configuration instance from the **Azure portal**. Like any other Azure resource, we can use the **Azure CLI** or **Azure PowerShell**. We will take the following steps:

1. Log in to the Azure portal using the `https://portal.azure.com` URL. Click on the **Create Resource** button or search for `App Configuration`. Then, click on the **Create** button, which will display a screen like this:

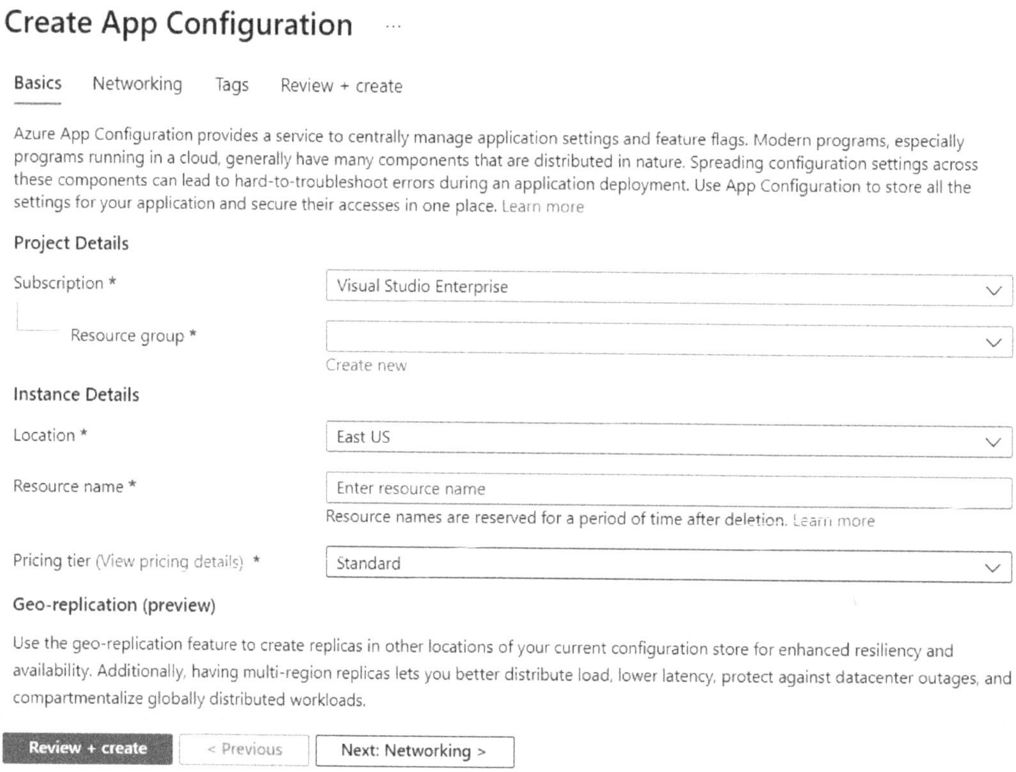

Create App Configuration   ...

Basics   Networking   Tags   Review + create

Azure App Configuration provides a service to centrally manage application settings and feature flags. Modern programs, especially programs running in a cloud, generally have many components that are distributed in nature. Spreading configuration settings across these components can lead to hard-to-troubleshoot errors during an application deployment. Use App Configuration to store all the settings for your application and secure their accesses in one place. Learn more

Project Details

Subscription *   Visual Studio Enterprise   ⌄

Resource group *   ⌄
                                        Create new

Instance Details

Location *   East US   ⌄

Resource name *   Enter resource name
                                        Resource names are reserved for a period of time after deletion. Learn more

Pricing tier (View pricing details) *   Standard   ⌄

Geo-replication (preview)

Use the geo-replication feature to create replicas in other locations of your current configuration store for enhanced resiliency and availability. Additionally, having multi-region replicas lets you better distribute load, lower latency, protect against datacenter outages, and compartmentalize globally distributed workloads.

Review + create   < Previous   Next: Networking >

Figure 9.1 – Create an Azure App Configuration instance

2. Next, we need to configure a resource group, location, and name for Azure App Configuration. Azure App Configuration comes with two pricing tiers – the **Standard tier** and the **Free tier**. For learning and testing purposes, we can use the Free tier. You can find more details about the different pricing tiers here: `https://azure.microsoft.com/en-us/pricing/details/app-configuration/`.

3. Once we choose the Free option for the pricing tier, the **Geo-replication** and **Recovery** options will be disabled.

4. Click on the **Next: Networking >** button to view the networking configuration. By default, the **Public Access** configuration will be set to **Automatic**. We can keep the value as the default and click on the **Review + create** button.

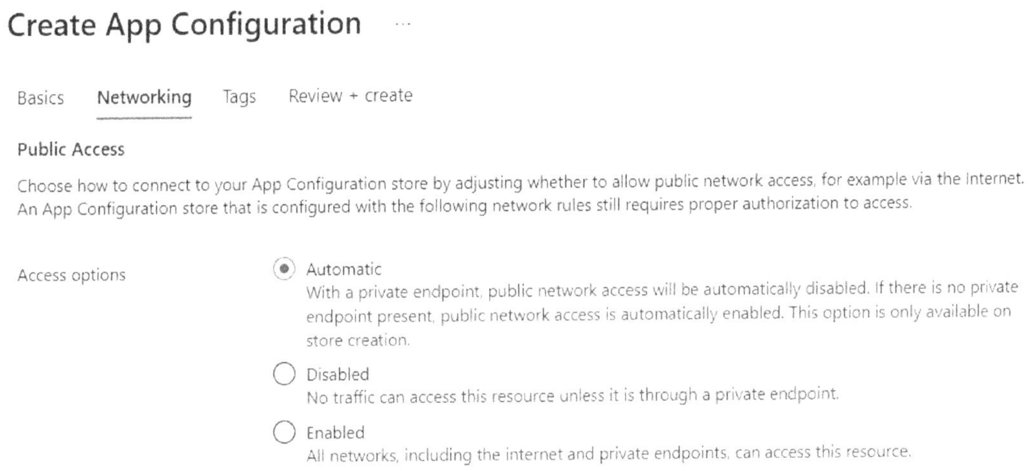

Create App Configuration   ⋯

Basics   **Networking**   Tags   Review + create

Public Access

Choose how to connect to your App Configuration store by adjusting whether to allow public network access, for example via the Internet. An App Configuration store that is configured with the following network rules still requires proper authorization to access.

Access options

    ⦿ Automatic
       With a private endpoint, public network access will be automatically disabled. If there is no private endpoint present, public network access is automatically enabled. This option is only available on store creation.

    ◯ Disabled
       No traffic can access this resource unless it is through a private endpoint.

    ◯ Enabled
       All networks, including the internet and private endpoints, can access this resource.

Figure 9.2 – Azure App Configuration – Networking

5. On the **Review + create** screen, Azure validates the configuration and displays the configured values. We can modify the configuration if any change is required; otherwise, we can click on the **Create** button to create the resource.

6. Next, we will add a configuration value to Azure App Configuration so that we can use it in the **ASP.NET Core** application. We will add a **SQL Server** database connection string. To do this, we need to click on **Azure App Configuration** and select the **Configuration explorer** menu option (see *Figure 9.3*).

7.   In **Configuration explorer**, click on the **+ Create** button and select the **Key-Value** option.

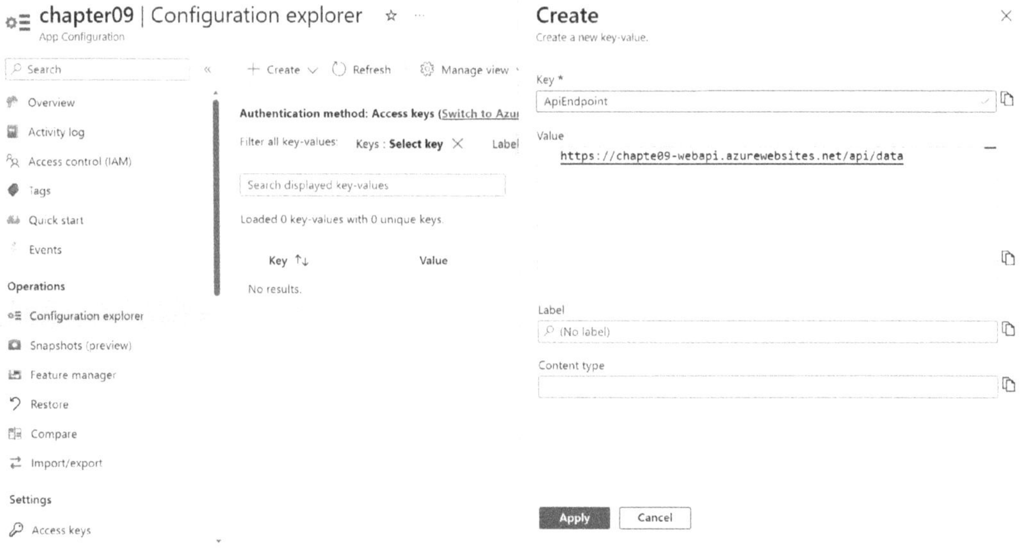

Figure 9.3 – Create a configuration in Azure App Configuration

8.   We can set the key and value. We can set **ApiEndpoint** as the configuration key and the web API endpoint for **Value**. Once it is done, click **Apply** to save the changes.

In this section, we created an Azure App Configuration resource using the Azure portal. In the next section, we will learn how to create an Azure App Configuration instance and set a configuration value using the Azure CLI.

Creating an Azure App Configuration instance using the Azure CLI

In this section, we will learn how to create an Azure App Configuration resource via the Azure CLI. We will take the following steps:

1.   We need to log in to the Azure CLI using the `az login` command.

2.   The following commands will create an Azure resource group and Azure App Configuration resource, and finally, set the key value:

```
> az group create --name Chapter09 --location eastus
> az appconfig create --name Chapter09  --location
eastus  --resource-group Chapter09 --sku free
> az appconfig kv set --name Chapter09 --key ApiEndpoint --value
" https://chapte09-webapi.azurewebsites.net/api/data"
```

3. This will create an Azure App Configuration instance with an Azure resource group and set the database connection string configuration.

In this section, we created an Azure App Configuration resource using the Azure portal and Azure CLI. In the next section, we will learn how to use Azure App Configuration from an ASP.NET Core application.

Using Azure App Configuration in ASP.NET Core

In this section, we will learn how we can use Azure App Configuration in ASP.NET Core. For the purposes of learning, we will be reading the database connection string created in the last section from Azure App Configuration. In this section, we are using the **dotnet CLI** to create the project and VS Code to develop and debug. You can use VS as well. Here are the steps we will follow:

1. First, we will be creating an **ASP.NET Core Web API** project using the `dotnet new webapi -minimal -o Chapter09 --framework net6.0` command.

2. Next, we need to add the **Microsoft.Azure.AppConfiguration.AspNetCore NuGet** packages to connect with Azure App Configuration and read the `ApiEndpoint` key from the configuration store. From the `commandline` or `terminal`, execute the `cd Chapter09` command, and then execute the `dotnet add package Microsoft.Azure.AppConfiguration.AspNetCore` command.

3. Now, we can open the project in **VS Code** in the same terminal window instance. We can do this with the `code` command.

4. Open the `appsettings.json` file in the project (referenced earlier in *Chapter 7, Writing and Reading Data from Azure SQL Database Using .NET Core*), where we will store the configuration values in this file. We will add the connection string to connect to Azure App Configuration. We can get it from the Azure App Configuration **Access keys** section.

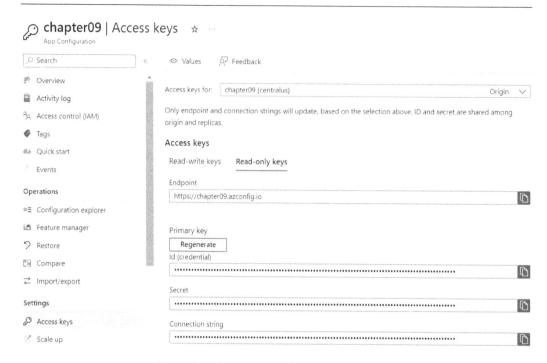

Figure 9.4 – Azure App Configuration access keys

5. Since we are only reading the configuration, it is better to use **Read-only keys**. We can copy the connection string from the screen and save it in `appsettings.json` like this:

```
"ConnectionStrings": {
  "AppConfig": "Endpoint=https://chapter09.azconfig.io;Id=1AgW-
14-s0:UhU4cqp2PHiF5SESK8G4;Secret=tiskPYaq2eRV/DjTmf/
On4EcSO2Q8AqyHH/szOVnd34="
}
```

6. Next, open the `Program.cs` file and add the following code after `var builder = WebApplication.CreateBuilder(args);`:

```
var appConfigConnectionString = builder.Configuration.
GetConnectionString("AppConfig");
builder.Configuration.
AddAzureAppConfiguration(appConfigConnectionString);
builder.Services.AddAzureAppConfiguration();
```

7. We need to add the `AppConfiguration` middleware as well. We can do this by adding the following code:

```
app.UseAzureAppConfiguration();
```

8. Now, our ASP.NET Core application is connected to Azure App Configuration and we have loaded all the key values. If we want to read the value of a key, say `ApiEndpoint`, we can do so like this:

```
var apiEndpoint = builder.Configuration.
GetValue<string>("ApiEndpoint")
```

9. For complex configurations with **child elements**, we can create a normal **C#** POCO class. Here is an example of a configuration:

```
"Smtp": {
  "Host": "smtp.sendgrid.com",
  "Username": "sendgrid-user",
  "Password": "secret007",
  "Port": "587"
}
```

The overall effect of these next commands is to set the configuration for an SMTP (email) service in the Azure App Configuration instance named `Chapter09`. The configuration includes the hostname of the SMTP server (`smtp.sendgrid.com`), a username (`sendgrid-user`), a password (`secret007`), and a port number (`587`).

10. The overall effect of these next commands is to set the configuration for an SMTP (email) service in the Azure App Configuration instance named `Chapter09`. The configuration includes the hostname of the SMTP server (`smtp.sendgrid.com`), a username (`sendgrid-user`), a password (`secret007`), and a port number (`587`):

```
> az appconfig kv set --name Chapter09 --key"Smtp:Host" --value
"smtp.sendgrid.com"  --yes
> az appconfig kv set --name Chapter09 --key "Smtp:Username"
--value "sendgrid-user" -yes
> az appconfig kv set --name Chapter09 --key "Smtp:Password"
--value "secret007"  --yes
> az appconfig kv set --name Chapter09 --key "Smtp:Port" --value
"587"  --yes
```

11. To consume it in the ASP.NET Core app, we need to create a C# class like this:

```
public class Smtp
{
    public string Host { get; set; } = default!;
    public int Port { get; set; }
    public string? Username { get; set; }
    public string? Password { get; set; }
}
```

12. Then, add the following code to read the configuration:

```
var appConfigConnectionString = builder.Configuration.
GetConnectionString("AppConfig");
builder.Configuration.
AddAzureAppConfiguration(appConfigConnectionString);
builder.Services.Configure<Smtp>(builder.Configuration.
GetSection("Smtp"));
 Similar to other services, we can consume the values using
IOptionsSnapshot interface, from Microsoft.Extensions.Options
namespace, which will be injected by ASP.NET Core runtime to
all the controllers or action methods. Here is an example, where
we are returning the value of Host configuration from Azure App
Configuration.app.MapGet("/smtp-host", (IOptionsSnapshot<Smtp>
options) => options.Value.Host);
```

13. Similar to other services, we can consume the values using IOptionsSnapshot interface, from Microsoft.Extensions.Options namespace, which will be injected by ASP.NET Core runtime to all the controllers or action methods. Here is an example, where we are returning the value of Host configuration from Azure App Configuration:

```
app.MapGet("/smtp-host", (IOptionsSnapshot<Smtp>

options) => options.Value.Host);
```

This way, we can consume a simple key-value pair configuration as well as complex configuration objects from Azure App Configuration in ASP.NET Core. In the next section, we will learn about dynamic configuration in ASP.NET Core.

Dynamic configuration in ASP.NET Core

So far, we have explored static configuration implementation – which means we need to restart the application to use the updated values. We can use the dynamic configuration option as well – which means not needing to restart the application to get the updated values. To implement dynamic configuration, we need to add a Sentinel key. A Sentinel key is a key that we need to modify once all other keys have been updated. We will configure our application to monitor this key, and if there is any update, reload all the other configurations.

So, let us add the Sentinel key using the Azure CLI:

```
> az appconfig kv set --name Chapter09 --key "Sentinel" --value
"1"  --yes
```

Next, we need to modify the ASP.NET Core project's `Program.cs` file, where we are connecting to Azure App Configuration like this:

```
builder.Configuration.AddAzureAppConfiguration(options =>
{
    options.Connect(appConfigConnectionString)
        .Select(KeyFilter.Any, LabelFilter.Null)
        .ConfigureRefresh(refreshOptions =>
        {
            refreshOptions.Register("Sentinel", refreshAll: true);
        });
});
```

In the preceding code snippet, we are configuring the application to monitor the changes in the Sentinel key, and if there is a change, refresh all the configuration values. Using the `Select` method, we can configure specific settings to reload. In our case, we are reloading all the configurations.

Next, run the application and verify the `/smtp-host` endpoint, which we implemented in the previous section. Also, verify we are getting the initial configuration value. Then, modify the configuration values for the `Smtp:Host` and Sentinel keys using the following commands:

```
> az appconfig kv set --name Chapter09 --key"Smtp:Host" --value
"smtp1.sendgrid.com"  --yes
> az appconfig kv set --name Chapter09 --key "Sentinel" --value
"2"  --yes
```

Now, browse the `/smtp-host` endpoint again and verify we are getting the updated value.

You have the option to incorporate a call to the `refreshOptions.SetCacheExpiration` function to define the shortest interval between configuration refreshes. If not specified, the default duration of 30 seconds is used. If the goal is to decrease the frequency of requests directed to your App Configuration store, consider configuring this option.

In this section, we learned about dynamic configuration in ASP.NET Core and how to update the configuration values dynamically. It will be applicable to feature toggles as well. In the next section, we will learn about feature flags and how to create them in Azure App Configuration.

Exploring feature toggles

Feature toggles, also known as **feature flags** or **feature switches**, are a technique used in software development to turn on or off specific features or functionality in a software application.

The purpose of feature toggles is to allow developers to release code changes to a production environment while minimizing risk and maintaining control over feature release. Instead of deploying all changes at once, developers can release new features gradually or selectively, and use feature toggles to enable or disable the new functionality as needed. Additionally, feature toggles allow developers to ship code that may not be readily available for use. By disabling the flag, the code can remain intact until development is complete and/or the decision is made to release.

Feature toggles can also be used to test new features with a small subset of users before making them available to everyone, allowing developers to gather feedback and make necessary improvements before a wider release.

Overall, feature toggles are a valuable tool for software development teams to manage the release of new features and ensure a seamless user experience.

Azure App Configuration helps us to configure feature toggles from a centralized location and access it from the **Azure SDK**. In this section, we learned about feature toggles. In the next section, we will learn how to consume them from ASP.NET Core and control the application features based on the various feature flags from Azure App Configuration.

Implementing feature toggles from ASP.NET Core

In a .NET Core or ASP.NET Core application, the **.NET Core Feature Management** libraries offer support for incorporating feature flags. To use Feature Management, we need to import the NuGet `Microsoft.FeatureManagement.AspNetCore` package. By using these libraries, we can declaratively incorporate feature flags into our code, removing the need for manual code writing to enable or disable features through `if-else` conditional statements.

In this section, we will learn how to implement feature toggles in ASP.NET Core. We will be reading the feature configuration from the `appsettings.json` configuration file. Here are the steps to follow:

1. First, let's create an ASP.NET Core **Model View Controller** (**MVC**) application with the following command: `dotnet new mvc -o Chapter09 -framework net6.0`. Once the application is created, we can open it with VS Code using the `code Chapter09` command.

2. Next, we need to add two NuGet packages to the project. We can do so using the following commands:

```
> dotnet add Chapter09 package Microsoft.Azure.AppConfiguration.
AspNetCore
> dotnet add Chapter09 package Microsoft.FeatureManagement.
AspNetCore
```

3. Next, open `appsettings.json` and add the following code:

```
"FeatureManagement" : {
  "FeatureA" : true,
  "FeatureB" : false
}
```

With the previous code, we are enabling `FeatureA` and disabling `FeatureB`.

4. Next, we need to inject the `IfeatureManager` interface using dependency injection into our `Program.cs` file. By doing so, we will be able to access the feature configuration from our **controllers** and **services**. The following code shows how to accomplish this:

```
using Microsoft.FeatureManagement;
var builder = WebApplication.CreateBuilder(args);
builder.Services.AddFeatureManagement();
builder.Services.AddControllersWithViews();
var app = builder.Build();
```

The `IFeatureManager` interface helps us to read the values of different features configured in `appsettings.json` or any other configuration, such as Azure App Configuration, by exposing the `IsEnabledAsync` method. This helps developers verify whether or not a feature is enabled.

5. In controllers, we can use the `IFeatureManager` interface in the constructor like in this example, where we are consuming the `IFeatureManager` interface in `HomeController`:

```
private readonly ILogger<HomeController> _logger;
private readonly IFeatureManager _featureManager;

public HomeController(ILogger<HomeController> logger,
IFeatureManager featureManager)
{
_logger = logger;
_featureManager = featureManager;
}
```

We can verify whether the feature is enabled or not like this:

```
public async Task<IActionResult> Index()
{
var isFeatureAEnabled =
await _featureManager.IsEnabledAsync("FeatureA");
if(isFeatureAEnabled)
{
    return View("View1");
}
return View();
}
```

We can manage the user interface or functionalities based on the feature. In the preceding code, if `FeatureA` is enabled, then we are returning a view with more options, and if it is not enabled, a normal view is returned.

In this section, we learned how to create and read feature toggles, as well as checking their availability using the `IFeatureManager` interface. In the next section, we will learn more about feature toggles by dealing with **controller actions**, **middleware**, **MVC filters**, and **ASP.NET Core MVC views**.

Controller actions

Earlier, we used the `IFeatureManager` interface to check whether a specific feature is enabled or not. In ASP.NET Core controllers, action methods are used to define the various endpoints or routes of your web application. These action methods handle incoming HTTP requests and return appropriate responses. The **Controller actions** option is useful when we want to toggle a controller action based on a feature. It means if the feature is enabled, we will be able to access the controller action; otherwise, we will get a `Not Found - 404` error. To enable this functionality, we start by adding the `FeatureGate` attribute to the controller action, as shown. This attribute is available in the `Microsoft.FeatureManagement.Mvc` namespace. We need to pass the name of the feature as the parameter to the attribute. In this scenario, we are checking whether `FeatureB` is enabled or not:

```
[FeatureGate("FeatureB")]
public IActionResult FeatureB()
{
    return View();
}
```

This attribute helps us control the feature availability with zero changes in the method implementation. We can also apply this attribute at the `Controller` level so that we can control entire controller actions based on the feature toggle. Here is how to apply the `FeatureGate` attribute to a `Controller` class:

```
[FeatureGate("FeatureB")]
public class HomeController : Controller
{
}
```

Middleware

The ASP.NET Core middleware is a feature of the ASP.NET Core framework that allows developers to incorporate modules or components for managing requests and responses in web applications. We can also use our feature toggles in order to control the middleware execution as well. Here is example code that returns the execution response time in the response headers:

```
public class ResponseTimeMiddleware
{
    private readonly RequestDelegate _next;
```

```
    public ResponseTimeMiddleware(RequestDelegate next)
    {
        _next = next;
    }
    public async Task InvokeAsync(HttpContext context)
    {
        var stopwatch = new Stopwatch();
        stopwatch.Start();
        context.Response.OnStarting(() =>
        {
            stopwatch.Stop();
            context.Response.Headers["X-Response-Time"] =
$"{stopwatch.ElapsedMilliseconds}ms";
            return Task.CompletedTask;
        });
        await _next(context);
    }
}
```

We can add this middleware to our `Program.cs` file by using the following command:

```
app.UseMiddleware<ResponseTimeMiddleware>();
```

Using feature flags, we can control the execution of this middleware like this:

```
app.UseMiddlewareForFeature<ResponseTimeMiddleware>("FeatureA");
```

So, instead of using the `UseMiddleware` method, we can use the `UseMiddlewareForFeature` method. If we want to control middleware execution based on a feature flag, we can do that using the following code:

```
app.UseForFeature("FeatureA", app =>
{
    app.UseMiddleware<ResponseTimeMiddleware>();
    //we can add more middleware here
});
```

This way, we can integrate a feature toggle with **ASP.NET Core middleware**.

MVC views

In ASP.NET Core MVC, views are responsible for generating the HTML or other content that is sent to the client's browser, rendering the user interface, and presenting data to users. In **MVC views**, we can use feature toggles by using the **feature toggle tag helpers**. Tag helpers help us to create custom **HTML** elements using C#. To do this, start by adding the **Feature Management tag helper** to _ViewImports.cshtml. This file is part of the ASP.NET Core MVC template, which we can find under the Views folder, under the project folder. Add the following code:

```
@addTagHelper *, Microsoft.FeatureManagement.AspNetCore
```

Next, we can modify the Index.cshtml file, under the **Views** | **Home** folder, with code like this:

```
<feature name="FeatureA">
    <p>This can only be seen if 'FeatureA' is enabled.</p>
</feature>
```

The <feature> HTML element mentioned previously is the tag helper. In ASP.NET Core, a tag helper is a feature that simplifies working with HTML tags and attributes in Razor views. To support the <feature> tag helper, we added the @addTagHelper snippet to the _ViewImports. cshtml file, which we can find under the Views folder. For more details about feature toggles in ASP.NET Core MVC, please visit https://learn.microsoft.com/en-us/azure/ azure-app-configuration/use-feature-flags-dotnet-core?tabs=core5x.

In this section, we learned how to use feature toggles in ASP.NET Core MVC. In the next section, we will learn about how to configure Azure App Configuration for feature management and how to use Azure App Configuration features from an ASP.NET Core application.

Using features from Azure App Configuration

Once we are able to run the application and manage the application logic with different features, we can start using the Azure App Configuration service instead of the appsettings.json file. Using the Azure App Configuration service, we will be able to manage the features from a centralized location. If we modify appsettings.json, we may need to restart the application to use the updated features, but with the help of Azure App Configuration, we will be able to do it at runtime; no application restart is required. First, we will discuss using the Azure CLI to configure features in Azure App Configuration, and then we will discuss using the Azure portal. Here are the steps we will follow:

1. Log in to the Azure CLI using and execute the az login command in your terminal. This will open the Azure login screen using your default browser. Once logged in, you will be able to see the subscription you're using. Then, you can close the browser window.

2. In the terminal window, execute the following command:

   ```
   az appconfig feature set --name chapter09 --feature featureB -y
   ```

   This will create a feature with the name featureB, and by default, it will be disabled.

3. We can enable this feature by executing the following command:

   ```
   az appconfig feature enable --name chapter09 --feature featureB
   -y
   ```

4. The -y flag informs the Azure CLI to show a confirmation prompt.

Up until this point, we have learned about configuring features in Azure App Configuration using the Azure CLI. Our next step is to learn about configuration features using the Azure portal by following these steps:

1. First, use the Azure portal to create a feature by going to the Azure portal, selecting the Azure App Configuration instance you created earlier in this chapter, and then selecting the **Feature Manager** menu option. Feature Manager will display the features configured and we will be able to manage different features.

2. To create a new feature, click on the + **Create** button on the **Feature Management** screen.

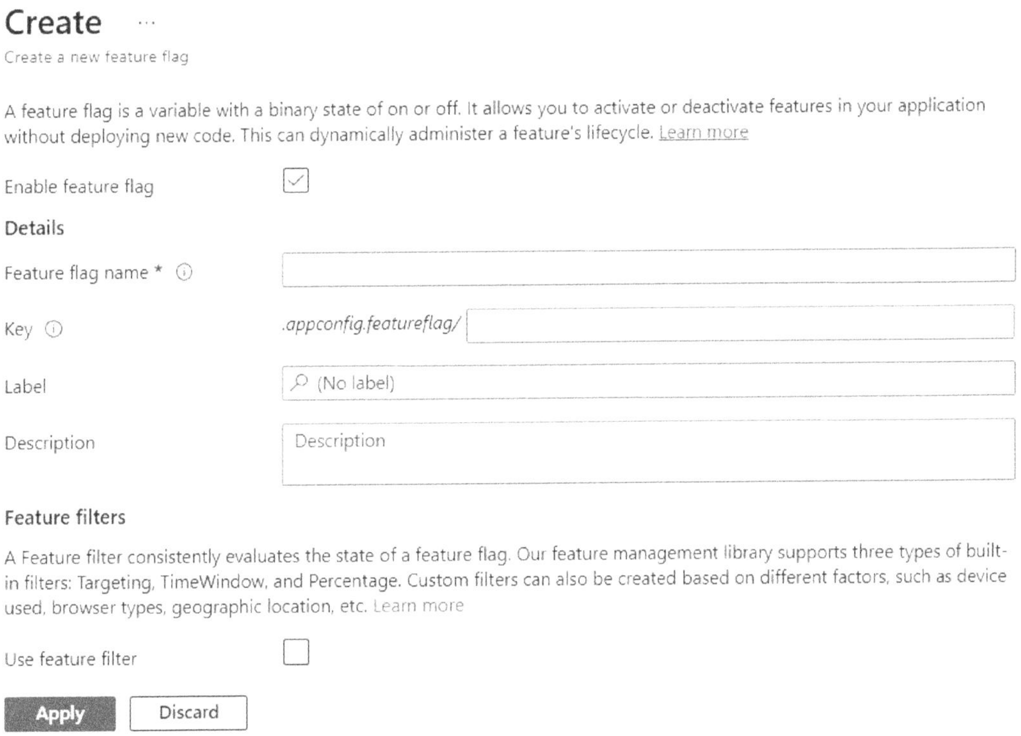

Create   ...
Create a new feature flag

A feature flag is a variable with a binary state of on or off. It allows you to activate or deactivate features in your application without deploying new code. This can dynamically administer a feature's lifecycle. Learn more

Enable feature flag   ☑

Details

Feature flag name * ⓘ   [   ]

Key ⓘ   .appconfig.featureflag/ [   ]

Label   🔍 (No label)

Description   [Description   ]

Feature filters

A Feature filter consistently evaluates the state of a feature flag. Our feature management library supports three types of built-in filters: Targeting, TimeWindow, and Percentage. Custom filters can also be created based on different factors, such as device used, browser types, geographic location, etc. Learn more

Use feature filter   ☐

[**Apply**]   [Discard]

Figure 9.5 – Azure App Configuration | Create new feature

3. Next, add a new feature, and we'll call that feature Beta. **Feature flag name** needs to have its value set to Beta. Also, select the **Enable feature flag** checkbox.

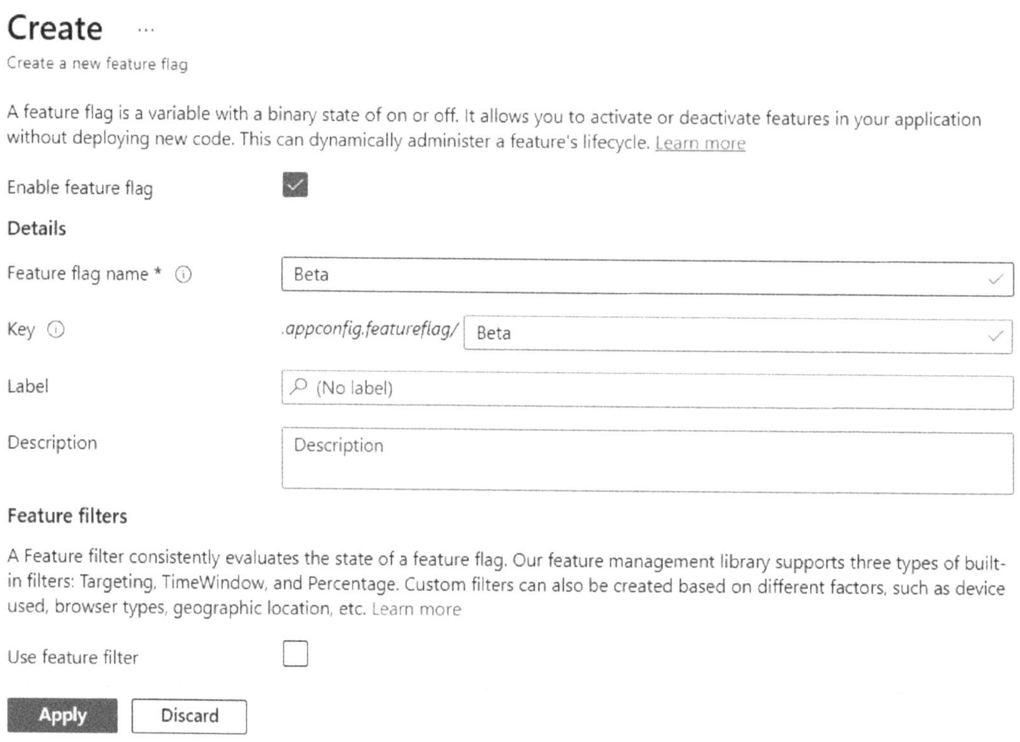

Create ...

Create a new feature flag

A feature flag is a variable with a binary state of on or off. It allows you to activate or deactivate features in your application without deploying new code. This can dynamically administer a feature's lifecycle. Learn more

Enable feature flag   ☑

Details

Feature flag name * ⓘ   Beta   ✓

Key ⓘ   .appconfig.featureflag/   Beta   ✓

Label   🔍 (No label)

Description   Description

Feature filters

A Feature filter consistently evaluates the state of a feature flag. Our feature management library supports three types of built-in filters: Targeting, TimeWindow, and Percentage. Custom filters can also be created based on different factors, such as device used, browser types, geographic location, etc. Learn more

Use feature filter   ☐

Apply   Discard

Figure 9.6 – Create new feature | Azure App Configuration

We will be using the name **Beta** in the code to verify the status of the flag in the application.

4. Next, modify `Program.cs` to include the code that reads the configuration and features from the Azure App Configuration service. The following is example code to do this:

```
using Microsoft.FeatureManagement;
var builder = WebApplication.CreateBuilder(args);
builder.Configuration.AddAzureAppConfiguration(options =>
{
options.Connect(builder.Configuration.
GetConnectionString("AppConfig"));
    options.UseFeatureFlags();
});
builder.Services.AddFeatureManagement();
```

The preceding code connects to Azure App Configuration using the `AppConfig` connection string, and the `UseFeatureFlags` method will then enable support for reading feature flags. The `AddFeatureManagement()` method injects the `IFeatureManager` interface via dependency injection.

5. In the `Controller` class itself, we can use the `IFeatureManager` interface like this:

```
public class HomeController : Controller
{
    private readonly ILogger<HomeController> _logger;
    private readonly IFeatureManager _featureManager;
    public HomeController(ILogger<HomeController> logger,
        IFeatureManager featureManager)
    {
        _logger = logger;
        _featureManager = featureManager;
    }

    public async Task<IActionResult> Index()
    {
        var isFeatureAEnabled =
            await _featureManager.IsEnabledAsync("Beta");
        if(isFeatureAEnabled)
        {
            return View("IndexBeta");
        }
        return View();
    }
}
```

Once we've explored Azure App Configuration, we can remove the resources to avoid Azure charges. We can either delete the resource group from the portal or execute the Azure CLI command:

```
az group delete --name chapter09
```

Please remember to validate that all the resources are deleted from your resource group so that you don't incur any unwanted fees.

In this section, we learned about feature toggles and how to use them in ASP.NET Core. We also learned about creating features in Azure App Configuration using the Azure CLI and the Azure portal.

Summary

In this chapter, we learned about Azure App Configuration – an Azure service that helps to manage application settings and configuration in a central location. In the first section, we learned how to create and configure different application configuration settings in Azure App Configuration. Then, we learned how to consume these configuration values from an ASP.NET Core Web API application. In the next section, we learned about feature flags or feature toggles – a software development technique that helps developers to roll out features without redeploying code. Then, we learned how to implement feature toggles in ASP.NET Core MVC applications. We also explored how to create features in Azure App Configuration using the Azure CLI and Azure portal, which will help us implement feature toggles for a distributed application.

In the next chapter, we will learn about the **Azure Event Hubs** service – a big data streaming platform and event ingestion service. This service helps us to process large volumes of data in seconds. We will learn about Azure Event Hubs, different patterns, and configuring security in Azure Event Hubs.

10
Processing Data with Azure Event Hubs

Welcome to your one-stop resource to navigate the exciting world of **Azure Event Hubs** as a **.NET** developer!

At its core, Azure Event Hubs is Microsoft Azure's response to the growing need for a robust **big data streaming platform** and **event ingestion service**. Picture your application generating millions of events every second. Now, imagine capturing, processing, and analyzing those events in real time.

In our rapidly digitizing world, the ability to process and analyze vast quantities of data in real time is no longer a luxury but a necessity. Applications for **Internet of Things (IoT)** devices, real-time analytics, and other digital services generate massive amounts of data. The key to success lies in harnessing, understanding, and making decisions based on this data. Azure Event Hubs can address this challenge for your .NET applications, allowing you to manage and analyze this torrent of information efficiently and effectively. Azure Event Hubs stands tall in this landscape. It's a solution that scales with you, capable of handling anything from a modest stream of data from a small application to a deluge of events from an enterprise-scale solution. Scalability isn't its only strength. Azure Event Hubs is a big data streaming platform and event ingestion service that efficiently captures and streams massive amounts of data, paving the way for subsequent real-time processing and analysis by other integrated services. It's part of the vibrant Azure ecosystem, integrating smoothly with various Azure services and third-party applications. Azure Event Hubs offer flexibility, allowing you to tailor it to your project's unique requirements and bringing Azure's reliability to your doorstep. With robust security, dependability, and Microsoft's support, you can trust Azure Event Hubs to support your data streaming needs.

This is the start of our journey into the heart of Azure Event Hubs for .NET developers. By leveraging the **Azure SDK for .NET**, you can harness the full capabilities of Azure Event Hubs in your applications. We'll walk you through key concepts, set up processes, and show you how to write .NET applications that fully utilize the power of event streaming.

So, let's dive in and unlock the power of real-time data processing with Azure Event Hubs! This chapter provides a detailed journey, from the basics to advanced usage of Azure Event Hubs, offering you the tools and knowledge to handle data in your .NET applications confidently.

In this chapter, we will cover the following topics:

- The key concepts of Azure Event Hubs
- How Azure Event Hubs handles event ingestion
- Event storage and retention
- Setting up an Azure Event Hubs client in .NET
- Routing, load balancing, and error handling
- Implementing retry policies and exponential backoff
- Dead-lettering and handling poison messages
- Monitoring and alerting for failures and errors
- Building robust applications with Azure Event Hubs
- Scaling and performance optimization

Key concepts of Azure Event Hubs

In the realm of event-driven architectures, where the seamless orchestration of event production, detection, consumption, and reaction is crucial, Azure Event Hubs emerges as a pivotal player. This architecture is particularly advantageous when dealing with massive real-time data streams, such as telemetry, which demands swift and reliable processing. Azure Event Hubs, a robust data streaming platform and event ingestion service within Microsoft Azure, is tailored to effectively handle such continuous data streams. It is especially well suited for scenarios such as IoT, where devices might send data at frequent intervals.

However, it's important to distinguish between telemetry data and discrete events. While Azure Event Hubs excels at ingesting large volumes of telemetry data, such as those generated in time-series patterns, Azure Event Grid and Service Bus are more apt to handle discrete, singular events. Event Grid is designed for high availability and consistent performance for event-based order of operations, allowing for reactive programming. Meanwhile, Service Bus is optimized for enterprise messaging, offering richer capabilities such as message sessions, topics, and subscriptions. The specific requirements of an application or system should determine which of these services to use.

This section will lead you through the foundational elements of Azure Event Hubs, equipping you with a solid understanding of its core concepts. As you navigate the ensuing headings, you'll gain insights into the pivotal roles of events, event producers, event consumers, partitions, and namespaces. This comprehension will serve as the bedrock for your journey into understanding how Azure Event Hubs ingests and processes events while exploring its integration within the broader Azure ecosystem.

Events

In the context of event-driven systems, events serve as the lifeblood of the entire process. These events often take the form of series data, particularly time-series data, which comprises a sequence of data points recorded at regular time intervals. These intervals are uniform, meaning the data points are spaced consistently over time.

For instance, think of data from a sensor that records temperature readings every minute or a heart rate monitor that tracks a user's heartbeat every second. Such data, collected over time, forms a time-series dataset and plays a crucial role in various applications, including monitoring, analytics, and real-time decision-making. These data points, when processed and analyzed, provide valuable insights and enable actions to be taken based on the evolving information.

When ingested through systems such as Azure Event Hubs, each data point becomes an event with its own payload (the actual reading) and metadata (information about when and where the reading was taken). In this context, Event Hubs is designed to handle the high velocity and volume of time-series data, ensuring that each event is captured and ready for subsequent processing or analysis.

Conversely, discrete events are singular occurrences and don't necessarily follow a consistent pattern or frequency – for instance, a user clicking on a web page, a machine completing its manufacturing cycle, or a stock trade occurring. These events are significant in their own right. They might be best processed with systems such as Azure Event Grid or Service Bus, tailored to handle such singular, significant occurrences.

Understanding the distinction between continuous time-series data and discrete events is crucial when architecting solutions, as the nature of the data dictates which tool or service is best suited for ingestion, processing, and reaction.

Event producers

Event producers are the sources of data that feed into Azure Event Hubs. In the event-driven scenario, they're the *talkers*, generating and sending data to the Event Hub. This could be anything from IoT devices, such as sensors and smart meters, to applications logging user activity, service logs from web servers, and so on. They create events, which Event Hubs then ingests. Understanding what an event producer is in your application is crucial to defining your event-driven data flow.

Event consumers

Conversely to event producers, we have **event consumers**. In our event-driven paradigm, these entities represent the *receptors* responsible for receiving and processing the data dispatched to the Event Hub by the producers. The diversity of event consumers is comparable to that of the producers – they can manifest as analytics systems performing complex calculations, databases archiving the incoming data, or applications programmed to respond to specific user activities, among other possibilities. By accurately defining your event consumers, you can pinpoint which components of your application are tasked with responding to the myriad events occurring within your system. This understanding is paramount in crafting a well-structured, efficient event-driven application.

Partitions

Partitions in Event Hubs are akin to lanes on a highway. They help manage the data flow, allowing multiple consumers to read data in parallel. Each partition maintains its chain of events and holds onto these events for a specified time, regardless of whether they've been read. This allows consumers to read from any point in the stored sequence of events, giving you a lot of flexibility in how you process your data.

Event Hubs namespaces

A **namespace** in Event Hubs is a way to group multiple event hubs. This is useful for organizations and for defining shared access policies. It's like a container for your event hubs, helping you to manage them more effectively.

Event ingestion and processing with Azure Event Hubs

Now that you understand the critical components of Event Hubs, let's look at how events are ingested and processed:

- **Event ingestion**: Event Hubs ingests data from event producers via a simple **HTTP POST**. Data can be sent individually or bundled together in batches. Batching can be more efficient, as it reduces the number of total requests made, but it's crucial to remember that there's a maximum size limit per batch (currently, 1 MB). Once ingested, the data is automatically sharded across the partitions in the Event Hub.

- **Event processing**: After data is ingested, it needs to be processed. Azure provides several services that integrate well with Event Hubs for this purpose, such as **Azure Stream Analytics** for real-time data stream processing, **Azure Functions** to execute **event-driven code**, and **Azure Logic Apps** for **workflows**.

Scaling and availability in Azure Event Hubs

Handling a large volume of data in real-time requires robust scaling capabilities. At the same time, ensuring that the data is always available is critical for many applications. Azure Event Hubs shines in both these aspects:

- **Scaling**: Scaling in Azure Event Hubs is primarily managed through throughput units. Each throughput unit allows a certain number of events (or total data size) per second. You can automatically scale the number of throughput units based on the needs of your application.

In addition, Event Hubs partitions allow data to be read and written in parallel, providing another layer of scalability.

- **Availability and reliability**: Event Hubs is designed to be highly **available** and **reliable**. It's a distributed service deployed across multiple data centers in all Azure regions, providing **built-in redundancy**. You can also configure Event Hubs to replicate data across multiple Azure regions, providing additional protection against regional failures. This high availability and reliability make Event Hubs a trustworthy backbone for any event-driven application.

Integrating Azure Event Hubs in the Azure ecosystem

Beyond functioning as a standalone service, Azure Event Hubs plays well with the broader Azure ecosystem. It can be integrated with several other Azure services, amplifying its value and offering more sophisticated data processing options. While Azure Event Hubs shines as a standalone powerhouse, its true potential is unveiled when harmoniously integrated into the broader Azure ecosystem. This integration expands its capabilities, allowing it to collaborate effortlessly with various Azure services to unlock sophisticated data processing avenues.

In the upcoming subsections, we'll delve into two notable integration points – Azure Event Grid and Azure Functions. These dynamic components will showcase how Azure Event Hubs extends its reach and synergizes with other Azure offerings, elevating your event-driven applications to new heights. Through these integrations, you'll witness firsthand how Azure Event Hubs transforms into a pivotal conduit, seamlessly connecting data flows, triggers, and actions for enhanced data management and processing.

Azure Event Grid

Azure Event Grid is a fully managed event routing service that works perfectly with Azure Event Hubs. Event Grid can distribute incoming data from Event Hubs to different destinations in a highly reliable and scalable manner. It can be used for scenarios such as **order processing**, **user telemetry processing**, and updating databases in response to changes in data.

Azure Functions

As you likely already know, **Azure Functions** is a serverless platform that enables the execution of modular code snippets, or *functions*, in a cloud environment. Due to Azure Functions' flexibility, various events – including those originating from Azure Event Hubs – can start these code snippets. Therefore, leveraging Azure Functions empowers you to run tailored code reacting to events within your designated Event Hub. The scope of these actions can range from manipulating data and invoking **external API calls** to conducting sophisticated computations, among other operations.

By now, you should have a solid understanding of Azure Event Hubs and its various components. You've learned about event producers, consumers, events, partitions, and namespaces. In the upcoming section, you will learn how Azure Event Hubs ingests and processes events and how it integrates with other Azure services.

How Azure Event Hubs handles event ingestion

Azure Event Hubs is a powerful platform for streaming big data and capturing events. It can handle and work with millions of events every second, making it the perfect solution for any application with **telemetry**, **distributed data streaming**, or **real-time analytics**. It enables multiple event producers to publish data to a central hub. Applications, or event consumers, can then retrieve this data in real time or later. Event ingestion in Azure Event Hubs is primarily based on two key components – **event producers** and **event consumers**. Event producers are entities that send data to Event Hubs. They can be any entity that produces data, such as a telemetry system on a vehicle, a website tracking page views, or a server monitoring system sending logs. Let's walk through an example together.

At the beginning of the ingestion process, event producers are responsible for creating and sending the events to the Event Hub. Event producers can be anything capable of creating and dispatching information. In an IoT scenario, for instance, an event producer can be a sensor monitoring temperature, whereas in a **logging** scenario, it might be an application reporting its internal state. Event producers send data to Event Hubs via **AMQP 1.0**, **HTTPS**, or **Apache Kafka** protocols. The data transmitted is typically small in size, and the body of the event data is the actual payload of the event itself. It could be as simple as a temperature reading from a sensor or more complex, such as a complete log file. Once an event is sent to an Event Hub, it gets assigned to a specific partition. When you send an event to an Event Hub, it's like putting it in a specific folder called a 'partition.' Event Hubs use partitions to handle lots of events quickly. Each partition is like a list of events in the order they arrive, with new events added to the end of the list.

The number of partitions in an Event Hub directly relates to its maximum throughput, so partitioning plays a crucial role in managing the scalability of your solution. Event Hubs use a concept called **Throughput Units** (**TUs**) to control the resources allocated for event processing. A TU guarantees a capacity of up to 1 MB per second for ingress and up to 2 MB per second for egress. Higher TUs provide higher capacity. This enables Event Hubs to scale dynamically based on the number of TUs, thus handling event ingestion effectively.

Let's illustrate event ingestion with a .NET code snippet that uses `EventHubProducerClient` to send events to an Event Hub:

```
string connectionString = "<< YOUR CONNECTION STRING >>";
string eventHubName = "<< YOUR EVENT HUB NAME >>";
await using (var producerClient = new
EventHubProducerClient(connectionString, eventHubName))
{
    using EventDataBatch eventBatch = await producerClient.
CreateBatchAsync();
```

```
    eventBatch.TryAdd(new EventData(Encoding.UTF8.GetBytes("First
event")));
    eventBatch.TryAdd(new EventData(Encoding.UTF8.GetBytes("Second
event")));
    eventBatch.TryAdd(new EventData(Encoding.UTF8.GetBytes("Third
event")));

    await producerClient.SendAsync(eventBatch);
}
```

This code creates an instance of `EventHubProducerClient`, which is used to send new events to the Event Hub. It creates a batch of events – in this case, three simple string messages – and then sends them to the Event Hub. This batch of events is then ingested by Azure Event Hubs, ready to be processed or consumed by any downstream services or applications.

In this section, we will learn about event storage and retention in Azure Event Hubs. While Event Hubs is primarily designed as a streaming platform for real-time data, it also offers event storage capabilities with configurable retention policies. We'll explore how events sent to an Event Hub are stored for a defined period and how the retention period can be customized.

Event storage and retention

Azure Event Hubs is primarily a streaming platform designed to handle real-time data, but it also features event storage capabilities and configurable retention policies.

When events are sent to an Event Hub, they are stored for a configured period. By default, the retention period is one day, but this can be set to a maximum of seven days in a standard tier Event Hubs namespace or longer with a dedicated tier.

It's crucial to note that Event Hubs follows a **log-based storage system**. This means once an event is written, it can't be changed or deleted until the retention period elapses. Also, events are read in the order they were added to the partition, following a **First In, First Out** (**FIFO**) model. In addition to its real-time data streaming capabilities, Azure Event Hubs offers essential features that ensure data reliability, fault tolerance, and scalability. Let's explore how Azure Event Hubs handles larger retention periods, its fault tolerance and reliability mechanisms, as well as its robust replication, high availability, and disaster recovery capabilities.

How Azure Event Hubs handles larger retention periods

For scenarios requiring long-term storage, event retention, replication, disaster recovery, and high availability, Event Hubs can be integrated with **Azure Blob Storage** or **Azure Data Lake Storage**. With this setup, events from Event Hubs can be automatically captured and written to these storage solutions. This feature is known as **Event Hubs Capture**. This feature is expensive and should be thoroughly vetted through a proof of concept to ensure it is a viable architectural decision for an organization.

Fault tolerance and reliability

Fault tolerance and **reliability** are critical aspects of any data platform. Azure Event Hubs is designed with multiple features to ensure high availability and reliability.

The following are the processes with which Azure Event Hubs ensures fault tolerance and reliability:

- **Replication**: In the background, Event Hubs automatically replicates all data three times within the same data center for redundancy. If one copy fails, there are still two other copies available.

- **Availability zones**: For an even higher level of resiliency, Azure Event Hubs supports **Availability Zones** (**AZs**). When enabled, they replicate data across three different data centers within the same region. Therefore, even if an entire data center goes down, your Event Hubs service remains unaffected.

- **Failovers**: In the event of a disaster, Azure Event Hubs provides support for regional disaster recovery failovers. You can pair two Event Hubs namespaces in different regions, and if there is a regional outage, you can manually fail over to the secondary namespace.

Replication, high availability, and disaster recovery capabilities

Azure Event Hubs ensures high availability by leveraging Azure's powerful features, such as AZs and Geo-Disaster recovery. AZs distribute Event Hub's infrastructure across multiple data center locations in a region, reducing the impact of hardware issues or maintenance disruptions. Additionally, Geo-Disaster recovery pairs primary and secondary Event Hubs namespaces across Azure regions, replicating vital entities such as event hubs and consumer groups – enabling smooth transitions to the secondary namespace during regional outages. While data isn't replicated, these strategies safeguard event streaming operations, guaranteeing uninterrupted service even in adverse circumstances.

For instance, to enable Geo-Disaster recovery, you must create an alias and associate two Event Hubs namespaces (primary and secondary) in different regions. Afterwards, all metadata operations go through the alias. This way, in the event of a **regional disaster**, you can manually initiate a failover to the secondary namespace via the alias without any changes required on the producer or consumer side.

Here's a brief code example of creating an Event Hubs namespace with **AZ support** via the **Azure CLI**:

1. Log in to Azure; if you are on your local development machine, you can set this command to log in:

    ```
    az login
    ```

2. Run the following command to create the primary Event Hub:

    ```
    az eventhubs namespace create \
        --name demoapp-telemetry-canadacentral \
        --resource-group demoapp-rg \
        --sku Standard \
    ```

```
--location canadacentral \
--zone-redundant true
```

With this command, you're creating an Event Hubs namespace named `demoapp-telemetry-canadacentral` within the `demoapp-rg` resource group. The Event Hubs namespace will be deployed in the `canadacentral` region and configured for zone redundancy.

3. Run the following command to create the backup Event Hub:

```
az eventhubs namespace create \
    --name demoapp-telemetry-canadaeast \
    --resource-group demoapp-rg \
    --sku Standard \
    --location canadaeast \
    --zone-redundant true
```

4. Finally, we need to configure the redundancy between the primary and backup Event Hubs; we will do this by creating a **Disaster Recovery (DR)** configuration alias as follows:

```
az eventhubs georecovery-alias create \
    --resource-group DR_Group \
    --namespace-name demoapp-telemetry-canadaeast \
    --alias demoapp-telemetry-canadawest-alias \
    --partner-namespace demoapp-telemetry-canadacentral \
    --partner-resource-group demoapp-rg \
    --partner-namespace-role Primary
```

This command helps you establish a Geo-DR configuration between two Event Hubs namespaces. The primary namespace, located in the `canadaeast` region, will have a Geo-DR alias (`demoapp-telemetry-canadawest-alias`) associated with it. The data from the primary namespace will be replicated to the partner namespace (`demoapp-telemetry-canadacentral`) located in the `canadacentral` region. The `Primary` role assigned to the partner namespace indicates that it will serve as the replication destination for the primary namespace's data, ensuring data redundancy and high availability.

Azure Event Hubs' robust design, backed by Azure's reliability features, ensures your real-time data ingestion and processing operations are highly reliable and fault-tolerant. This empowers you to focus on building applications that drive your business, knowing your data pipeline will be resilient and always available. With all this theory completed, let's now focus our efforts on setting up an Azure Event Hubs client in .NET.

Setting up an Azure Event Hubs client in .NET

When working with Azure Event Hubs in .NET, establishing a connection to the Event Hub is the first crucial step before sending or receiving events. This section will explore setting up an Azure Event

Hubs client using the `Azure.Messaging.EventHubs` NuGet package. With the client in place, you can seamlessly interact with the Event Hub, enabling efficient data streaming and processing in real-time applications.

Establishing a connection to an Event Hub

You need to establish a connection to an Event Hub before sending or receiving events. The first step is to install the **Azure.Messaging.EventHubs NuGet package**. After installing it, you can establish the connection using the following code:

```
using Azure.Messaging.EventHubs;
string connectionString = "<Your Event Hubs connection string>";
string eventHubName = "<Your Event Hub name>";

await using var client = new EventHubProducerClient(connectionString,
eventHubName);
```

The provided code demonstrates how to establish a connection to an Azure Event Hub using the `Azure.Messaging.EventHubs` NuGet package in a .NET application. Before delving into the mechanics of connecting to an Azure Event Hub in a .NET environment, let's unpack the essentials of the code structure and the sequence of operations that it entails:

- **Importing the necessary namespace**: The code begins by importing the required namespace. `Azure.Messaging.EventHubs` contains the classes and components needed to work with Event Hubs.

- **Connection details**: The `connectionString` and `eventHubName` variables are used to store the connection string and the name of the specific Event Hub you want to connect to. These values are crucial for the client to know which Event Hub to interact with.

- **Creating an Event Hub client**: The `EventHubProducerClient` class is used to create a client that can send events to the Event Hub. `EventHubProducerClient` is initialized with the `connectionString` and `eventHubName` values, effectively establishing a connection to the specified Event Hub.

- **Using a statement and asynchronous operation**: The code uses the `await-using` statement, which ensures the proper disposal of resources when the client is no longer needed. The `await` keyword indicates that the operation is asynchronous, allowing other application parts to continue executing while the connection is established.

In summary, this code snippet sets up an `EventHubProducerClient` object, enabling the application to interact with the specified Event Hub. Once this connection is established, the application can send events to the Event Hub for further processing and distribution.

Sending events to an event hub using the Event Hubs client

After setting up a connection to Azure Event Hubs, the next step is to use the client to send data. In real-time systems, this data, called an *event*, can represent anything from a button click in an app to a reading from a device, or even a completed financial transaction. It's crucial to send these events quickly and effectively so that other system components can analyze or use them. In this section, we'll walk you through how to send one of these events using the Event Hubs client.

Here's how you can send a single event:

```
using Azure.Messaging.EventHubs;
using Azure.Messaging.EventHubs.Producer;
string connectionString = "<Your Event Hubs connection string>";
string eventHubName = "<Your Event Hub name>";
await using var client = new EventHubProducerClient(connectionString,
eventHubName);
var eventData = new EventData(Encoding.UTF8.GetBytes("This is a test
event."));
await client.SendAsync(eventData);
Console.WriteLine("Event sent.");
You can also batch multiple events together to optimize network
utilization:
using Azure.Messaging.EventHubs;
using Azure.Messaging.EventHubs.Producer;
string connectionString = "<Your Event Hubs connection string>";
string eventHubName = "<Your Event Hub name>";
await using var client = new EventHubProducerClient(connectionString,
eventHubName);
using EventDataBatch eventBatch = await client.CreateBatchAsync();
eventBatch.TryAdd(new EventData(Encoding.UTF8.GetBytes("First
event")));
eventBatch.TryAdd(new EventData(Encoding.UTF8.GetBytes("Second
event")));
await client.SendAsync(eventBatch);
Console.WriteLine("Batch of events sent.");
```

The code illustrates how to send events to an Azure Event Hub using `EventHubProducerClient` from the `Azure.Messaging.EventHubs` namespace. Initially, it establishes a connection using specified connection details and then sends a single `EventData` instance with a test message. Following that, the code demonstrates a more efficient approach – batching events. It creates an empty batch with `CreateBatchAsync`, populates it with multiple events, and sends them collectively. Both approaches provide a console confirmation upon successful transmission, highlighting the flexibility in dispatching individual or batched events to the Event Hub.

For receiving events, you can use EventProcessorClient, which is also part of the **Azure. Messaging.EventHubs.Processor NuGet package**. Here's how you can use it to receive events:

```
using Azure.Messaging.EventHubs.Consumer;
using Azure.Messaging.EventHubs.Processor;
using Azure.Storage.Blobs;
string connectionString = "<Your Event Hubs connection string>";
string eventHubName = "<Your Event Hub name>";
string blobStorageConnectionString = "<Your blob storage connection
string>";
string blobContainerName = "<Your blob container name>";
```

The preceding code begins by importing the required libraries using the using statements. These statements allow the code to utilize classes and functionalities from the aforementioned namespaces.

Next, placeholder variables (connectionString, eventHubName, blobStorage ConnectionString, and blobContainerName) need to be replaced with actual values specific to your setup. Using the BlobContainerClient provides a streamlined way to interact with Azure Blob Storage in your application. When you initialize this client, you'll need to provide blobStorageConnectionString, which gives you the specifics of your Azure Blob Storage connection, and blobContainerName, which identifies a specific blob container within that storage. This is showcased in the following example:

```
BlobContainerClient storageClient = new
BlobContainerClient(blobStorageConnectionString, blobContainerName);
```

A new EventProcessorClient instance is created, responsible for processing events from the specified Event Hub. The constructor takes several arguments:

- storageClient: The previously created BlobContainerClient instance, which will be used for checkpointing.

- EventHubConsumerClient.DefaultConsumerGroupName: The default consumer group name for the Event Hub. Consumer groups allow multiple consumers to independently read from the same Event Hub.

- connectionString: The connection string for the Azure Event Hub.

- eventHubName: The name of the specific Event Hub from which events will be consumed.

Let us now implement these arguments in the following code snippet:

```
EventProcessorClient processor = new
EventProcessorClient(storageClient, EventHubConsumerClient.
DefaultConsumerGroupName, connectionString, eventHubName);
```

Event handlers are registered for the `ProcessEventAsync` and `ProcessErrorAsync` events of the processor instance. These event handlers (`ProcessEventHandler` and `ProcessErrorHandler`) will be invoked when events are received and when errors occur during event processing:

```
processor.ProcessEventAsync += ProcessEventHandler;
processor.ProcessErrorAsync += ProcessErrorHandler;
```

The `StartProcessingAsync()` method is called on the processor instance, initiating the event processing. The processor will start consuming events from the specified Event Hub and trigger the registered event handlers when events are received or errors occur:

```
await processor.StartProcessingAsync();
```

The `ProcessEventHandler` method is an asynchronous method that takes a `ProcessEventArgs` argument. This method is registered as the event handler for processing events. Within this method, the received event's content is extracted and printed to the console using `Encoding.UTF8.GetString()`. After processing the event, the `UpdateCheckpointAsync()` method is called on `eventArgs` to update the checkpoint in the blob storage. This ensures that the event processor can resume from the appropriate point if there are restarts:

```
async Task ProcessEventHandler(ProcessEventArgs eventArgs) { Console.
WriteLine("\tReceived event: {0}", Encoding.UTF8.GetString(eventArgs.
Data.Body.ToArray())); }
async Task ProcessErrorHandler(ProcessErrorEventArgs eventArgs) {
Console.WriteLine($"\tError occurred: {eventArgs.Exception.Message}");
return Task.CompletedTask; }
```

The `ProcessErrorHandler` method is an asynchronous method that takes a `ProcessErrorEventArgs` argument. This method is registered as the event handler to handle errors. Within this method, the error message from the exception is extracted and printed to the console. The method returns `Task.CompletedTask`, indicating that error handling is complete.

In summary, this code sets up an event processor to consume events from an Azure Event Hub using the Azure SDK. It creates `EventProcessorClient`, registers event and error handlers, and initiates event processing. The event handler processes received events and updates checkpoints, while the error handler handles errors that occur during event processing. Now, let's see how to process and handle events in a .NET application.

Processing and handling events in a .NET application

The event processing and handling are covered in the `ProcessEventAsync` handler shown in the preceding code. In this method, you can add your logic to process the events. Here, we will just print the event data. After processing an event, it's a good practice to update the checkpoint, as shown in the preceding code, so that if there is a failure, you can start from where you left off.

Remember to call `await processor.StopProcessingAsync();` when you want to stop processing events:

```
await processor.StartProcessingAsync();  async Task
ProcessEventHandler(ProcessEventArgs eventArgs) { Console.WriteLine("\
tReceived event: {0}", Encoding.UTF8.GetString(eventArgs.Data.Body.
ToArray())); // Update the checkpoint after processing the event.
await eventArgs.UpdateCheckpointAsync(); }
async Task ProcessErrorHandler(ProcessErrorEventArgs eventArgs) {
Console.WriteLine($"\tError occurred: {eventArgs.Exception.Message}");
return Task.CompletedTask; }await processor.StopProcessingAsync();
```

These code examples give you a basic understanding of using Azure Event Hubs in a .NET application. However, you can explore many advanced concepts, such as routing events to different partitions, balancing the load among multiple consumers, and handling failures, in the upcoming section.

In the context of Azure Event Hubs and stream processing, a checkpoint is a record that the event processor creates to denote the position in the event stream where it last successfully processed events. This position is often referred to as an *offset*. The offset represents the location of an event within a partition of the Event Hub. By saving this offset, the processor can remember its position in the stream.

Why is this important? In distributed systems and especially in stream processing scenarios, failures are a given (e.g., system crashes and network issues). Without a mechanism such as checkpointing, if an event processor restarts (due to a crash or any other reason), it wouldn't know from what point to continue processing. This could lead to the following:

- **Duplicate processing**: If the processor starts from an earlier position than where it left off, it might process some events more than once

- **Missing events**: If, for any reason, the processor starts ahead of where it left off, it might skip some unprocessed events

As the event processor processes each event, it periodically records a checkpoint, which is the offset of the most recently processed event. These checkpoints are stored in a durable store – in this case, Azure Blob Storage. If the event processor restarts, it reads the checkpoint from Blob Storage to know where to resume processing.

Checkpointing too frequently (e.g., after processing every single event) can introduce overhead due to the constant writes to the durable store. Conversely, checkpointing too infrequently can mean more duplicate processing if a failure occurs, as events since the last checkpoint would need to be reprocessed. Depending on the exact requirements and the nature of the processing involved (idempotent operations versus non-idempotent ones), developers should choose an appropriate checkpointing frequency.

Routing, load balancing, and error handling

Azure Event Hubs provides a real-time event streaming platform that can reliably handle millions of events per second. It's an essential tool in the Azure ecosystem to build data-driven applications and analytics pipelines. While we have covered the basics of using Azure Event Hubs in the previous sections, this section will delve into some advanced topics – **routing** events to different partitions, **balancing** the load among multiple consumers, and **handling failures**. We will also provide .NET code examples for developers.

Routing events to different partitions

Partitions are a fundamental concept in Event Hubs. They are essentially independent *streams* within an Event Hub and help to provide concurrent processing of events. By default, when events are sent to an Event Hub, they are distributed to different partitions in a round-robin manner, providing equal load among all partitions. However, there are scenarios where you might want to send specific events to a particular partition. This can be done using a **partition key** or directly using a **partition ID**. Here's how you can do it using .NET:

```
using Azure.Messaging.EventHubs;
using Azure.Messaging.EventHubs.Producer;
string connectionString = "<Your Event Hubs connection string>";
string eventHubName = "<Your Event Hub name>";
await using var client = new EventHubProducerClient(connectionString,
eventHubName);
var options = new CreateBatchOptions { PartitionKey = "partition-key"
};
using EventDataBatch eventBatch = await client.
CreateBatchAsync(options);
eventBatch.TryAdd(new EventData(Encoding.UTF8.GetBytes("First
event")));
eventBatch.TryAdd(new EventData(Encoding.UTF8.GetBytes("Second
event")));
await client.SendAsync(eventBatch);
Console.WriteLine("Batch of events sent.");
```

In the preceding code, all events in the batch will be sent to the same partition that matches `partition-key`. It's important to note that a *partition key* is not the same as a *partition ID*. While a *partition ID* directly determines the target partition, a *partition key* provides a hint to Event Hubs to route events to the same partition for better event ordering, but it doesn't guarantee the exact partition.

Similarly, you can send events to a specific partition using a *partition ID*:

```
var options = new CreateBatchOptions { PartitionId = "0" };
using EventDataBatch eventBatch = await client.
CreateBatchAsync(options);
eventBatch.TryAdd(new EventData(Encoding.UTF8.GetBytes("First
event")));
eventBatch.TryAdd(new EventData(Encoding.UTF8.GetBytes("Second
event")));
await client.SendAsync(eventBatch);
Console.WriteLine("Batch of events sent.");
```

The concept of partitioning plays a crucial role in Azure Event Hubs, acting as separate streams within the Event Hub to enable concurrent event processing. By default, events are evenly distributed across partitions using a round-robin approach. However, scenarios may arise where you must direct specific events to particular partitions. This can be achieved through either a partition key or a partition ID. Here's how this can be done using .NET:

```
using Azure.Messaging.EventHubs;
using Azure.Messaging.EventHubs.Producer;
using System.Text;
class Program
{
    static async System.Threading.Tasks.Task Main(string[] args)
    {
        string connectionString = "<Your Event Hubs connection
string>";
        string eventHubName = "<Your Event Hub name>";
         await using var client = new
EventHubProducerClient(connectionString, eventHubName);
        using var batchWithPartitionKey = await client.
CreateBatchAsync(new CreateBatchOptions { PartitionKey = "partition-
key" });
        batchWithPartitionKey.TryAdd(new EventData(Encoding.UTF8.
GetBytes("Event data with partition key")));
        await client.SendAsync(batchWithPartitionKey);
        string specificPartitionId = "partition-id";
        using var batchWithPartitionId = await client.
CreateBatchAsync(new CreateBatchOptions { PartitionId =
specificPartitionId });
        batchWithPartitionId.TryAdd(new EventData(Encoding.UTF8.
GetBytes("Event data for a specific partition")));
        await client.SendAsync(batchWithPartitionId);
    }}
```

The code utilizes the Azure SDK for Event Hubs, including necessary imports for `EventHubProducerClient` and `CreateBatchOptions`. A connection string and event hub name are required for configuration.

Events are grouped into a batch using `CreateBatchAsync` with the `partition-key` partition key. This ensures that all events within the batch are directed to the same partition based on the provided key. It's important to understand that a partition key serves as a hint for routing, enhancing event ordering within a partition without guaranteeing the exact partition.

Similarly, the partition ID can direct events to a specific partition. A batch is created with a designated partition ID, and events are added to it. Upon sending the batch, events are directed to the partition associated with the provided ID.

In summary, the provided code exemplifies how to route events to different partitions within Azure Event Hubs. It showcases the usage of partition keys and partition IDs to control the distribution of events, enhancing event processing and organization within the hub. We can handle the load by balancing events through multiple consumers, which we will explore in the upcoming section.

Balancing the load among multiple consumers

Event Hubs allows multiple consumers to read events concurrently. This can be done using **consumer groups**. A consumer group is a view of the entire Event Hub, and each consumer group has a separate set of offset or sequence numbers for each partition. This allows each consumer group to read the stream independently at its own pace and with its own offsets.

When using multiple instances of `EventProcessorClient` (for example, on different servers), these client instances can collaborate and distribute the partitions among themselves; each client instance will own and process events from a subset of partitions. Event Hubs ensures that only one `EventProcessorClient` instance processes each partition by coordinating this distribution through the storage account (used for checkpointing).

Here's how you can use `EventProcessorClient` with a specific consumer group:

```
string consumerGroup = "<Your consumer group>";
var processorOptions = new EventProcessorClientOptions
{
    DefaultStartingPosition = EventPosition.Earliest,
    PrefetchCount = 100,
    LoadBalancingStrategy = LoadBalancingStrategy.Greedy // or
LoadBalancingStrategy.Balanced
};
EventProcessorClient processor = new EventProcessorClient(
    checkpointStore, consumerGroup, connectionString, eventHubName,
processorOptions);
processor.ProcessEventAsync += ProcessEventHandler;
processor.ProcessErrorAsync += ProcessErrorHandler;
await processor.StartProcessingAsync();
```

In the preceding code, the `LoadBalancingStrategy` option offers control over the load-balancing behavior of the `EventProcessorClient` instances. When set to `LoadBalancingStrategy.Greedy`, the instances aim to own as many partitions as possible. Conversely, when set to `LoadBalancingStrategy.Balanced`, they endeavor to distribute the partitions more evenly among them.

Handling failures

In the ever-evolving realm of event-driven architectures, anticipating challenges is as crucial as harnessing opportunities. Azure Event Hubs, a powerhouse in data streaming, is a testament to this. Designed with robustness at its core, it's not immune to the unpredictable nature of software ecosystems. So, as with any sophisticated system, failures loom large. It's not about avoiding them but mastering their management. However, here's the silver lining – armed with the right strategies and insights, these challenges become stepping stones, not stumbling blocks. Like all distributed systems, Event Hubs isn't exempt from challenges. Recognition and management of these failures are crucial to guaranteeing the consistent performance of your application. To gain a comprehensive understanding of Azure Event Hubs, it is crucial to extensively examine specific domains that often play crucial roles in resilient event-driven systems. These subjects are not merely abstract concepts but, rather, the foundational principles upon which dependable applications are constructed. The following list outlines the primary domains that will be examined:

- **Ensuring data consistency and reliable event processing**:

  - **Idempotency**: Consider this a way to ensure that recurring tasks yield the same outcome on every occasion. It's akin to replaying your preferred musical track and expecting an identical melody with each iteration.

  - **Duplicate events**: Accidentally receiving two identical copies of a book when you only need one, leading to redundancy and potential inefficiencies in data processing and storage. Understanding the causes and implementing strategies to mitigate duplicate events is crucial for maintaining the reliability and performance of your event-driven system.

- **Ensuring reliability and data integrity**:

  - **Error handling and retries**: Errors are an inevitable part of a process. We shall acquire the skills to identify them, log their occurrences, and adeptly manage them to avert any disruptions.

  - **Handling failures and bad data**: Occasionally, things take an undesirable turn, or data becomes untidy. We shall navigate through an array of tools and methodologies, such as task pausing or utilization of schema registries, to uphold data integrity and sustain seamless system operations.

Idempotency

Azure Event Hubs, a cloud-based event ingestion service, provides a powerful solution to collect and process large volumes of data in real time. However, in distributed systems such as Event Hubs, ensuring data consistency and preventing unintended side effects due to duplicate events is a crucial challenge. This is where the concept of idempotency comes into play. In this section, we will delve into the significance of idempotency in the context of Azure Event Hubs and how developers can implement it effectively to ensure reliable event processing.

Idempotency is the property that an operation, when applied multiple times, produces the same result as if it were applied only once. In the world of distributed systems and event-driven architectures, idempotency becomes vital to maintain data integrity and prevent data inconsistencies caused by network glitches, retries, and message duplication.

Azure Event Hubs follows an "at least once delivery" model, meaning that events are guaranteed to reach their destination, but they might be delivered multiple times due to various factors. This reliability ensures that no events are lost in transit, but it introduces the challenge of handling duplicate events on the consumer side. When developing applications that consume events from Azure Event Hubs, ensuring that your consumers are idempotent becomes paramount. Idempotent consumers guarantee that processing the same event multiple times does not lead to unintended consequences or inconsistent data updates. This is especially crucial to maintain the correctness of your application's state.

To implement idempotency, developers need to track which events have been processed. Azure Event Hubs provides metadata such as `SequenceNumber` and `EventId` that can be leveraged for this purpose. By persistently storing information about processed events in a reliable storage system such as a database or a distributed cache, developers can identify and skip events that have already been processed.

We'll explore a sample implementation of an idempotent event processing function using Azure Functions and .NET. This example demonstrates how to consume events from Azure Event Hubs and ensure that each event is processed only once:

```
var telemetryClient = new TelemetryClient();
try
{
    string eventBody = "Hello, Event Hub!";

    using EventDataBatch eventBatch = await producerClient.
CreateBatchAsync();
    eventBatch.TryAdd(new EventData(Encoding.UTF8.
GetBytes(eventBody)));

    var eventId = eventBatch.TryAdd(new EventData(Encoding.UTF8.
GetBytes(eventBody)));
    var blobClient = containerClient.GetBlobClient(eventId.
ToString());

    if (await blobClient.ExistsAsync())
    {
        telemetryClient.TrackTrace("Event already processed.
Skipping.");
    }
    else
    {
```

```
        try
        {
            await producerClient.SendAsync(eventBatch);
            await blobClient.UploadAsync(new MemoryStream());
            telemetryClient.TrackTrace("Event sent successfully.");
        }
        catch (Exception ex)
        {
            telemetryClient.TrackException(ex);
        }
    }
}
catch (Exception ex)
{
    telemetryClient.TrackException(ex);}
```

This code demonstrates how to securely retrieve the Azure Event Hub connection string from Azure Key Vault using managed identity authentication. The retrieved connection string is then used to configure `EventHubBufferedProducerClient`, with features such as idempotent retries, concurrency control, event buffering, and wait time management. We have also included logging to the application insights instead of typical writing to the console as output. The result is a reliable and efficient method to send events Azure Event Hubs while maintaining high data integrity and security. To view the full code example, visit the code repository at `https://github.com/PacktPublishing/A-Developer-s-Guide-to-.NET-in-Azure` for the full example.

Thorough testing is crucial when working with idempotency in Azure Event Hubs. Developers should test scenarios involving duplicate events, network failures, and concurrent processing. By simulating these scenarios, you can ensure that your idempotent processing logic holds up and maintains data integrity under different conditions. While idempotency is essential for data consistency, developers should be aware of the trade-offs. Stricter idempotency checks might introduce additional processing overhead or complexity. Balancing these trade-offs requires careful consideration of your application's requirements and performance goals.

In the realm of distributed systems and event-driven architectures, idempotency is a critical concept to ensure reliable event processing. In the context of Azure Event Hubs, where events might be delivered more than once, idempotency helps developers maintain data consistency and prevent unintended side effects. By understanding the nuances of idempotency, leveraging event metadata, and designing effective processing logic, developers can build robust and resilient applications that can gracefully handle duplicate events and ensure data integrity.

Duplicate events

Duplicate events present a common challenge within event-driven architectures, necessitating comprehensive strategies to ensure accurate and reliable event processing. While offering powerful event streaming capabilities, Azure Event Hubs demands an understanding of scenarios, leading to duplicate events and the application of effective deduplication techniques to maintain data integrity and optimize system functionality.

Here are some scenarios that can lead to duplicate events:

- **Checkpointing**: Azure Functions employs checkpoints to mark the progress of event consumption. Imagine an event-driven application that crashes before reaching a checkpoint. Upon recovery, the function resumes from the last checkpoint, reprocessing previously handled events. This situation can lead to the duplication of events in the processed data. Let's say an IoT application processes temperature data from sensors. If a crash occurs after processing sensor data from timestamp X but before creating a checkpoint, the system reprocesses data from timestamp X upon recovery, resulting in duplicated temperature records.

- **Missing acknowledgments**: In scenarios where **acknowledgments (ACKs)** from services are not received despite successful outgoing requests, duplicate events can be inadvertently published – for instance, a function processes payment events and sends a confirmation to an external service. If the confirmation ACK is lost in transit, the function might initiate retries, potentially causing the same payment event to be processed multiple times. Consider an e-commerce application that processes orders. If an outgoing request to update inventory succeeds but the confirmation ACK is lost, the function might assume the update failed and initiate retries. This could lead to multiple updates of the same order, impacting inventory accuracy.

Checkpoint strategies

To optimize event-driven systems and mitigate duplicate events, developers must implement a well-defined checkpoint strategy that considers the frequency of checkpoint creation. Configuring checkpoints at optimal intervals ensures the establishment of recovery points without inadvertently causing excessive duplication during failure and recovery scenarios. Consider a logistics application that processes shipment events. The application utilizes Azure Functions and Azure Event Hubs for event processing. The checkpoint strategy is defined as creating a checkpoint after processing every batch of 100 events or every 5 minutes, whichever comes first. This approach strikes a balance between frequent checkpoints to ensure minimal data loss and avoiding overly frequent checkpoints that might lead to duplicate processing. In the event of a failure, the system can recover and resume processing from the most recent checkpoint, minimizing the potential for duplicate events in the processed data.

Deduplication techniques

To mitigate the impact of duplicate events, developers should employ effective deduplication techniques. One of these techniques involves looking for duplicates before processing an event. This approach performs pre-processing validations to determine whether the event should undergo further processing. This step involves confirming the event's continued relevance and validity. For instance, consider a financial application that processes transactions. In this context, events older than a certain time threshold might be stale and can be skipped. Consider a social media platform where events are generated for user actions such as *liking* a post. Over time, such events lose their relevance. The event timestamp is validated against a predefined threshold before processing to handle this. If an event's timestamp indicates that it's too old to impact the system's current state, the processing function can intelligently skip such events, preventing irrelevant duplicates from influencing the system.

In conclusion, addressing duplicate events in Azure Event Hubs requires a nuanced understanding of the scenarios that lead to duplication and applying effective deduplication techniques. By adopting a proactive approach that combines pre-processing checks and well-defined checkpoint strategies, developers can optimize the reliability and accuracy of their event-driven applications, mitigating the impact of duplicate events on data integrity and system performance. Let's now move on to the topic of retry policies; mastering the art of retry management stands as a pivotal component to achieving fault tolerance and guaranteeing the eventual delivery of events.

Retry policy

One key failure-handling strategy is a *retry with exponential backoff*. `EventHubProducerClient` and `EventProcessorClient` automatically retry transient failures with an exponential backoff policy. An exponential backoff policy is a strategy used in computer science and networking to handle retries when there's a need to communicate with a service, system, or resource that might be temporarily unavailable or experiencing issues. This policy helps avoid overloading the target system with repeated requests, especially during transient failures, giving it time to recover. Here's how an exponential backoff policy typically works:

- **Initial retry**: When a request for a service fails for reasons such as network congestion, timeouts, or service unavailability, instead of immediately retrying, the requester waits for a brief period.

- **Increasing delays**: If the first retry doesn't work, the requester waits longer before trying again. The time between each retry keeps getting longer, usually following a set time specified in the configurations. According to the configuration settings, with a maximum number of retries defined, if you started waiting for 1 second, for instance, you might wait for the next try for 2 seconds, the one after that for 4 seconds, and so on. After several failed attempts, the requester might stop retrying and consider the operation permanently unsuccessful.

- **Resetting the backoff**: If a retry attempt is successful, the policy resets, and the requester can resume sending requests normally.

The exponential increase in delay between retries allows for a *grace period*, during which the target service might recover from its temporary issues. It also prevents a flood of retry requests that could worsen a situation. Exponential backoff policies are commonly used in various networking protocols, cloud services, and distributed systems to handle intermittent failures gracefully and ensure efficient use of resources while maintaining system reliability. We can build this into our instance of our previously built `EventHubBufferedProducerCLientOptions` client, as shown here:

```
var producerOptions = new EventHubBufferedProducerClientOptions
{
```

```
    RetryOptions = new EventHubsRetryOptions(
        maximumRetries: 5,
        delay: TimeSpan.FromSeconds(2),
        maximumDelay: TimeSpan.FromSeconds(30)),
};
```

Let's analyze the code to understand the configuration created. The `var producerOptions = new EventHubBufferedProducerClientOptions` line initiates a new setup for the Event Hub producer client's behavior using the `EventHubBufferedProducerClientOptions` class. This class allows us to configure how the producer handles its actions. The next part, `RetryOptions = new EventHubsRetryOptions(...)`, focuses on defining the way the producer will respond when temporary errors or failures occur while sending events. Specifically, `maximumRetries: 5` indicates that the producer will attempt to resend an event up to five times if there is a temporary failure. The `delay: TimeSpan.FromSeconds(2)` introduces a two-second pause before the initial retry, providing a brief moment for recovery. Additionally, `maximumDelay: TimeSpan.FromSeconds(30)` establishes a limit of 30 seconds as the maximum interval between retry attempts. This prevents excessively long delays. Overall, these settings manage how a producer reacts to temporary problems. If there's an issue sending an event due to a short-term problem, the producer will automatically try sending it again up to the specified maximum retries. These retries are designed to improve the odds of successful event delivery, even if there are sporadic problems. It's important to choose suitable values for `maximumRetries`, `delay`, and `maximumDelay` based on your system's needs and infrastructure characteristics. Remember, the choice of these values can significantly influence your system's dependability and performance.

In summary, while Azure Event Hubs provides a simple interface to ingest and process large volumes of events, it also provides a rich set of features to handle advanced scenarios, such as **custom routing**, **load balancing**, and **error handling**. By using these features effectively, developers can build highly scalable, robust, and complex event-driven applications on Azure.

Let's dive into common failures that can occur in event processing now that we've seen how to handle logging these details via code.

Understanding common failure scenarios in event processing

In Azure Event Hubs, several failure scenarios can disrupt the event processing flow. These typically fall into four main categories:

- **Network interruptions**: Network interruptions are disruptions in connectivity between your application and Azure Event Hubs. These can occur due to a wide range of factors, from local network congestion or failures in networking equipment to broader issues, such as service outages in networking providers.

- **Service outages**: Service outages are periods during which Azure Event Hubs is unavailable. This can be due to various reasons, such as platform upgrades, unexpected server crashes, or larger-scale Azure service issues.

- **Resource constraints**: Resource constraints in Azure Event Hubs occur when the allocated resources, such as throughput units, are fully utilized. This can lead to **throttling**, which impacts the performance and responsiveness of your event processing operations.

- **Misconfigured entities**: A misconfigured entity in Azure Event Hub results from the incorrect setup of event producers or consumers. This could be due to invalid connection strings, incorrect event hub names, faulty routing setup, or other similar issues.

Understanding these common failure scenarios is the first step toward building resilient applications with Azure Event Hubs. Knowing what can go wrong allows us to create solutions to handle those situations and keep our applications running smoothly.

As a .NET developer working with Azure Event Hubs, understanding the `EventHubsException.FailureReason` enumeration and its different options is crucial to handling exceptions effectively and building robust event-driven applications. This enumeration provides insights into the reasons behind specific failure scenarios, allowing you to tailor your error-handling strategies accordingly:

- `ClientClosed`: This reason indicates that an operation was attempted using an Event Hubs client instance already closed. It's important to handle this scenario gracefully and ensure that you don't attempt any further operations on a closed client.

- `ConsumerDisconnected`: This reason occurs when a client is forcibly disconnected from an Event Hub instance. This often happens when another consumer with a higher OwnerLevel asserts ownership over the partition and consumer group. To handle this, consider implementing logic to recover or retry the operation gracefully.

- `GeneralError`: This reason represents a general error within the client library. While this reason is broad, it's crucial to log and analyze these exceptions to identify potential issues and improve overall reliability.

- `InvalidClientState`: This indicates that the client is in an invalid state from which it cannot recover. The recommended approach is to close and recreate the client to force reinitialization of its state.

- `MessageSizeExceeded`: This reason is triggered when a message exceeds the maximum size allowed for its transport. You should handle this scenario by either adjusting your message size or implementing a strategy to break down more significant messages into smaller chunks if necessary.

- `ProducerDisconnected`: Similar to `ConsumerDisconnected`, this reason applies to producers. It occurs when a producer client is forcefully disconnected due to another producer with a higher OwnerLevel. Handling this requires similar considerations to consumer disconnections.

- QuotaExceeded: This is important when interacting with the Azure Event Hubs service. It indicates that a quota applied to an Event Hub resource has been exceeded. This could impact sending or receiving messages, so implementing appropriate retry logic or alert mechanisms is crucial.

- ResourceNotFound: When an Event Hubs resource such as an Event Hub, consumer group, or partition cannot be found, this reason is triggered. You should implement error handling that provides meaningful feedback to users or administrators about the missing resource.

- ServiceBusy: If the Azure Event Hubs service reports that it's busy responding to a client request, this reason is raised. Implementing retry mechanisms with incremental backoff can help alleviate the effects of a busy service.

- ServiceCommunicationProblem: This reason indicates a general communication error when interacting with the Azure Event Hubs service. Implementing appropriate logging and retry strategies can help manage such scenarios.

- ServiceTimeout: When an operation or request times out while interacting with the Azure Event Hubs service, this reason is triggered. You should implement timeout handling and retry strategies to handle service timeouts gracefully.

In the process of interacting with Azure Event Hubs, exceptional situations may arise that require tailored handling. The following code exemplifies a structured approach to handling different EventHubsException scenarios. Using the ex.Reason property to identify the reason behind the exception, developers can implement precise error-handling strategies and ensure the robustness of their event-driven applications. The following switch case provides more details:

```
try{
}
catch (EventHubsException ex){
    switch (ex.Reason){
  case EventHubsException.FailureReason.ClientClosed:
            break;
        case EventHubsException.FailureReason.ConsumerDisconnected:
            break;
        case EventHubsException.FailureReason.
MessageSizeExceeded:          break;
        case EventHubsException.FailureReason.
QuotaExceeded:          break;
        case EventHubsException.FailureReason.ResourceNotFound:
            break;
        case EventHubsException.FailureReason.ServiceBusy:
            break;
        case EventHubsException.FailureReason.
ServiceCommunicationProblem:
            break;
```

```
        case EventHubsException.FailureReason.ServiceTimeout:
            break;
        default:
            break;
    }}
```

In summary, comprehending the `EventHubsException.FailureReason` options empowers you to design more resilient applications. By implementing targeted error handling and recovery strategies for each failure scenario, you can ensure the reliability and stability of your Azure Event Hub-based event-driven systems.

In the next section, we will look at strategies to handle transient errors and network interruptions to increase the resilience of our Azure Event Hubs applications.

Strategies to handle transient errors and network interruptions

Transient errors and **network interruptions** are temporary issues that often resolve themselves quickly. However, they can significantly disrupt your application if not handled properly. Here, we will discuss a few strategies to handle these issues in the context of Azure Event Hubs.

Circuit breaker pattern

The **circuit breaker pattern** is another effective way to handle transient errors. It's a bit like an electrical circuit breaker – after several consecutive failures, it *trips* and stops all attempts to execute the operation for a period of time. Once this *cool-down* period has elapsed, the operation can be attempted again.

Here are some of the key benefits of using the circuit breaker pattern:

- **Failing fast**: This allows the application to promptly handle a fault rather than wait for a timeout.

- **Preventing an overload**: Stopping all outgoing calls to a service that is down prevents the system from being overwhelmed with requests that are likely to fail.

- **Recovering gracefully**: After a predefined period, the circuit breaker allows a limited number of requests to pass through to see whether the service has recovered. This way, the system can promptly resume normal operations once the issue is resolved.

Here's a more in-depth code snippet demonstrating a circuit breaker in action:

```
  bool isCircuitOpen = false;
int exceptionsCount = 0;
try{
    await foreach (PartitionEvent partitionEvent in consumerClient.
ReadEventsAsync(cancellationTokenSource.Token)){
        if (!isCircuitOpen){
            ProcessEvent(partitionEvent);
```

```
        } }}
catch (EventHubsException ex)
{
    if (ex.Reason == EventHubsException.FailureReason.
ServiceCommunicationProblem || ex.Reason == EventHubsException.
FailureReason.ServiceUnavailable){
        exceptionsCount++;
        if (exceptionsCount >= 3) {
            isCircuitOpen = true;
            await Task.Delay(TimeSpan.FromMinutes(1),
cancellationTokenSource.Token);
            isCircuitOpen = false;
        }}    else
    {
    }}
```

In this code, we manually track the circuit state, `isCircuitOpen`, and the count of exceptions, `exceptionsCount`. When the defined threshold of exceptions is reached, the circuit is opened, a delay is introduced, and then the circuit is reset. This mimics the behavior of the circuit breaker pattern without using the Polly library.

These are some ways you can handle transient errors and network interruptions in Azure Event Hubs. Applying these strategies to your applications will help ensure they remain robust and reliable, even in the face of temporary issues. In the upcoming section, we will focus on implementing retry policies and setting up exponential backoff if a system experiences any intermittent issues or downtime.

Dead-lettering and handling poison messages

Dead letters and poison messages are essential components in many messaging systems and serve as fundamental feedback in the **Advanced Message Queuing Protocol (AMQP)**. In the world of message processing, a poison message is a message that can't be dealt with because something is wrong with its content. Continuously attempting to handle these problematic messages can use up resources and potentially disrupt the processing of other messages that are perfectly fine. Because of this, it's critical to handle these messages correctly to ensure the dependability of our applications. In Azure Event Hubs, this task is achieved through a procedure known as **dead-lettering**.

Dead-lettering

Messages that can't be processed are moved to a separate **dead-letter queue** where they can be reviewed and handled accordingly. While Event Hubs itself does not have native support for dead-lettering, you can implement a similar concept in your application. When a poison message is encountered, you can move it to a separate storage or logging system instead of repeatedly attempting to process it.

Here is a .NET example of how you might implement this:

```
Try
{
    ProcessEvent(partitionEvent);
}
catch (Exception ex){
DeadLetterEvent(partitionEvent, ex);
}
void DeadLetterEvent(PartitionEvent partitionEvent, Exception ex)
{
    var deadLetter = new
    {
        Exception = ex.Message,
        EventData = partitionEvent.Data
    };
    string deadLetterJson = JsonSerializer.Serialize(deadLetter);
    var blobClient = new BlobClient(connectionString, "deadletters",
$"{partitionEvent.Data.SequenceNumber}.json");
    blobClient.Upload(new MemoryStream(Encoding.UTF8.
GetBytes(deadLetterJson)));
}
```

In this code snippet, we try to process an event with the `ProcessEvent` method. If an exception occurs (simulating a poison message), we catch it and call the `DeadLetterEvent` method. This method serializes the event and exception details into a JSON string and writes it to a separate storage system – in this case, Azure Blob Storage.

We can create a dead letter queue in our Event Hub from the previous CLI example. To do this, we need to create a consumer group and also enable DLQ on a subscription:

```
az eventhubs consumer-group create \
    --resource-group demoapp-rg \
    --namespace-name demoapp-telemetry-canadacentral \
    --eventhub-name telemetry-alerts-dlq \
    --name dlq-consumer-group
```

This command allows you to create a consumer group named `dlq-consumer-group` within a specified Event Hub. This consumer group will be designated to manage messages that are sent to the dead-letter queue. It's essential to have a separate consumer group for the dead-letter queue to ensure effective processing and management of messages that couldn't be processed in the main subscription. Then, we have to enable the DLQ on a subscription:

```
az eventhubs subscription update \
    --resource-group demoapp-rg \
```

```
--namespace-name demoapp-telemetry-canadacentral \
--eventhub-name telemetry-alerts-dlq \
--topic-name telemetry-alerts-topic \
--name dlq-subscription \
--dead-letter-on-filter-exceptions true
```

In this example, you use the Azure CLI to update the properties of a subscription named `dlq-subscription` within the `telemetry-alerts-dlq` Event Hub, located in the `demoapp-telemetry-canadacentral` namespace and the `demoapp-rg` resource group. This subscription is associated with the `telemetry-alerts-topic` topic.

By setting `--dead-letter-on-filter-exceptions true`, you ensure that any messages failing the subscription's filters will be directed to the dead-letter queue, `telemetry-alerts-dlq`, for closer examination and analysis.

This command is part of the configuration process to effectively handle messages that couldn't be processed by the subscription and route them to the dead-letter queue for further investigation.

Handling poison messages

In the context of event-driven architectures and Azure Event Hubs, handling poison messages is critical to ensure the reliability and integrity of your message processing pipeline. When a message cannot be successfully processed, it's moved to a separate dead-letter queue. This allows you to focus on investigating and resolving the issues causing the message processing failure. Let's explore how to effectively handle poison messages and enhance your event-driven application's resilience:

- **Log poison messages**: Implement comprehensive logging for your message processing logic. When a message is moved to the dead-letter queue, log relevant details such as the message content, metadata, and exceptions encountered during processing.

- **Analyze message content**: Carefully examine the content of poison messages. Check for data inconsistencies, unexpected formats, missing fields, or any data that could lead to processing failures.

- **Review processing logic**: Evaluate the processing logic that handles incoming messages. Ensure that it can gracefully handle different scenarios, including unexpected or invalid data. Verify that your application's validation and error-handling mechanisms are effective.

- **Correlate with source**: If poison messages originate from specific sources or events, correlate them with the data source. Investigate whether changes to the source or upstream processes contributed to the issues.

- **Compare with successful messages**: Compare the content and structure of poison messages with successfully processed messages. Look for patterns or differences that might explain the processing failures.

- **Testing and debugging**: Recreate the scenario locally for testing and debugging. Simulate the conditions under which poison messages failed to identify whether the issue could be replicated. This helps to narrow down the problem and validate potential fixes.

- **Data validation**: Strengthen data validation mechanisms. Implement stricter rules to prevent invalid data from reaching the processing logic. This helps catch potential poison messages before they cause processing failures.

- **Error handling and recovery**: Review error-handling mechanisms. Ensure exceptions are caught and logged correctly – design recovery mechanisms to allow your application to proceed smoothly after encountering issues with specific messages.

- **Collaboration**: Engage the investigation's relevant team members, including data producers and stakeholders. Their insights might shed light on changes that could trigger the issues.

- **Documentation**: Document findings, investigation steps, and solutions. This documentation is a valuable resource for future troubleshooting and helps others understand how to handle similar situations.

Following a systematic investigation approach, you can identify and address the root causes of poison messages, enhancing your application's stability and reliability. Handling poison messages effectively contributes to the overall quality of your event-driven system and ensures seamless message processing.

Monitoring and alerting for failures and errors

Monitoring your application and setting up alerts for failures and errors is vital to maintaining a robust and reliable system. Azure provides several tools and services that can help you monitor your Event Hubs application and set up alerts for specific conditions. Keeping a watchful eye on your application and establishing alerts for potential failures and errors is crucial to maintaining a resilient and dependable system.

Azure Monitor

Azure Monitor is a comprehensive service that provides telemetry and insights into the performance and health of your applications and resources in Azure.

With Azure Monitor, you can collect and analyze metrics and logs from your Event Hubs to identify trends and spot issues. For instance, you can monitor the `IncomingMessages` metric to track the volume of events being sent to your Event Hub, or the `ServerErrors` metric to catch any internal errors occurring within the service.

Here is an example of how to log custom metrics with Azure Monitor in a .NET application:

```
var telemetryClient = new TelemetryClient(TelemetryConfiguration.
CreateDefault());
try
```

```
{
    ProcessEvent(partitionEvent);
}
catch (Exception ex)
{ telemetryClient.TrackException(ex); }
```

Now, let's move on to Azure alerts. We will explore how to proactively monitor your Azure resources and applications by setting up personalized alerts based on specific conditions and thresholds.

Azure alerts

In conjunction with Azure Monitor, you can use **Azure alerts** to receive notifications when certain conditions are met. For instance, you can set up an alert to be triggered when the number of server errors exceeds a certain threshold, allowing you to quickly respond to potential issues.

Creating an alert rule involves specifying a target resource (your Event Hub), a condition to evaluate (such as the `ServerErrors` metric over a certain threshold), and an action to take when the condition is met (such as sending an email or calling a webhook).

Now, let's explore building robust applications with Azure Event Hubs.

Building robust applications with Azure Event Hubs

Building robust applications requires a deep understanding of the platform and tools at our disposal. Azure Event Hubs, combined with other Azure services, provides a powerful platform to build resilient, scalable, and reliable applications. It's now up to us as developers to leverage these tools effectively and create applications that can gracefully handle failures and continue to function reliably.

Configuring access control and permissions for Event Hubs

Securing your Azure Event Hubs involves not only securing the connections but also setting appropriate permissions and access controls. Azure uses **Shared Access Signatures** (**SASs**) for this purpose as well.

Understanding SAS permissions

When defining a shared access policy for your Event Hubs namespace or a specific Event Hub, you can specify one or more of the following permissions:

- **Send**: Allows the policyholder to send events to the Event Hub
- **Listen**: Allows the policyholder to listento (read) the events from the Event Hub
- **Manage**: Allows the policyholder to manage the Event Hub, including reading events, sending events, and modifying the Event Hub's configuration

Using SAS permissions

In your .NET code, you'd use the appropriate policy and key depending on what the client needs to do. This way, you can restrict what each client can do with your Event Hub, thereby following the principle of least privilege. Using SAS permissions is a powerful approach to controlling access and securing your Azure Event Hubs. By providing different policies and keys to clients based on their specific needs, you can enforce the principle of least privilege, ensuring each client has the necessary permissions for their intended operations.

For sending messages to the Event Hub, you can create a connection string with the "SendPolicy" policy and key. This allows the client to send events to the Event Hub securely. Conversely, to receive messages from the Event Hub, you can create a separate connection string with the ListenPolicy policy and key. This restricts the client only to listening and receiving events, providing the necessary security and isolation for the read-only operation:

```
var sendConnectionString = new EventHubsConnectionStringBuilder(new
Uri("amqps://your-namespace.servicebus.windows.net"), "your-eventhub-
name", "SendPolicy", "send-key");
var sendClient = EventHubClient.
CreateFromConnectionString(sendConnectionString.ToString());
```

To receive messages from the Event Hub, you can create a connection string with the ListenPolicy policy and key. This configuration allows the client to securely listen and receive events from the Event Hub, ensuring read-only access and providing the necessary security and isolation for this operation:

```
var receiveConnectionString = new EventHubsConnectionStringBuilder(new
Uri("amqps://your-namespace.servicebus.windows.net"), "your-eventhub-
name", "ListenPolicy", "receive-key");
var receiveClient = EventHubClient.
CreateFromConnectionString(receiveConnectionString.ToString());
```

In your .NET code, you can then use these connection strings to create the appropriate client instances, allowing your application to interact with the Event Hub while adhering to the specified access permissions. This approach adds an extra layer of security, reduces the risk of accidental misuse or unauthorized actions by clients, and overall enhances the security posture of your event processing system.

By carefully configuring SAS permissions, you can achieve a fine-grained level of control over clients' actions on your Event Hub. This is especially important in scenarios where different parts of your application have distinct roles and responsibilities. For instance, you may have one component responsible for generating events and another component responsible for handling event processing. With SAS permissions, you can ensure that each component only has the necessary access rights, reducing potential attack surfaces and limiting the scope of any security breaches.

It is essential to manage your SAS keys securely. Treat them as sensitive information, and avoid hardcoding them directly into your code or source control. Instead, consider using environment variables or a configuration management system to securely store and inject the keys at runtime.

Additionally, regularly rotate your keys to minimize the impact of potential key compromises, and maintain a high level of security for your Event Hub.

Remember that SAS tokens are time-limited, and you can set their expiration to a specific duration that aligns with your security requirements. This enables you to automatically revoke access to clients once their tasks are complete or when their permissions are no longer needed.

In the next section, we will delve into the world of Azure AD and explore how it can be seamlessly integrated with messaging services, providing a secure and streamlined authentication experience for your applications.

Using Azure Active Directory for authentication and authorization

Azure Active Directory (**AAD**) is Microsoft's cloud-based identity and access management service. It allows you to use **role-based access control** (**RBAC**) with Azure resources, including Event Hubs.

Understanding AAD and RBAC

In the context of Azure Event Hubs, RBAC allows you to assign specific roles to users, groups, and applications at different scopes. There are several predefined roles available, such as **Azure Event Hubs Data Sender** and **Azure Event Hubs Data Receiver**.

Configuring AAD and RBAC

To assign a role to a user or application in the Azure portal, navigate to your Event Hubs namespace, select **Access control (IAM)** from the menu, and click **+ Add role assignment**. You can then choose the role, assign it to a user or application, and specify the scope.

Using AAD and RBAC

In a .NET application, instead of using an SAS key in the connection string, you can use the `DefaultAzureCredential` class provided by the **Azure.Identity** package to authenticate using AAD. Here's an example:

```
var fullyQualifiedNamespace = "your-namespace.servicebus.windows.
net"; var eventHubName = "your-eventhub-name"; var producerClient =
new EventHubProducerClient(fullyQualifiedNamespace, eventHubName, new
DefaultAzureCredential());
```

In this example, the application will authenticate using the Azure credentials configured in its environment. This can be a **managed identity** when running in Azure, or a developer's credentials when running locally.

Encrypting data in transit and at rest

Azure Event Hubs provides built-in mechanisms to ensure your data is secure, both while it's being transmitted over the network (*in transit*) and while it's stored (*at rest*).

Data in transit

All data sent to or received from Event Hubs is automatically encrypted using the latest **Transport Layer Security** (**TLS**) version, such as TLS 1.2. This encryption guarantees that the connection between your application and Event Hubs is secure, ensuring that intercepted data during transmission cannot be deciphered.

Azure Event Hubs employs robust, built-in encryption mechanisms to safeguard your data during transit and at rest. This means you can confidently transmit and store your data, knowing it remains shielded from potential security threats. Using native encryption provides a strong layer of protection, significantly enhancing the overall security posture of your event-driven applications.

You can confidently transmit and store your data by leveraging these encryption measures provided by Azure Event Hubs. This security feature plays a pivotal role in safeguarding sensitive information, making it integral to maintaining the integrity and confidentiality of your application's data.

Data at rest

Azure Event Hubs also encrypts data at rest using **Azure Storage Service Encryption**. This encryption uses **256-bit AES encryption**, one of the strongest block ciphers available.

This feature is enabled by default and doesn't require any action from you; however, if your corporation manages its own keys, you can also utilize them. All data written to Azure Storage by Event Hubs, including event data and metadata, is encrypted before it's written to the disk and decrypted when read.

With data encryption in transit and at rest, Azure Event Hubs ensures a robust security foundation for your event streaming solution. The encryption mechanisms and access control through shared access signatures and event filtering bolster the overall security posture. However, in a production environment, it's essential to implement additional best practices to enhance the security of your Event Hubs implementation. Let's explore some of these best practices to secure Event Hubs in a production environment.

Best practices to secure Event Hubs in a production environment

Securing your Azure Event Hubs involves a combination of the methods we've discussed above, along with some additional considerations. Here are a few best practices to ensure your Event Hubs are secure in a production environment:

- **Rotate keys regularly**: It's a good practice to regularly rotate your SAS keys. You can do this in the Azure portal by navigating to your Event Hubs namespace or specific Event Hub, going to the **Shared access policies** section, selecting a policy, and clicking **Regenerate Primary Key** or **Regenerate Secondary Key**.

- **Use managed identities**: When running your application in Azure (for example, in Azure Functions or Azure App Service), consider using managed identities to authenticate to Event Hubs. This eliminates the need to manage SAS keys in your application.

As an example, we have gone into our created Event Hub and clicked on **Identity** on the left-hand side, switched the **Status** toggle to **On**, and created a managed identity that we can now assign to a resource.

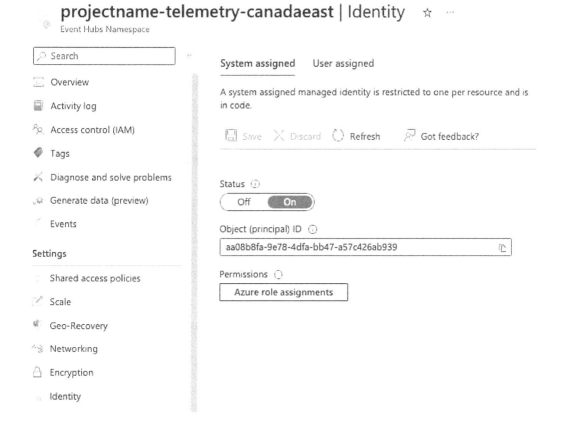

Figure 10.1 – Setting up a managed identity (MI) in Event Hubs

- **Limit permissions**: Apply the principle of least privilege when assigning permissions. Use the appropriate SAS permissions or RBAC roles to ensure that users, applications, and services have only the permissions they need and nothing more.

- **Network isolation**: Consider using **Azure Private Link** to access your Event Hubs over a private network connection. Also, use IP firewall rules to restrict access to your Event Hubs namespace.

- **Monitor and respond to security threats**: Use Azure Monitor, **Azure Security Center**, and **Azure Sentinel** to monitor your Event Hubs for security threats and respond to them quickly. Set up alerts for suspicious activities, such as an unusual volume of data being sent or received.

In this section, we went in depth into various aspects of Azure Event Hubs security, including securing connections, access control, using AAD, and encryption. We also looked at some best practices to secure Event Hubs in a production environment. With these techniques, you can ensure that your Event Hubs applications are secure and resilient.

Scaling and performance optimization

In an era of rapidly growing data and real-time analytics, the ability to scale your event streaming platform becomes crucial. Azure Event Hubs, Microsoft's fully managed, real-time data ingestion service, is no exception. Scaling and performance optimization are fundamental to maintaining a robust and efficient data pipeline, ensuring your application can handle an increasing workload, accommodate traffic spikes, and deliver events promptly.

We will dive into the art of scaling Azure Event Hubs both vertically and horizontally, optimizing throughput for event processing, and managing consumer groups for effective load distribution. We'll also look into monitoring and fine-tuning performance metrics, and discuss auto-inflate and auto-expiration policies – features unique to Azure Event Hubs.

By understanding and leveraging these concepts, you'll be equipped to design and manage scalable, performant, and cost-effective event-driven .NET applications on Azure. Whether you're broadcasting a small number of sizable events or dealing with millions of tiny ones, the techniques and best practices covered in this chapter will guide you toward achieving optimal performance in your Azure Event Hubs implementation. Now, let's explore mastering scaling and performance optimization with Azure Event Hubs.

Techniques to scale event hubs horizontally and vertically

To achieve high throughput and scalability in high-velocity event scenarios, partitioning is a critical technique. Azure Event Hubs employs partitions to distribute incoming data across several storage units, enabling concurrent processing. Each partition is an ordered sequence of events, and the number of partitions influences the system's capability to handle concurrent workloads. With more partitions, parallelism increases, leading to higher throughput.

When designing an event hub, it is crucial to consider the optimal number of partitions based on your expected data ingress rate and processing requirements. More partitions may lead to hotspots, where a small number of partitions receive most of the data, limiting scalability. Conversely, too many partitions can increase management overhead and lead to underutilization of resources. As a best practice, you can start with a reasonable number of partitions and monitor the ingress and egress rates. If some partitions consistently receive more data than others, you can dynamically scale the number of partitions to balance the workload.

Optimizing throughput and performance for event processing

Optimizing throughput and performance in Azure Event Hubs becomes a top priority in high-velocity event scenarios. Achieving high throughput is crucial to efficiently processing and managing the large volume of incoming data. To do this effectively, consider the following strategies.

Horizontal scaling

Let us explore how horizontal scaling and strategic consumer group adjustments optimize throughput and streamline data processing:

- **Partitioning for high throughput**: Horizontal scaling through partitioning is critical to achieving high throughput in Azure Event Hubs. Partitions distribute incoming data across multiple storage units, enabling concurrent processing. As partitions increase, parallelism grows, leading to higher throughput. Correctly choosing the number of partitions based on data ingress rates and processing needs is vital. Scaling the number of partitions dynamically can balance the workload and avoid bottlenecks.

- **Scaling consumer groups**: Scaling consumer groups horizontally ensures that different processing pipelines can effectively manage specific tasks. By distributing the workload across multiple consumer groups, independent applications or components can process data streams according to their unique requirements. This enhances efficiency and resource utilization.

Vertical scaling

Now, let us discuss some options for vertical scaling:

- **Optimizing throughput**: Achieving optimal performance and throughput requires strategic considerations. Pre-purchased throughput units offer controlled ingress and egress rates. These units can be scaled automatically to prevent throttling, dynamically adapting to varying workload demands.

- **Processing units in the premium tier**: In the premium tier, **processing units** (**PUs**) provide isolation at the CPU and memory levels, enhancing control over workloads. Different PU levels offer improved performance based on factors such as producers, consumers, and processing rates. This tiered approach ensures that resources are efficiently allocated for maximum performance.

Shared concepts

Horizontal and vertical scaling options share a few concepts, as follows:

- **Evaluating publisher rate and consumer capabilities**: Irrespective of horizontal or vertical scaling, evaluating the publisher rate and consumer capabilities is crucial. Monitoring tools can provide insights into event publication frequency and throughput metrics. Assessing consumer application processing capabilities helps to identify performance constraints and optimize processing strategies.

- **Batching for performance**: Batching offers a performance boost by grouping multiple events into a single send operation regardless of scaling direction. This reduces overhead from network calls, achieving higher throughput and lower latency, which is particularly valuable for high-velocity data streams.

In summary, achieving efficient scalability in Azure Event Hubs involves horizontal and vertical strategies. Partitioning and scaling consumer groups horizontally enhances parallelism while optimizing throughput, utilizing PUs, and evaluating performance considerations to enable effective vertical scaling. These techniques collectively ensure Azure Event Hubs can efficiently handle varying workloads while maintaining high performance and throughput.

By leveraging these strategies in combination, you can ensure that your Azure Event Hubs implementation performs optimally and efficiently when handling high-velocity event streams. Efficient throughput and performance are vital to building scalable and responsive event-driven architectures, making Azure Event Hubs essential in modern cloud-based solutions.

Monitoring and fine-tuning performance metrics

Monitoring the performance and behavior of your Azure Event Hubs solution is crucial to ensure its optimal operation and swiftly identify potential issues. Azure equips you with an array of monitoring tools, including Azure Monitor and Azure Event Hubs Capture, which play a pivotal role in gathering vital performance metrics. These metrics include ingress and egress rates and event counts for incoming and outgoing data and event sizes. Such metrics serve as vital performance indicators that offer insights into the health and efficiency of your system. By scrutinizing these metrics, you gain the power to fine-tune parameters such as partition counts, consumer group configurations, and optimization settings, such as multiplexing and prefetching.

Here's an overview of the key categories of Azure Event Hub monitoring metrics:

- **Requesting metrics for data and management operations**:
  - **Requests received**: Tracks data and management requests directed at the Event Hubs service, spanning both namespace and entity-level requests
  - **Requests successfully processed**: Reflects the count of requests effectively handled by the Event Hubs service, a clear indicator of operational robustness

- **Metrics for throttled requests**:
  Monitors requests that encounter throttling due to exceeding operational limits or other constraints

- **Messaging incoming and outgoing metrics**:
  - **Incoming communications**: Quantifies the events or communications sent to an Event Hub during a specific timeframe
  - **Outgoing communications**: Captures the number of events or communications dispatched from an Event Hub in a given period

- **Captured messages**: Tallies the number of captured messages

- **Incoming bytes**: Measures the incoming data volume in bytes for an Event Hub over a defined interval

- **Outgoing bytes**: Measures the volume of data transmitted from an Event Hub during a specified time

- **Capturing metrics**:

  - **Captured communications**: Tracks the count of captured communications

  - **Captured bytes**: Quantifies the volume of data captured in bytes

  - **Capture overflow**: Monitors potential capture overflow within an Event Hub

- **Metrics for connection**:

  - **Active connections**: Offers a snapshot of active connections at the namespace and entity levels

  - **Open connections**: Counts the active connections

  - **Connections closed**: Records the count of closed connections

- **Error monitoring KPIs**:

  - **Server errors**: Reflects the number of requests that could not be processed due to Event Hub service errors

  - **User errors**: Quantifies the requests left unprocessed due to user errors

  - **Quota exceeded errors**: Tracks errors arising from exceeding specified quotas

Each metric is enriched with specific dimensions, such as entity names, providing vital context to the metric data. Furthermore, Event Hubs enables you to capture logs across categories such as operational, auto-scale, virtual network connection events, and customer-managed key user logs.

Leveraging these comprehensive monitoring capabilities, you can meticulously optimize your Azure Event Hubs deployment, swiftly identify anomalies, and ensure a seamless operation for your technically proficient audience of .NET developers. This proactive monitoring and optimization strategy ensures end users receive a reliable and efficient experience.

Considerations for auto-inflate and auto-expiration policies

Consider implementing auto-inflate and auto-expire policies when working with Azure Event Hubs to manage resources and maintain optimal system performance efficiently. Auto-inflate policies enable your event hub throughput units to scale automatically based on load, ensuring your application can manage increased traffic without requiring manual intervention. This dynamic scaling helps prevent performance bottlenecks during traffic spikes while automatically scaling down during periods of lower demand to optimize costs.

Alternatively, auto-expiration policies allow you to control data retention in your event centers. By configuring expiration policies, you can specify how long data should be stored in the hub before being deleted automatically. This is especially useful for compliance and data retention, as it prevents your event center from accumulating unnecessary data over time. By carefully configuring auto-inflate and auto-expire policies in your Azure Event Hubs deployment, you can balance resource efficiency, cost-effectiveness, and data management.

Here's a small piece of code that demonstrates how you can update these settings, using the `EventHubManagementClient` from the `Microsoft.Azure.Management.EventHub` namespace:

```
var tokenCredentials = new TokenCredentials("access token");
var eventHubManagementClient = new
EventHubManagementClient(tokenCredentials){
    SubscriptionId = "your subscription id"
};
var parameters = new EHNamespace(){
    Location = "East US",
    Sku = new Sku()
    {
        Name = SkuName.Standard,
        Tier = SkuTier.Standard,
        Capacity = 2 // Increasing Throughput Units to 2
    },
    IsAutoInflateEnabled = true,
    MaximumThroughputUnits = 10
};
var result = await eventHubManagementClient.Namespaces.
CreateOrUpdateAsync(resourceGroupName, namespaceName, parameters);
```

In this snippet, we create or update an Event Hubs namespace with auto-inflate enabled, and we set the maximum TUs to 10.

Having grasped these concepts, you're now better equipped to maximize the potential of Azure Event Hubs. You'll be able to build robust, scalable, and highly performant event-driven .NET applications that can accommodate growth and fluctuations in traffic while maintaining cost efficiency.

Remember, optimizing a real-time data ingestion service such as Azure Event Hubs is not a one-time task. It's a continuous process that involves constant monitoring, fine-tuning, and adapting to changes. Keep exploring, stay curious, and don't shy away from experimentation.

As we conclude this chapter, we hope you've found the information insightful and are eager to apply these strategies to your own .NET projects. The exciting journey to master Azure Event Hubs doesn't end here – there's always more to learn and discover.

Summary

In conclusion, Azure Event Hubs is a robust and reliable event streaming platform, catering to the high demands of real-time data ingestion and processing in modern cloud-based applications. Its robust features, including partitioning, event capture, and advanced scalability, empower developers to quickly build efficient and responsive systems that can handle massive volumes of data.

Scaling is a core strength of Azure Event Hubs, enabling seamless handling of high-velocity event streams. Event Hubs achieves parallel processing by distributing data across multiple partitions, ensuring that a system can handle large workloads. Understanding how to partition event data effectively is essential to achieve the desired scalability and performance.

Handling events efficiently is crucial in real-time applications, and Azure Event Hubs provides various mechanisms to optimize event processing. Features such as batching and prefetching improve throughput and reduce latency, enabling fast and responsive event processing.

Reliability is a cornerstone of Azure Event Hubs, ensuring no data is lost during message processing. By following a log-based storage system and adhering to a FIFO model, Event Hubs guarantees that events are processed in the order they were added to the partition, maintaining data integrity.

The .NET SDK for Azure Event Hubs provides a set of APIs and client libraries, making it easy for .NET developers to interact with Event Hubs. The SDK supports both synchronous and asynchronous programming models and offers a wide range of functionality to work with data in Event Hubs. The SDK simplifies managing events in Event Hubs, from creating and querying data to updating and deleting it.

Next, we will delve into another essential component of Azure's messaging services – Azure Service Bus. We will explore its key features, design considerations, and best practices to craft robust enterprise solutions, exchanging data and messages in a distributed environment efficiently. Understanding Azure Event Hubs and Azure Service Bus equips developers with powerful tools to build scalable, reliable, and secure cloud applications that drive innovation and enhance the user experience. By leveraging the capabilities of these services, organizations can unlock new opportunities for growth and success in the ever-evolving digital landscape.

11

Designing Ready-Made Solutions with Azure Service Bus

In this chapter, we will embark on a journey to explore the powerful capabilities of Azure Service Bus and its significance in designing enterprise-ready solutions. As businesses continue to rely on distributed systems and interconnected applications, the need for reliable and scalable messaging becomes paramount. Azure Service Bus is a robust and efficient messaging service that caters to these critical requirements.

Reliable and scalable messaging is the backbone of seamless information exchange in today's complex business landscape. Enterprises heavily depend on distributed systems and related applications, necessitating a messaging infrastructure that can handle large volumes of data without compromising performance. Azure Service Bus rises to the challenge, providing a reliable and flexible communication channel. It empowers different applications or distributed system components to exchange information seamlessly, enabling collaboration and operational efficiency.

Throughout this chapter, we will delve into the following key aspects of Azure Service Bus:

- Understanding Azure Service Bus
- Considerations to design enterprise solutions using Azure Service Bus
- Delving into topics and subscriptions
- Scaling and High Availability in Azure Service Bus
- Optimizing Service Bus performance
- Integrating Azure Service Bus with enterprise architectures
- Creating an Azure Service Bus via a CLI

By the end of this chapter, you will have gained a comprehensive understanding of Azure Service Bus and its diverse applications in modern enterprise scenarios. Armed with this knowledge, you will be better equipped to design and implement robust, scalable, and high-performing messaging solutions to meet the communication needs of your enterprise.

Understanding Azure Service Bus

In this rapidly evolving digital era, seamless communication between applications is necessary. One technology that stands out in this domain is Azure Service Bus. In this detailed guide, we'll dive deep into what Azure Service Bus is, its key features and capabilities, and how it fares compared to other messaging technologies.

Azure Service Bus, a powerful messaging service offered by Microsoft Azure, empowers organizations to build enterprise-ready solutions. It boasts essential features such as **message queuing**, **publish/ subscribe patterns**, support for various protocols, and advanced message routing mechanisms. By comparing Azure Service Bus with other messaging technologies, we can gain insights into its unique advantages and use cases. This understanding enables organizations to make informed decisions when designing their messaging infrastructure, ensuring optimal performance and scalability.

Message queues

Azure Service Bus provides first-in, first-out messaging infrastructure with **message queues**. Each message is read by a single recipient and removed from the queue, ensuring no message is processed more than once.

Topics and subscriptions

Azure Service Bus also supports a **publish/subscribe model** with **topics** and **subscriptions**. Here, **senders (publishers)** send messages to a topic, while **receivers (subscribers)** receive these messages from one or more associated subscriptions.

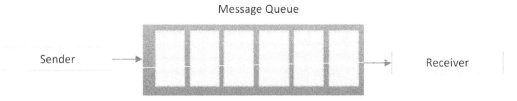

Figure 11.1 – A Service Bus message queue

Dead-letter queues

Azure Service Bus provides **dead-letter queues** to handle messages that cannot be delivered or processed. It helps ensure that no message is lost in the process of transmission.

Scheduled delivery

With the **scheduled delivery** feature, Azure Service Bus allows you to schedule messages for future delivery. It's like setting a timer for your messages.

The unique capabilities of Azure Service Bus

Beyond its main features, Azure Service Bus offers several unique capabilities, including the following:

- **Transaction support**: Azure Service Bus supports transactional operations on messages, making it an excellent choice for applications requiring high consistency

- **Batching**: This supports sending or receiving multiple messages in a single operation, improving overall efficiency

- **Auto-forwarding**: This feature enables you to chain together queues and topics, thus automatically forwarding messages from one queue or subscription to another

Azure Service Bus versus other messaging technologies

Several messaging technologies, such as RabbitMQ and Kafka, are prevalent today. While Azure Service Bus brings unique advantages, it's essential to note that platforms such as RabbitMQ also offer fully managed instances and powerful features. Azure Service Bus boasts advanced features such as dead-letter queues, scheduled delivery, and transaction support. However, it's worth noting that any platform with **Advanced Message Queuing Protocol** (**AMQP**) support, including RabbitMQ, will likely have these capabilities. Furthermore, as a part of the Azure ecosystem, Azure Service Bus can seamlessly integrate with other Azure services, making it a compelling choice for businesses already invested in Azure.

When evaluating Azure Service Bus as a messaging solution, weighing its potential drawbacks or limitations against other options is crucial. While Azure Service Bus is robust, certain specialized messaging technologies offer performance advantages in specific scenarios. For instance, while Azure Service Bus supports the global AMQP standard, specific use cases might benefit from other protocols or proprietary solutions. Kafka is best suited for high-throughput stream processing, log aggregation, and event sourcing. RabbitMQ excels in decoupling applications, traditional message brokering, and ensuring message delivery with complex routing. Azure Service Bus integrates well with the Azure ecosystem, supports enterprise messaging patterns, and offers robust security and compliance features. In essence, choose Kafka for distributed data streaming, RabbitMQ for flexible and reliable messaging, and Azure Service Bus for Azure-centric enterprise messaging needs.

From exploring the advantages of Azure Service Bus over other messaging technologies, it is evident that it offers a range of powerful features, seamless integration with Azure services, and a fully managed infrastructure. However, it is essential to evaluate all aspects and considerations when designing enterprise solutions carefully. In the following section, we will delve into specific considerations to leverage the capabilities of Azure Service Bus to design robust, scalable, and efficient enterprise solutions. From understanding messaging patterns and applying best practices to ensuring security and optimal performance, these considerations will empower you to harness the full potential of Azure Service Bus in your architectural decisions. Let's now explore the essential considerations for designing enterprise solutions using Azure Service Bus.

Considerations for designing enterprise solutions using Azure Service Bus

Several crucial factors come into play when designing enterprise solutions with Azure Service Bus. Organizations must carefully consider message patterns and communication models to determine how messages flow between sender and receiver components. **Scalability** and **throughput** requirements must be assessed to ensure efficient handling of large message volumes. Message durability and reliability are vital aspects that guarantee message delivery even in critical scenarios. Security and access control considerations are significant in protecting sensitive data and ensuring compliance with industry regulations. **Monitoring**, **diagnostics**, and **error handling** are essential to maintain a healthy messaging infrastructure. Crafting enterprise solutions that are scalable, efficient, and secure requires strategic design considerations. This becomes particularly crucial when leveraging a robust messaging platform such as Azure Service Bus. This section will explore the critical design elements to create effective enterprise solutions.

Message patterns and communication models

When designing an enterprise solution with Azure Service Bus, it's essential to understand the different message patterns and communication models. Azure Service Bus supports **point-to-point** (**queue**), **load leveling** (**queue**), **competing consumer** (**queue**), and **publish-subscribe** (**topic**) communication models. Point-to-point is a **unicast method** where the sender, or publisher, is agnostic of its recipients, meaning that it doesn't need to know who the subscribers are. Messages are sent to a topic, and any number of subscribers can choose to receive messages from that topic without the publisher having to be aware of them. This decoupling of publishers and subscribers makes the system more flexible and future-proof, as subscribers can be added or removed without affecting the publisher's operation. Choosing the suitable communication model depends on your business requirements. If you need to communicate with a single recipient, you may opt for queues. If you need to broadcast a message to multiple subscribers, topics would be your go-to choice.

Scalability and throughput requirements

Azure Service Bus is built to cater to various scalability and throughput requirements. However, it's crucial to understand your business needs to ensure optimal performance. A highly scalable system will manage an increasing load efficiently, but it may have additional cost implications. Similarly, a system with high throughput can process large volumes of data but may require more resources. Therefore, it's critical to balance these two aspects according to your requirements. For instance, to manage high-volume scenarios, you can leverage the **Azure Service Bus Premium tier** that offers dedicated resources, or use features such as **partitioning** and **sharding** to distribute your messages across multiple entities. To view more details about the different pricing tiers, you can visit this link: `https://azure.microsoft.com/en-ca/products/service-bus`.

In Azure Service Bus, partitioning is a key feature that enhances scalability and availability. Azure Service Bus automatically distributes the messages across multiple message brokers and stores when partitioning is enabled for a queue or topic. This parallelism allows higher throughput, as multiple producers and consumers can send and receive messages concurrently. If one message broker or store becomes unavailable, the remaining partitions continue functioning, ensuring availability. To maintain message ordering, Service Bus uses the `SessionId` or `PartitionKey` properties of messages to control the distribution of messages to specific partitions. While Service Bus itself doesn't explicitly support "sharding," as seen in databases, a similar load distribution can be achieved by creating multiple Service Bus namespaces, each with its own set of queues and topics, or by leveraging topics and subscriptions to distribute messages to different sets of consumers. These techniques collectively enable Azure Service Bus to handle large volumes of messages efficiently and reliably.

Message durability and reliability

When designing enterprise solutions, message **durability** and **reliability** should never be compromised. Azure Service Bus ensures this with features such as **duplicate detection** and dead-letter queues.

Azure Service Bus's duplicate detection and dead-letter queue features enhance the reliability and durability of your messaging system. Duplicate detection allows Azure Service Bus to recognize and remove any duplicate messages sent to a queue or topic, ensuring the reliability of your system by preventing redundant processing. Conversely, dead-letter queues are a special kind of queue where messages that cannot be delivered are stored. This ensures that no message is lost during transmission, contributing to the durability of your messages. However, it's important to note that the dead-letter queue doesn't automatically resolve issues; it essentially acts as a holding area for messages that can't be processed. Someone needs to monitor this queue and determine how to handle the messages – whether they should be fixed, discarded, or forwarded to another queue or system. So, while dead-letter queues help preserve messages that could not be processed, they require manual intervention or additional logic to fully ensure system reliability and message durability.

Security and access control considerations

Security is paramount in any enterprise solution, and Azure Service Bus is no exception. It provides various security and access control features that you can leverage.

Azure Service Bus integrates with **Azure Active Directory** for identity and access management. It also supports **Shared Access Signature** (**SAS**) authentication, which allows you to control the level of access for different users.

In addition to its scalability and availability features, Azure Service Bus strongly emphasizes security, providing robust mechanisms to safeguard your data. It supports IP filtering, allowing you to control the network addresses that can access your Azure Service Bus namespaces, limiting exposure to unauthorized users. Moreover, Azure Service Bus ensures the confidentiality of your messages through encryption. It supports encryption at rest, where data is secured when stored on the disk. For this encryption, you can choose to use Microsoft-managed keys or, for more control, your customer-managed keys. **Bring Your Own Key** (**BYOK**) for encryption is a significant competitive advantage, as it provides you with direct control over the keys used to protect your data, satisfying stringent regulatory and compliance requirements.

Monitoring, diagnostics, and error handling

Lastly, an effective enterprise solution must have robust **monitoring**, **diagnostics**, and **error-handling** mechanisms.

Azure Service Bus comes with **Azure Monitor**, which helps track your resources' performance and activity. It also provides built-in logging and diagnostics for troubleshooting.

The **dead letter queue** (**DLQ**) feature in Azure Service Bus aids in error handling by preserving messages that encounter processing or delivery issues. It isolates problematic messages, allowing for easy debugging and troubleshooting, which is crucial for identifying and resolving errors or misconfigurations. DLQs also facilitate controlled retries of failed messages once underlying issues are corrected, ensuring that no data is lost and that system stability is maintained. This feature provides valuable visibility into error-causing messages, enabling efficient error resolution without disrupting the entire system.

In this section, we explored the critical design elements to craft effective enterprise solutions using Azure Service Bus. We discussed the importance of message patterns and communication models, scalability and throughput assessment, message durability and reliability, security and access control considerations, as well as monitoring, diagnostics, and error-handling strategies. Now, let's delve into another fundamental aspect of Azure Service Bus – topics and subscriptions.

Delving into topics and subscriptions

Azure Service Bus encompasses a multitude of services and capabilities. Among them, the concepts of **topics** and **subscriptions** stand out for their ability to facilitate **one-to-many** and **many-to-many communication**. Let's delve into the details of topics and subscriptions, their usage, and their intricacies.

In Azure Service Bus, a topic acts as a message channel where senders (publishers) push messages. Conversely, one or more subscriptions can be associated with a topic and act as a virtual queue, enabling recipients (subscribers) to pull these messages.

The beauty of this model lies in its flexibility – a single topic can have multiple subscriptions, and each subscription can have multiple subscribers. This allows a single message sent to a topic to be received by multiple subscribers, thereby facilitating efficient one-to-many communication.

In the upcoming section, we will address the following nuances and aspects of topics and subscriptions in Azure Service Bus:

- **Publishing and subscribing to topics**: We will cover the process of publishing messages to a topic and how subscribers can receive these messages through their associated subscriptions. This will include an in-depth look at the sender and receiver components.

- **Filters and rules for message routing**: We will explore how filters and rules can be applied to subscriptions to enable selective message retrieval based on specific criteria. This will allow subscribers to receive only messages that match their defined filtering conditions.

The **Competing Consumers pattern** is a powerful design pattern in messaging systems that allows multiple consumers to simultaneously process messages from a shared resource, ensuring efficient load balancing and parallel processing. While it's commonly associated with subscriptions, it's essential to understand that this pattern isn't limited to just that:

- **Queues and Competing Consumers**: The Competing Consumers pattern can be applied to simple queues. When multiple receivers dequeue from the same queue, they inherently compete to process the messages. This ensures that if one consumer is slow or encounters an error, another consumer can pick up the slack, ensuring that the processing of messages doesn't lag.

- **Load leveling**: Intimately connected with the Competing Consumers pattern is the concept of load leveling. The system can distribute the "load" of processing messages across various consumers by having multiple consumers. This not only ensures efficiency but also provides a level of fault tolerance. If one consumer fails, others can continue processing, ensuring no downtime or lag.

- **Subscriptions and Competing Consumers**: While the pattern applies to queues, subscriptions in a topic-based system add another layer of complexity. In such systems, multiple subscribers can listen to a topic, and each can have multiple consumers competing to process the messages. This allows the efficient processing of messages based on topic filters, ensuring that messages relevant to a particular subscriber are processed efficiently.

In conclusion, while subscriptions are an everyday use case for the Competing Consumers pattern, it's crucial to understand its broader applicability. Whether you work with simple queues or complex topic-based systems, understanding and effectively leveraging the Competing Consumers pattern can significantly enhance the efficiency and reliability of your messaging system.

By understanding these nuances, developers can optimize their use of topics and subscriptions in Azure Service Bus, enabling them to design efficient and flexible communication patterns for their enterprise solutions.

Publishing and subscribing to topics

Publishing a message to a topic in Azure Service Bus is simple – the publisher sends a message to the topic, and Azure Service Bus takes care of the rest. The service ensures that the message is delivered to all active subscriptions associated with that topic.

Subscribing to a topic is equally straightforward – subscribers receive messages from a particular subscription associated with the topic. When a message arrives, subscribers can *pull* it from the subscription for processing.

Let's think of Azure Service Bus as a post office. Imagine *topics* as the postbox where you drop letters (messages), and *subscriptions* as the recipients' addresses. A topic can have multiple subscriptions, signifying that a single message sent to a topic is received by multiple subscriptions, thereby enabling one-to-many communication. To establish this in .NET, follow these steps:

1. We first need to install the **Azure Service Bus SDK** using **NuGet**:

    ```
    Install-Package Azure.Messaging.ServiceBus
    ```

    Before using the Service Bus functionality, the first step is to install the required NuGet package called `Azure.Messaging.ServiceBus` in your .NET project. This package provides the necessary classes and methods to interact with the Azure Service Bus.

2. Next, you need to set up the connection string and provide names for the topic and subscription you want to create. The connection string allows your application to authenticate and interact with Azure Service Bus:

    ```
    string connectionString = "<your_connection_string>";
    string topicName = "sampleTopic";
    string subscriptionName = "sampleSubscription";
    ```

3. Replace <your_connection_string> with the actual connection string obtained from your Azure Service Bus resource.

4. The `ServiceBusAdministrationClient` manages the Service Bus entities (e.g., topics and subscriptions). It is initialized with the connection string:

```
ServiceBusAdministrationClient administrationClient =
new(connectionString);
```

5. The code then proceeds to create a topic using the `CreateTopicAsync` method of `administrationClient`. A topic in Azure Service Bus is a logical entity that allows publishers to send messages to it. Subscribers can then receive these messages from subscriptions:

```
await administrationClient.CreateTopicAsync(topicName);
```

6. Next, a subscription is created for the previously created topic using the `CreateSubscriptionAsync` method of `administrationClient`. A subscription represents a filter on the messages from a topic, allowing subscribers to receive only the messages that match specific criteria:

```
await administrationClient.CreateSubscriptionAsync(topicName,
subscriptionName);
```

That's it! After executing the preceding code, you'll have a topic named `sampleTopic` and a subscription named `sampleSubscription` set up in your Azure Service Bus instance, ready to send and receive messages.

The preceding example provides the essential steps to create a simple messaging infrastructure using Azure Service Bus, which can be further expanded and customized to meet the needs of your application.

Filters and rules for message routing

Azure Service Bus offers a powerful feature to direct specific messages to specific subscriptions – **filters** and **rules**. These can be applied to each subscription, and the Azure Service Bus uses them to determine whether a message published on a topic should be sent to a particular subscription.

Rules consist of a filter and an optional action. The filter is a condition the message must meet to be added to the subscription. If a message satisfies the condition, the action (if any) is applied to the message before it is added to the subscription.

Filters and rules in Azure Service Bus allow for complex and sophisticated message routing scenarios. A rule comprises a filter expression and an associated action. When a message arrives at a topic, the filter is applied, and if it matches, the action is executed.

Filters can be of three types – `SqlFilter`, `CorrelationFilter`, and `MatchAll/MatchNone`.

Let's illustrate the use of `SqlFilter` in .NET:

1. In the provided code snippet, we illustrate the use of `SqlRuleFilter` in .NET for Azure Service Bus. `SqlRuleFilter` is a type of filter that allows us to define SQL-like expressions to selectively route messages, based on specific criteria:

    ```
    var ruleDescription = new CreateRuleOptions
    {
        Name = "Priority1",
        Filter = new SqlRuleFilter("Priority = '1'"),
    };
    await administrationClient.CreateRuleAsync(topicName,
    subscriptionName, ruleDescription);
    ```

    We begin by creating a `ruleDescription` object of type `CreateRuleOptions`. This object will be used to define the properties of the rule we want to create for the subscription.

2. We set the `Name` property of the rule as `Priority1`. This will be the name of the rule we will create.

3. The critical part is the `Filter` property. Here, we create an instance of `SqlRuleFilter` and pass it a SQL-like expression as a string – `"Priority = '1'"`. This expression is essentially a condition that specifies that only messages with a property named `Priority` that have a value of 1 will pass through the filter.

4. Next, we call the `CreateRuleAsync` method on `administrationClient` to create the rule. We pass in `topicName`, `subscriptionName`, and the `ruleDescription` object as parameters. This will create the rule with the specified properties for the given topic and subscription.

5. Once the rule is created, it will be applied to the subscription specified by `subscriptionName`. From this point on, only messages that meet the condition defined in the SQL-like expression will be delivered to this particular subscription.

In summary, the provided code demonstrates how to use `SqlRuleFilter` in .NET to create a rule that filters messages based on a specific condition. In this case, the rule filters messages to only allow those with a `Priority` property set to 1 to pass through and be delivered to the associated subscription.

Let's continue with another example, this time on how to use `CorrelationFilter`. In an IoT scenario where multiple devices send telemetry data, you might use `CorrelationFilter` in Azure Service Bus to set up a specific subscription that receives messages only from a particular device, thereby enabling targeted processing of device-specific data:

```
CorrelationFilter correlationFilter = new CorrelationFilter
{
    Label = "Telemetry",
    CorrelationId = "Device1"
```

```
};
namespaceManager.CreateSubscription("TelemetryTopic",
"Device1Subscription", correlationFilter);
```

In this example, only messages with a `Label` property set to `Telemetry` and `CorrelationId` set to `Device1`will be delivered to `Device1Subscription`.

With the `MatchAll` filter in Azure Service Bus, you can set up a default subscription that receives all messages sent to a topic, regardless of their properties, which is useful for scenarios such as logging or archiving every message that passes through the system:

```
SqlFilter matchAllFilter = new SqlFilter("1=1");
namespaceManager.CreateSubscription("AllEventsTopic",
"ArchiveSubscription", matchAllFilter);
```

In this example, all messages sent to `AllEventsTopic` will be delivered to the `ArchiveSubscription`, since the `1=1` filter condition is always `true`. Now, let's look at the final case of the `MatchNone` filter. In Azure Service Bus, the `MatchNone` filter allows you to configure a subscription that generally does not receive any messages, making it useful for scenarios such as troubleshooting or special handling of exceptional cases in your messaging system:

```
SqlFilter matchNoneFilter = new SqlFilter("1=0");
namespaceManager.CreateSubscription("AllEventsTopic",
"NoMessagesSubscription", matchNoneFilter);
```

In this example, no messages will be delivered to `NoMessagesSubscription` under normal circumstances, since the `1=0` filter condition is always false.

> **Guidance on filter selection**
>
> Here's some guidance on filter selection when working with Azure Service Bus:
>
> a. **Performance versus flexibility**: Your choice of filter should balance performance needs and flexibility. While SQL filters are the most flexible, they come with a performance cost. Conversely, Boolean and correlation filters are more performant but offer less flexibility.
>
> b. **Use case specificity**: Boolean filters are the best choice for simple scenarios where you want to route all or no messages to a subscription. If you have specific properties you want to match against, correlation filters are ideal. SQL filters are the way to go for complex conditions and maximum flexibility.

Imagine you have messages with a `MessageType` property. If you want to route only messages with `MessageType` set to `'Alert'` to a specific subscription, you could do one of the following:

- Use a correlation filter with `Properties["MessageType"] = 'Alert'` for optimal performance.

- Use a SQL filter with the `MessageType = 'Alert.'` condition. This provides flexibility – for instance, if you later add more conditions, such as `MessageType = 'Alert' AND Priority = 1`. However, remember that this comes with a slight performance overhead.

When setting up filters and rules in Azure Service Bus, it's crucial to understand the trade-offs between performance and flexibility. You can ensure efficient and effective message routing in your system by aligning your filter choice with your specific use case and performance needs.

The Competing Consumers pattern with subscriptions

Azure Service Bus can also handle the Competing Consumers pattern with subscriptions. In this pattern, multiple consumers or receivers connect to a single subscription and compete to process messages. When a receiver retrieves a message from the subscription, that message is locked and not available to other receivers.

This pattern can be beneficial for load balancing and improving message processing speed, especially when dealing with high-volume scenarios.

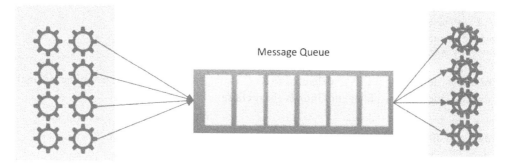

Figure 11.2 – The Competing Consumers pattern

To create an Azure Service Bus client in .NET 6, the `ServiceBusClient` class is your gateway to all ServiceBus entities. This top-level client facilitates interactions with Service Bus, providing a shared AMQP connection for lower-level types such as `ServiceBusSender` and `ServiceBusReceiver`. Disposing of `ServiceBusClient`, achieved through the `DisposeAsync()` method during application shutdown, properly cleans up network resources and unmanaged objects. Creating an instance of the `ServiceBusClient` involves several constructors that accommodate different authentication methods, such as `AzureNameKeyCredential`, `AzureSasCredential`, and `TokenCredential`. These constructors, bearing various parameters, enable you to tailor your client instantiation to your authentication and configuration needs. Once `ServiceBusClient` is instantiated, you gain access to many methods. These methods cover a wide range of tasks, from accepting sessions and session receivers to creating processors for message handling.

The `CreateReceiver` and `CreateSender` methods are especially noteworthy, allowing you to create instances of `ServiceBusReceiver` and `ServiceBusSender` for efficient message receiving and sending.

Here's an example of how to set up different authentication methods and then the competing consumers in .NET:

```
using Azure.Identity;
using Azure.Messaging.ServiceBus;
using System;
using System.Threading.Tasks;
class Program {
    static async Task Main(string[] args) {
        string fullyQualifiedNamespace = "<Your_Fully_Qualified_
Namespace>";
        string topicName = "<Your_Topic_Name>";
        string subscriptionName = "<Your_Subscription_Name>";
        string clientId = "<Your_Azure_AD_Client_ID>";
        string clientSecret = "<Your_Azure_AD_Client_Secret>";
        string tenantId = "<Your_Azure_AD_Tenant_ID>";
        ClientSecretCredential adCredential = new
ClientSecretCredential(tenantId, clientId, clientSecret);
        await using (ServiceBusClient client = new
ServiceBusClient(fullyQualifiedNamespace, adCredential, new
ServiceBusClientOptions()))
        {
            ServiceBusReceiver receiver1 = client.
CreateReceiver(topicName, subscriptionName);
            ServiceBusReceiver receiver2 = client.
CreateReceiver(topicName, subscriptionName);
            Task receiveTask1 = ReceiveMessagesAsync(receiver1);
            Task receiveTask2 = ReceiveMessagesAsync(receiver2);
            await Task.WhenAll(receiveTask1, receiveTask2);
        } }
    static async Task ReceiveMessagesAsync(ServiceBusReceiver
receiver) {
        await foreach (ServiceBusReceivedMessage message in receiver.
ReceiveMessagesAsync())
        {
            Console.WriteLine($"Received message: {message.Body}");
            await receiver.CompleteMessageAsync(message);
        }}}
```

We have added code to create two `ServiceBusReceiver` instances for the same topic subscription and then start competing consumers to receive messages from that subscription. The ReceiveMessagesAsync method is used to receive messages from the subscription asynchronously, and the logic in the `ReceiveMessagesAsync` method processes received messages and completes them. Replace the placeholders in the code with your actual configuration details. This extended example demonstrates how to create competing consumers for a subscription, using `ServiceBusReceiver` instances with Azure AD authentication.

The two receivers, `receiver1` and `receiver2`, act as competing consumers; in the preceding example, the two receivers are created for the same subscription, allowing them to act as competing consumers. This setup ensures efficient load distribution and enhanced message processing capabilities, making it an excellent strategy to achieve greater application performance and scalability.

Here's what happens in the scenario we described, where `receiveTask1` gets the message before `receiveTask2`:

- `receiveTask1` consumes the message: When a message arrives in the subscription, `receiveTask1` and `receiveTask2` are both candidates to receive that message. In our scenario, `receiveTask1` receives and processes the message first.

- No more messages for `receiveTask2`: Because `receiveTask1` already received and processed the message, there are no more messages left for `receiveTask2` to process at that moment. Service Bus ensures that a message sent to a subscription is processed by only one receiver when competing consumers exist.

- `Task.WhenAll` (`receiveTask1` and `receiveTask2`) behavior: `Task.WhenAll` creates a task that will be completed when all of the supplied tasks are completed. In this case, it waits for both `receiveTask1` and `receiveTask2` to complete.

    Let's suppose `ReceiveMessagesAsync` is designed to keep running and polling for new messages until some condition is met (such as a cancellation token is triggered). In that case, `receiveTask2` will just keep waiting for messages to arrive, even if `receiveTask1` has already processed a message.

    Let's suppose `ReceiveMessagesAsync` is designed to complete after processing a single message or after a certain period. In that case, `receiveTask2` will complete when it meets its designed condition, even if it hasn't processed any messages.

- `Task.WhenAll` completion: `Task.WhenAll` completes when both `receiveTask1` and `receiveTask2` have completed, regardless of whether `receiveTask2` actually processed any messages.

- Exception handling (if applicable): If any of the tasks (in this case, `receiveTask1` or `receiveTask2`) throws an error, the task returned by `Task.WhenAll` will also throw an error, and the exceptions can be observed and handled.

So, in summary, if `receiveTask1` reaches a message before `receiveTask2`, `receiveTask2` won't see that message and will continue to wait for new messages to arrive or until its own completion condition is met. `Task.WhenAll` will wait for both `receiveTask1` and `receiveTask2` to complete, regardless of how many messages each task processed.

As you venture deeper into Azure Service Bus, it's essential to understand the concept of dead lettering and its significance in the reliable message-processing landscape. The **Dead-Letter Queue (DLQ)** is a holding area for messages that couldn't be delivered or processed successfully. Azure Service Bus ensures that no message gets lost in the ether by placing it in the DLQ, whether it's due to exceeded delivery attempts, expiration, or any other exception. Next, we'll delve into why messages end up in the DLQ, how to retrieve these messages, and the best practices to manage and process dead-letter messages. This knowledge is crucial to building resilient systems that can withstand unexpected hiccups and continue to operate efficiently. Next up, we will introduce another useful pattern when working with Azure Service Bus called the **fan-in and fan-out pattern**.

The fan-in and fan-out pattern

The fan-in and fan-out patterns are important messaging patterns in distributed systems that deal with message processing and distribution. These patterns play a significant role in optimizing communication and resource utilization. The following subsections provide a technical explanation of both patterns.

The fan-in pattern

The fan-in pattern refers to a scenario where multiple sources or senders channel their messages into a single destination, such as a queue or a topic. Consolidating messages from various sources into a single entity allows for centralized processing or analysis. The term *fan-in* originates from the idea that multiple input streams come together like the blades of a fan converging at a single point. In the context of Azure Service Bus, this is how the fan-in pattern works:

- Multiple senders or producers send messages to a common destination, such as a queue or topic
- The destination acts as a hub, collecting messages from different sources
- This pattern is often used when multiple data sources need to be aggregated and processed together. For example, different microservices might send events to a central topic, where those events are processed together

Let's dive into an example utilizing the fan-in pattern:

```
using Azure.Messaging.ServiceBus;
using System;
using System.Threading.Tasks;
class Program
{
    static async Task Main(string[] args)
    {
        string fullyQualifiedNamespace = "<Your_Fully_Qualified_
Namespace>";
```

```
        string topicName = "<Your_Topic_Name>";
        string sender1 = "<Sender1_Name>";
        string sender2 = "<Sender2_Name>";
        await using (ServiceBusClient client = new
ServiceBusClient(fullyQualifiedNamespace))
        {
            ServiceBusSender sender1 = client.CreateSender(sender1);
            ServiceBusSender sender2 = client.CreateSender(sender2);
            ServiceBusMessage message1 = new
ServiceBusMessage("Message from Sender 1");
            ServiceBusMessage message2 = new
ServiceBusMessage("Message from Sender 2");
            await sender1.SendMessageAsync(message1);
            await sender2.SendMessageAsync(message2);
        }}}
```

In this code, you start by specifying the fully qualified namespace of your Azure Service Bus and creating two sender instances, using `client.CreateSender(sender1)` and `client.CreateSender(sender2)`. Then, you create two messages, `message1` and `message2`, each containing a specific message content. Finally, you use the `SendMessageAsync` method of each sender to send the respective messages to the Azure Service Bus namespace. This code allows you to efficiently send messages from different senders to the same namespace, facilitating asynchronous communication between different components or services. Let's continue and learn about the fan-out pattern and its use cases.

The fan-out pattern

The fan-out pattern is the opposite of the fan-in pattern. It involves a single source sending messages to multiple destinations, usually multiple subscribers or consumers. This pattern allows parallel processing and the distribution of messages to multiple recipients. The term *fan-out* is derived from the concept of spreading messages outwards like the blades of a fan.

In the context of Azure Service Bus, this is how to fan-out pattern works:

- A single sender or producer sends messages to multiple destinations (subscribers or consumers)

- Each destination independently processes the messages it receives

- This pattern is useful when distributing data to multiple consumers for parallel processing. For instance, a central topic might broadcast events to subscribers who perform specific actions based on the events

These patterns are particularly relevant when decoupling components and achieving parallelism are essential goals. Azure Service Bus provides the infrastructure to implement the fan-in and fan-out patterns efficiently. Whether you're consolidating data from various sources or distributing messages to multiple consumers, these patterns help optimize communication, resource utilization, and scalability in distributed applications. We can see this with the following example:

```csharp
using Azure.Messaging.ServiceBus;
using System;
using System.Threading.Tasks;
class Program{
static async Task Main(string[] args)
    {
        string fullyQualifiedNamespace = "<Your_Fully_Qualified_
Namespace>";
        string topicName = "<Your_Topic_Name>";
        string subscription1 = "<Subscription1_Name>";
        string subscription2 = "<Subscription2_Name>";
        await using (ServiceBusClient client = new
ServiceBusClient(fullyQualifiedNamespace))
        {
            ServiceBusSender sender = client.CreateSender(topicName);
            ServiceBusMessage message = new ServiceBusMessage("Message
for Subscribers");
            await sender.SendMessageAsync(message);
            ServiceBusReceiver receiver1 = client.
CreateReceiver(topicName, subscription1);
            ServiceBusReceiver receiver2 = client.
CreateReceiver(topicName, subscription2);
            await ReceiveMessagesAsync(receiver1);
            await ReceiveMessagesAsync(receiver2);
        }}
    static async Task ReceiveMessagesAsync(ServiceBusReceiver
receiver)
    {
        await foreach (ServiceBusReceivedMessage message in receiver.
ReceiveMessagesAsync())
        {
            Console.WriteLine($"Received message: {message.Body}");
            await receiver.CompleteMessageAsync(message);
        }}}
```

The provided code example highlights the usage of `Azure.Messaging.ServiceBus` to interact with Azure Service Bus topics and subscriptions. This messaging pattern involves sending messages to a topic and distributing them to multiple subscriptions. The code connects to the Service Bus client and sends a message to a specified topic. It then creates two subscribers (receivers) for the topic's subscriptions and asynchronously retrieves messages from each subscription using the `ReceiveMessagesAsync` method. The received messages are processed and marked as completed, ensuring their removal from the subscription. This approach facilitates efficient asynchronous communication between different components or services, through the publish-subscribe messaging model offered by Azure Service Bus.

Handling dead-letter messages

Azure Service Bus provides a robust mechanism for addressing messages that cannot be successfully delivered or processed. These messages find a home in a dedicated sub-queue linked to each subscription, aptly named the **dead-letter queue** (**DLQ**). This safeguard ensures that no message is inadvertently lost during transit. By examining these messages, you can understand why they weren't processed or delivered as expected and take corrective measures accordingly.

While Azure Service Bus employs an automatic system-level approach to dead-letter messages under specific conditions, it's paramount to recognize that developers also wield explicit control over dead-lettering. During processing, if a receiver determines a message to be non-compliant or infeasible for processing due to specific business rules or other reasons, the receiver can proactively direct the message to the DLQ. This proactive strategy enhances error handling in a resource-efficient manner. Instead of permitting Service Bus to engage in repetitive delivery attempts (up to 10 times by default) while observing the receiver crash on each occurrence, developers can assume command and directly initiate the dead-lettering of the problematic message. This approach contributes to efficient error diagnosis and conserves compute resources not squandered on fruitless delivery attempts.

Furthermore, considering the critical nature of messages within the DLQ, it's considered best practice to monitor DLQs closely. Utilizing tools such as Azure Monitor, vigilant observation of the DLQ ensures swift responses to potential issues. This practice fortifies the reliability and resilience of your messaging system.

A crucial aspect to highlight is that developers can explicitly dead-letter a message. Beyond the inherent system-level dead-lettering, application receivers can independently designate a message as dead-lettered. This is particularly beneficial when a message is non-compliant or infeasible to process due to reasons specific to your application's business logic. By doing so, developers prevent the inefficient consumption of computing resources. Instead of letting the Azure Service Bus make multiple futile delivery attempts (up to 10 times) and potentially witnessing the receiver crash repeatedly, you can proactively intervene. By explicitly dead-lettering the message, you ensure precise error handling and conserve precious compute resources.

Building on this understanding, let's delve deeper and explore an example that shows how to manage and process these dead-letter messages effectively in .NET:

```
ServiceBusReceiver deadLetterReceiver = client.
CreateReceiver(topicName, subscriptionName, new
ServiceBusReceiverOptions
{
    SubQueue = SubQueue.DeadLetter
});
while (true){
```

```
ServiceBusReceivedMessage receivedDeadLetterMessage = await
deadLetterReceiver.ReceiveMessageAsync();
    if (receivedDeadLetterMessage != null)
    {
        if (receivedDeadLetterMessage.Label == "CreateCustomer")
        {
            Console.WriteLine("Creating customer: " +
receivedDeadLetterMessage.Body.ToString());
        }
        else if (receivedDeadLetterMessage.Label ==
"AddToCustomerList")
        {
            Console.WriteLine("Adding customer to list: " +
receivedDeadLetterMessage.Body.ToString());
        }
        await deadLetterReceiver.
CompleteMessageAsync(receivedDeadLetterMessage);
    }
    else
    {
        await Task.Delay(TimeSpan.FromSeconds(10));
    }
}
```

This code continuously checks the DLQ for messages. When a message is received, it checks the type or content of the message and processes it accordingly. If the message order matters, you should implement logic to ensure prerequisites are met before processing (e.g., ensuring a customer object exists before adding it to a list).

However, this is a basic example. In a real-world scenario, you'd also want to incorporate logging and error handling, integrating with other systems or databases to ensure data consistency. Properly handling out-of-sequence messages involves re-queuing specific messages, stashing them for later processing, or notifying administrators of potential issues.

DLQs are a crucial feature of Azure Service Bus and a part of the AMQP specification, and they help ensure that no messages are lost during message processing. When a message encounters an issue during processing, such as reaching its maximum delivery count without being successfully processed or expiring, it gets moved to the DLQ.

We create a receiver specifically for the DLQ to process dead-letter messages. In the code, we use `client.CreateReceiver()` to create `deadLetterReceiver`, which will target the dead-letter sub-queue for the specified subscription.

Once the receiver is set up, we use the `ReceiveMessageAsync()` method to fetch a single dead-letter message from the DLQ. The received message is stored in the `receivedDeadLetterMessage` variable.

After retrieving the message, we can perform any necessary processing or analysis. In this example, we print the body of the dead-letter message to the console using `Console.WriteLine (receivedDeadLetterMessage.Body.ToString()`

Then, to complete the processing of the dead-letter message, we call `CompleteMessageAsync()` on `deadLetterReceiver`, passing in the received message as the parameter. This informs the Azure Service Bus that the message has been successfully handled, and that the message is removed from the DLQ.

When receiving messages from the DLQ, you need to set the `SubQueue` option of `ServiceBusReceiverOptions` to `SubQueue.DeadLetter` – eliminating the need to manually construct the DLQ name, as was done with `Microsoft.Azure.ServiceBus`.

Here's how to implement this with code:

```
ServiceBusReceivedMessage receivedMessage = await receiver.
ReceiveMessageAsync();

await receiver.DeadLetterMessageAsync(receivedMessage, "sample
reason", "sample description");

ServiceBusReceiver dlqReceiver = client.CreateReceiver(queueName, new
ServiceBusReceiverOptions
{
    SubQueue = SubQueue.DeadLetter
});
ServiceBusReceivedMessage dlqMessage = await dlqReceiver.
ReceiveMessageAsync();

string reason = dlqMessage.DeadLetterReason;
string description = dlqMessage.DeadLetterErrorDescription;
```

This approach simplifies the process of handling dead-letter messages and accessing their associated metadata, providing more convenient methods and properties for developers. The provided code snippet illustrates the handling of dead-letter messages using the `Azure.Messaging.ServiceBus` library. It first receives a message from a queue and then dead-letters it, with an optional reason and description. A separate receiver is explicitly created to retrieve messages from the DLQ, and a dead-letter message is received from it. The code shows how to access dead-letter metadata, such as a reason and description, providing valuable insights into why a message ended up in the DLQ.

Effective monitoring with Azure Monitor

In the realm of monitoring, DLQs take center stage. These queues are prime candidates for vigilant observation, and Azure Monitor serves as a potent tool for this purpose. By keeping a watchful eye on DLQs, you gain insights into the health and performance of your messaging system. This proactive monitoring approach allows you to swiftly detect and address any anomalies or issues that may arise.

Monitoring DLQs ensures seamless message processing, enabling your application to maintain its optimal responsiveness and reliability.

By integrating automatic and proactive dead-lettering strategies, developers can establish messaging systems that thrive on resilience and resource efficiency. DLQs present a valuable opportunity for developers to tackle message processing challenges effectively, reducing downtime and maximizing system dependability.

Handling dead-letter messages is vital to maintain the integrity and reliability of message processing in any messaging system. It allows developers to analyze and address the root causes of message processing failures, ensuring that no message goes unprocessed or unaccounted for. Developers can implement robust and resilient messaging solutions by leveraging the capabilities of DLQs in Azure Service Bus.

Scaling and high availability in Azure Service Bus

Building resilient applications in the cloud demands a strong emphasis on scalability and high availability. These aspects are often interrelated and form the bedrock of efficient cloud solutions. As a powerful messaging platform, Azure Service Bus excels in addressing these vital concerns through various features and capabilities. In this section, we will explore how Azure Service Bus tackles the challenges of scalability and high availability.

Firstly, we will delve into scaling and how Azure Service Bus enables applications to handle varying message workloads efficiently. Azure Service Bus's scalability is anchored around **Throughput Units (TUs)** in its Premium tier, which bundles CPU and network bandwidth resources. You can allocate a fixed number or let them auto-inflate based on demand. For enhanced throughput, entities such as queues and topics can be partitioned, distributing messages across multiple copies. In extreme load scenarios, spreading a workload across several Service Bus namespaces can be beneficial. The Premium tier also offers Geo-Disaster Recovery for high availability across regions. On the application side, multiple instances of consuming services can process messages concurrently, and Azure services such as Load Balancer can help distribute this load. However, scaling, costs, and message ordering are essential factors. Azure Service Bus offers a suite of tools and strategies to scale efficiently based on your messaging workload, ensuring performance and resilience.

Geographic redundancy is a vital consideration that we'll delve into in this section. Azure Service Bus can replicate its entities across different Azure regions. This ensures that the structure of your messaging system, such as queues and topics, remains intact and available, even in the face of regional outages or disasters. However, it's crucial to note that while the entities are replicated for high availability, the messages within those entities are not. This feature, specifically referring to geographic redundancy, primarily ensures the integrity and availability of your Azure Service Bus's structure and configuration, minimizing the potential for service disruptions.

Furthermore, we will examine the concept of zone redundancy, which takes availability a step further. By distributing message replicas across availability zones within a single region, Azure Service Bus ensures resilience against single points of failure. Availability zones are physically separate data centers with independent infrastructure, bolstering the reliability of message processing.

Throughout this section, we will analyze the design considerations and best practices to effectively leverage Azure Service Bus's scaling, geographic redundancy, and zone redundancy capabilities. By the end of this exploration, you will be equipped with the knowledge and insights to design and implement highly available and scalable messaging solutions on the Azure cloud platform. Let's begin our journey into scaling and high availability in Azure Service Bus.

Scaling out and partitioning with Service Bus

Scalability refers to the capacity of a system to handle growing amounts of work or its potential to be enlarged to accommodate growth. Azure Service Bus offers several mechanisms to scale your messaging solution, including partitioning. Partitioning is the process of splitting a single logical entity (in our case, a topic or queue) into multiple parts that can be managed and accessed independently. By enabling partitioning when creating a queue or topic, Service Bus can distribute and handle messages across multiple message brokers and message stores, effectively improving scalability and availability.

Let's consider a .NET example of creating a partitioned queue:

```
var createQueueOptions = new CreateQueueOptions("sampleQueue")
{
    EnablePartitioning = true
};
await administrationClient.CreateQueueAsync(createQueueOptions);
```

In this code, we create a queue with partitioning enabled, which allows Service Bus to spread the load across multiple message stores. Enabling partitioning on a Service Bus entity such as a queue or topic involves breaking it into smaller, independently manageable segments called partitions. Partitions allow for better scalability and throughput. However, the management of partitions and their internal distribution is handled transparently by Azure Service Bus. From a client perspective, you don't interact with partitions directly; you deal with the entity as a whole. When you publish or send a message to a partitioned queue or topic, Azure Service Bus internally decides which partition the message should be placed in. This decision is often based on factors such as message properties or routing keys. The partitioning logic aims to distribute messages evenly across partitions. Partitioning doesn't directly address the issue of preventing a message from being received by multiple subscribers. Instead, this issue is typically handled through message duplication or unique message identifiers. Here's how you can approach it:

- **Message deduplication**: To ensure that different subscribers do not process a message multiple times, you can use message deduplication techniques. This involves generating a unique identifier for each message, and before processing a message, a subscriber checks whether it has seen this identifier before. If it has, the message is considered a duplicate and can be ignored.

- **Message correlation**: Another approach is to include a correlation ID or other metadata in the message properties. Subscribers can then check this correlation ID to determine whether they need to process the message. This approach allows multiple subscribers to process the same message but act differently, based on the correlation ID.

- **DLQ**: If multiple subscribers process a message, due to partitioning or other factors, and it's undesirable for them all to process it, you can handle this scenario by using a DLQ. Subscribers can examine the message content and determine whether it's suitable for processing. If not, they can move the message to a DLQ, which acts as an error queue where such messages can be further analyzed or discarded.

In summary, while partitioning enhances scalability and throughput, ensuring message uniqueness and preventing multiple subscribers from processing the same message is typically managed through message deduplication, message correlation, or DLQs. These mechanisms help maintain the integrity of message processing across different subscribers and partitions.

Load balancing and message distribution across namespaces

Balancing load across different namespaces is another effective technique to improve scalability. By distributing your queues and topics across different namespaces, you can distribute the messaging load evenly, thus increasing throughput and reducing the likelihood of bottlenecks. To create a new namespace, you would typically use the **Azure portal**, the **Azure CLI**, or **ARM templates**. Once created, you can distribute your queues and topics among these namespaces.

However, when using multiple namespaces, it is essential to consider how your application connects to each one. One effective approach is using a load balancer, which can distribute connections across multiple namespaces based on strategies such as **round-robin** or **least connections**.

In a .NET application, you can implement the concept of distributing connections across multiple Azure Service Bus namespaces using a load balancer approach. While Azure Service Bus doesn't offer an out-of-the-box load balancer, you can simulate this behavior using code.

Here's a simple example demonstrating how you could achieve this using the round-robin strategy:

```
int messageCount = int.Parse(Environment.
GetEnvironmentVariable("MessageCount") ?? "10");
string queueName = Environment.GetEnvironmentVariable("QueueName") ??
"<Your_Default_Queue_Name>";
var senders = clients.ToDictionary(client => client, client => client.
CreateSender(queueName));
List<Task> tasks = new List<Task>();
for (int i = 0; i < messageCount; i++){
    ServiceBusClient currentClient = clients[i % clients.Count];
    ServiceBusSender sender = senders[currentClient];
    ServiceBusMessage message = new ServiceBusMessage($"Message {i +
1}");
```

```
        tasks.Add(SendMessageAsync(sender, message, i,
serviceBusNamespaces[i % clients.Count]));
}
await Task.WhenAll(tasks);foreach (var sender in senders.
Values){    await sender.DisposeAsync(); }async Task
SendMessageAsync(ServiceBusSender sender, ServiceBusMessage message,
int messageId, string namespaceName){
    try{       await sender.SendMessageAsync(message);
        telemetryClient.TrackTrace($"Sent message {messageId + 1}
using namespace {namespaceName}");
    }
    catch (Exception ex){
        telemetryClient.TrackException(ex, new Dictionary<string,
string> {
            { "MessageId", messageId.ToString() },
            { "Namespace", namespaceName }
        }); }}
```

Note that this is a simplified example for illustration purposes. In a real-world scenario, you'd need to handle errors and retries and implement more advanced load-balancing strategies, based on the specific requirements of your application. The preceding code serves as an example of the round-robin strategy of distributing messages across multiple Azure Service Bus namespaces. Let's break down the code step by step:

1. **Using directives**: The code begins with the necessary using directives to import required namespaces from the `Azure.Messaging.ServiceBus` library.

2. **Main method**: The entry point of the application is the main method.

3. **List of namespaces**: `serviceBusNamespaces` is created to hold the names of the Azure Service Bus namespaces you want to work with. Replace the placeholders with the actual namespace names.

4. **Creating ServiceBusClient instances**: The code creates a list of `ServiceBusClient` instances by iterating through each namespace name in the `serviceBusNamespaces` list. For each namespace, a `ServiceBusClient` instance is created using the corresponding connection string.

5. **Simulating a round-robin strategy**: The code simulates sending 10 messages using the round-robin strategy across different namespaces. The current namespace index is calculated using the modulo operator (`i % clients.Count`), ensuring round-robin distribution.

6. **Create a sender**: For each message, a `ServiceBusSender` instance is created using `currentClient`. Then, `ServiceBusMessage` is created with unique message content.

7. **Sending a message**: The message is sent using the `SendMessageAsync` method of the sender.

8. **Output**: The console prints a message, indicating which message was sent and with which namespace. This visualization helps us understand the round-robin distribution.

9. **Closing clients**: After sending the messages, the code disposes of each `ServiceBusClient` in the clients list, using `DisposeAsync` to release resources.

This code example demonstrates how to use the round-robin strategy to distribute messages across multiple Azure Service Bus namespaces evenly. It shows a common pattern for load balancing when working with multiple namespaces.

Availability and disaster recovery considerations

Ensuring high availability is just as crucial as scalability in a cloud environment. High availability ensures that a service remains available and operational for as long as possible, even in the face of failures and unforeseen circumstances. Azure Service Bus has built-in disaster recovery capabilities through a feature known as **paired namespaces**. Paired namespaces allows you to configure your namespaces in pairs, where the primary namespace accepts incoming requests, and the secondary namespace acts as a failover if there is an outage in the primary namespace. You would typically use the Azure portal or Azure CLI to pair two namespaces for disaster recovery. However, you can also create an alias to abstract the pair of namespaces within your .NET application, as shown in the following example:

```
ServiceBusAdministrationClient aliasClient = new
ServiceBusAdministrationClient("<connection_string>", "<alias>");
// Failover to secondary namespace
await aliasClient.PairWithNamespaceAsync("<secondary_namespace>");
```

In this example, if the primary namespace fails, the application can fail over to the `secondary namespace` using the `alias`. Now, we will discuss geographic and zone redundancy to ensure our service is functional if there is an outage or disaster.

Using geographic redundancy and zone redundancy

Azure Service Bus uses **geographic redundancy** to replicate its entities, such as queues and topics, across two or more distinct data centers in different geographical regions. This replication ensures that your messaging structure remains intact, even during a region-wide outage. Notably, this approach replicates only the entities, not the messages they hold. In contrast, **zone redundancy** provides a more detailed approach within a single Azure region. In this method, Azure Service Bus replicates your data and the messages they contain across multiple availability zones in a particular region. This means that if one zone experiences an outage, the presence of data in other zones keeps your messaging system running.

The difference between these two methods is crucial to grasp. Geographic redundancy casts a broader safety net by covering multiple regions but does not replicate messages. In contrast, zone redundancy focuses on a single region but replicates both entities and their messages. Complexities emerge, particularly in scenarios that demand ordered message processing. For instance, if a region encounters an outage and your system needs to transition to a backup region, you might face a sequence gap because only the entities were replicated, not the messages. This inconsistency can create problems.

As an example, a system might lose a "create" message but later receive an "update" message for the same entity. To address such challenges, you must design your system meticulously, possibly employing patterns such as compensating transactions or sagas to maintain data integrity and consistency.

Geographic redundancy doesn't deal with a single queue's settings but, rather, with your entire Service Bus namespace being replicated in a different region. Here's how you can set it up using code:

```
var primaryNamespaceConnectionString =
"YourPrimaryNamespaceConnectionString";
var secondaryNamespaceConnectionString =
"YourSecondaryNamespaceConnectionString";
var administrationClientPrimary = new
ServiceBusAdministrationClient(primaryNamespaceConnectionString);
var administrationClientSecondary = new
ServiceBusAdministrationClient(secondaryNamespaceConnectionString);
var createQueueOptions = new CreateQueueOptions("sampleQueue")
{
    EnablePartitioning = true,
    RequiresDuplicateDetection = true
};
 await administrationClientPrimary.
CreateQueueAsync(createQueueOptions);
await administrationClientSecondary.
CreateQueueAsync(createQueueOptions);
```

The preceding code outlines a procedure to achieve geographic redundancy with Azure Service Bus by utilizing two distinct namespaces, primary and secondary ones, possibly situated in different Azure regions. Each namespace has its connection string, serving as the unique identifier and access mechanism.

To manage these namespaces, the preceding code employs `ServiceBusAdministrationClient`. This tool is pivotal to generating or deleting queues within Azure Service Bus. The queue, aptly named `sampleQueue`, is designed with two pivotal features. Firstly, the `EnablePartitioning` property ensures that messages are distributed across varied partitions, optimizing scalability. Secondly, the `RequiresDuplicateDetection` property safeguards against repetitive messages by automatically identifying and removing them.

For redundancy, the same queue, with its defined properties, is instantiated in both the primary and secondary namespaces. This dual setup acts as a safety net. If the primary region encounters disruptions, the system can seamlessly switch to or leverage the secondary region, ensuring uninterrupted service. In essence, this code meticulously crafts a mirrored queue structure in two separate regions, underpinning the robustness and resilience of the messaging system.

Here's an example of creating a queue with zone redundancy enabled:

```
using Azure.Messaging.ServiceBus.Administration;
var administrationClient = new
ServiceBusAdministrationClient(connectionString);
CreateQueueWithProperties("sampleQueue", true, true);
private async Task CreateQueueWithProperties(string queueName, bool
enablePartitioning, bool requiresDuplicateDetection)
{
    var createQueueOptions = new CreateQueueOptions(queueName)
    {
        EnablePartitioning = enablePartitioning,
        RequiresDuplicateDetection = requiresDuplicateDetection
    };
    try
    {
        await administrationClient.
CreateQueueAsync(createQueueOptions);
        Console.WriteLine($"Queue {queueName} created successfully.");
    }
    catch (Exception ex)
    {
        Console.WriteLine($"Error creating queue {queueName}. Error:
{ex.Message}");
    }
}
```

The code offers a methodical approach to creating a new queue within Azure Service Bus with tailored properties. Here's a breakdown.

An administration client, `ServiceBusAdministrationClient`, is initialized using a given connection string, acting as the gateway to manage and control Azure Service Bus.

The core function, `CreateQueueWithProperties`, is crafted to streamline the creation of a queue. This function accepts three parameters:

- queueName: This specifies the unique name for the queue

- enablePartitioning: This dictates whether the queue's messages should be spread across multiple partitions, enhancing scalability

- requiresDuplicateDetection: This indicates the necessity to discern and eliminate repetitive messages

A `CreateQueueOptions` object is defined within this function, encapsulating the queue's name and two properties. A try-catch block is employed to execute the queue creation, ensuring errors are gracefully caught and communicated, providing feedback on the success or failure of the operation.

In essence, this code elegantly scripts creating a custom Azure Service Bus queue, equipped with error handling, making the queue creation process efficient and user-friendly.

In conclusion, Azure Service Bus provides a wide array of features and options to ensure your messaging solutions' scalability and high availability. As .NET developers, it is essential to understand these features and leverage them effectively in your applications to ensure robustness and resilience. The next section will delve into optimizing performance in Azure Service Bus, another crucial aspect to maintain healthy and efficient cloud solutions.

Optimizing Service Bus performance

When it comes to messaging solutions, performance is a crucial factor that directly impacts the responsiveness and scalability of your applications. With its robust and feature-rich messaging capabilities, **Azure Service Bus** offers various optimization techniques that empower developers to achieve high throughput and low latency. This section will explore three essential aspects of optimizing Service Bus performance:

- **Partitioning**: As mentioned earlier, enabling partitioning on your queues and topics can help improve scalability and performance
- **Batching**: Service Bus allows you to send or receive multiple messages in a single operation, reducing the number of network calls and improving performance
- **Prefetching**: This feature allows you to fetch messages in advance, reducing the latency in message retrieval and improving throughput

As we explore various techniques to optimize Azure Service Bus performance, it's essential to consider specific design considerations that can further enhance the efficiency of your messaging solution. You can fine-tune your application to achieve peak performance and responsiveness by implementing the following strategies, which we will cover next.

Design considerations for optimal performance

As you fine-tune your messaging solution with Azure Service Bus, specific design considerations are crucial in achieving optimal performance and ensuring seamless message delivery. By implementing the following strategies and best practices, you can maximize the efficiency and responsiveness of your application.

Choosing the right tier

Azure Service Bus offers different service tiers, each tailored to meet specific requirements and workloads. When designing your messaging solution, carefully evaluate each tier's capabilities and performance characteristics to select the one that best aligns with your application's needs. Let's take a closer look at the available tiers:

- **Basic tier**: Ideal for development and testing scenarios, the Basic tier provides limited features and is suitable for applications with relatively lower message throughput requirements.

- **Standard tier**: Well-suited for most production workloads, the Standard tier offers advanced features such as topics, subscriptions, and dead-lettering. It is designed to handle moderate to high message throughput.

- **Premium tier**: Geared toward high-demand, mission-critical applications, the Premium tier offers enhanced performance, features such as message partitioning, and support for high message volumes with low latency. It also includes zone redundancy and geo-replication if there is a disaster.

By choosing the right tier, you can ensure that your messaging solution is both cost-effective and capable of handling your expected message load efficiently. To learn more, you can visit the Azure Service Bus page for more information about the tiers and pricing: `https://azure.microsoft.com/en-ca/pricing/details/service-bus/`.

Monitoring performance metrics

To maintain the health and efficiency of your Azure Service Bus implementation, it is essential to monitor its performance metrics regularly. Azure Service Bus provides a wealth of performance indicators that offer insights into various aspects of your messaging solution. Key metrics to monitor include the following:

- **Message throughput**: This metric reveals the rate at which messages are processed, providing an essential measure of your system's responsiveness.

- **Latency**: Monitoring message latency allows you to assess the time taken for messages to be sent and received, aiding in the identification of potential bottlenecks. To monitor message latency, you can use Application Insights to instrument your application and track custom events.

- **Resource utilization**: Tracking resource usage, such as CPU and memory, helps optimize the allocation of resources to meet performance demands.

- **DLQ length**: Monitoring the DLQ can highlight issues with message processing, such as message errors or delivery failures.

By analyzing these performance metrics regularly, you can proactively identify potential bottlenecks or issues and take corrective action promptly. Additionally, monitoring enables you to make informed decisions about optimizations and capacity planning, ensuring that your messaging solution maintains optimal performance under varying workloads.

Azure Service Bus best practices

To ensure smooth and efficient message delivery, following best practices that promote robustness, security, and resilience is essential. Let's delve deeper into some of the key best practices to use Azure Service Bus effectively:

- **Using DLQs**: DLQs act as a safety net for messages that cannot be delivered successfully to their intended destination. When a message encounters a delivery failure for reasons such as message expiration or exceeding maximum delivery attempts, it gets moved to the DLQ. It's crucial to regularly monitor the DLQ and process these messages to identify any potential issues in your application or messaging flow. Handling messages in the DLQ ensures that no message is lost during transmission, and it allows you to take corrective actions or investigate the root cause of message delivery failures.

- **Implementing retry policies**: Temporary issues, such as network connectivity problems or transient service outages, can occur during message transmission. Retry policies can help your application handle these transient failures gracefully, reducing overall application performance and message delivery impact. Azure Service Bus SDKs offer built-in support to implement retry policies, which can automatically retry message delivery if there is a failure. Configuring appropriate retry intervals and maximum retry attempts can strike a balance between achieving successful message delivery and preventing excessive retries that may overload a system.

Let us explore this with an example!

Exponential retry policy

The following code block shows the configuration of `ServiceBusClient`, with retry options set to an exponential delay between retries, capped by a maximum delay. The specifics of this configuration include the following:

```
ServiceBusClient client = new ServiceBusClient(connectionString, new
ServiceBusClientOptions
{
    RetryOptions = new ServiceBusRetryOptions
    {
        Mode = ServiceBusRetryMode.Exponential,
        MaxRetries = 5,
        Delay = TimeSpan.FromSeconds(1),
        MaxDelay = TimeSpan.FromSeconds(30)
    }
});
```

In this code segment, an exponential retry policy is configured using the Azure Service Bus SDK. `ServiceBusClientOptions` is set to employ an exponential delay strategy to retry operations. This means that if a transient failure occurs during message transmission, the system will automatically wait for an increasing duration before each retry. The MaxRetries parameter limits the number of retry attempts to five, ensuring that if the operation is unsuccessful after the specified number of retries, it will not be retried further. The initial delay of one second gradually increases with each retry, while the MaxDelay parameter caps the maximum delay at 30 seconds, preventing excessive delays.

Fixed retry policy

Illustrating the fixed retry policy, this code block presents the setup of ServiceBusSender, with retry options configured for a fixed delay between retries:

```
ServiceBusSender sender = client.CreateSender(queueName, new
ServiceBusSenderOptions
{
    RetryOptions = new ServiceBusRetryOptions
    {
        Mode = ServiceBusRetryMode.Fixed,
        MaxRetries = 3,
        Delay = TimeSpan.FromSeconds(2)
    }
});
```

Here, the fixed retry policy is applied to the ServiceBusSender component. This policy enforces a consistent delay between retry attempts. The MaxRetries parameter specifies a maximum of three retries for the operation. If a transient failure occurs, the system will wait for two seconds before each subsequent retry, ensuring a stable but relatively quick recovery from such failures.

Custom retry policy

Illustrating the fixed retry policy, this code block presents the setup of ServiceBusSender, with retry options configured for a fixed delay between retries:

```
ServiceBusReceiver receiver = client.CreateReceiver(queueName, new
ServiceBusReceiverOptions
{
    RetryOptions = new ServiceBusRetryOptions
    {
        Mode = ServiceBusRetryMode.Custom,
        MaxRetries = 10,
        Delay = TimeSpan.FromSeconds(5),
        CustomRetryPolicy = myCustomRetryPolicy
    }
});
```

In this code portion, the custom retry policy is utilized for `ServiceBusReceiver`. `ServiceBusReceiverOptions` is configured to use a custom retry policy delegate, denoted by `myCustomRetryPolicy`. This allows you to define a retry delay based on your specific logic. In the given example, the custom retry policy is defined in the `myCustomRetryPolicy` method. It calculates the retry delay by raising 2 to the power of the attempt number, causing the delay to increase exponentially with each retry. The `MaxRetries` parameter is set to `10`, and the `Delay` parameter is initialized to 5 seconds. This approach provides a flexible and adaptive retry mechanism.

These three code blocks show the diverse retry policies available in the Azure Service Bus SDK, allowing you to tailor the retry behavior to best suit your application's requirements and the characteristics of the underlying service:

- **Securing your Azure Service Bus**: Ensuring the security of your Azure Service Bus is paramount to protecting your data and maintaining the integrity of your application. Follow these security best practices:

  - **Authentication and authorization**: Use **Azure Active Directory** (**Azure AD**) to authenticate and authorize users and applications accessing the Service Bus. This ensures that only authorized entities can send or receive messages.

  - **Secure connection strings**: Connection strings contain sensitive information and should be treated carefully. Avoid hardcoding connection strings in your application code or configuration files. Instead, leverage Azure Key Vault or environment variables to securely store and retrieve connection strings. An example of storing and retrieving a secret in Azure Key Vault is as follows:

    ```
    var secretClient = new SecretClient(new Uri(keyVaultUrl), new
    DefaultAzureCredential());
    await secretClient.SetSecretAsync("MyConnectionSecret",
    "my-connection-string-value");
    KeyVaultSecret retrievedSecret = await secretClient.
    GetSecretAsync("MyConnectionSecret");
    string connectionString = retrievedSecret.Value;
    ```

  By implementing these practices, you not only enhance the security of your application but also adhere to best practices. This additional section provides developers with practical insights into securing their connection strings and other sensitive information effectively. For now, we've provided a small snippet to get you thinking about security; in the next chapter, we will cover Azure Key Vault in more detail.

- **Network security**: Configure **network security groups** (**NSGs**) and firewalls to restrict access to your Azure Service Bus namespace. This helps prevent unauthorized access and minimizes the attack surface.

- **Use shared access policies**: When working with Service Bus from devices or applications that do not support Azure AD authentication, leverage shared access policies to generate signatures with controlled **Role-Based Access Control** (**RBAC**) permissions. This approach ensures limited and time-bound access to designated resources, aligning with best practices to securely interact with Service Bus components. By utilizing shared access policies, you can maintain finer-grained control over access and enhance the security of your messaging infrastructure.

- **Throughput calculation**: In the context of Azure Service Bus, throughput is a data transfer rate measurement, accounting for both incoming (ingress) and outgoing (egress) data. Smaller message payloads are conducive to higher throughput due to reduced bandwidth and processing requirements. To assess the expected throughput for specific scenarios, leveraging benchmarking tools that involve sending and receiving messages can provide valuable insights.

- **Protocols**: In communication with Azure Service Bus, the **Advanced Message Queuing Protocol** (**AMQP**) stands out as an efficient choice, primarily due to its ability to maintain a persistent connection, which leads to enhanced performance. AMQP offers advantageous features such as support for batching and prefetching, resulting in reduced round trips to the Service Bus service and improved overall efficiency. Conversely, the **Service Bus Messaging Protocol** (**SBMP**) caters specifically to .NET Framework and serves as an alternative protocol to interact with Service Bus.

- **Concurrent operations**: Efficient handling of concurrent messages hinges on adopting asynchronous operations. Asynchronous operations enable the execution of multiple tasks concurrently, optimizing resource utilization and overall efficiency. Reusing factories responsible for creating clients and instances of clients, such as senders and receivers, is a best practice that contributes to efficient connection management and minimizes unnecessary overhead.

- **Receive modes**: Service Bus offers two primary receive modes. The PeekLock mode allows receivers to preview a message, lock it, perform processing, and complete the operation. Conversely, the ReceiveAndDelete mode combines the receive and complete operations into a single step, reducing round trips to the Service Bus. While the ReceiveAndDelete mode boosts throughput by minimizing interactions with Service Bus, it lacks transaction handling capabilities present in the PeekLock mode.

- **Prefetching**: Prefetching is a strategy that involves proactively loading additional messages from the Service Bus service while a receiver is active, caching them locally for subsequent processing. Doing so reduces the frequency of round trips between the client and the Service Bus service, enhancing overall efficiency. The effectiveness of prefetching is determined by the `PrefetchCount` parameter, which dictates the number of messages fetched in advance and directly influences cache size and message-handling efficiency.

- **Partitioned namespaces**: Partitioned namespaces offer a scalable solution to enhance performance by distributing a workload across multiple partitions. This approach involves allocating lower **Messaging Units** (**MUs**) to each partition, resulting in optimal resource utilization and improved system performance. The benefits of partitioning extend to improved parallel processing capabilities and efficient resource allocation, which collectively contribute to enhanced scalability.

In this subsection, we explored the best practices for Azure Service Bus to ensure reliable and efficient messaging between applications and services. We learned the importance of DLQs in safeguarding messages and how retry policies can handle transient failures gracefully. Additionally, we emphasized the significance of securing Service Bus with Azure AD, secure connection strings, and network security. Planning for high availability and monitoring performance were also highlighted to maintain the robustness of messaging solutions. While optimizing the performance and functionality of Azure Service Bus is crucial, understanding its cost management and available pricing tiers is equally essential. Now, we will dive into the cost considerations associated with using Azure Service Bus.

Cost management and pricing tiers

Cost management is fundamental to any cloud-based solution, and Azure Service Bus is no exception. As organizations leverage the powerful messaging capabilities of Azure Service Bus, it becomes imperative to understand the cost implications and optimize resource allocation effectively. Azure Service Bus offers different pricing tiers tailored to specific needs and workloads. These pricing tiers include Basic, Standard, and Premium. The choice of pricing tier can significantly impact cost, performance, and feature availability. To optimize costs in Azure Service Bus, organizations can adopt various strategies. One essential approach is choosing the right pricing tier that aligns with the application's needs, avoiding unnecessary features that might lead to overprovisioning. Organizations can also leverage the auto-inflate feature, which automatically adjusts the number of messaging units based on the message throughput, ensuring efficient resource utilization and cost-effectiveness. Regularly monitoring performance metrics and message throughput is essential to identify potential bottlenecks and ensure cost-effective operations. Organizations can adjust settings and resource allocations to optimize performance and cost by gaining insights into message patterns and throughput trends. Ultimately, understanding the cost management aspect of Azure Service Bus empowers organizations to make informed decisions, striking the right balance between performance, scalability, and cost-effectiveness. Organizations can leverage Azure Service Bus to build robust, scalable, and cost-efficient messaging solutions by choosing the appropriate pricing tier and employing cost optimization strategies. Let's learn about the various pricing tiers and cost optimization strategies in Azure Service Bus to make informed decisions that balance performance, scalability, and cost-effectiveness.

Understanding pricing tiers

Azure Service Bus offers three pricing tiers – Basic, Standard, and Premium. Each tier provides different capabilities and is priced accordingly:

- **Basic**: This tier offers basic queueing features and is suitable for simple workloads. It is charged per operation.

- **Standard**: This tier provides additional features such as topics, subscriptions, sessions, and duplicate detection. It is also charged per operation.

- **Premium**: This tier offers all the features of the Standard tier plus additional performance and resource isolation. It is charged per messaging unit per hour.

Cost optimization strategies

There are several strategies to optimize costs in Azure Service Bus:

- **Choose the right tier**: As mentioned earlier, choose the tier that best suits your workload to avoid paying for unnecessary features.

- **Use Auto-inflate**: Auto-inflate automatically adjusts the number of messaging units as needed, preventing you from over-provisioning resources.

- **Efficient message handling**: Implement practices such as message batching to minimize operations and optimize costs.

- **Continuous monitoring and optimization**: Regularly monitor performance and throughput, fine-tuning settings for cost-effective and efficient operations. You can achieve a cost-effective and high-performance Azure Service Bus implementation by carefully considering the pricing tiers, applying cost optimization strategies, and efficiently managing your messaging workloads. Next, we will explore integrating Azure Service Bus with enterprise architecture to gain a more holistic understanding of the solution. You can utilize Azure Monitor to collect and track metrics to better understand the utilization and performance of your system.

Integrating Azure Service Bus with enterprise architectures

Hybrid cloud scenarios have become increasingly popular among organizations seeking to leverage the benefits of both on-premises infrastructure and cloud-based services. In such setups, some critical resources reside on local servers or private data centers, while others are hosted in the cloud. This combination allows businesses to maintain sensitive data on-premises while taking advantage of cloud services' flexibility, scalability, and global reach. However, managing and securely connecting these distributed resources can pose significant challenges.

One such option is the Azure Relay service. It is an intermediary bridging the gap between on-premises **Windows Communication Foundation** (**WCF**) services and cloud-based applications. With the Relay service, you can expose your WCF services running on local machines or private networks to the cloud without opening ports in your firewall. This capability ensures that sensitive services protected behind your organization's firewall remain shielded from external threats while still being accessible to authorized cloud applications. The Relay service efficiently forwards messages between your on-premises services and cloud-based clients, eliminating the need for complex networking configurations and simplifying the integration process.

The following code demonstrates how to use the Azure Service Bus Relay service to expose a WCF service running on a local machine to the cloud. This enables secure access to the service from cloud-based applications without the need to open ports in the local firewall.

The following code segment encapsulates the core mechanism behind securely exposing a locally hosted WCF service to cloud-based applications, effectively circumventing the need to configure firewall ports at the local level:

```
    static void Main(string[] args) {
  string relayNamespace = "<your_relay_namespace>";
        string relayName = "<your_relay_name>";
        string connectionString = "<your_shared_access_key_connection_
string>";
        Uri serviceUri = new Uri($"sb://{relayNamespace}/
{relayName}");
        TokenProvider tokenProvider = TokenProvider.
CreateSharedAccessSignatureTokenProvider("<your_shared_access_key_
name>", "<your_shared_access_key>");
        var listener = new HybridConnectionListener(serviceUri,
tokenProvider);
        listener.OpenAsync().GetAwaiter().GetResult();
        while (true){            var connection = listener.
AcceptConnectionAsync().GetAwaiter().GetResult();
            ProcessConnection(connection);
        }}    static void ProcessConnection(HybridConnectionStream
connection)
    {
    }}
```

Another vital connectivity option is Hybrid Connections. This feature enables secure communication between your corporate network and Azure App Service applications. In many enterprises, critical business processes and data remain in corporate networks, and securely connecting these resources with cloud-based applications can be a priority. Hybrid Connections allow you to achieve this goal without exposing your corporate network to the internet or compromising security. Hybrid Connections enable seamless data exchange and integration by creating a bidirectional, encrypted connection between your on-premises infrastructure and your Azure App Service applications. This feature proves especially valuable when you have legacy applications or databases on your corporate network that need to interact with cloud-hosted applications.

The following code demonstrates how to use Hybrid Connections to securely connect resources within your corporate network to Azure App Service applications:

```
class Program{
static void Main(string[] args){
TelemetryConfiguration.Active.DefaultTelemetrySink = new
TraceTelemetrySink();
TelemetryConfiguration.Active.InstrumentationKey = "<your_
instrumentation_key>";
string relayNamespace = "<your_relay_namespace>";
string relayName = "<your_relay_name>";
```

```
string connectionString = "<your_shared_access_key_connection_
string>";
Uri serviceUri = new Uri($"sb://{relayNamespace}/{relayName}");
TokenProvider tokenProvider = TokenProvider.
CreateSharedAccessSignatureTokenProvider("<your_shared_access_key_
name>", "<your_shared_access_key>");
var listener = new HybridConnectionListener(serviceUri,
tokenProvider);
listener.OpenAsync().GetAwaiter().GetResult();
TelemetryClient telemetryClient = new TelemetryClient();
while (true){
var connection = listener.AcceptConnectionAsync().GetAwaiter().
GetResult();
ProcessConnection(connection, telemetryClient);
}}
static void ProcessConnection(HybridConnectionStream connection,
TelemetryClient telemetryClient){
using (var reader = new StreamReader(connection)){
string message = reader.ReadLine();
DisplayReceivedMessage(message, telemetryClient);}
static void DisplayReceivedMessage(string message, TelemetryClient
telemetryClient){
telemetryClient.TrackTrace($"Received message: {message}");}}
```

Both code sets share a similar structure, as they're designed to achieve the same goal of establishing secure connectivity between on-premises resources and cloud-based applications, using Azure Relay and Hybrid Connections. Here's a breakdown of the common components:

- **Configuration**: Replace placeholders such as <your_relay_namespace>, <your_relay_name>, <your_shared_access_key_name>, and <your_shared_access_key> with actual values

- **Service URI**: Construct the service URI using the relay namespace and name

- **Token provider**: Create a token provider with shared access signature credentials

- **Listener creation**: Create HybridConnectionListener using the service URI and token provider

- **Listener opening**: Open the listener to start accepting incoming connections

- **Connection acceptance**: Use a loop to continuously accept incoming connections

- **Connection processing**: Inside the loop, accept the connection, and then process the data received from the connected client or service

The main difference between the two examples lies in the `ProcessConnection` method, with the Azure Relay example leaving it as a placeholder for custom processing, while the Hybrid Connections example demonstrates reading data from the connection stream using `StreamReader`.

These code sets provide a foundation to set up secure connectivity between on-premises and cloud resources, using Azure Relay and Hybrid Connections. In practice, you would customize the `ProcessConnection` method to handle your specific data exchange and application logic.

By incorporating these code examples into your applications, you can easily leverage the power of the Relay service and Hybrid Connections to achieve secure and efficient communication in hybrid cloud scenarios. To further explain how topics and subscribers communicate, we will cover the differences between event-driven architectures and **publish/subscribe (pub/sub)**, which Azure Service Bus can be utilized for.

Service Bus and event-driven architectures

Event-Driven Architectures (EDAs) are software architectures designed to respond in real time to events or changes happening in a system. The responsiveness of an EDA largely hinges on the behavior of the event producer, specifically whether it queues its events immediately or employs a different strategy. Azure Service Bus plays a pivotal role in EDAs, acting as the mediator between event producers and consumers. One primary usage of Service Bus in EDA is through its support for topics and subscriptions. A system can send an event to a topic, and any interested consumers can listen to these events through a subscription. Azure's Event Grid, featuring system and custom topics, actively positions itself as a first-class player in the EDA landscape. It provides robust capabilities that drive event-driven integrations and workflows, seamlessly integrating the business logic of subscribers.

Here is an example of how you would publish an event (message) to a topic:

```
string connectionString = "<your_connection_string>";
string topicName = "sampleTopic";
var client = new ServiceBusClient(connectionString);
var sender = client.CreateSender(topicName);
await sender.SendMessageAsync(new ServiceBusMessage("Hello, world!"));
And this is how another part of the system would subscribe to the
event:

string connectionString = "<your_connection_string>";
string topicName = "sampleTopic";
string subscriptionName = "sampleSubscription";
var client = new ServiceBusClient(connectionString);
var receiver = client.CreateReceiver(topicName, subscriptionName);
var message = await receiver.ReceiveMessageAsync();
Console.WriteLine(message.Body.ToString());
```

The difference between EDA and pub/sub

Service Bus and an EDA versus the pub/sub model are concepts that often overlap, but they serve different purposes and have distinct characteristics. Let's break down the differences:

- **Conceptual level**:

  - **EDA**:

    - EDA is a broader architectural pattern where events determine the flow of the program. These events can be user actions, system outputs, or sensor outputs.

    - EDA doesn't dictate how these events are communicated between components. It can be through polling, interruptions, or message passing (such as pub/sub).

    - EDA focuses on the production, detection, consumption, and reaction to events.

  - **The pub/sub model**:

    - Pub/sub is a messaging pattern where senders (publishers) categorize published messages into classes without knowing which subscribers (if any) there might be. Similarly, subscribers express interest in one or more classes and only receive messages of interest without knowing who published them.

    - Pub/sub is a pattern that can be used to implement EDA, but not all EDA systems use it.

- **Implementation**:

  - A service bus, especially Azure Service Bus, is a managed communication system that can use multiple patterns, including queues (point-to-point) and topics/subscriptions (pub/sub).

  - It provides features such as dead-lettering, message deferral, sessions, and transactions.

  - A service bus is a tool or platform, while pub/sub is a pattern. You can implement the pub/sub pattern using Azure Service Bus's topics and subscriptions.

- **Granularity and use cases**:

  - **EDA**:

    - EDA is often used when loose coupling, scalability, and real-time responsiveness are required.

    - It's common in microservices architecture to ensure that services can operate, evolve, and scale independently.

    - Examples include real-time analytics, monitoring systems, and complex business processes.

- **Pub/sub**:

    - Pub/sub is commonly used in scenarios where you want to broadcast information to multiple interested parties. It's about disseminating data to all interested subscribers.

    - Examples include chat systems, live sports updates, and newsletter distributions.

- **Decoupling**: Both EDA and pub/sub use decoupling, but they do so in slightly different ways:

    - EDA decouples system components based on when they process events. Components can operate independently and interact primarily through events.

    - Pub-sub decouples the sender from the receiver. The sender doesn't need to know about its subscribers, and subscribers don't need to know about the details of the publishers.

While there's overlap between Service Bus, an EDA, and the pub/sub model, they serve different layers of abstraction. An EDA is a high-level architectural style, pub/sub is a messaging pattern, and a service bus is a platform that can be used to implement both. Understanding the distinctions helps make informed decisions when designing and implementing distributed systems.

To conclude the chapter, we will cover EDAs and provide real-world examples that utilize Azure Service Bus.

Real-world use cases and examples of Azure service bus integration

Azure Service Bus is used extensively in various real-world scenarios:

- **Order processing systems**: Azure Service Bus can be used to decouple the order-taking and order-processing systems in an e-commerce application. This ensures that the order-taking system doesn't slow down even when the order-processing system is under heavy load.

- **Real-time updates**: Applications that require real-time updates from various systems can use Azure Service Bus. For instance, an IoT application can have thousands of devices sending updates to a topic, and various parts of the system can listen to these updates through subscriptions.

- **Inter-organization communication**: Azure Service Bus can be used for secure inter-organization communication. Since it supports **AMQP 1.0**, organizations using different platforms can communicate with each other using it.

The service is a versatile and powerful messaging system that fits well into various enterprise architectures, from hybrid cloud scenarios to EDAs. As .NET developers, understanding and leveraging these features in your applications can ensure robust, scalable, and maintainable solutions. In the next subsection, we will discuss an important real-world scenario of message versioning that is a crucial practice in microservices architecture. It involves adding a version identifier within messages to ensure compatibility and seamless transitions during upgrades or changes to the message payload, enabling the independent evolution of components while maintaining effective communication.

Message versioning

Different components often communicate through messages in complex and decoupled systems such as microservices. However, as a system evolves, changes to the structure or content of these messages can lead to compatibility issues between older senders and newer subscribers, or vice versa. Message versioning addresses this challenge by introducing a version identifier within the message itself. This version identifier serves as metadata, indicating the message's structure and format.

The advantages of message versioning

Message versioning in microservices architecture offers several advantages that enhance communication between components, while ensuring seamless evolution and compatibility:

- **Compatibility**: Introducing a version property in messages ensures that old and new components can communicate effectively. Subscribers can interpret the version and adapt their processing logic accordingly.

- **Decoupled evolution**: In microservices architecture, different components can evolve independently. With message versioning, a new component can communicate with an old version using the appropriate version of the message.

- **Smooth upgrades**: During upgrades or deployments, you can update individual components individually, ensuring a system continues functioning without abrupt interruptions.

- **Error handling**: When a message with an unsupported or unexpected version is encountered, subscribers can handle it gracefully by logging an error or taking other appropriate actions.

- **Clear documentation**: By including a version property in messages, you're effectively documenting the schema and structure of the message, making it easier for developers to understand the message payload.

- **Incremental changes**: Message versioning encourages making incremental changes to messages, which can lead to more manageable and controlled updates.

Message versioning facilitates compatibility, decoupled evolution, smooth upgrades, error handling, clear documentation, and incremental changes in microservices, contributing to a robust and flexible system. Let's review a practical implementation together.

Practical implementation

Consider an example of an order processing system in microservices architecture. As the system evolves, the structure of the `order_created` event message might change. Here's how versioning can be implemented:

- **Original message (version 1.0.0)**:

    ```
    {
        "version": "1.0.0",
    ```

```
        "event": "order_created",
        "data": {
            "orderId": "12345",
            "customerName": "John Doe",
            "totalAmount": 100.0
        }
    }
```

- **Updated message (version 2.0.0)**:

```
    {
        "version": "2.0.0",
        "event": "order_created",
        "data": {
            "orderId": "12345",
            "customer": {
                "firstName": "John",
                "lastName": "Doe"
            },
            "totalAmount": 100.0,
            "currency": "USD"
        }
    }
```

In this example, if a subscriber is designed to handle version 1.0.0 messages, it can filter messages based on that version and process them accordingly. Similarly, a new subscriber version can be developed to handle version 2.0.0 messages with an updated structure.

Message versioning is a strategy that empowers distributed systems to evolve while maintaining compatibility and smooth transitions. By including a version property in messages, you provide a clear and flexible mechanism to manage changes in message payloads. This approach supports decoupled evolution, incremental updates, and graceful handling of different versions, making it a fundamental practice in designing resilient and adaptable systems.

Creating an Azure Service Bus via the CLI

While understanding the theory behind Azure Service Bus is crucial, putting that knowledge into action by creating your own Service Bus infrastructure is equally important. In this section, we'll jump right into creating an Azure Service Bus namespace, topic, and subscription using the Azure **Command-Line Interface** (**CLI**). This hands-on approach will enable you to see the concepts in action and set up a functional messaging system efficiently. In our scenario involving financial services, we've chosen names that reflect the purpose of each resource. `finance-transactions-namespace` signifies the namespace where all financial transaction-related entities reside. Within this namespace, `finance-transactions-topic` represents a communication channel dedicated to financial transactions. The `high-value-alerts` subscription is indicative of its role in receiving alerts for high-value transactions. By following this naming convention, developers and administrators can quickly grasp the function of each resource, facilitating efficient management and collaboration across a team. Additionally, adhering to a well-defined naming convention simplifies troubleshooting and maintains a structured environment, promoting best practices in cloud resource management.

Now that we have set the stage, let's dive into an example of creating a service bus using the CLI:

1. **Access the Azure CLI**: Log into your Azure portal and open the cloud shell in the top-right corner (it looks like a >_ symbol). Click on it to open a CLI directly within the portal. You can also utilize the Azure CLI on a local machine you previously downloaded and log into Azure, utilizing the following script:

   ```
   az login
   ```

2. **Create an Azure Service Bus namespace**: Let's start by creating a Service Bus namespace. This namespace acts as a container for your messaging entities such as topics and queues:

   ```
   az servicebus namespace create \
       --name finance-transactions-namespace \
       --resource-group demoapp-rg \
       --location canadacentral \
       --sku Standard \
       --tags "environment=dev" \
       --min-tls 1.2
   ```

   Let us break down what each parameter does:

   - `--name`: Sets a unique name for your namespace
   - `--resource-group`: Specifies the resource group where your resources will be organized
   - `--location`: Chooses the geographic region for your namespace (e.g., `canadacentral`)
   - `--sku`: Selects the pricing tier for the namespace
   - `--tags`: Assigns tags to categorize and manage your resources (optional)
   - `--min-tls`: Sets the minimum **Transport Layer Security** (**TLS**) version for communication

3. **Create an Azure Service Bus topic**: Now, let's create a topic within the namespace. Topics are channels through which messages can be sent and received:

   ```
   az servicebus topic create \
       --name finance-transactions-topic \
       --namespace-name finance-transactions-namespace \
       --resource-group demoapp-rg
   ```

Here's what each parameter does:

- `--name`: Names your topic

- `--namespace-name`: Specifies the existing namespace where the topic will reside

- `--resource-group`: Reiterates the resource group name

4. **Create an Azure Service Bus subscription**: Finally, we'll create a subscription for the topic. Subscriptions are endpoints that receive messages from topics based on filtering rules:

```
az servicebus topic subscription create \
  --name high-value-alerts \
  --namespace-name finance-transactions-namespace \
  --resource-group demoapp-rg \
  --topic-name finance-transactions-topic \
  --max-delivery-count 10 \
  --enable-dead-lettering-on-message-expiration true\
    --status Active
```

Let us take a look at the CLI parameters in detail:

- `az servicebus topic subscription create`: The `az servicebus topic subscription create` command is used to establish a new subscription for an Azure Service Bus topic, enabling seamless message processing within a topic-based communication system.

- `--name high-value-alerts`: This flag designates the chosen name for the subscription, making it easily identifiable. For instance, in this instance, the subscription is labeled `high-value-alerts`.

- `--topic-name finance-transactions-topic`: By specifying the `--topic-name` parameter, you indicate the target topic to which this subscription is linked. Replace `finance-transactions-topic` with the actual name of your topic.

- `--max-delivery-count 10`: With the `--max-delivery-count` parameter, you can define the threshold for message delivery attempts before relegating a message to the DLQ. In this context, messages will be given up to 10 attempts for successful delivery.

- `--enable-dead-lettering-on-message-expiration true`: This parameter, when set to `true`, enacts a mechanism that redirects messages to the DLQ if they expire before consumption. It provides an additional layer of reliability to your message handling.

- `--status Active`: The subscription's status is determined by the `--status` parameter. In this case, the subscription is instantiated in the Active state, ready to process incoming messages effectively.

Figure 11.3: The created Service Bus name and topic

By seamlessly weaving together these parameters, you can effortlessly generate a subscription within the Azure Service Bus ecosystem, tailored to your needs. Remember to input your own values for the topic name and resource configurations as needed.

Congratulations! By following the outlined steps and utilizing the Azure CLI, you've effectively established a robust Azure Service Bus infrastructure perfectly tailored for financial transactions. Let's recap what you've achieved:

- **A Service Bus namespace**: You've created a dedicated namespace, `finance-transactions-namespace`, providing a secure container for your messaging entities.

- **A topic for financial transactions**: Within the namespace, the `finance-transactions-topic` topic has been set up, offering a centralized channel for transaction-related messages.

- **A subscription for high-value alerts**: You've successfully crafted a subscription named `high-value-alerts` within the topic. This subscription is now primed to process high-value transaction alerts with its carefully configured parameters.

With your Azure Service Bus infrastructure in place, your applications and services can now communicate seamlessly, enhancing the efficiency, reliability, and scalability of your solutions. Messages will flow effortlessly through the designated channels, ensuring your financial transactions are managed with the utmost precision.

Now that you've laid a solid foundation using the Azure CLI, feel free to explore advanced features, experiment with different configurations, and continue to fine-tune your messaging system to meet the specific demands of your financial services applications.

Summary

As we wrap up this exploration of Azure Service Bus and its pivotal role in modern enterprise solutions, it's worth revisiting some of the critical points we've touched upon.

We've traversed a range of topics, discussing Azure Service Bus's fundamental building blocks, queues, and topics and delving deeper into concepts such as message routing, dead-lettering, scaling, high availability, and integration with enterprise architectures. Throughout these discussions, we've seen .NET examples showing the application of these concepts in code, thereby bridging the gap between theory and practice.

From creating robust, partitioned queues to balancing load across namespaces, and from ensuring disaster recovery through paired namespaces to implementing geographic and zone redundancy, we've seen that Azure Service Bus is equipped to handle the demands of enterprise-scale applications. It not only provides the tools to build reliable and scalable messaging architectures but also integrates seamlessly with hybrid cloud scenarios and EDAs.

In the interconnected world of modern enterprises, the ability to communicate effectively between systems is paramount. Reliable messaging is critical in this communication, acting as the backbone for data exchange and system integration. Azure Service Bus shines as a reliable messaging service that ensures your messages get to where they need to be, in the proper order, without getting lost or duplicated. It provides robust delivery assurances, from *at-most-once* to *exactly-once* delivery, catering to the varied needs of enterprise applications. The importance of this reliability cannot be overstated. It means that your application's various components can communicate confidently, focusing on their core business logic rather than on the intricacies of message delivery.

Azure Service Bus is more than just a messaging system; it's a powerful service enabling resilient, scalable, and related applications. As .NET developers, mastering Azure Service Bus opens the doors to designing robust enterprise solutions, both for on-premises and cloud scenarios. As we conclude this chapter, we hope that you, as a developer or architect, feel empowered to leverage Azure Service Bus in your projects effectively. We've seen its capabilities, its flexibility, and its resilience. Now, it's over to you to harness these strengths and build efficient, reliable enterprise applications.

Remember, the journey of learning never truly ends. Continue exploring, practicing, and pushing the boundaries of what you can achieve with Azure Service Bus. The world of software development is ever-evolving, and staying adaptable is the key. Keep coding, keep learning, and above all, enjoy the journey!

As we conclude our discussion on Azure Service Bus and its powerful messaging capabilities, we will now focus on another integral service within the Azure suite – Azure Key Vault.

Azure Key Vault is a robust cloud service engineered to secure cryptographic keys and secrets that cloud applications and services use. This includes sensitive data such as database connection strings, API keys, and other critical credentials that your cloud applications and services need to function securely and efficiently.

In the upcoming chapter, we will delve into the world of Azure Key Vault, highlighting its main features, its role in securing sensitive data, and how it operates in harmony with other Azure services to provide an enhanced level of security and management for your keys and secrets.

By gaining a solid understanding of Azure Key Vault, you can implement robust security measures and safeguard sensitive application data, thereby building more secure and scalable cloud applications. Let's begin our exploration of Azure Key Vault, unlocking its potential to fortify security and compliance in your Azure cloud environment.

12

Enhancing Data Protection with Azure Key Vault

Azure Key Vault is a service from Microsoft Azure that helps to unify the storage and management of application secrets, which could be API keys, passwords, or certificates. For example, if we are using an **Azure SQL Server database** in our application, instead of configuring the connection string in the application configuration, we can store the connection string securely in Azure Key Vault – this reduces the chances of accidentally leaking the connection string information. Azure Key Vault serves as a crucial asset for securely handling cryptographic keys and secrets in the cloud. Centralizing sensitive data and utilizing hardware security modules improves the security of our applications and services, minimizing the chances of unintentional disclosure and streamlining secret management throughout their life cycle. In this chapter, we will learn how to create a key vault, how to set up a secret in Azure Key Vault, and finally, how to configure our application to access Azure Key Vault using C# code.

In this chapter, we're going to cover the following main topics:

- Azure Key Vault overview
- Creating an Azure Key Vault service
- Setting up secrets, certificates, and keys
- Setting up authentication in Key Vault

Technical requirements

In this chapter, we will implement examples using **ASP.NET Core**, so we need to install **.NET SDK**. For building and debugging, we need either **Visual Studio** or **VS Code**. For creating and working with Azure Key Vault, we need an active Azure subscription as well.

Introducing Azure Key Vault

In this section, we will learn about the Azure Key Vault service and the various advantages of Azure Key Vault. As mentioned earlier, Azure Key Vault serves as a crucial asset for securely handling cryptographic keys and secrets in the cloud. With Azure Key Vault, you can easily manage and control access to your secrets and keys, including certificates, connection strings, passwords, and API keys, which are used to authenticate and authorize access to your resources and data.

The advantages of using Azure Key Vault include the following:

- **Enhanced security**: Azure Key Vault provides a secure and tamper-resistant storage environment that is designed to meet the most stringent security requirements. The keys and secrets stored in Azure Key Vault are encrypted using industry-standard algorithms, and access to them can be restricted to only authorized users and applications.

- **Simplified key management**: Azure Key Vault simplifies the key management process by providing a central location for all your keys and secrets. We can easily create, store, and securely manage cryptographic keys and secrets and control their access and usage across multiple applications and services.

- **Integration with Azure services**: Azure Key Vault integrates seamlessly with other Azure services such as **Azure Virtual Machines** and **Azure App Service**, making it easy to deploy and manage applications that require secure access to keys and secrets.

- **Compliance**: Azure Key Vault helps us meet regulatory and compliance requirements by providing auditing logs, access controls, and other security features that are required to meet industry-specific regulations and standards.

- **Cost-effective**: Azure Key Vault is a cost-effective solution for managing cryptographic keys and secrets, as it eliminates the need for expensive hardware and software infrastructure and reduces the risk of data breaches and security incidents.

- **Scalability and availability**: Azure Key Vault is designed to be highly scalable and available, with built-in redundancy and automatic failover, ensuring that users' keys and secrets are always accessible and secure.

Overall, Azure Key Vault is a highly secure and reliable solution for managing keys and secrets in the cloud and can help you enhance the security of your applications and services while simplifying the key management process.

In the next section, we will learn how to create an Azure Key Vault service from the **Azure portal** and using the **Azure CLI**.

Creating an Azure Key Vault service

In this section, we will learn how to create an Azure Key Vault instance using the Azure portal and the Azure CLI. Most of the configuration and settings are similar to other Azure resources. Unlike other resources, we need to configure the number of days to retain the deleted vaults – we can configure this for 7 to 90 days and we will be able to recover the key vault during this period. We will access secrets from Azure Key Vault in our ASP.NET Core application.

Creating a key vault from the Azure portal

We can create a key vault from the Azure portal just as with any other Azure resource. We do this as follows:

1. Sign in to the Azure portal – `https://portal.azure.com` – with a Microsoft account and click on the **Create resource** button. On the **Create resource** screen, search for `Key Vault`.

2. In the Azure portal, we have the option to see Azure services only, from which we can select **Key Vault**. Then, click on the **Create** button and select **Key Vault**, as shown in the following figure:

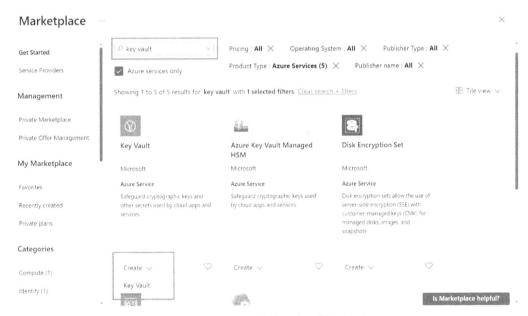

Figure 12.1 – Azure Marketplace | Key Vault

3. On the **Create a key vault** screen, we need to select the **Subscription** option and create/select **Resource group**. Then, we need to configure the key vault name, **Region** (select one near to you), **Pricing tier** (**Standard** tier), and finally we need to configure the days for which to retain deleted vaults – we can keep the default – we can select something in the range of 7 to 90 days, but once it is configured, we can't change it back. Azure Key Vault comes with two pricing tiers – Standard tier and Premium tier. The main difference between these two tiers is that the

Standard tier supports only software-protected keys, while the Premium tier supports both software-protected and **hardware security module (HSM)**-protected keys. HSM-protected keys are more secure and offer higher performance than software-protected keys. Software-protected keys are more suitable for test/dev environments, while HSM-protected keys are more suitable for production environments and high-value keys. We can find more information on the HSM from the Microsoft Learn documentation – `https://learn.microsoft.com/azure/key-vault/managed-hsm/?WT.mc_id=DT-MVP-5002040`.

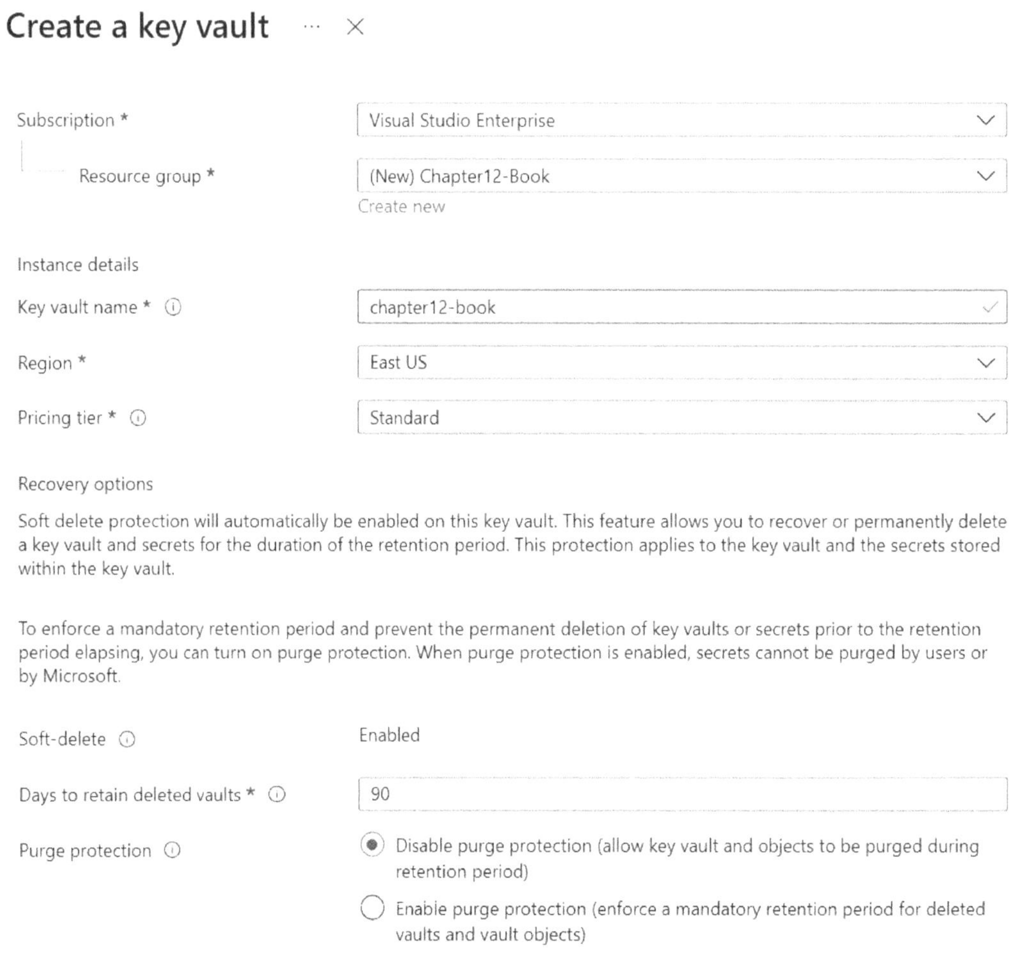

Create a key vault   ⋯ ✕

Subscription *	Visual Studio Enterprise ⌄
Resource group *	(New) Chapter12-Book ⌄
	Create new

Instance details

Key vault name * ⓘ	chapter12-book ✓
Region *	East US ⌄
Pricing tier * ⓘ	Standard ⌄

Recovery options

Soft delete protection will automatically be enabled on this key vault. This feature allows you to recover or permanently delete a key vault and secrets for the duration of the retention period. This protection applies to the key vault and the secrets stored within the key vault.

To enforce a mandatory retention period and prevent the permanent deletion of key vaults or secrets prior to the retention period elapsing, you can turn on purge protection. When purge protection is enabled, secrets cannot be purged by users or by Microsoft.

Soft-delete ⓘ	Enabled
Days to retain deleted vaults * ⓘ	90
Purge protection ⓘ	⦿ Disable purge protection (allow key vault and objects to be purged during retention period)
	◯ Enable purge protection (enforce a mandatory retention period for deleted vaults and vault objects)

Figure 12.2: Creating an Azure Key Vault instance

4. Next, click on the **Review + create** button to confirm the configuration and then click on **Create** button to create the key vault. We will configure the other tabs such as **Access Policy** and **Networking** later.

5. Once the key vault has been created, we can see its details as follows. We can see the options to add **Keys**, **Secrets**, and **Certificates**, as shown in the following figure:

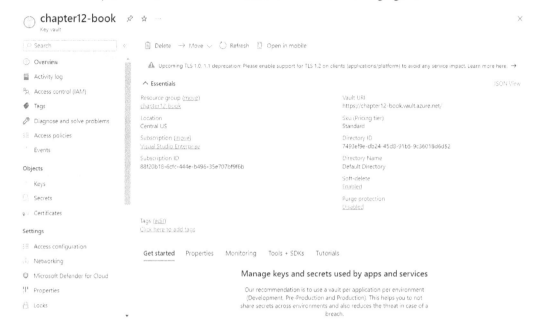

Figure 12.3 – Overview of Azure Key Vault

6. We can delete the resources created by deleting the resource group, which helps to avoid Azure resource charges.

We have seen how to create a key vault using the Azure portal. Next, let's see how we can use the Azure CLI to create a key vault.

Creating a key vault using the Azure CLI

In the earlier section, we created a key vault using the Azure portal. The Azure CLI is a better choice if we want to provision Azure resources quickly. Here are the steps we can follow to create a key vault using the Azure CLI:

1. Open your favorite terminal window, such as PowerShell, Bash, or any other terminal. We can log in to our Azure account using the Azure CLI with the `az login` command, which will open a browser window. Once the Azure account is logged in, we will be able to see the details of the Azure subscription in the console window.

2. Next, we need to run the command to create an **Azure resource group**. We can execute the following command to create an Azure resource group in the Central US location – as mentioned earlier, we need to provision Azure resources near our users, so if the application

users are from the US, it is a better choice to provision it in the US, and if the customers are in Europe, provision it in the Europe region. If we provision a resource in the US region and try to access it from India, there may be some latency – this is because the application is running in a different region/data center:

```
> az group create --name "keyvaultdemo-chapter12" --location
"CentralUS"
```

3. Finally, execute the following command to create to a key vault:

```
> az keyvault create --name "keyvaultdemo-chapter12" --resource-
group "keyvaultdemo-chapter12" --location "CentralUS"
```

4. Once the command has executed successfully, it will display the details of the key vault we created.

5. We can delete the Azure resource group using the following command:

```
> az group delete --name "keyvaultdemo-chapter12"
```

This way, we can create an Azure Key Vault using the Azure portal and Azure CLI. In the next section, we will learn about setting up secrets, certificates, and keys in Azure Key Vault.

Setting up secrets, certificates, and keys

In the previous section, we learned about Azure Key Vault and how to create a key vault using the Azure portal and Azure CLI. In this section, we will learn how to set up secrets, certificates, and keys in Azure Key Vault. We can configure Azure Key Vault access with two permission models – **Azure Key Vault access policies** and **Role-Based Access Control (RBAC)**. Azure Key Vault access policies are used to control access to specific resources (keys, secrets, and certificates) within a key vault, providing fine-grained control over who can perform specific operations within the vault. RBAC, on the other hand, is a broader Azure-wide access control mechanism for managing permissions on various resources, including key vaults, and is beneficial when you need a unified access control framework across your entire Azure environment. Choose access policies for detailed control within a key vault, especially when managing individual resources, and use RBAC when you require consistent access control across multiple Azure services and resources, considering your organization's specific security and governance needs. For Azure Key Vault, it is recommended to use RBAC over access policies, and RBAC is used by default. Since we have not configured any permissions, we will use RBAC permissions. When we configure secrets, we need to set RBAC permissions for the current user.

Configuring RBAC permissions for Azure Key Vault

In this section, we will learn how to configure RBAC permissions for Azure Key Vault using the Azure portal, which will help us to access the key vault from other Azure sevices:

1. Open the key vault we created and select **Access Control (IAM)**. Then, click on the **Add role assignment** option.

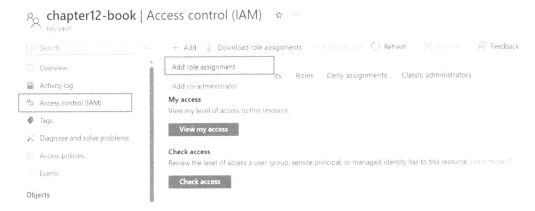

Figure 12.4: Azure Key Vault – Access control (IAM)

2. In **Add role assignment**, select **Key Vault Administrator**.

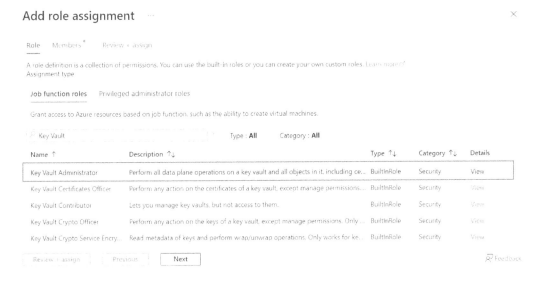

Figure 12.5: Add role assignment

3. Click on the **Next** button.

4. On the **Add role assignment** | **Members** screen, click on the **Select members** link, which will open the **Select members** screen. On the **Select members** screen, search for your username, and click on the **Select** button.

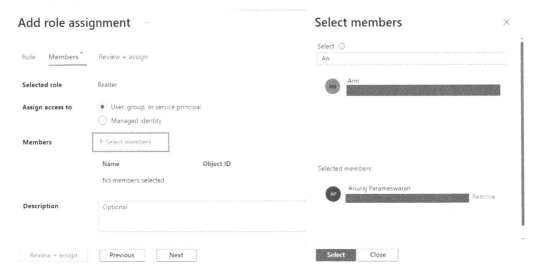

Figure 12.6 – The Select members screen

5. Click on the **Review + assign** button.

6. On the **Review + assign** screen, click on the **Review + assign** button again. This will assign the Key Vault Administrator role to the logged-in user.

Now we have configured the Azure Key Vault Administrator role for the currently logged-in user. Without configuring this role, we will not be able to manage secrets, certificate, or keys in Azure Key Vault.

Setting and retrieving a secret from Azure Key Vault

In the earlier sections, we provisioned Azure Key Vault using the Azure portal and the Azure CLI. In this section, we will learn how we can set and retrieve a secret from Azure Key Vault. We will use these secrets while working with ASP.NET Core code:

1. Log in to the Azure portal at `https://portal.azure.com` and go to the key vault we created earlier.

2. Click on the **Secrets** menu, which will open the **Secrets** page, where we can see the secrets we created in the key vault.

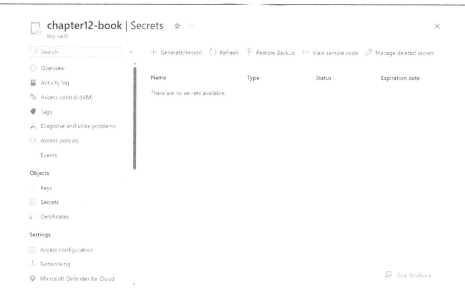

Figure 12.7: Secrets stored in our key vault

3. To create a new secret, click on the + **Generate/Import** button, which will display the **Create a secret** screen (see *Figure 12.8*):

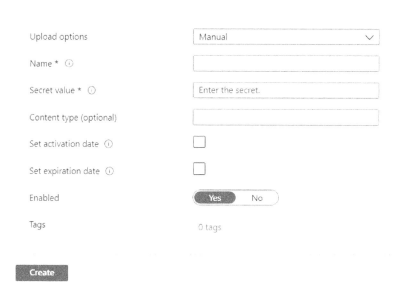

Figure 12.8 – Azure Key Vault | the Create a secret screen

4. On the **Create a secret** screen shown in the preceding figure, the **Name** and **Secret value** fields are mandatory. All other fields are optional. Under **Upload options**, we will keep **Manual** as the selected value. The other option is **Certificate** – uploading a certificate via this screen has been deprecated now. We need to give the **Name** value of the secret that we will use in the code to access **our secret's value**. We also need to set **Secret value**. Since we are using the Azure portal, it only supports single-line secret values. For multiline secrets, we need to use **Azure PowerShell**. If the secret we are using has an expiration or activation date, we can configure it here. These fields are for information purposes only. Azure Key Vault will not throw an error if the user tries to access an expired or deactivated secret. To handle expired secrets in Azure Key Vault, regularly identify and delete them using the Azure CLI or API, reducing security risks. For non-activated secrets, set activation dates using the same tools, ensuring they become valid when needed. Automation via scripts or Azure services can streamline these processes, and proper access policies, RBAC, and auditing should be in place. Additionally, implement secret rotation to enhance security, maintain documentation, and monitor secret status for comprehensive management.

5. Once we have set all the configurations, click on the **Create** button to set the secret. The secrets will be listed on the **Secrets** screen, as shown in the following figure:

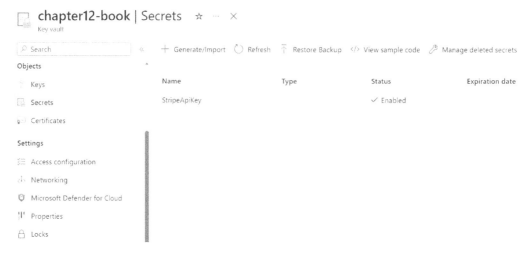

Figure 12.9 – Azure Key Vault | the Secrets screen

6. To retrieve the secret, we can click on the secret name, which will display the selected secret versions screen – the versioning helps us to do secret rotation. **Secret rotation** is the process of creating a new secret version with a new value and updating the applications that use the secret to point to the new version. This helps to improve the security and compliance of your secrets by reducing the risk of compromise or leakage. *Figure 12.7* shows the details of the current version of the secret. If we add a new version, it will be displayed here.

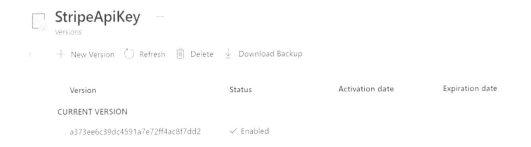

Figure 12.10: Azure Key Vault – Secret version screen

7. Click on **CURRENT VERSION** (see *Figure 12.7*), and will be able to see the details of the selected version, including when it was created, when it was modified, and its secret identifier URI. We can also configure the activation date, expiration date, content type, and enable or disable tags (see *Figure 12.8*). Clicking on the **Show Secret Value** button will display the secret value we configured earlier in the **Secret value** textbox and, if required, we can copy it.

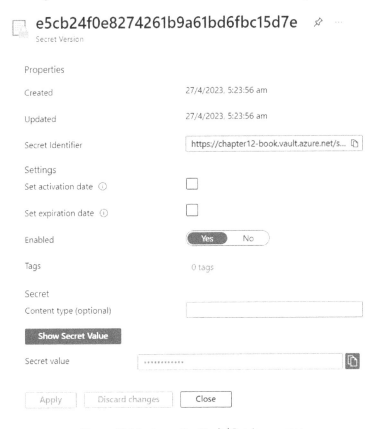

Figure 12.11– Azure Key Vault | Retrieve secret

This way, we can set and retrieve secrets from Azure Key Vault using the Azure portal. We will learn how to do so via the Azure CLI later in the *Setting up authentication in Azure Key Vault* section. Next, we will set and retrieve a certificate from Azure Key Vault.

Setting and retrieving a certificate from Azure Key Vault

An Azure Key Vault certificate support helps us to manage **X.509 certificates**. An X.509 certificate is a digital document that verifies the identity of a person, organization, or device on the internet. It is used for secure communication and authentication purposes. We can upload the **Secure Sockets Layer** (**SSL**) certificates to Azure Key Vault and reference them in an Azure App Service. We will create an SSL certificate (self-signed) and we can associate it with an Azure App Service or Azure VM:

1. Log in to the Azure portal at `https://portal.azure.com` and go to the key vault we created earlier.

2. Click on the **Certificates** menu, which will display all the certificates available in our key vault.

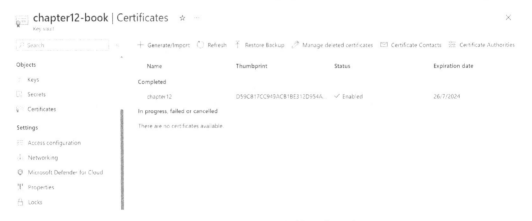

Figure 12.12 – Azure Key Vault | list of certificates

3. Click on the **+ Generate / Import** button to create a certificate. This screen will help us to create a self-signed certificate with Azure Key Vault.

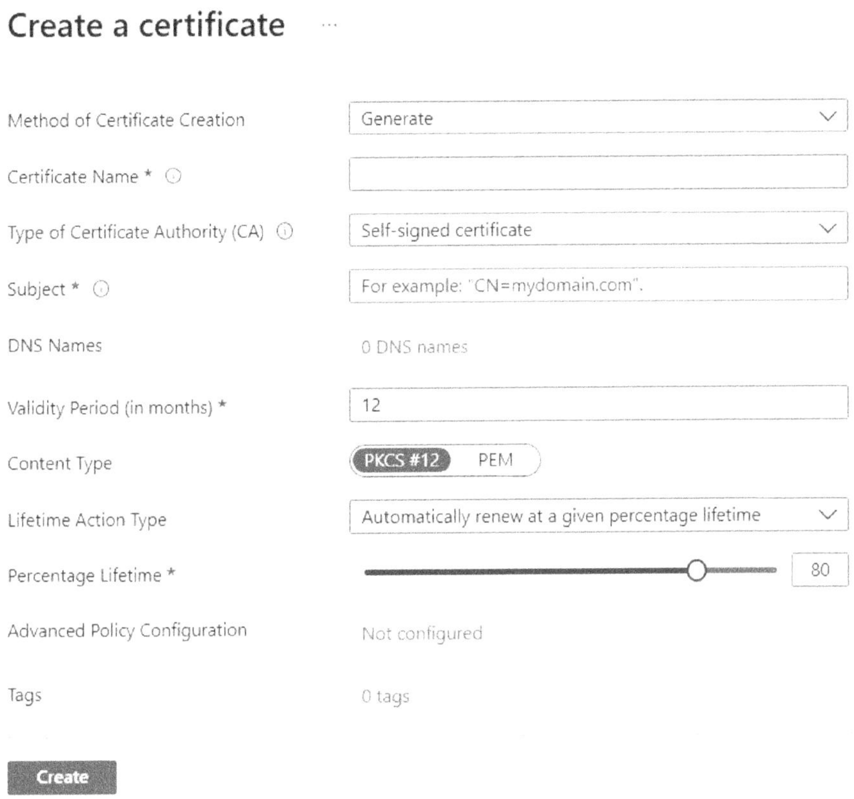

Create a certificate ...

Method of Certificate Creation	Generate ⌄
Certificate Name * ⓘ	
Type of Certificate Authority (CA) ⓘ	Self-signed certificate ⌄
Subject * ⓘ	For example: "CN=mydomain.com".
DNS Names	0 DNS names
Validity Period (in months) *	12
Content Type	(PKCS #12 PEM)
Lifetime Action Type	Automatically renew at a given percentage lifetime ⌄
Percentage Lifetime *	───────────●───── 80
Advanced Policy Configuration	Not configured
Tags	0 tags

Create

Figure 12.13 – Azure Key Vault | Create a certificate

4. In this example, we are creating a self-signed certificate, which can be used in applications for authentication, but we can't use self-signed certificates for a web application that is available on the public internet because they lack third-party validation and trust. These certificates aren't verified by recognized certificate authorities, leading to security warnings and eroding user trust. Without the green padlock icon and due to vulnerability to man-in-the-middle attacks, visitors may perceive the site as unsafe, impacting user experience and the site's credibility. Learn more about self-signed certificates in applications at this URL – `https://learn.microsoft.com/en-us/azure/active-directory/develop/howto-create-self-signed-certificate`. On the screen (see *Figure 12.10*), we need to fill in **Certificate Name** and **Subject**; for all the other configuration values, we can use the defaults. Click on the **Create** button. Once it is created, it will be available on the **Certificates** page.

5. As with secrets, we can click on the certificate name and view the version of the certificate. The current version of the certificate will be used by applications such as Azure VMs and/or Azure App Service instances.

Figure 12.14 – Azure Key Vault | selected certificate | Versions

6. When we click on the certificate version under the **CURRENT VERSION** listing (see *Figure 12.14*), we can find more details that we configured earlier (see *Figure 12.15*) and other details, such as **Serial Number** and **Thumbprint**, and we can enable and disable the certificate. We also get options to download the certificate in various formats, such as CER and PEM/PFX.

Figure 12.15 – Azure Key Vault | certificate details

7. We can use the **Create a certificate** screen to generate SSL certificates from different **certification authorities (CA)** as well – such as **GoDaddy.com** or **Digicert.com**. We need to configure the certificate authority before configuring the certificate.

8. To configure the certificate authority, click on the **Certificate Authorities** button on the certificates listing page.

Figure 12.16 – Certificates listing – Certificate Authorities

9. On the **Certificate Authorities** page, click on the + **Add** button to configure a new certificate authority – which will open the **Create a certificate authority** screen, where we need to set the name, provider(Digicert or GlobalSign), account ID, account password, and organization ID.

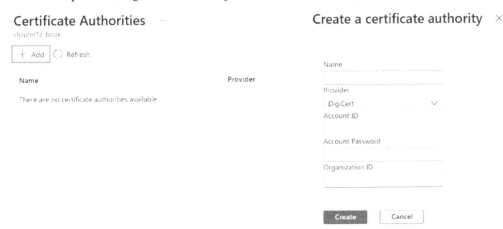

Figure 12.17 – Create a certificate authority

10. We can create the certificate using the Azure CLI. We can use the following commands:

```
> az keyvault certificate get-default-policy | Out-File
-Encoding utf8 defaultpolicy.json
> az keyvault certificate create --vault-name "chapter12-book"
-n "ExampleCertificate" --policy `@defaultpolicy.json
```

In the preceding code, we get the default policy from Azure Key Vault in the first line and then use the default policy to create a certificate.

11. To list all the certificates, we can use the following commands:

```
> az keyvault certificate list  --vault-name "chapter12-book"
```

This way, we can set and retrieve a certificate from Azure Key Vault using the Azure portal and Azure CLI. Next, we will set and retrieve keys from Azure Key Vault.

Setting and retrieving a key from Azure Key Vault

The main purpose of keys in Azure Key Vault is to provide a secure and centralized location for storing cryptographic keys, such as **encryption keys**, **signing keys**, and secrets. These keys can be used by Azure applications and services, as well as external clients, to perform cryptographic operations, such as encrypting and decrypting data, signing and verifying digital signatures, and authenticating messages. By using Azure Key Vault, users can manage and safeguard their cryptographic keys more effectively, as well as ensure compliance with security and regulatory requirements. We can follow these steps to create and retrieve a key from Azure Key Vault:

1. Log in to the Azure portal at `https://portal.azure.com` and go to the key vault we created earlier.

2. Click on the **Keys** menu, which will display all the keys we have created so far. Click on the **+ Generate/Import** button.

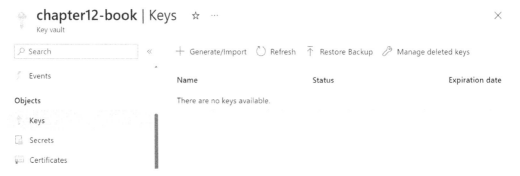

Figure 12.18: Azure Key Vault – Keys

On the **Create a key** screen shown, we need to set the name of the key; for all the other fields, we can use the default values – so we will be creating an **RSA key** with a key size of **2048**. **Rivest–Shamir–Adleman** (**RSA**) is a widely employed public-key cryptosystem utilized to ensure secure data transmission.

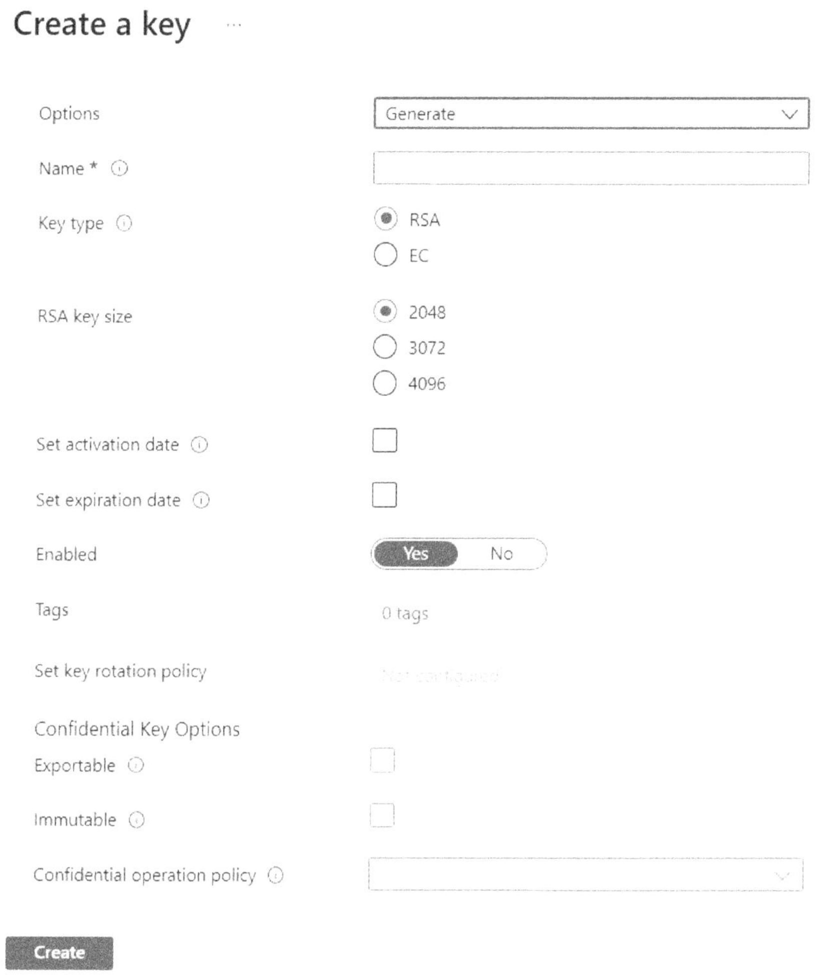

Create a key ...

Options	Generate ⌄
Name * ⓘ	
Key type ⓘ	⦿ RSA ◯ EC
RSA key size	⦿ 2048 ◯ 3072 ◯ 4096
Set activation date ⓘ	☐
Set expiration date ⓘ	☐
Enabled	(**Yes** No)
Tags	0 tags
Set key rotation policy	Not configured
Confidential Key Options	
Exportable ⓘ	☐
Immutable ⓘ	☐
Confidential operation policy ⓘ	⌄

Create

Figure 12.19 – Azure Key Vault | the Create a key screen

3. Once we have created the key, it will be available on the **Keys** page (see *Figure 12.18*). As with *secrets* and *certificates*, we can see the versions of the key by clicking on the key name, and we can see the other details of the key by clicking on the version. On the key version screen (see *Figure 12.19*), as with secrets and certificates, we can configure activation and expiration dates. We can also configure different operations in which we can use the key, such as for encryption, decryption, and so on.

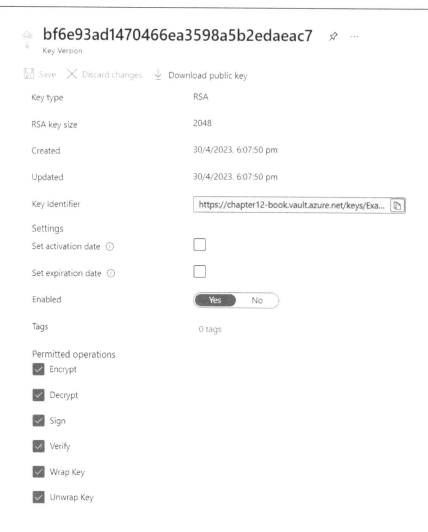

Figure 12.20 – Azure Key Vault | Details of the key

4. We have seen, so far, how to create and view the key in Azure Key Vault using the portal. Next, let's learn how to do this using the Azure CLI with the following commands:

```
> az keyvault key create --vault-name "chapter12-book" -n
ExampleKey
> az keyvault key show --name "ExampleKey" --vault-name
"chapter12-book"
```

This way, we can create keys in Azure Key Vault using the Azure portal and the Azure CLI. In the next section, we will learn about setting up authentication in Azure Key Vault and how to access Azure Key Vault from **ASP.NET Core**.

Setting up authentication in Azure Key Vault

Azure Key Vault's authentication is carried out in collaboration with **Azure Active Directory** (**Azure AD**), which is accountable for verifying the identity of a security principal. A **security principal** refers to an entity, such as a user, group, service, or application that seeks permission to access Azure resources. Each security principal is assigned a distinct object ID by Azure. An individual with a profile in Azure AD is recognized as a user security principal. On the other hand, a **group security principal** is used to identify a collection of users that are established in Azure AD. When roles or permissions are assigned to the group, all members within the group receive them. A **service principal** is a security principal type that represents an application or service instead of a user or group. The object ID of a service principal serves as its username, and its client secret serves as its password. In the following section, we will learn how to configure authentication in Azure Key Vault and access the secrets and keys from the ASP.NET Core application. We will use the Azure SDK to access the key vault from Azure App Service.

Using a system-assigned identity

For Azure Key Vault access, it is recommended to use a **system-assigned managed identity**. We already learned about creating identities in *Chapter 7* in the *Entity Framework core migrations* section. In Azure, a system-managed identity (also known as a **Managed Service Identity** (**MSI**)) is automatically created and managed by Azure for specific Azure resources such as Virtual Machines or Azure Functions. It allows these resources to authenticate with Azure services and resources without exposing credentials. On the other hand, a user-assigned identity is a standalone identity that can be created independently and associated with one or more Azure resources. It provides more flexibility as you can assign it to multiple resources, allowing them to authenticate and access other Azure services securely, while a system-managed identity is tied to a specific resource and can only be used by that resource.

In this section, we will create an Azure App Service and enable a **managed identity** for the App Service. Then, we will enable access permissions in Azure Key Vault for the managed identity. Finally, we will read a secret value from Azure Key Vault from the **ASP.NET Core web app**.

First, we can create a secret in the Azure Key Vault. We can do it either via the portal or via the CLI:

1. In the portal, click on the **Secrets** menu, and, on the **Secrets** page, click on the + **Generate/Import** button (see *Figure 12.4* in the *Setting and retrieving a secret from Azure Key Vault* section).

2. On the **Create a secret** screen, we need to configure the **Name** and **Secret value** field. We can keep **Upload options** as the default, **Manual**. For this example, I am using an API key for **SendGrid** (which is an email service provider). We can use any kind of secret here – for example, if we were using Azure Cognitive Services, we could use that API key here.

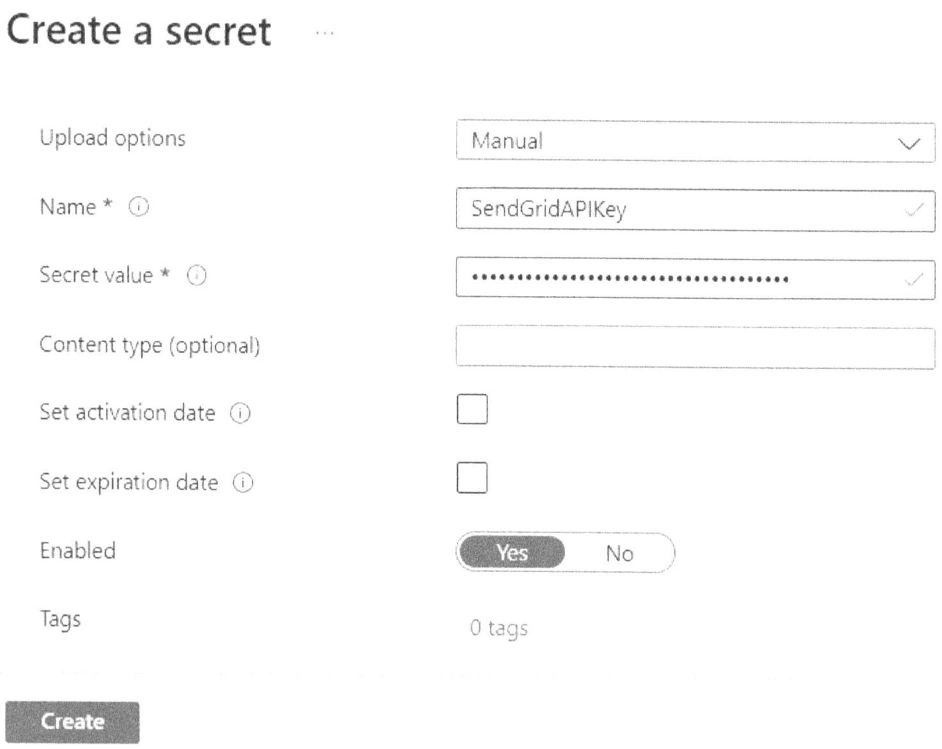

Create a secret ...

Upload options	Manual ∨
Name * ⓘ	SendGridAPIKey ✓
Secret value * ⓘ	•••••••••••••••••••••••••••••••• ✓
Content type (optional)	
Set activation date ⓘ	☐
Set expiration date ⓘ	☐
Enabled	Yes No
Tags	0 tags

Create

Figure 12.21 – Azure Key Vault | Create a secret

3. All the other fields are optional. If the secret we are using has an expiration or activation date, we can configure it here. These fields are for information purposes only. Remember that Azure Key Vault will not throw an error if a user tries to access an expired or unactivated secret.

4. Once the configuration is complete, we can click on the **Create** button to create the secret. After creating the secret, we can click on the secret name and view the secret value.

5. We can use the following Azure CLI command to create and retrieve the secret value from Azure Key Vault:

```
> az keyvault secret set --vault-name "chapter12-book"
--name "SendGridAPIKeyCLI" --value "3944a6af-6b3d-4733-bcf4-
7df36692ef86"
> az keyvault secret show  --name "SendGridAPIKeyCLI" --vault-
name "chapter12-book" --query "value"
```

This way, we can set and read secrets from Azure Key Vault using the Azure portal and Azure CLI.

Next, to access a secret from Azure Key Vault in an application, we will be creating an Azure App Service instance – we could create any other Azure service as well, such as Azure Functions or Azure Virtual Machines, but in this example, we will enable identity for the App Service instance and configure

Azure Key Vault access for the identity. Later, we will set up an **ASP.NET Core web application** to read the secret in the application code. Here are the steps to be followed:

1. First, let's create an Azure resource group, and then create an Azure App Service instance inside the resource group. We are using the Azure CLI. The following command will create an Azure resource group called `chapter12-rg` in the Central US location:

    ```
    > az group create --name "chapter12-rg" --location "CentralUS"
    ```

2. We can create the Azure App Service plan next, using the `CLI` command. We need to create an App Service plan before creating the Azure App Service instance. The following command will create an App Service plan, in the resource group we created in the previous step called `Chapter12-asp`. Since it is for demo purposes, we can use the Free pricing tier:

    ```
    > az appservice plan create --name "chapter12-asp" --resource-
    group "chapter12-rg" --sku FREE
    ```

3. We can create the Azure App Service instance using the Azure CLI with the following command:

    ```
    > az webapp create --resource-group "chapter12-rg" --plan
    "chapter12-asp" --name "chapter12-webapp-demo"
    ```

4. For the Azure App Service instance to access Azure Key Vault, we need to create an Azure App Service identity. We can do it with the following command:

    ```
    > az webapp identity assign --name "chapter12-webapp-demo"
    --resource-group "chapter12-rg"
    ```

5. Finally, we need to configure Azure Key Vault to give access permission to the Azure App Service identity with the following command:

    ```
    > az keyvault set-policy --name "chapter12-book" --resource-
    group "chapter12-book" --object-id "fcbc650d-59bf-449a-b7fd-
    4a9fd2608274" --secret-permissions get list
    ```

6. When we create the Azure App Service identity (*step 4*), we get the `-object-id` parameter. To read the secret, we need the `GET` and `LIST` permissions for the identity. We can get the `-object-id` parameter using the following command as well:

    ```
    > az webapp list --resource-group "chapter12-book" --query "[].
    {id: id}" --output tsv
    ```

Now we have completed the Azure resource configurations for accessing the Azure Key Vault secret from Azure App Service. Next, we will write ASP.NET Core code to access the secret value:

1. We create an ASP.NET Core web application project using the following command:

    ```
    > dotnet new web -o Chapter12.ReadSecret --framework net6.0
    ```

2. For interacting with the Azure Key Vault, we need to add the following NuGet packages to the `dotnet` project. We can execute the following commands to install the NuGet packages:

```
> dotnet add package Azure.Identity
> dotnet add package Azure.Security.KeyVault.Secrets
```

3. Once the NuGet packages have been added, we can modify the ASP.NET Core application code as follows to connect to and access the secret.

Open the project in VS Code or Visual Studio and modify the `Program.cs` file as follows:

```
using Azure.Identity;
using Azure.Security.KeyVault.Secrets;

var builder = WebApplication.CreateBuilder(args);
var app = builder.Build();

var client = new SecretClient(new Uri("https://chapter12-book.
vault.azure.net/"),
    new DefaultAzureCredential());

KeyVaultSecret secret = client.GetSecret("SendGridAPIKey");

string secretValue = secret.Value;
app.MapGet("/", () => "Hello World!");
app.MapGet("/secret", () => $"The value of secret is:
{secretValue}");
app.Run();
```

In the code, we are creating an instance of the `SecretClient` class, which we can use to connect to Azure Key Vault. The `DefaultAzureCredential` object enables us to establish a connection to Azure Key Vault using the identity context. In a development setting, this utilizes the Azure account credentials we've used to log in via the Azure CLI, while in a hosted environment or in Azure, it leverages the identity of the Azure App Service instance or the service that hosted this application.

Once we have created the client instance, we can use the `GetSecret` method to read the value of the secret we configured earlier.

4. Save the changes in `Program.cs`, run the application with the `dotnet run` command, and browse to the `localhost` URL with `/secret` endpoint – we should be able to see the secret value. If there is any error while running the `dotnet run` command, make sure you are logged in to the Azure CLI.

5. Next, we can deploy the application to the Azure App Service and verify that the application is able to read the secret from Azure Key Vault. Either we can deploy the project to Azure App Service from VS Code or Visual Studio or we can deploy it using the Azure CLI. In earlier

chapters, we explored how we can deploy the ASP.NET Core application from VS Code and Visual Studio. We can use the command-line tools to deploy the application to Azure. We need to execute the following commands:

I.   This command will build the application and the published application will be copied to the `Publish` folder:

```
> dotnet publish --configuration Release --output Publish
```

II.   Next, we need to compress the `Publish` folder to deploy the Azure App Service instance. We can do this with the `Compress-Archive` PowerShell command like this:

```
> Compress-Archive -Path .\publish\* -DestinationPath publish.zip
```

III.   And finally, we can execute the `deploy` command to deploy the zip file to Azure App Service, like this:

```
> az webapp deployment source config-zip  -g "chapter12-rg" -n  "chapter12-webapp-demo"  --src .\publish.zip
```

In this command, the `-g` parameter is the resource group, `-n` will be the name of the Azure App Service instance, and the `-src` parameter should be the zip file we created earlier.

Now, browse the application with the Azure App Service URL. For the / endpoint, we will get a text response of Hello World, and for the `/secret` endpoint, we will get the value of the secret we configured earlier.

In the preceding example, we used the Azure App Service system-assigned identity. We can use the user-assigned identity as well – the advantage of a user-assigned identity is we can manage the lifetime of the identity. If it is a system-assigned identity, it will get removed when we remove the associated Azure resource. For example, the system-assigned identity we created earlier in this section will be removed if we remove the Azure App Service resource. So far, we have used the system-assigned identity. In the next section, we will use the user-assigned managed identity. For a user-assigned managed identity, there are some code changes required in the application.

Using a user-assigned managed identity

We will explore how to create a user-assigned identity and how to use it with Azure App Service and Azure Key Vault. We can follow these steps to create a user-assigned managed identity. Unlike a system-assigned identity, we need to create it explicitly:

1.   As with other Azure resources, for a user-assigned managed identity, we need a resource group. We can use any existing resource group or we can create a new resource group and use it. We create it the same way we create any other resource; from the home page, search for `Managed Identities`, and select the **Managed Identities** service.

2. Next, we can click on the + **Create** button to create the managed identity.

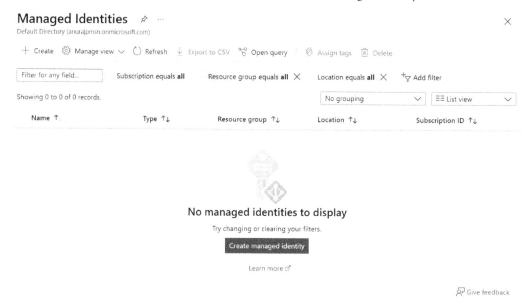

Figure 12.22: Azure Managed Identities screen

3. On the **Create User Assigned Managed Identity** screen in the following figure (see *Figure 12.23*), we need to fill in the **Subscription**, option select the **Resource group**, **Region**, and **Name** fields. Then, we can click on the **Create** button to create the resource; we can also add tags if required.

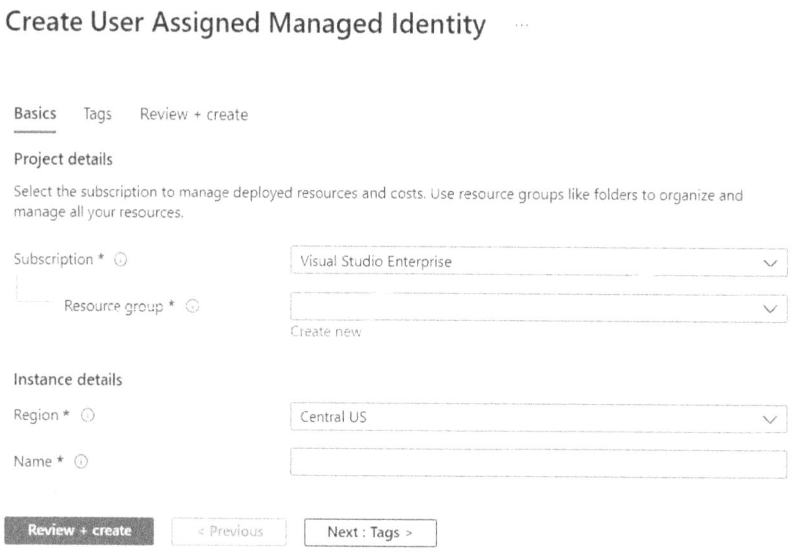

Figure 12.23 – Settings to create a user-assigned managed identity

4. Once the identity has been created, we can configure the identity for the Azure App Service instance. To do this, we can click on the **Identity** menu, and click on the **+ Add** button, as shown in the following figure. From the list of identities, select the one we created.

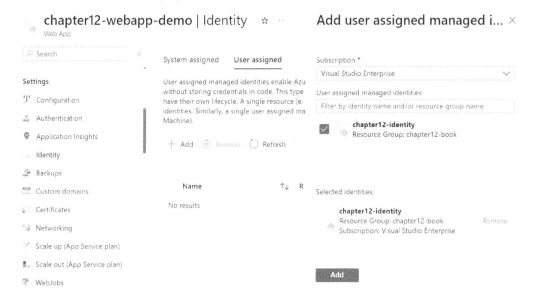

Figure 12.24 – Azure App Service | configuring the identity

Click on **Add** to associate the identity with Azure App Service.

5. Next, we need to open the key vault and click on the **Access Policies** menu. Then, click on the **+ Create** button. First, we will see **Create an access policy**, as shown in the following figure. On the screen, we need to select **Secret permissions** – **Get** and **List**. Then, click on the **Next** button.

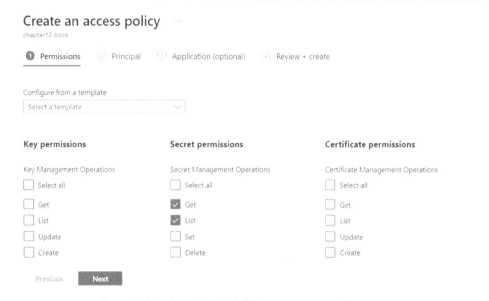

Figure 12.25 – Azure Key Vault | Create an access policy

6. Next, we need to search for the identity name, select it, and click on the **Next** button, as shown in the following figure:

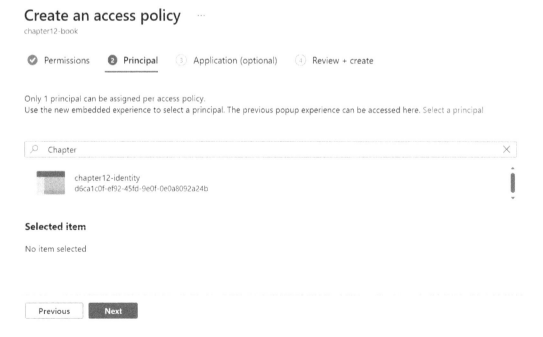

Figure 12.26 – Azure Key Vault | creating an access policy | selecting an identity principal

7. Next, we need to select the application. Since the App Service instance is already associated with the identity, we can click on the **Next** button.

8. On the final screen, click on the **Create** button to associate the identity with the key vault. We can see all the configuration we did earlier, review it, and then click on the **Create** button to create the access policy.

9. Once it is done, the configuration is completed. We can modify the web application code to use the user-assigned managed identity as follows:

```
using Azure.Identity;
using Azure.Security.KeyVault.Secrets;
var builder = WebApplication.CreateBuilder(args);
var app = builder.Build();
app.MapGet("/secret", async (response) =>
{
    string userAssignedClientId = "b7debcfd-ad7e-4e2f-ab5b-
b5c276462835";
    var credential = new DefaultAzureCredential(new
DefaultAzureCredentialOptions
    {
        ManagedIdentityClientId = userAssignedClientId
    });
    var client = new SecretClient(new Uri("https://chapter12-
book.vault.azure.net/"), credential);
    KeyVaultSecret secret = client.GetSecret("SendGridAPIKey");
    string secretValue = secret.Value;
    await response.Response.WriteAsync(secretValue);
});
app.MapGet("/", () => "Hello World!");
app.Run();
```

In the preceding code, we are creating an endpoint with the URL /secret, and, in the implementation, we are creating an instance of the DefaultAzureCredential class with the client ID of the user-assigned managed identity we created earlier. We are using it to authenticate against the key vault. Then, we read the value from the key vault and write it as output. Now, we can run the application and verify the /secret endpoint – it should return the value of the secret we configured earlier.

This way, we can set up authentication in Azure Key Vault and access the secret value from ASP.NET Core web applications.

Azure Key Vault references in Azure App Service

Key vault references in Azure App Service allow us to securely access secrets, certificates, or keys stored in Azure Key Vault from our web applications. By referencing key vault secrets in the Azure App Service configuration settings or code, we can keep sensitive information separate from our application code and configuration, enhancing security and simplifying key rotation. These references are managed as environment variables within the App Service instance, dynamically fetching the secrets from the key vault during runtime, ensuring that your application always uses the latest secret values without exposing them in plaintext. This feature facilitates secure and efficient management of sensitive information in your web applications hosted on Azure App Service.

To configure the Azure Key Vault references in Azure App Service, we need to configure the identity of the application and then we need to add the reference to the key vault secret under Azure App Service | **Configuration**.

Figure 12.27 – Configuring the Azure app settings

The name is required to identify the secret value within Azure Key Vault and the value should be something like this:

```
@Microsoft.KeyVault(SecretUri=https://<azure-key-value-name>.
vault.azure.net/secrets/<secret-name>)
```

We can access the secret value in the same way we access the Azure app configuration, as follows:

```
app.MapGet("/", () => $"Send Grid Api Key : {Environment.
GetEnvironmentVariable("SendGridAPIKey")}");
```

Or like this:

```
app.MapGet("/via-config", (IConfiguration configuration) => $"Send
Grid Api Key : {configuration["SendGridAPIKey"]}");
```

Now we can browse the / endpoint or the /via-config endpoint and will be able to see the value of SendGridAPIKey. This way, we can use the Azure Key Vault reference in Azure App Service. The Azure Key Vault reference helps us to access secrets and keys without modifying the application code. We need to make sure the Azure App Service identity can access the key vault and has enough permissions to read. Currently, for demo purposes, we are using the Azure Key Vault Administrator role for the Azure App Service identity.

Summary

In this chapter, we learned about Azure Key Vault – an Azure service that helps to unify the storage and management of application secrets. In the first section, we learned about Azure Key Vault, followed by learning how to create and configure a key vault using the Azure portal and the Azure CLI. In the next section, we learned how to set and read secrets, certificates, and keys from Azure Key Vault in the Azure portal and using the Azure CLI. In the final section, we learned about setting up authentication in Azure Key Vault. We covered both system-assigned managed identities and user-assigned managed identities, which will help us to decide which approach we need to choose when designing and provisioning Azure resources. We also learned how to access the secret value from Azure Key Vault in an ASP.NET Core web application. This will help us to keep important values such as connection strings, API keys, and tokens securely in a centralized location.

In the next chapter, we will learn about **Azure Active Directory B2C**, which is an Azure service that assists in the administration of customer and consumer access to your **business-to-consumer** (**B2C**) applications. We will get an overview of Azure AD B2C and how to create and configure an Azure AD B2C tenant. We will also learn how to use Azure AD B2C in ASP.NET Core and **single-page applications**.

13

Managing Access with Azure Active Directory B2C

The significance of web application security has increased significantly due to the heightened risks of unsecured applications, data breaches, and hacks. These vulnerabilities have the potential to cause severe consequences, ranging from detrimental impacts on a company's reputation to financial losses substantial enough to bankrupt even well-known businesses. In this chapter, we will learn about Azure **Active Directory** (**AD**) B2C. It is an Azure service that assists in the administration of customer and consumer access to your **business-to-customer** (**B2C**) applications. Leveraging the robust capabilities of Azure AD B2C, we can seamlessly implement robust web application security, reducing the necessity for custom code development in authentication and authorization processes.

In this chapter, we're going to cover the following main topics:

- Introducing Azure AD B2C
- Creating and configuring Azure AD B2C
- Using Azure AD B2C in ASP.NET Core applications
- Using Azure AD B2C in single-page applications
- Configuring social login with Azure AD B2C

Technical requirements

In this chapter, we will be creating **ASP.NET Core MVC** applications, so we need to install the **.NET SDK**. For debugging purposes, we need either **Visual Studio** (**VS**) **Code**. To create Azure AD B2C instance, we need an active Azure subscription.

Introducing Azure AD B2C

Azure AD **Business to Customer** (**B2C**) is a cloud-based identity and access management solution provided by Microsoft Azure. It enables organizations to manage user identities and access to their applications, whether they are web or mobile, with a focus on consumer-facing scenarios. Azure AD B2C is designed to help organizations to deliver secure authentication and authorization services to their customers or external partners, without requiring them to have their own identity infrastructure.

Azure AD B2C is constructed on the foundation of Azure AD, which provides core identity services. It relies on industry-standard protocols such as **OpenID Connect** (**OIDC**) and **Open Authorization** (**OAuth**) 2.0 for secure authentication and authorization. It supports various identity providers, including social and enterprise providers, and allows custom policies for tailored authentication flows. Additionally, Azure AD B2C offers multi-factor authentication, user self-service capabilities, extensive APIs and SDKs, and robust analytics, and leverages Azure's scalability and reliability while maintaining strong security and compliance standards, making it a versatile and secure identity management solution for customer-facing applications.

With Azure AD B2C, organizations can provide their customers with the ability to sign up, sign in, and manage their profiles using social media accounts or traditional email and password credentials. They can also customize the user interface and user flows to match their branding and user experience requirements.

Azure AD B2C has the ability to establish connections with identity providers that are compatible with the OAuth 1.0, OAuth 2.0, OIDC, and SAML protocols for federated authentication and authorization processes. However, certain features of these protocols are not supported by Azure AD B2C. For example, the resource owner password credentials grant feature of OAuth 1.0 is not supported by Azure AD B2C.

While working with Azure AD B2C, it is important to know about the OAuth and OIDC protocols. OAuth and OIDC are essential protocols used in Azure AD B2C. OAuth facilitates secure access to APIs and resources by allowing applications to obtain access tokens after user authentication. On the other hand, OIDC enhances authentication by providing identity tokens, confirming user identity, and supplying user information. In Azure AD B2C, OAuth handles authorization, while OIDC manages authentication, ensuring a comprehensive identity and access management solution. These protocols enable customization of authentication and authorization experiences and integration with various identity providers for diverse application needs.

Azure AD B2C offers a range of features, including multi-factor authentication, password reset, and integration with popular social identity providers, such as Facebook, Google, and Microsoft accounts. It also supports custom policies, which allow organizations to define their own authentication and authorization rules and workflows.

Overall, Azure AD B2C is a powerful identity management solution that helps organizations to improve the security and user experience of their customer-facing applications.

In this section, we learned about Azure AD B2C. In the next section, we will learn about how to create an Azure AD B2C instance and configure it.

Different authentication flows

The authorization process in identity management encompasses several distinct flows, each tailored to different application scenarios.

Firstly, the authorization code flow is ideal for web and mobile apps capable of securely storing a client secret. In this approach, the application triggers an authorization request, directing the user to the authorization server (such as Azure AD B2C). After the user logs in and grants permissions, the authorization server issues an authorization code to the app. This code is then exchanged for both an access token and a refresh token, empowering the app to access protected resources and renew tokens if they expire. Optionally, this flow can incorporate **Proof Key for Code Exchange** (**PKCE**) for added security, requiring the app to generate a random code verifier and challenge for each request.

Secondly, the implicit flow suits **single-page applications** (**SPAs**) incapable of storing client secrets. Following an authorization request, the user is redirected to the authorization server, signs in, and consents to permissions. Unlike the authorization code flow, the authorization server directly returns an access token (and optionally an ID token) in the URL fragment. However, it lacks a refresh token, requiring the app to request a new access token upon expiration. This method, while supported by Azure AD B2C, is considered less secure than the authorization code flow with PKCE.

Thirdly, the resource owner password credentials flow is designed for trusted applications capable of collecting user credentials (username and password). These credentials are then forwarded to the authorization server, which validates them and provides both an access token and a refresh token. Although supported by Azure AD B2C, it's not recommended due to potential security and privacy concerns associated with users sharing their credentials with the app, and it lacks support for various advanced features.

Fourthly, the client credentials flow is suitable for confidential applications acting independently, not on behalf of users. These apps authenticate themselves with the authorization server using their client ID and secret, requesting an access token for a specific scope. The authorization server validates the credentials and issues an access token, enabling the app to access the protected resource. However, Azure AD B2C is not compatible with this flow, as it's tailored for user-centric scenarios, not service-to-service interactions.

Finally, the device code flow is ideal for devices with limited input capabilities or without a browser, such as smart TVs or IoT devices. These devices initiate an authorization request and display a user code and verification URL to the user, who then accesses the URL on another device, completes the authorization, and provides the device with access and refresh tokens. Azure AD B2C supports this flow but has some limitations, such as a lack of support for social or federated identity providers and custom policies.

Creating and configuring Azure AD B2C instance

In this section, we will be creating Azure AD B2C instance. We will be doing this from the Azure portal. First, we will create an Azure AD B2C resource, then we will create an application that will help us to integrate Azure AD B2C into our ASP.NET Core web application.

Creating an Azure AD B2C resource

We can follow these steps to create an Azure AD B2C resource:

1. Open the browser, navigate to `https://portal.azure.com`, and log in with your Azure account if you're not logged in already.

2. Click on the **Create a resource** button, and in the **Search services and marketplace** textbox, type `Azure Active Directory B2C`. From the search results (*Figure 13.1*), select **Azure Active Directory B2C**, click on the **Create** button, and select **Azure Active Directory B2C** again from the list.

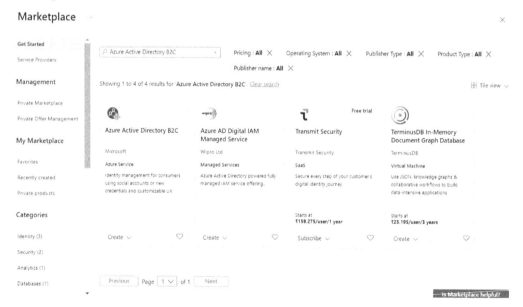

Figure 13.1 – Azure Active Directory B2C – search results

3. On the next screen (*Figure 13.2*), choose the first option – **Create a new Azure AD B2C Tenant**. The second option, **Link an existing Azure AD B2C Tenant to my Azure subscription**, is required once we have an Azure AD B2C tenant and we want to link it to the current Azure subscription for billing purposes.

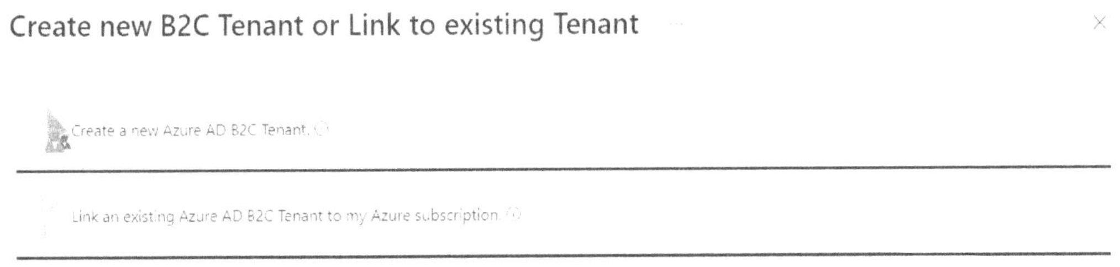

Create new B2C Tenant or Link to existing Tenant   ✕

Create a new Azure AD B2C Tenant.

Link an existing Azure AD B2C Tenant to my Azure subscription.

Figure 13.2 – Create new or link existing Azure AD B2C

4. Once we click on the **Create a new Azure AD B2C Tenant** option, we will be redirected to a **Configuration** screen (*Figure 13.3*), where we need to provide an organization name, initial domain name, and location. By default, it will be **United States**. We also need to choose an Azure subscription and select or create a resource group as well.

5. Unlike other resources, the Azure AD B2C resource doesn't support tags. Once we configure the values, we can click on the **Review + create** button (*Figure 13.3*) to review the changes and create the resource after that – this might take a few minutes.

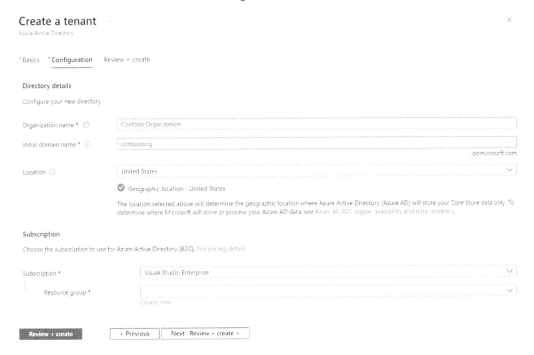

Figure 13.3 – Azure AD B2C Configuration screen

6. We can click on the Azure AD B2C resource name in the **Notifications** pane and go to the Azure AD B2C details page (*Figure 13.4*). It may prompt you to log in again. We can log in with our Azure credentials.

Figure 13.4 – New Azure AD B2C tenant created

7. Once you have logged in, we will be able to see the Azure AD B2C overview page, as shown in the following figure:

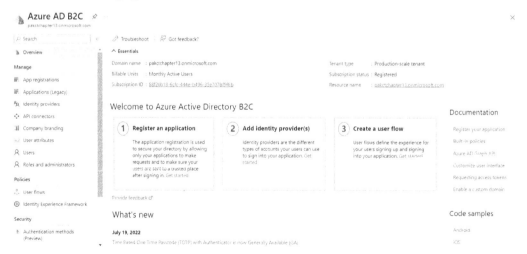

Figure 13.5 – Azure AD B2C – overview page

On this screen, you will be able to customize and configure the login and registration pages for your application.

In this section, we learned about provisioning Azure AD B2C resources and accessing them. In the next section, we will learn about registering a web application in Azure AD B2C.

Registering a web application to Azure AD B2C

In this section, we will learn how to register a web application to Azure AD B2C. We need to register applications in Azure AD B2C so that the **ASP.NET Core** application can interact with Azure AD B2C. Azure AD B2C supports different types of applications, such as web applications built using **server-side application logic**, **SPAs**, and **mobile applications**.

To register an application, we can take the following steps:

1. Log in to the Azure portal using `https://portal.azure.com`.

2. Search for Azure AD B2C instance you created by typing the name in the search textbox. Another option is to click on the **Directories + subscriptions** button (*Figure 13.6*) or using the `https://portal.azure.com/#settings/directory` link. Click on the **Switch** button next to the Azure AD B2C instance created earlier in this chapter.

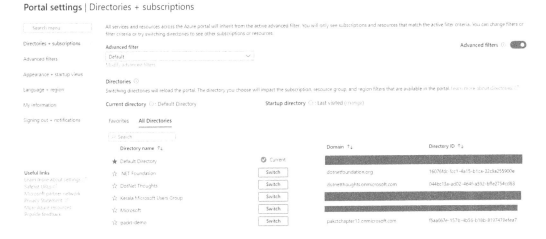

Figure 13.6 – Select the Azure AD B2C instance

3. On the portal screen, search for Azure AD B2C, which will open the newly created Azure AD B2C instance.

4. From the **Azure AD B2C** screen, click on the **App registrations** menu option and select the **+ New registration** button.

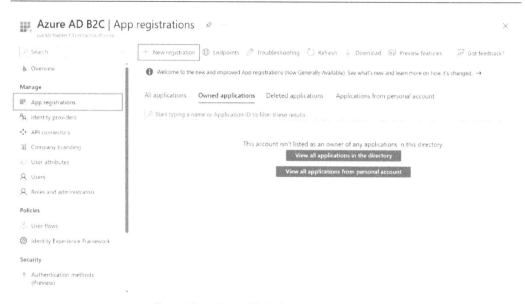

Figure 13.7 – Azure AD B2C – App registrations

5. On the screen (*Figure 13.8*), we need to configure **Name**, select the supported account types – we will use the default selected one – and configure the redirect URI – which is optional but recommended; we need to configure the ASP.NET Core application URL here. We can do it later as well. The **Grant admin consent to openid and offline_access permissions** checkbox is selected by default. We will keep it as it is – the openId permission is required for Azure AD B2C to sign the user in to the application. The offline_access permission is required to issue refresh tokens to the user. For more details about various tokens, use this link: https://learn.microsoft.com/en-us/azure/active-directory-b2c/tokens-overview.

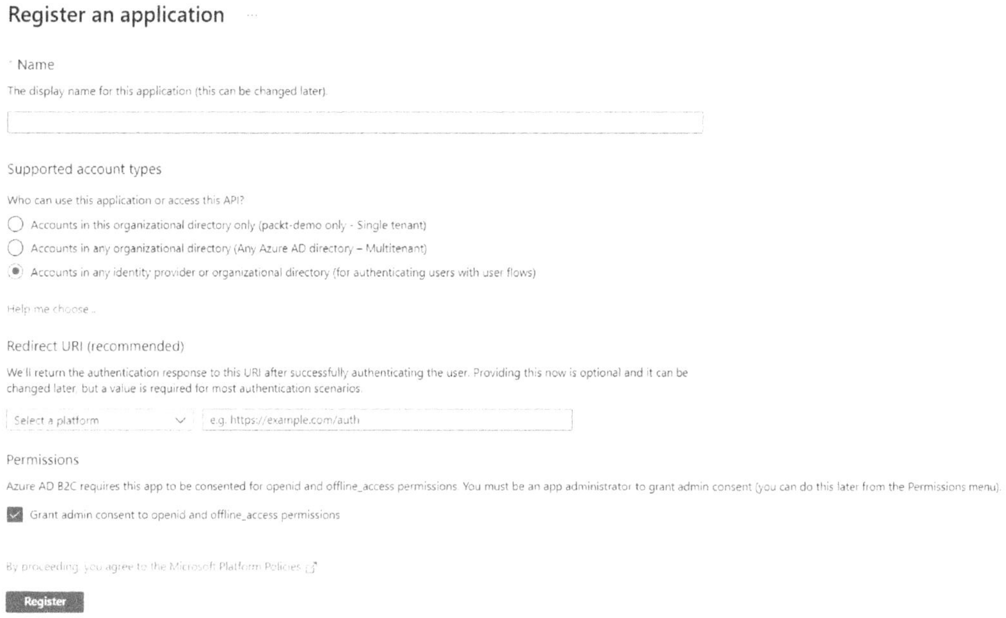

Register an application

Name

The display name for this application (this can be changed later).

Supported account types

Who can use this application or access this API?

○ Accounts in this organizational directory only (packt-demo only - Single tenant)

○ Accounts in any organizational directory (Any Azure AD directory – Multitenant)

◉ Accounts in any identity provider or organizational directory (for authenticating users with user flows)

Help me choose...

Redirect URI (recommended)

We'll return the authentication response to this URI after successfully authenticating the user. Providing this now is optional and it can be changed later, but a value is required for most authentication scenarios.

Select a platform   ⌄   e.g. https://example.com/auth

Permissions

Azure AD B2C requires this app to be consented for openid and offline_access permissions. You must be an app administrator to grant admin consent (you can do this later from the Permissions menu).

☑ Grant admin consent to openid and offline_access permissions

By proceeding, you agree to the Microsoft Platform Policies ↗

Register

Figure 13.8 – Register an application screen

6. Once we configure the name, we can keep the default values and click on the **Register** button (*Figure 13.8*). After the Azure AD B2C app is created, we will get a screen that will display values for configuring the ASP.NET Core application, as shown in the following figure:

Figure 13.9 – Azure AD B2C – app registration screen

7. Once the ASP.NET Core application is created, we can use the **Authentication** menu and configure the platform and callback URLs.

In this section, we learned about app registration in Azure AD B2C. In the next section, we will create user flows for sign-up and sign-in, which we will be using in the ASP.NET Core application for registration and login purposes.

Creating and configuring user flows

In Azure AD B2C, we have the ability to establish procedural rules that users must adhere to in order to access our application. These rules can include the specific steps that users must follow during activities such as signing in, signing up, modifying a profile, or resetting a password. Upon successful completion of the prescribed steps, the user will be granted a token that allows them access to your application.

We can follow these steps to create a user flow:

1. Log in to the Azure portal using `https://portal.azure.com`.

2. Search for the Azure AD B2C instance you created by typing the name in the search textbox. Another option is to click on the **Directories + subscriptions** button or use the `https://portal.azure.com/#settings/directory` link. Then, click on the **Switch** button in the Azure AD B2C instance created earlier in this chapter.

3. Then, click on the **User flows** menu option, which will display a screen like this:

Figure 13.10 – User flows screen

4. Click on the + **New user flow** button to create a new user flow. Clicking on the button will open up the **Select a user flow type** screen, as in *Figure 13.11*, where we need to select the user flow we want to create. We can select the **Sign up and sign in** workflow. When selected, it will display a version selection option, where we can select the **Recommended** version. Click on the **Create** button.

Create a user flow

User flows are predefined, configured policies that you can use to set up authentication experiences for your end users. Select a user flow type to get started. Learn more.

Select a user flow type

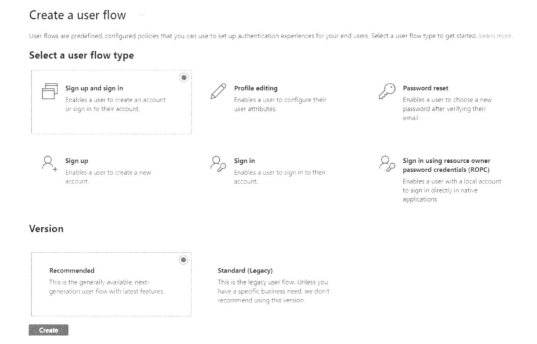

Sign up and sign in
Enables a user to create an account or sign in to their account.

Profile editing
Enables a user to configure their user attributes.

Password reset
Enables a user to choose a new password after verifying their email.

Sign up
Enables a user to create a new account.

Sign in
Enables a user to sign in to their account.

Sign in using resource owner password credentials (ROPC)
Enables a user with a local account to sign in directly in native applications

Version

Recommended
This is the generally available, next-generation user flow with latest features.

Standard (Legacy)
This is the legacy user flow. Unless you have a specific business need, we don't recommend using this version.

Create

Figure 13.11 – Select user flow type and version

5. On the **Create** screen, we need to provide a name for the user flow, which we will be using in the code. We also need to select the identity providers; currently, only the **Email signup** option is available. We will be configuring a social provider later in this chapter. We need to configure the Name and Identity providers parameters, while the others are optional. We can configure user attributes and token claims, which will be displayed on the **Sign up** screen, and the values will be part of the claim when a user signs up or signs in to the application with the user flow, which we can access from the application code. We can keep the other configuration as the default. Click on the **Create** button.

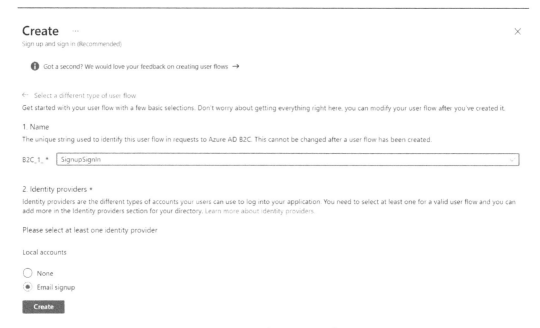

Figure 13.12 – Create a user flow

6.   Once we've created the user flow, we can click on it and view the details, as shown in the following figure. With the application we created in the last section, we are able to test the workflow using the **Run user flow** option.

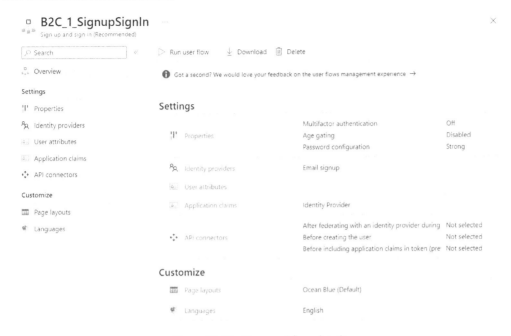

Figure 13.13 – User workflow details

Now we have created sign-up and sign-in user workflows, which can be used for user registration to the application and for the user to sign in to the application.

In this section, we learned how to create an Azure AD B2C instance, Azure AD B2C applications, and user workflows. In the next section, we will learn how to use an Azure AD B2C application and user workflow in an ASP.NET Core MVC application. As mentioned earlier in this chapter, we need the user workflow name, application ID, and Azure AD B2C tenant ID to configure the ASP.NET Core application to use the Azure AD B2C sign-in and sign-up user workflows.

Using Azure AD B2C in ASP.NET Core applications

In the last section, we configured Azure AD B2C and user workflows. In this section, we will be configuring an ASP.NET Core MVC application to use the user workflow to support user sign-up and sign-in with Azure AD B2C.

We will be using the **dotnet CLI** to create the application with ASP.NET Core MVC. We will be using the dotnet new mvc command with some extra parameters for supporting authentication using Azure AD B2C. We can follow the steps and start integrating the Azure AD B2C application into ASP.NET Core:

1. First, we need to copy the application ID we created in Azure AD B2C. Then, we need to copy the Azure AD B2C tenant ID – we can get both of these values from the Azure AD B2C application overview page, as shown in the following figure:

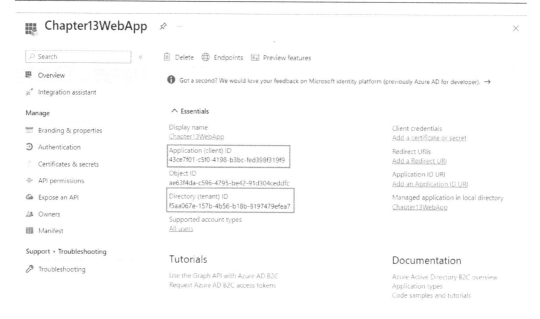

Figure 13.14 – Application overview page

2. We need to copy the user workflow name from the **User flows** list.

3. Next, open the terminal and execute the following command:

```
> dotnet new mvc -o Chapter13.MVC --framework net6.0 --auth
IndividualB2C --aad-b2c-instance https://pakctchapter13.
b2clogin.com  --susi-policy-id B2C_1_SignupSignIn --domain
pakctchapter13.onmicrosoft.com --SignedOutCallbackPath /signout/
B2C_1_SignupSignIn  --client-id 43ce7f01-c5f0-4198-b3bc-
fed398f319f9 --tenant-id f5aa067e-157b-4b56-b18b-8197479efea7
--callback-path /signin-oidc
```

4. The client ID, tenant ID, domain, and `susi-policy-id` need to be replaced with your Azure AD B2C values.

5. Once the application is created, we can open the application in VS Code or VS and run it. We need to identify the URL of the application and configure the Azure AD B2C application registration redirect URI.

6. Next, we need to configure the application redirect URI. We can copy the ASP.NET Core MVC URL and append `/signin-oidc`. We will be using this URL as the redirect URL in the Azure AD B2C application.

7. Open Azure AD B2C, select the **App registrations** menu option, and click on the application created earlier. On the application overview page, click on the **Add a Redirect URI** link shown in the following figure:

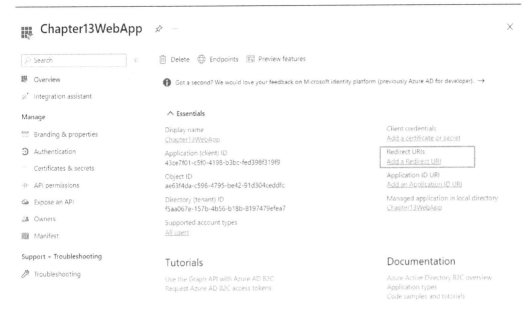

Figure 13.15 – Azure AD B2C application overview page

8. Clicking on the **Add a Redirect URI** link will open up the **Authentication** screen, where we need to add the platform configurations – in our case, we need to select the **Web** option under **Web Applications**.

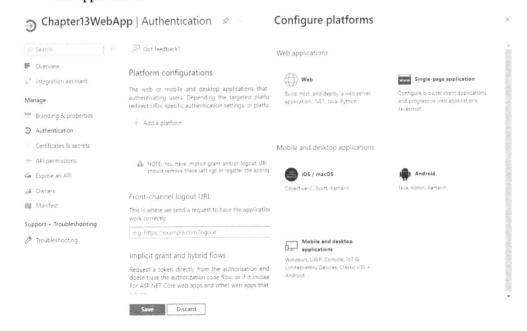

Figure 13.16 – Add and configure platform

9. Once the **Web** application type is selected, we will be able to see the configuration screen where we can configure the redirect URI (*Figure 13.17*), which is the application URL we collected in *step 6*. We also need to select the different tokens to be issued as part of the authentication workflow. We need to select both tokens – **Access tokens** and **ID tokens**.

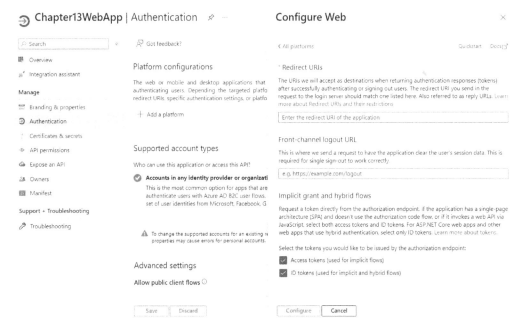

Figure 13.17 – Configure redirect URL

10. Once the redirect URI is configured, we can either run the application using the **IDE/editor** or, in the terminal, we can execute the `dotnet run` command.

11. Open the web application in the browser with the HTTPS URL displayed on the screen from the `dotnet run` command. Click on the **Sign In** button on the home page to sign in or sign up for an ASP.NET Core application using the Azure AD B2C user workflow.

12. Once we've logged in, the application will show the email we signed in. Since we didn't configure any application claims in the workflow, only the default claim – email – will be displayed. We can modify the user workflow and add some other claims, such as the user's object ID, whether the user is new, and the display name. We can also add some user attributes so that we can collect that information from the sign-up screen. We can click on the **Sign up and sign in** user workflow we created earlier. On the screen, we will be able to choose the user attributes and application claims, which will help us to configure the fields on the sign-up/sign-in page and the application claims.

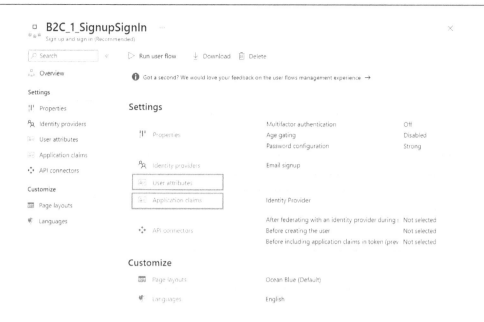

Figure 13.18 – User workflow overview page

13. Click on the **User attributes** link, and on the screen (*Figure 13.19*), select **Country/Region**, **Display Name**, and **Email Address** and save the changes. This will start displaying the sign-up form with the new fields.

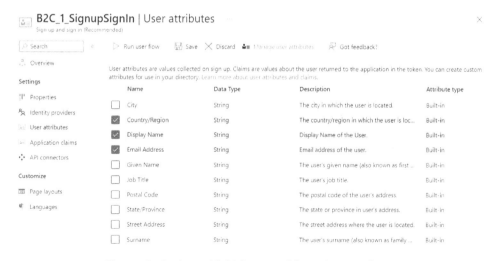

Figure 13.19 – Azure AD B2C user workflow – User attributes

14. After adding the user attributes, we can add the application claims. We can click on the **Application claims** link, and on the screen, we can add the **User's Object ID**, **User is new**, **Display Name**, and **Country/Region** fields, as shown in the following figure:

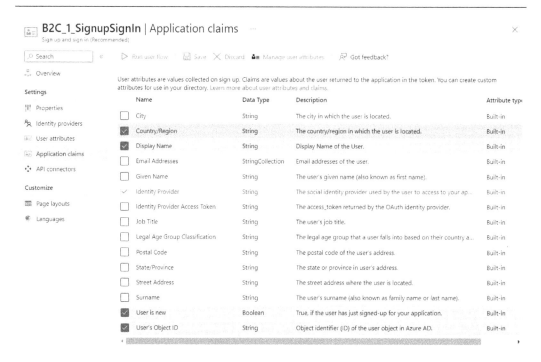

Figure 13.20 – Azure AD B2C user workflow – Application claims

Now we can register a new user and log in with the user workflow, and we will be able to see new form fields and the display name we used in the application.

15. To store the logged-in user's information in the application database, we can modify the Program.cs code like this:

```
builder.Services.
Configure<OpenIdConnectOptions>(OpenIdConnectDefaults.
AuthenticationScheme, options =>
{
    options.Events = new OpenIdConnectEvents()
    {
        OnTicketReceived = async (context) =>
        {
            await OnTicketReceived(context);
        }
    };
});
```

16. In the `OnTicketReceived` method, we will be reading the `objectidentifier` claim and checking it in the database using the database context. Here is the implementation:

```
async Task OnTicketReceived(TicketReceivedContext context)
{
var applicationDbContext = scope.ServiceProvider.
GetRequiredService<ApplicationDbContext>();
    var objectidentifier = context.Principal.
FindFirstValue("http://schemas.microsoft.com/identity/claims/
objectidentifier");
    var isUserExists = await applicationDbContext.
ApplicationUsers
        .AnyAsync(u => u.ObjectIdentifier == objectidentifier);
    if (!isUserExists)
    {
        await RegisterUser(context, objectidentifier);
    }
}
```

17. In the `RegisterUser` method, we will be adding the user to the database like this:

```
async Task RegisterUser(TicketReceivedContext context, string
objectidentifier)
{
    using (var scope = context.HttpContext.RequestServices.
CreateScope())
    {
        var applicationDbContext = scope.ServiceProvider.
GetRequiredService<ApplicationDbContext>();
        var nameidentifier = context.Principal.
FindFirstValue(ClaimTypes.NameIdentifier);
        var name = context.Principal.FindFirstValue("name");
        var user = new ApplicationUser()
        {
            ObjectIdentifier = objectidentifier,
            NameIdentifier = nameidentifier,
            Name = name
        };
        await applicationDbContext.ApplicationUsers.
AddAsync(user);
        await applicationDbContext.SaveChangesAsync();
    }
}
```

Now, we know how to use Azure AD B2C in an ASP.NET Core MVC application. Let's take a quick look at the three main types of tokens in the authentication and authorization systems.

Different types of tokens

In this section, we selected an option to choose both the ID token and access token. In authentication and authorization systems, there are three main types of tokens we need to know about:

- **Access token**: This is a short-lived credential granted to an application after a user successfully logs in. It authorizes the app to access specific resources, such as APIs or services, on behalf of the user. Access tokens are used to make secure requests to these resources, ensuring that only authorized applications can access them.

- **ID token**: Often used in OIDC, an ID token contains information about the authenticated user, such as their name and email address. It helps verify the user's identity and is used in single sign-on scenarios, providing user profile data to applications.

- **Refresh token**: Refresh tokens are long-lived and used to obtain new access tokens once the original one expires. They enable seamless and secure access for extended periods without the user having to re-enter their credentials. However, they should be safeguarded as they hold higher privileges. In Azure AD B2C, to get the refresh tokens, we need to include the `offline_access` scope.

Together, these tokens form the backbone of secure authentication and resource access in modern applications, ensuring both user privacy and system security.

We now know how to sign up and sign in using an Azure AD B2C user workflow and finally store the logged-in user's information in the database. In the next section, we will learn how to create a SPA and use authentication to connect to the **ASP.NET Core Web API** to access the authenticated data.

Using Azure AD B2C in single-page applications

In an earlier section, we learned how to integrate Azure AD B2C user workflows into an ASP.NET Core MVC application, and how to use them to sign up and sign in to the application. In this section, we will learn how to use Azure AD B2C in a SPA. For simplicity, we are using **vanilla JavaScript** in this section to create a SPA. We can use any other **JavaScript framework**, such as **Angular**, **React**, or **Vue.js**. In this implementation, we will be using the **Azure AD B2C JavaScript SDK** to log in to an application using Azure AD B2C. We can refer to the Azure AD B2C JavaScript SDK from Microsoft CDN using this URL: `https://alcdn.msauth.net/browser/2.35.0/js/msal-browser.min.js`. Since we are using vanilla JavaScript, we can include the JavaScript SDK using the URL in the script tag in HTML. We can follow these steps to create JavaScript SDK authentication using Azure AD B2C:

1. First, we will create an empty **ASP.NET web application** – this is for hosting the client application. We can do this using the - `dotnet new web --framework net6.0 -o Chapter13.Web` command, and then open the application in VS Code/VS.

2. Create a `wwwroot` folder in the project root along with the `Program.cs` file. Create an `index.html` file in the `wwwroot` folder.

3. Modify the `Program.cs` file like this, which will help to serve the `index.html` file for all the requests:

```
var builder = WebApplication.CreateBuilder(args);
var app = builder.Build();
app.UseStaticFiles();
app.MapFallbackToFile("index.html");
app.Run();
```

4. Before writing the code in the `index.html` file, we need to do an App Registrationin Azure AD B2C, like we did it in the Registering a web application to Azure AD B2C section earlier this chapter. We already created an Azure AD B2C application earlier in this chapter. Earlier, we added the web platform and configured the redirect URI. For the SPA, we need to add the SPA platform and configure the redirect URI – the URL of the ASP.NET Core application.

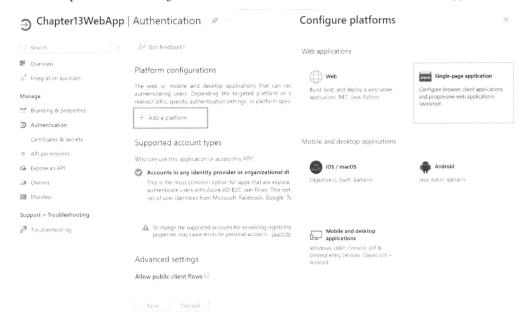

Figure 13.21 – Adding a SPA as a platform

5. Once we've registered the application, we need to copy the client ID. We already set the other configuration values in an earlier section.

6. Now, we will modify `index.html` to include various JavaScript libraries and HTML code. We will be using the **Microsoft Authentication Library** (**MSAL**) for JavaScript and including the **Bootstrap library** for the user interface. Here is the HTML code:

```html
<!doctype html>
<html lang="en">
<head>
    <meta charset="utf-8">
    <meta name="viewport" content="width=device-width, initial-
scale=1">
    <title>Chapter 13 - SPA Demo</title>
    <link rel="stylesheet" type="text/css"    href="https://cdn.
jsdelivr.net/npm/bootstrap@5.2.3/dist/css/bootstrap.min.css">
</head>
<body>
    <div class="container">
        <h1>Chapter 13 - SPA Demo</h1>
        <p>This is a demo of a Single Page Application (SPA)
using the Microsoft Authentication Library (MSAL) for
            JavaScript.</p>
        <button id="signinsignoutbutton" class="btn btn-primary"
onclick="signIn()">Sign In</button>
    </div>
    <div class="container">
        <h3>User</h3>
        <p id="user"></p>
    </div>
    <script src="https://cdn.jsdelivr.net/npm/bootstrap@5.2.3/
dist/js/bootstrap.bundle.min.js"></script>
    <script type="text/javascript" src="https://alcdn.msauth.
net/browser/2.35.0/js/msal-browser.min.js"></script>
</body>
</html>
```

The preceding HTML code will download the **Bootstrap JavaScript**, the **CSS** (which is optional), and the `msal-browser` JavaScript file, which is the JavaScript SDK to connect and authenticate with Azure AD B2C. We will be using a **Sign In** button, which will help users to sign in to the application.

7. Next, we need to write the JavaScript code that will help us to sign in to the application. We can include the following code inside the `<body>` element after all the script declarations. The following code is initializing the MSAL public application object with the configuration values – we need to replace them with the Azure AD B2C application:

```javascript
const msalConfig = {
    auth: {
```

```
            clientId: '66d2c6c2-f036-470d-accb-b70f2784458a',
            authority: 'https://pakctchapter13.b2clogin.com/
    pakctchapter13.onmicrosoft.com/B2C_1_SignupSignIn/',
            knownAuthorities: ["pakctchapter13.b2clogin.com"]
        }
    };
    const msalObject = new msal.PublicClientApplication(msalConfig);
    msalObject["browserStorage"].clear();
    var accountId = '';
```

The `SignIn()` function will be invoked when the user clicks on the **Sign In** button:

```
async function signIn() {
    try {
        const loginResponse = await msalObject.loginPopup();
        console.log(loginResponse);
        accountId = loginResponse.account.homeAccountId;
        document.getElementById('user').innerHTML =
loginResponse.account.idTokenClaims.name;
        document.getElementById('signinsignoutbutton').innerHTML
= 'Sign Out';
document.getElementById('signinsignoutbutton').
setAttribute('onclick', 'signOut()');
    } catch (error) {
        console.log(error);
    }
}
```

Once the user is signed in, the button text will be displayed as **Sign out**, and the **click event handler** will change to the `Signout()` function:

```
function signOut() {
    const currentAcc = msalObject.getAccountByHomeId(accountId);
    msalObject.logout(currentAcc);
    document.getElementById('signinsignoutbutton').innerHTML =
'Sign In';
    document.getElementById('signinsignoutbutton').
setAttribute('onclick', 'signIn()');
}
```

8. Now we are ready to run the application. On the web page, click on the **Sign In** button, which will open the pop-up **Sign in** window, as shown in the following figure. Once we sign in with the Azure AD B2C credentials created earlier, we will be able to see the **Display Name** field of the user on the screen.

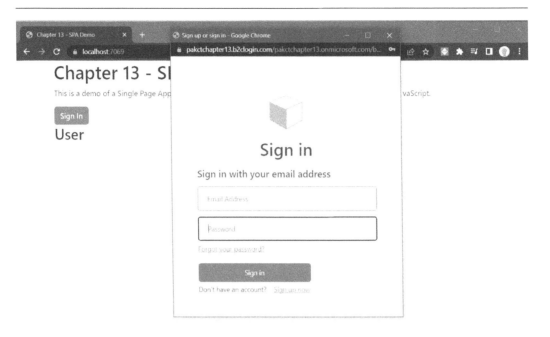

Figure 13.22 – Azure AD B2C SPA Sign in pop-up window

9. Similar to the Azure AD B2C ASP.NET Core integration, in a SPA integration model, we will also be able to sign up to the application.

In this section, we learned how we can integrate Azure AD B2C application authentication into SPAs. We can find more details about how to use other SPA frameworks such as Angular, React, and Vue. js here: `https://learn.microsoft.com/en-us/azure/active-directory-b2c/index-spa`.

In the next section, we will learn how to configure a **social media provider** for signing in and signing up to the Azure AD B2C application so that users need not keep another set of credentials for logging in/signing up to the application.

Configuring social media login with Azure AD B2C

In this section, we will learn how to configure social media login to Azure AD B2C. We can configure multiple social media providers. First, we need to configure identity providers in Azure AD B2C. We can do so using the following steps:

1. First, we need to log in to the Azure AD B2C instance.

2. Next, we need to click on the **Identity providers** menu, as shown in the following figure. In this section, we will be able to see different social media providers.

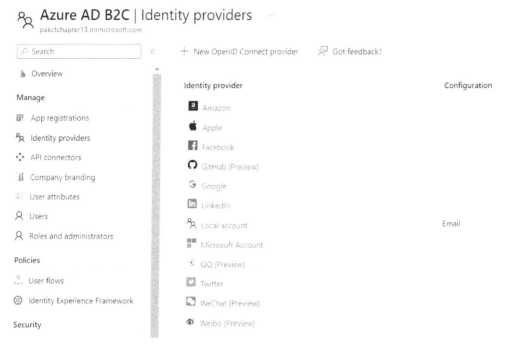

Figure 13.23 – Azure AD B2C | Identity providers

3. We will use the **Google identity provider**. Click on the **Google** option and then copy the callback URL, shown in the following screenshot – we need this URL in configuring the Google project.

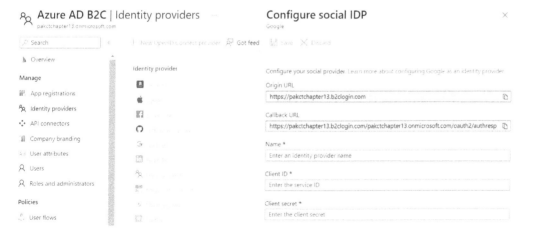

Figure 13.24 – Google identity provider | configure client ID and client secret

4. To use the Google identity provider, we need to create a project in the **Google Cloud console**. We can visit this page: `https://console.cloud.google.com/apis/dashboard`. Log in with your Google credentials.

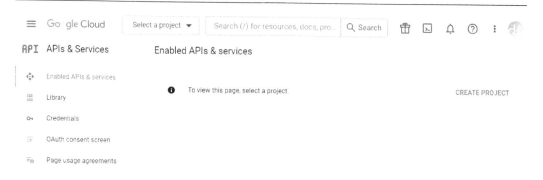

Figure 13.25 – Google Cloud console dashboard

5. Click on **CREATE PROJECT**. We need to configure the project name. Then, click on the **Create** button. Once the project is created, click on the **OAuth consent screen** menu option. Select the **External** option and click on **Create**. On the **App Information** screen, we need to provide the app name, user support email – which we need to select from the list – and authorized domains. Use b2clogin.com for the domain and set the email address to Developer contact information. Then, click on the **Save and continue** button. On the next three screens, we can click on the **Save and continue** button. There is no need to configure any values.

6. Next, click on the **Credentials** menu option, and then click on the **CREATE CREDENTIALS** option and select **OAuth client ID**. In the **Application type** dropdown, select **Web Application**. We can also configure the name. We need to set the value Authorized redirect URIs from the Azure AD B2C Google identity provider Callback URL. Click on the **Create** button.

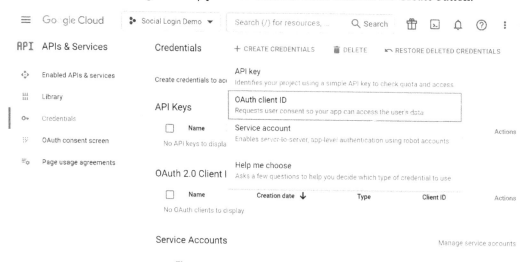

Figure 13.26 – Create OAuth client ID

7. Once the OAuth client is configured, the Google console will display the client ID and client secret and we need to configure it in Azure AD B2C. Save the configuration.

8. Once the Azure AD B2C Google identity provider is configured, we need to modify the user flow we created earlier in this chapter. Select the user flow and click on **Identity providers**, which will display different identity providers; we can select **Google**, as shown in the following figure. Click on the **Save** button to save the changes.

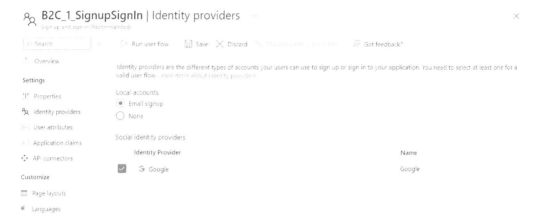

Figure 13.27 – Google identity provider configuration

9. Now we can run the application again and we will be able to see the Google login option on the login page or in the login pop-up dialog, as shown in the following figure (*Figure 13.28*):

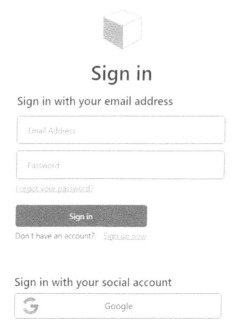

Figure 13.28 – Google social login on Azure AD B2C login page

10. Users can sign up and sign in using the **Google** button.

Now, we know how to configure social providers to Azure AD B2C.

Summary

In this chapter, you learned about Azure AD B2C. Azure AD B2C is an application service from Azure that helps in the administration of customer and consumer access to your B2C applications. We learned how to create an Azure AD B2C tenant and how to create and customize user flows – which will be useful for signing up and signing in users to the ASP.NET Core application. Then, we learned about configuring sign-up and sign-in to ASP.NET Core MVC applications using the web application client. Then, we explored implementing authentication in SPAs using Azure AD B2C and JavaScript. Finally, we learned about configuring social providers with Azure AD B2C with Google. The Azure AD B2C service helps us to configure a secure and customizable identity service so that we don't need to write application code for managing authentication and authorization. With the help of various SDKs and REST APIs, we can also incorporate Azure AD B2C into any kind of application, such as web, mobile, and console or service-based applications.

This book has taken us on a journey through cloud computing and the vast possibilities of Microsoft's Azure platform and .NET Core 6.0. We explored Azure services, serverless computing, and microservices for agile, scalable apps. Understanding data management and security enables optimized, data-driven applications. With examples and exercises, we're now equipped to build innovative, secure cloud solutions. This book has empowered you to unlock the cloud's potential and shape technology's future with confidence.

Index

Symbols

D

Other Books You May Enjoy

If you enjoyed this book, you may be interested in these other books by Packt:

Azure for Developers - Second Edition

Kamil Mrzygłód

ISBN: 978-1-80324-009-1

- Identify the Azure services that can help you get the results you need
- Implement PaaS components – Azure App Service, Azure SQL, Traffic Manager, CDN, Notification Hubs, and Azure Cognitive Search
- Work with serverless components
- Integrate applications with storage
- Put together messaging components (Event Hubs, Service Bus, and Azure Queue Storage)
- Use Application Insights to create complete monitoring solutions
- Secure solutions using Azure RBAC and manage identities
- Develop fast and scalable cloud applications

FinOps Handbook for Microsoft Azure

Maulik Soni

ISBN: 978-1-80181-016-6

- Get the grip of all the activities of FinOps phases for Microsoft Azure
- Understand architectural patterns for interruptible workload on Spot VMs
- Optimize savings with Reservations, Savings Plans, Spot VMs
- Analyze waste with customizable pre-built workbooks
- Write an effective financial business case for savings
- Apply your learning to three real-world case studies
- Forecast cloud spend, set budgets, and track accurately

Packt is searching for authors like you

If you're interested in becoming an author for Packt, please visit `authors.packtpub.com` and apply today. We have worked with thousands of developers and tech professionals, just like you, to help them share their insight with the global tech community. You can make a general application, apply for a specific hot topic that we are recruiting an author for, or submit your own idea.

Share Your Thoughts

Now you've finished *A Developer's Guide to .NET* in Azure, we'd love to hear your thoughts! Scan the QR code below to go straight to the Amazon review page for this book and share your feedback or leave a review on the site that you purchased it from.

`https://packt.link/r/1837633010`

Your review is important to us and the tech community and will help us make sure we're delivering excellent quality content.

Download a free PDF copy of this book

Thanks for purchasing this book!

Do you like to read on the go but are unable to carry your print books everywhere?

Is your eBook purchase not compatible with the device of your choice?

Don't worry, now with every Packt book you get a DRM-free PDF version of that book at no cost.

Read anywhere, any place, on any device. Search, copy, and paste code from your favorite technical books directly into your application.

The perks don't stop there, you can get exclusive access to discounts, newsletters, and great free content in your inbox daily

Follow these simple steps to get the benefits:

1. Scan the QR code or visit the link below

https://packt.link/free-ebook/9781837633012

2. Submit your proof of purchase

3. That's it! We'll send your free PDF and other benefits to your email directly

www.ingramcontent.com/pod-product-compliance
Lightning Source LLC
Chambersburg PA
CBHW060640060326
40690CB00020B/4468